When Right Really Means Left:
A Case Study of Anti-Communist Dictatorships as Collectivist Regimes
By Nevin Gussack

Executive Summary

Perhaps one of the most seldom studied aspects of the history of the Cold War and various anti-communist dictatorships which existed in the 20th Century was the fact these regimes actually represented a variant of collectivism where the role of the state was often paramount to that of economic freedom. Such an attachment to a collectivistic philosophy arose from a number of reasons which depended on the historical background and dictatorship(s) in question. For example, governments such as the Republic of South Africa (1948 to the 1980s), General Francisco Franco, and Premier Antonio Salazar all arose from extreme nationalist collectivist movements against forces that atomized their societies. Such atomizing forces included liberal free market capitalism, communism, and colonialism. The philosophies and regimes of Franco, Salazar, and the early Nationalist Party leaders in South Africa were all affected in varying degrees by the Nazi and Italian Fascist movements. This included corporative structuring of the economy, creation of state-owned enterprises, establishment of mass movements to mobilize support for the regimes in question, and occasional bouts of anti-American and anti-US outbursts. The collectivist aspects of the South Korean military dictatorships also had their roots in the ideologies of the Japanese militarists. The dictatorship of General Chiang Kai-shek had certain ideological and philosophical commonalities with the Soviet Union and Nazi Germany.

Many of these regimes also viewed state-led developmentalist economic policies as the best path to modernize their respective nations and achieve what they believed as social justice. Somoza's Nicaragua, the Shah's Iran, Batista's Cuba, South Korea, Taiwan, and Diem's South Vietnam were only some of many examples of governments that chose state-directed economic development policies as a matter of pragmatism and ideology. Other regimes used a collectivist ideology to justify their looting of their respective nation's wealth. General Rafael Trujillo was a notorious example of this point. Some anti-communist dictatorships also explicitly asserted that their ideologies were neither Right nor Left. Zaire under General Mobutu Sese Seko was an outstanding example of such a regime that rejected the conventional Western political spectrum. Other dictatorships even incorrectly asserted that they represented capitalism and Western values, such as Malawi under President Hastings Kamazu Banda.

Even more surprising was the evidence that I encountered of these anti-communist dictatorships trading and even sometimes cooperating with the Soviets, Red Chinese, Cubans, and other communist or radical socialist despotisms that were adversaries of the United States. The evidence pointed to several reasons for communist relations with dictatorships such as General Franco's Spain, Salazar's Portugal, South Africa under the Nationalists, and the Shah's Iran. These anti-communist regimes cooperated with various Red countries for reasons of garnering economic benefits, spiting the United States, uniting against common enemies, and maintaining the image of Non-Alignment on the global stage. Governments such as Salazar's Portugal, Stroessner's Paraguay, and Spain under General Franco were quite upset at the United States for criticism of their human rights abuses and colonial policies and informed Washington DC of their extreme displeasure. The Salazar and Franco regimes also had ideologically fascistic roots which always exhibited a bias against the Western and American political and economic systems and a somewhat favorable opinion towards the Axis Powers. Anti-communist dictatorships such as Chile under General Pinochet or Pakistan under General Mohammed Zia al-Haq also maintained close relations with Red China out of the mistaken belief that Beijing's brand of communism was inflexibly against the interests of Moscow. Beijing's continued alignment with the interests of world communism and even many aspects of Moscow's long range goals are covered in my book Golitsyn Vindicated?: A Second Look at "Splits" in the Communist World During the Cold War. The ultimate purpose of this book is to correct the historical record and prove that even the anti-communist "friends" of the United States played both sides in the Cold War and also represented collectivist values and not capitalism and free markets. Unfortunately, a number of liberal and conservative anti-communists acted more as apologists for collectivist dictatorships that were ostensibly anti-Moscow or anti-Beijing. One outstanding example of conservative, anti-communist apologia for the Franco, Salazar, Chiang Kai-shek and Syngman Rhee regimes was a compilation of The New American articles that were published in a book titled Twentieth Century Heroes. This collection of well-written historical articles was edited by Gary Benoit and focused on the positive and pro-American attributes of these leaders, while ignoring their collectivist ideologies, policies, and double-dealings with the communists.[1] One friendly reviewer actually stated that these anti-communist dictators "fought dirigisme's tyranny."[2] Amazingly, anti-free market leaders such as Franco, Salazar, and Chiang Kai-shek were lumped together with true classical liberals such as Ludwig von Mises and American nationalist anti-communists such as Robert Welch, Senator Joseph McCarthy (R-WI), and General George Patton. Much of the political Left and international communist forces portrayed these anti-communist dictatorships as simply extensions of landowning oligarchs, rich industrialists, and other fat cats. This book will dispel some of the myths which emanated from the Left regarding the anti-communist collectivist regimes. Furthermore, it will serve as a caution to political scientists and scholars who argued that the United States should unconditionally support "authoritarian" governments against the forces of communist totalitarianism.[3]

I categorically reject the traditional political spectrum of the Right and Left, which was initially originated in the French National Assembly soon after the Revolution. The term "Right" is particularly troublesome, since both collectivists and individualists are lumped in that camp. Obviously, one cannot seriously lump the political cultures of the neo-Nazis and the Tea Party into a single ideological camp. Neo-Nazis are radical collectivists, while the Tea Partiers are either constitutional conservatives or libertarians. Yet they are erroneously termed "right wing" movements. Hence, I subscribe to the following political spectrum/formula:

Left (Total Government)

Center (Government with Checks and Balances)

Right (Anarchy)

---

[1] Benoit, Gary. 20th Century Heroes (American Opinion Books 2000). Item can be purchased at http://www.amazon.com/20th-Century-Heroes-Compilation-Originally/dp/0964567911

[2] Stove, R.J. "Twentieth Century Heroes" The National Observer March 22, 2001 Accessed From: http://www.thefreelibrary.com/Twentieth-Century+Heroes.+(Book+Reviews).-a080057200

[3] One well known case of such rationalizations was former Ambassador Jeanne Kirkpatrick's essay titled "Dictatorships and Double Standards." The article was published in Commentary Magazine in 1979 and could be accessed here: https://www.commentarymagazine.com/article/dictatorships-double-standards/

Based on the political formula mentioned above, the governments covered in this book all exhibit attributes of the Left in the following areas:

1) Heavy state involvement in the economy.
2) Mass mobilization (depending on the anti-communist dictatorship in question).
3) Ideological discourse which rejects liberal capitalism and endorses a nationalist form of collectivism.
4) Centralization of the police, communications, and other basic functions of government.
5) In some cases, the employment of social revolutionary rhetoric and *"anti-imperialism."*

However, these governments differed from the conventional, Marxist Left on the following issues:

1) Solid, ideological anti-communism.
2) Upholding of religious traditionalism (particularly in Latin America and much of the Middle East).
3) Rejection of internationalism and support for nationalism.
4) Rejection of the struggle between the classes within a given nation.

While the anti-communist collectivists strongly rejected Marxism-Leninism, this did not automatically translate into blind support for the traditional private oligarchies. Many of the anti-communist, collectivist dictatorships developed competing elites whose power and influence were detrimental to the established classes in the countries mentioned below. The countries discussed in this book are: Greece, Portugal, Spain, Chile, Argentina, Bolivia, Dominican Republic, Haiti, Paraguay, Venezuela, China, South Korea, Indonesia, Pakistan, Saudi Arabia, Iran, and South Africa.

Greece Under the Military Junta (1967-1974)

In 1967, a group of Greek military officers led by Colonel Papadopoulos overthrew the democratic government and established what was initially thought to be a populist, anti-communist, and traditionalist dictatorship. However, it quickly melded fascistic ideology with Greek Orthodox traditionalism, extreme nationalism, and a strong anti-communism. The Papadopoulos dictatorship made a specific point to distance itself from the wealthy classes and identify itself with the Greek workers and especially the peasants. The military dictatorship's civilian Prime Minister Kollias noted that *"we belong to no political party and we do not intend to give advantage to any political group at the expense of another. We do not belong to the economic oligarchy…We belong to the class of toil. And we stand by the side of our poor brothers…We seek to abolish corruption…From this moment there do not exist rightists, centrists, or leftists. There exist only Greeks who believe in Greece…We will march forward on the path of duty to the Motherland and of Virtue. Towards radical change. Towards prosperity and progress. Our basic objective is social justice. The just distribution of the national income. The moral and material improvement of society as a whole and especially of the peasants and workers and of the poorer classes…"* The ex-communist turned extreme nationalist theoretician George Georgalas wrote in the Ideology of the Revolution that the military revolutionaries were the children of the *"working people"* and were not descended *"from the aristocracy, nor from the plutocracy, nor from any kind of closed caste."*[4]

The Papadopoulos regime retained three ex-communist (KKE) activists as official theoreticians of the dictatorship: George Georgalas, Savvas Konstantopoulos, and Theophylaktos Papakonstantinou. Georgalas fancied himself the theorist of the *"decline of the consumer society"* and even had his essays published in a book written in 1970. Even more incredible was the fact that the book that contained Georgalas' essays was published alongside Eldridge Cleaver's works. The Papadopoulos regime also took a strong stand against personal, economic, and political individualism and believed that Greek citizens needed to be remolded into collectivist nationalists. The military dictatorship in Greece believed that *"the people has been liberated from itself, that is to say, it has been saved from the egotistical mentality."* The government noted that *"the people who compose Greek society must again become social beings."* An end must be made to the *"Blow you Jack, I'm all right"* worldview and to the *"anarchism of the jungle."* Georgalas stated that the regime believed in class harmony and not class struggle. He also added that *"the individual must stretch out to the whole. He must be socialized in the good meaning of the word."*[5] The regime also took a strong stand against the existence of political parties and limited government in Greece. In 1969, Papadopoulos denounced *"the anarchy of the Western world"* and that the politicians *"must forget the interests of their own parties..."*[6] The regime denounced representative forms government as corrupt and inefficient.[7]

While the Papadopoulos dictatorship strongly supported private enterprise, government controls proliferated over the Greek business community. Furthermore, the Greek military regime opposed economic liberalism in its purist form, feeling that such a philosophy atomized the people into stratified social classes. Loulis summarized the Papadopoulos government's economic ideology very nicely in an article in Encounter Magazine: *"Strangely enough the Colonels were far from being free marketers let alone individualists. Dictator George Papadopoulos had in fact stressed the need to 'socialize our individual aims' and for the state that would 'guide' the economy."*[8] Since 1967, the Papadopoulos regime controlled all trade unions, syndicates, corporations, and cartels. The representatives of the workers and management in industries were appointed by the government. Special commissars were appointed to investigate the operations of industry at all levels. These commissars made important decisions and businessmen were not allowed to ignore their wishes. The regime also engaged in public works programs.[9]

Labor conditions and prices were also controlled by the military dictatorship. Interior Minister Pattakos decreed that dismissal of employees and workers was forbidden and that employers must pay salaries, wages, and Easter bonuses. Infringements of this order were punishable by courts-martial. The government decreed that *"no price increase will be allowed*

[4] Clogg, Richard and Yannopoulos, George. Greece Under Military Rule (Basic Book, 1972) pages 37-39.
[5] Ibid, pages 42-49.
[6] "Greek Leader Hits Back At West's Anarchy" Times (London) December 16, 1969 page 7.
[7] Hayes, Paul M. Fascism (George Allen and Unwin, 1973) pages 186-187.
[8] Loulis, John. "The Greek Malaise" Encounter July/August 1986 pages 69-70.
[9] Hayes, Paul M. Fascism (George Allen and Unwin, 1973) pages 186-187.

for any kind of commodity" and that all goods must be sold at pre-April 21st prices.[10] The regime also enacted policies that seemed to favor the Greek peasantry, who were viewed as a bulwark of traditionalism against the degeneration and corruption rampant in the cities. In 1968, Papadopoulos forgave all the debts owed by peasants before 1967. He stated in a speech that such assistance *"will help redeem yourselves from the corrupt past and start out on a new road to prosperity."*[11]

Elements of the extreme nationalist, Nazi-like Greek fringe supported the Papadopoulos dictatorship as an authentic Greek revolution against Western and American decadence, imperialism, and the machinations of the CIA. Furthermore, the military regime was also portrayed as supportive of the aspirations of the workers and peasants against the Left and the American-supported oligarchy of capitalists and bankers. One right-wing nationalist website described pre-1967 Greece as having *"a split population, an obvious decline in public morals, a failing economy, strikes and street protests, squabbling politicians, pompous speech making, institutionalized lying, threats, and endless other problems created by the democratic system had the Greek people outraged, and the coup was received with cheers from the population, as is normal and ordinary for these sorts of events…Arrogant politicians were arrested en masse as the creators of Greek poverty and misery."* It was noted that the Greek military junta consisted of members *"of the agricultural classes and looked to the city with disdain. For them, the city was the basis of corruption, big money and oppression. As always, the Establishment, both left and right, was close to big money and was thus an urban phenomenon…Unsurprisingly, the U.S. immediately condemned the coup, referring to it as a 'rape of democracy.' The coup itself was supported by lower level officers and rejected by the upper brass, including all politicians, who saw their power ebbing away to the increasingly wild cheers of the population."* The website remarked that *"The junta, or the Revolutionary Council, as they termed themselves, faced opposition from the United States, the middle classes (read urban intellectuals and businessmen) and international finance. They were strongly supported by labor and, especially, agriculture."* The website also further noted that the Colonels *"were ideologically driven in the best of senses, as they saw Greece government by a small urban clique allied with international finance and capitalism. They saw, as a result, the despoliation of labor and agriculture, both created and resulting from the disastrous economic policies of the previous democratic oligarchy."* The website noted that the Colonels *"had the utmost contempt for bankers and leftists, but certainly had no truck with the 'conservatives' represented by Constantine and 'moderate' elements."*[12]

Despite the denunciations of the threat of the Greek Communist Party (KKE) and the Soviet Union, the Papadopoulos regime seemed to perform an *"about face"* on their earlier positions regarding Moscow and its allies. This was all the more surprising given the Greek military leadership's commitment to NATO and the American-led anti-Soviet alliance. In 1969, Papadopoulos alleged that *"Communism is no longer a danger in the world."*[13] In January 1970, Papadopoulos noted that communism was *"no longer appearing to be a great danger."* Greek businessmen and Papadopoulos government officials desired an increase in profitable trade relations with the USSR and many of their clients in Eastern Europe. One report opined that

---

[10] Schwab, Peter and Frangos, George D. Greece Under the Junta (Facts on File, 1970) page 28.

[11] "Debt Relief for Greek Farmers" Times (London) April 1, 1968 page 4.

[12] Johnson, Matthew Raphael. "The Greek Military Junta of 1967-1974" Accessed From: http://thattimehascome.blogspot.com/2011/05/greek-military-junta-of-1967-1974.html

[13] "Greek Leader Hits Back At West's Anarchy" Times (London) December 16, 1969 page 7.

"The Soviet Union, its Eastern European allies, and Greece's two socialist neighbors --Albania and Yugoslavia --appear to have realized that there are profits to be made by adjusting commercial and political policies that would allow for friendlier ties with Athens…most of the nine nations in question have responded on some level to Athens' willingness to bury the ideological hatchet at the market place." The Greeks also desired a détente with its communist neighbors, such as Bulgaria, Yugoslavia, and Albania as a means of easing pressure on its northern border. In addition, it was reported that the Greek junta's closer ties with the USSR and the Eastern Bloc could have been *"result of an effort by the Greek military to put pressure on the United States to resume full military aid to Greece rather than from a sudden emergence of affection for communists."*[14]

In January 1970, the Greek militarist regime unilaterally reduced tariffs on certain Soviet imports by about 50%. Soviet technicians visited northern Greece to prospect for the potential exploitation of peat deposits. The Greeks granted Most Favored Nation (MFN) trade status to the USSR. Despite these early efforts, Greek trade with the Soviet Union fell from 55 million rubles in 1967 to 44.5 million in 1968. The Greeks exported their surplus tobacco to the Soviet Union in exchange for goods. The Papadopoulos dictatorship also improved economic relations with its Soviet satellite neighbor Bulgaria. Radio Sofia (Bulgaria) noted that *"Our relations with Greece are correct and businesslike. A number of agreements of mutual interest have been signed and implemented during the last few years. Economic and trade relations are expanding. Both nations are looking for new forms of technical cooperation."* Greek Foreign Minister Panagiotis Pipinelis remarked in January 1968 that *"our relations with Bulgaria are better than those with the Soviet Union"* and that *"the stand of the Bulgarian press is much better than the Soviet one."* Pipinelis noted in March 1970 that the Bulgarian state-owned press and radio avoided *"provocative statements"* regarding the Greek military regime. Furthermore, the Greek militarist regime even asserted that coomunist Bulgaria displayed a better attitude about Papadopoulos than a free country like Sweden. Two-way Bulgarian-Greek trade totaled $33 million in 1968 and then fell to $15 million in 1969. Greek-Czechoslovak trade generally totaled $20 million per year. Czechoslovakia imported citrus fruits, tobacco, cotton, raw skins and hides, juices and currants from Greece. The Czech Communists exported timber, sugar, machinery, coal and coke, agricultural tractors, and chemical products to Greece under the military dictatorship. Under the Colonels' junta, the Hungarians held a trade fair at the Athens Hilton Hotel, which was described as *"the first trade exhibition in Athens by any communist country since the Papadopoulos government came to power in 1967."* In 1967 and 1968, Poland participated in the Salonika Trade Fair. The Polish state-owned press did not report Poland's presence at the Fair. Prime Minister Constantine Kollias noted to Radio Free Europe in June 1967 that Greece would like to continue peaceful trade relations with Poland. In October 1968, Greece and Poland signed a trade agreement and in 1969, two-way trade increased by 40%. Another trade agreement was signed between Poland and Greece in October 1969 which involved the exchange of goods which totaled $26 million. Poland shipped items such as coal, sulfur, meat, chemicals, and industrial products to Greece in exchange for Greek tobacco, citrus fruits, dried fruits, cotton, hides, and skins. In early 1970, the Greek and Albanian Chambers of Commerce signed a trade agreement in Paris, France. This trade agreement called for a two- way trade worth a little less than $1

---

[14] "The Colonels and the Comrades Greek Relations with Socialist Countries Thaw" Radio Free Europe/Radio Liberty Research Institute Accessed From: http://www.osaarchivum.org/greenfield/repository/osa:0b3ab581-d32a-4c02-a104-d2af9408dae1

million each way. The Albanian communist newspaper Bashkimi noted in February 1970 its intention for "*normalization*" of the Greek-Albanian relationship. The Albanian desire for trade was laid out in an article in Bashkimi. According to Bashkimi, the ruling communists had "*abided by and is still abiding by the principle of trade based on mutual advantage, without obstacles and discriminations with all countries which desire such a thing.*" In 1969, Yugoslavia exported $31 million worth of goods to Greece. Yugoslavia imported $33 million worth of goods from Greece. In September 1969, Yugoslavia and Greece signed a trade agreement and the two dictatorships were generally supportive of expanded economic relations.[15]

Portugal Under Dr. Antonio Salazar

In 1926, the Portuguese Republic moved along the path towards a military dictatorship. By the early 1930s, Dr. Antonio Salazar became the Prime Minister and established a highly authoritarian regime under his personal control. It was officially called the *Estado Novo* or New State and the ruling political party was known as the National Union (*Uniao Nacional* or UN). The Salazar dictatorship adhered to political and economic fascism, the regimentation of all sectors of the population, Catholic traditionalism, and opposition to communism and liberal capitalism.

The ideological statements, speeches, and documents that were issued by spokesmen and theorists of the Salazar regime consistently opposed free market liberal capitalism and supported class collaboration through agencies of the corporative state. Furthermore, the New State also strongly prescribed state interventionism into the private economy and even the establishment of state-owned enterprises. The ultimate goals of the economic policy of the Salazar regime were maximized production, economic modernization, social solidarity, and the creation of a utopian fascist state. The Portuguese Constitution of 1933 stipulated that "*The economic organisation of the State has as its principal duty the maximisation of production and useful social wealth, and to establish a collective life that will empower the State and ensure justice for all citizens...The State will regulate the nation's economic relations with other countries in accordance with the principle of adequate co-operation without prejudicing specially obtained commercial advantages or the nation's indispensable ability to defend itself from external threats or attacks...The State has the right and obligation to co-ordinate and to regulate social and economic life for the attainment of the following objectives: To establish an equilibrium of professions, occupations, capital and labour within the population; To defend the national economy from agricultural, industrial and commercial exploitation of a parasitical nature, or of a nature that is incompatible with the superior interests of human life...The State will favour private economic activities that, when all other things are equal, are more profitable without prejudice to the social benefits therefore attributed and the subsequent protection of small domestic industries...The State may only intervene directly in the management of private economic interests when it has to finance them for the attainment of social benefits superior to those that could be achieved without State intervention...*"

Specific policy measures prescribed in the Salazar-era Constitution included the "*formation and the development of the national corporatist economy, ensuring that its several*

[15] "The Colonels and the Comrades Greek Relations with Socialist Countries Thaw" Radio Free Europe/Radio Liberty Research Institute Accessed From: http://www.osaarchivum.org/greenfield/repository/osa:0b3ab581-d32a-4c02-a104-d2af9408dae1

elements do not establish between them a system of competition that is unregulated and contrary to society's and their own just objectives, but rather that they collaborate mutually as members of the same collective..."

The role of private property in the New State was remarkably similar to that of the National Socialists in Germany and the Italian Fascists: *"Property, capital and labour fulfill a social function within a regime of economic co-operation and solidarity..."* The state-sanctioned corporations were also recognized as the bodies that were tasked to negotiate labor contracts and relations between employers and employees: *"The economic corporations that are recognised by the State may negotiate collective contracts of employment. Such contracts will be invalid if they have been agreed without their intervention...All litigation relating to labour relations are the competence of special tribunals...No party to the relations between labour and capital are permitted to suspend their activity in furtherance of their demands...The State will promote and favour institutions of solidarity, welfare, co-operation and mutuality."*[16]

In 1934, Salazar noted in a speech before the First Congress of the *Uniao Nacional* that the ideology of the New State was *"as distinct from the individualistic liberalism of some countries and from internationalism of the Left, as it is from other theoretical and practical systems that have originated abroad as a reaction against liberalism and internationalism."*[17] Salazar remarked at a meeting of the *Uniao Nacional* that *"...We want to dignify labor and harmonize property with society. We want to move towards a new economy working in harmony with human nature under the authority of a strong state capable of defending the nation's superior interests its wealth and its labor be it from capitalist excesses be it from destructive Bolshevism. We want to satisfy proletarian demands within order, justice, and national balance to a greater degree than was done by those who promised everything."*[18]

The anti-free market rhetoric continued after World War II and even after Salazar left office in 1968 due to ill health. For example, one Portuguese propaganda booklet asserted in 1945 that *"The inhuman selfishness of liberal economy has been replaced by a more fertile and a stronger ideal of social solidarity."*[19]

Salazar's successor and fellow New State architect Marcello Caetano continued to support the ideological foundations of the corporative state and state interventionism in the economy. Caetano stated in 1968 that *"...private interests must be subordinate to the general: the profession, production or the Nation. The corporative organization disciplines competition and seeks to maintain harmony and balance within each sector...Corporativism must be lived and put into practice by the whole nation. It must dominate the guidelines of companies and*

---

[16] 1933 Political Constitution of the Portuguese Republic Official edition published by the National Press, Lisbon (1933) Accessed From: http://www.cphrc.org/index.php/documents/docnesta/167-1933-02-22-political-constitution-of-the-portuguese-republic-part-1#section 4

[17] Salazar's speech to the 1st Congress of the Uniao Nacional Lisbon, 26 May 1934 Accessed From: http://www.cphrc.org/index.php/documents/docnesta/84-1934-05-26-salazars-speech-to-the-first-congress-of-the-uniao-nacional

[18] De Meneses, Filipe. Salazar: A Political Biography (Enigma Books 2013) pages 109-110.

[19] Secretariado Nacional da Informacao. The National Revolution 20 Years of Mighty Achievements May 28, 1926-May 28, 1945 (Editions SNI, 1945) page 10.

settle deep into the consciousness of the workers."[20] In 1970, Caetano observed that Portugal did not experience real capitalism. He stated that the corporative system took care of the workers and asserted that there was little worker dissatisfaction.[21] Caetano even admitted in 1970 that the New State fulfilled some of the goals of socialism: "*As I have stressed more than once, not the least merit of corporativism in Portugal is that it has built up a network of protection for the worker as the national economy has developed without any need for the open strife and painful suffering that in other countries the workers had to undergo to gain the rights of labor...**the corporative state has in effect carried out what the socialist parties set out to achieve in those countries where they exist and it has the capacity to continue to put it into practice**. General legislation and the norms of collective work agreements regulate work, condition, and restrict the action of employers and protect the worker.*"[22]

One particularly unpleasant feature of the Salazar dictatorship was its tilt towards the European Axis Powers for much of the 1930s and early 1940s. While Portugal remained officially neutral during World War II, the Salazar regime engaged in cooperation with Nazi Germany, Fascist Italy, and Franco's Spain. The Portuguese secret police's (PDVE) first agents were trained by the Nazi Gestapo. In fact, one of the PDVE's first chiefs, Neves Graca, was a student of the infamous SS *Obersturmbannfuhrer* Josef Kramer.[23] Furthermore, the PDVE approached and harassed British nationals in Portugal.[24] In 1937, Fascist Italy dispatched four OVRA[25] advisors to train the PDVE under the terms of a technical accord.[26]

Other Portuguese institutions were the subjects of Nazi attention and even praise. The German Ambassador Baron von Hoyningen-Huene was pleased that the paramilitary Portuguese Legion expressed interest in using the Nazi SA and SS as the model of its development. He noted that "*It is undoubtedly in our interest that Portugal follows our model in this organization as well, because by it one can expect progress in the promotion of appreciation for National Socialist Germany.*"[27] Henceforth, the Portuguese Legion and Youth were supplied with German advisers.[28] Elements of the Portuguese New State also contained outright pro-Nazi personalities. For example, the pro-Nazi, racialist Santos Costa was the Minister of Defense.[29] Portugal also purchased weapons from the Axis countries. For example, during a 1937 parade of Portuguese Youth and Legion members, German-built Ju-52 bombers flew overhead. After the suicide of

---

[20] Makler, Harry M. "The Portuguese Industrial Elite and Its Corporative Relations: A Study of Compartmentalization in an Authoritarian Regime" Economic Development and Cultural Change April 1976 pages 495 and 518.

[21] "Caetano Sets His Face Against Socialism" Times (London) February 23, 1970 page 4.

[22] Caetano, Marcello. The Time Has Come for Action (Secretaria de Estado da Informacao e Turismo, 1970) pages 15-16.

[23] Angelo Del Boca and Mario Giovana. Fascism today: a world survey (Pantheon Books, 1969) page 252.

[24] Nicholas Booth. ZigZag: The Incredible Wartime Exploits of Double Agent Eddie Chapman (Skyhorse Publishing 2013)

[25] The OVRA was the Fascist secret police force under Mussolini.

[26] L. F. Bruyning. Italy – Europe (Rodopi, 1990) page 102.

[27] De Meneses, Filipe. Salazar: A Political Biography (Enigma Books 2013) page 143.

[28] Free Europe Volume 5 1942 page 31.

[29] Angelo Del Boca and Mario Giovana. Fascism today: a world survey (Pantheon Books, 1969) page 252.

Adolf Hitler, the Salazar government declared a period of official mourning. A monarchist writer named Alfredo Pimenta noted in a letter to Salazar that he supported the censorship by the New State in order to eliminate "*insult and injury to Germany and Hitler or commentaries based on war news which compromise Portugal's neutral position.*" Pimenta also noted that this censorship did not go far enough since "*all of this misplaced love for England and France serves only to mask the hatred of regimes founded on Authority.*" The monarchist daily A Voz accused the *Uniao Nacional* publication Diario da Mamba of pro-Nazi sympathies. A German resident of Portugal wrote a letter to the official Nazi publishing which stated that "*Dr. Salazar is a friend of the Germans but the English do not like this and try to create internal difficulties.*"

Films were shown of the German conquest of Poland to leaders in the Portuguese armed forces, Portuguese Youth, and the press at the German Legation in Lisbon.[30] The Portuguese Anti-British Youth was formed and published a review called Chains of Fire. Another group called the Anti-British League published a manifesto. The British Embassy noted in 1940 that "*The Germans...made a determined effort to persuade the Portuguese government that the very existence of Dr. Salazar's regime was being threatened by the country's pro-British sympathies. They pointed out that the cause of the Allies was being hailed as the cause of the democracies and was being invoked by Dr. Salazar's political enemies in the hope of bringing about his downfall.*"[31] In 1941, the German Legation published the pamphlet titled I Accuse England, which examined British-Portuguese relations through the lens of anti-Semitism.[32] In 1942, the PDVE broke up a British spy ring which involved a number of employees of the Shell oil company.[33] During World War II, pro-German feelings existed in the Portuguese armed forces, the Portuguese Legion, the international police, the secret police, and the youth movement. In 1941, the Legion issued an order that announced its solidarity with Germany.[34]

In May 1941, Ambassador Huene conversed with Salazar and reported to his superiors that the Portuguese dictator leaned towards the Axis Powers. Ambassador Huene noted that Salazar was "*more emphatic than ever before in embracing the cause of the reorganization of Europe and it was incomprehensible to him that England should fail to recognize it....Salazar showed great interest in the effects of future intra-European economic cooperation and asked detailed questions about the experiences to date, particularly in the matter of a central clearing system.*"[35] In early 1943, Salazar noted that "*an American victory...signified the triumph of the materialism of Wall Street and the immorality of Hollywood, not to mention the threat posed to the Atlantic Islands.*"[36]

Along with the nationalist and corporative Integralists, the other quasi-fascist organization that initially aligned itself with the Salazar regime was the National Syndicalists (NS). The NS were radicals whose opposition to liberal capitalism and free government was laden with radical, revolutionary quasi-Nazi rhetoric. The NS believed that financial capital led

---

[30] De Meneses, Filipe. Salazar: A Political Biography (Enigma Books 2013) pages 229-233.
[31] Ibid, pages 229-233.
[32] Ibid, pages 250-251.
[33] Ibid, pages 229-233.
[34] Leitz, Christian. Nazi Germany and Neutral Europe During the Second World War (Manchester University Press, 2000) pages 151-156.
[35] De Meneses, Filipe. Salazar: A Political Biography (Enigma Books 2013) pages 229-233.
[36] Leitz, Christian. Nazi Germany and Neutral Europe During the Second World War (Manchester University Press, 2000) pages 151-156.

"to the death of small employers and to the proletarianisation of the working masses" which in turn would *"lead to the rebellion of the modern slaves."* The NS leader Francisco Rolao Preto noted that *"In order to dominate politics, liberal-democracy centralises and concentrates the profits of governing the country in a few hands."*

According to the NS, private enterprise was to serve the state and certain sectors of the economy would even be nationalized. The NS recognized that private property *"is a natural right but one that must be defined in accordance with social utility…the nation's public and private economies must be disciplined and directed by the State that has a duty to control them and intervene whenever the public and collective good, equity or social justice so demand."* The State, according to the NS, was *"the leader of national production."* The NS would ensure *"the common good"* and *"the entire socio-economic nation will be constructed in harmony with its moral and material interests representing labour and the nation's civic life through its hierarchies."* The NS attacked employers for noncompliance with working hour legislation, paying poor wages, and an unwillingness to collaborate with employees. The *"Nationalist State"* of the NS called for the government to *"nationalize"* capital, discipline its owners, and ensure *"social harmony,"* minimum salaries, retirement benefits and social security. The NS northern zone secretariat supported *"a policy of decisive protection for agriculture, including obligatory agricultural labour, the enforced unionization of all social classes, and State control of the banks."* The publication <u>Revolucao</u> engaged in various *"anti-plutocratic"* campaigns. The radical faction of the NS led by Antonio Tinoco supported more socialism, *"anti-capitalism,"* and less respect for private property. The Guimaraes delegation of the NS noted its opposition to *"financiers and plutocrats who are, to a greater or lesser degree, irresponsible. National Syndicalism is against capitalism, that is, it is against that organization of production that has established predominance, more than a predominance, the tyranny of property and capital over technique and labour."* The NS was to establish *"organic collectivism"* to battle the *"internationalist and red"* ideology of the communists. The NS commented that *"When we note the danger represented by the ever-increasing threat of communism there are very few conservatives who do not shrug their robust shoulders in disdain, certain that there is nothing to it."* In September 1932, the NS created *"union houses"* throughout Portugal to serve as social, education, and propaganda centers. A NS leader Francisco Moreira stated: *"I will never cease to be a revolutionary against the bourgeois and capitalist society which has to this date only sought to exploit the working class. Here I am today, ready once more for battle in defence of the principles which are proclaimed by National Syndicalism."*

Even the Integralists became radicalized in the 1930s and moved in a more pronounced anti-capitalist direction. Salazar regime figures sought to co-opt the radicals of the NS and Integralists into government-controlled mass organizations. An Integralist named Brigadier Joao de Almeida expressed his disdain for *"the exploitation by capitalists who don't work…while workers of all categories remain in the darkest misery."* Pedro Teotonio Pereira, a top Integralist and Under-Secretary of State for Corporations, called for NS members and leaders to construct a corporative state in collaboration with the Salazar regime. NS members were recruited by Salazar as civil servants employed at the National Labor and Welfare Institute (INTP) and militants of the government-controlled labor unions (the *sindicatos*). NS members openly aligned themselves with the Axis Powers during World War II. The NS facilitated pro-Axis events in Portugal and disseminated pro-Nazi propaganda. For example, the NS commission in Coimbra distributed pro-Nazi propaganda in December 1939. These NS activities were aided by German and Italian agents. Even in 1943, NS members wrote for Portuguese journals that were in turn funded by Germany. During this period of time, the NS maintained close relations with the Italian and German Embassies. Delegations of the Italian Fascist and German Nazi Parties regularly attended NS rallies.[37] Relations with the international fascist organization CAUR was maintained by the Vanguard Students' Action (AEV) which was controlled by the government's National Propaganda Secretariat (SPN). The novelist Eca de Queiroz represented Salazar's Portugal and the National Syndicalists at the Comitati d'Azione per l'Universalita di Roma (CAUR) international fascist congress at Montreaux in 1934.[38]

The Salazar regime also opened modern Portugal to the concept of the highly interventionist state in the realm of the private economy. At least one historian pointed this fact out in a very articulate fashion. The Portuguese historian A.H. de Oliveira Marques observed that the statist and even socialist legacy of the Salazar-Caetano period shaped modern Portugal in a leftist fashion: "***But it seems beyond doubt that the corporative state shaped a new Portugal very much in the socialist way, which will be hard to destroy. Regardless of its faults and poor results in production and standard of living the corporate system built up an economically organized country an interventionist state essentially different from the liberal, laissez faire Republican order. Almost forty years of actual performance have made the Portuguese accustomed to, and more and more dependent on the state***."[39]

At first, independent labor unions and employers' organizations were either suppressed or subjected to strict government oversight. In 1931 and 1932, the General Confederation of Labor (CGT) was abolished and trade unions were placed under government control. In 1931, the employers' organizations were transformed into *gremios*. A Superior Council for the National Economy was formed, which extended state control to farming, labor, and industry.[40] In 1933, Salazar promulgated the National Labor Statute which forbade strikes and lockouts. Business and labor were organized into corporative bodies called *gremios* and *sindicatos*. Both bodies denounced class warfare and liberal capitalism.[41] By 1934, it was already reported that the Portuguese economy could be characterize as a state-controlled economy in private hands. During this time, the Portuguese government lent money to needy private firms as a means of stabilizing various economic sectors. Meanwhile, by 1934, the Salazar regime created a state-owned tobacco company, while government ownership of the railroads was maintained. The government controlled the sales tax rates on goods, while state-sanctioned cartels were formed in the fruit and fish export industries. Such compulsory cartelization subjected these sectors to the regimentation of government decrees.[42]

Early in the Salazar regime, independent, private businesses and industrialists protested the strong government regulations and intrusions into the Portuguese economy. The Salazar regime also formed the Organizations of Economic Coordination, which imposed fines, taxes, dues, stamps, and permits on businesses. As of 1937, the Organizations for Economic

---

[37] Pinto, Antonio Costa. The Blue Shirts (Social Science Monographs Boulder 2000) Accessed From: http://antoniocostapinto.eu/docs/books/The%20Blue%20Shirts_832172.pdf

[38] De Meneses, Filipe. Salazar: A Political Biography (Enigma Books 2013) pages 250-251.

[39] Marques, A.H. de Oliveira. History of Portugal (Columbia University Press 1972) page 183.

[40] Wiarda, Howard J. Corporatism and Development (University of Massachusetts Press, 1977) page 98.

[41] Gallagher, Tom. Portugal: a twentieth-century interpretation (Manchester University Press, 1983) page 76.

[42] "Portugal Opposed to All Radicalism" The New York Times September 23, 1934 page E2.

Coordination regulated the wheat, wine, fishing, import-export, canning, mining, cork, and other industries. As of 1934, the state owned the tobacco, oil, and railroad enterprises. More monopolies and oligopolies were also formed under the control of the state. Wiarda noted that such policies and decrees were examples of *"state capitalism."* Wiarda observed that *"a system of capitalism was thus created by the government often over the violent objections and reluctance of the 'capitalist class' itself."* The government controlled the *gremios* through the approval of their charters, regulation of their elections, budgeting their activities, and controlling their political participation.[43]

In 1936, the Corporative Technical Council of Commerce and Industry was formed to provide a corporative character to the administration of business and industry. Cadres of *"negotiators"* were utilized by the Council to further manage trade and commerce in the years prior to World War II. By the late 1930s, new government agencies proliferated in Salazar's New State. Such agencies included the Subsecretariat of State for Corporations, the National Institute of Labor and Social Welfare, the National Foundation for Joy at Work, national labor tribunals, and massive numbers of juntas, commissions, offices, and agencies that regulated and controlled the day-to-day operations of the economy.[44]

In October 1939, the Ministry of Commerce and Industry was given full powers to regulate the economy. The Ministry used the existing corporative agencies and bureaucracies to control the Portuguese economy. New regulatory bodies for the control of chemicals, pharmaceuticals, food, vegetable oils, and metals were created by 1939. In June 1940, these regulatory bodies took full control of the *gremios* in an effort to *"discipline"* prices and production. Increasingly, agriculture was centralized and controlled by the Salazar regime. During World War II, food and consumer goods were rationed, while decrees were issued that banned hoarding. Peasant crop prices were fixed by the state, while the Salazar government suppressed the black market and illegal slaughterhouses. In April 1943, the government decreed the right to regulate all salaries and working conditions of all employees. The government used the *gremios* to enforce price controls, payments, production schedules, and taxes. In February 1943, the Portuguese government assumed increased powers to fully mobilize all essential industries, enterprises, and labor.[45]

From 1946 through the 1950s, the corporative system was retained from the World War II period. In 1966, Salazar bragged that *"in our century we are the only corporative revolution that triumphed."* In the 1960s, the corporative agencies reportedly became bureaucratic sinecures for career officials. This growth in bureaucracy absorbed a whopping 1/3 of the national budget. The Salazar dictatorship used the *gremios* to:

1) Transmit directives to the landowners and industrialists on what products could be manufactured or grown.
2) How much these businesses could produce.
3) The customers that these capitalist could sell their products to.
4) The fixing of sale prices.[46]

---

[43] Wiarda, Howard J. Corporatism and Development (University of Massachusetts Press, 1977) pages 141-143.
[44] Ibid, pages 151-155.
[45] Ibid, pages 165-169.
[46] Ibid, pages 229-231.

After Marcello Caetano became the new Portuguese dictator, the corporative state and the regulated economy were retained as institutional features of the New State. In June 1969, Caetano's government mandated direct negotiations between the employers and workers concerning labor contracts. The state still intervened in the relations between the *sindicatos* and *gremios* and rewrote labor-management contracts.[47]

Predictably, the regulations and corporative policies were heartedly circumvented and opposed by the business and landowning classes in Portugal. In 1933, The New York Times commented that if the policies of the Portuguese corporate state were transferred to the United States, it would provoke *"violent opposition on the part of American business men and trade unionists."*[48] Years later, the situation in Portugal did not improve. A Portuguese shopkeeper noted in 1961 *"You're all right if you're rich and you're all right if you're poor, but if you're in the middle class it is taxes, taxes. Pay this, pay that. We are the oppressed class here."*[49] Historian Tom Gallagher reported that *"Many landowners and industrialists recognized the corporative agencies for what they were, networks of state surveillance, through which the government sought to dilute any real interest group or class based action."*[50]

Harry Makler authored a study on the relations between the business community and the corporative agencies of the New State. He observed that businessmen continuously complained about the *gremios* in Portugal. Industrialists viewed the *gremios* as ineffective bodies that were ignored by the government. Furthermore, Makler also reported that the government was insensitive to any pro-business claims of the *gremios*. One owner of a textile firm in northern Portugal reported that *"I go to the gremio to discuss problems of general interest that are fundamental to our industry such as the labor contract which was written without us being consulted. We only were officially informed there should be a 40% raise in salaries one week, after the Government's decision."* An owner of a Lisbon metallurgical products factory noted that *"The gremio presents its reports to the Corporacao da Industria which takes them to the Government. However, the Government does as it pleases paying no attention to these reports. Instead of asking the opinion of people with experience in the field they would rather confer with technocrats."*[51]

Even in the post-World War II period, the Salazar regime engaged periodically in anti-Western and anti-American propaganda and took positions in direct conflict to Washington's official Cold War stances. The catalysts for such Portuguese anti-US positions was the American opposition to Lisbon's colonialism and invasion of Goa in India. In 1961, Portuguese newspapers carried out an anti-US campaign, which contrasted the violent race problems in

---

[47] Williamson, Peter J. Varieties of Corporatism (Cambridge University Press, 1985) pages 113-114.

[48] "Portugal Builds Corporate State" New York Times December 3, 1933 page N4.

[49] Welles, Benjamin. "Salazar's Critics Score Tax Burden" New York Times January 30, 1961 page 2.

[50] Gallagher, Tom. Portugal: a twentieth-century interpretation (Manchester University Press, 1983) page 69.

[51] Makler, Harry M. "The Portuguese Industrial Elite and Its Corporative Relations: A Study of Compartmentalization in an Authoritarian Regime" Economic Development and Cultural Change April 1976 pages 495 and 518.

Alabama with that of loyal, happy African citizens in Portugal's colonies that demonstrated their support of the Salazar regime.[52]

New York Times writer Benjamin Welles opined that Salazar's Portugal was contemplating a shift to the Left in foreign policy by opening relations with China and the Soviet Union. An editorial in a Portuguese newspaper asserted that *"Portugal is not an enemy of the Soviet Union or of communist China, but only of communism."* Portugal was considering recognition of Red China as a means of securing its continued control over Macao and deepening its anti-Western foreign policy. Portugal also allowed the Red Chinese to utilize Macao in order to smuggle embargoed goods.[53] The Portuguese even justified Red China's invasion of India in 1962. An official of the Salazar regime commented that *"China's action against India has nothing to do with communism. Any government in Peking might have started it because it responds to old Chinese national aspirations."*[54] Portugal even suspended its commitment to the anti-communist alliance and disengaged itself from close relations with Taiwan (Nationalist China). Under pressure from Red China, Portugal shut down the Nationalist Chinese diplomatic missions in Macao under pressure from Red China in 1965.[55]

In 1966, Salazar asserted that NATO should no longer expect *"automatic cooperation"* from Portugal. He also elaborated that *"as to our relations with the Eastern countries, we continue our policy of seeking to broaden the economic and commercial contacts, which do not necessarily exclude other types of relations with those with whom they would be the most convenient if these turn out to be possible or mutually advantageous."* Lisbon also sought new markets in the communist world for their export-oriented businesses. Portugal also maintained *"normal commercial and diplomatic relations"* with communist Cuba and traded with several Eastern Bloc states.[56] Foreign Minister Alberto Nogueira opened Portuguese trade relations with Romania, Poland, Hungary, Czechoslovakia, and Yugoslavia. This trade was handled through banks which served as intermediaries in such commercial transactions.[57]

In all fairness, the communist threat to Portugal was real. On the one hand, the Soviets and their allies sought to separate the Salazar regime away from NATO and the United States based on Washington's critique of Lisbon's colonialism and human rights violations. On the other hand, Moscow sought to subvert the Salazar and Caetano dictatorships through the Communist Party of Portugal and the Armed Forces Movement, which came into being by 1973. The communist road to almost absolute power was paved by a relatively popular revolution against the fascistic regime of Caetano. The Soviets and their allies penetrated the Portuguese armed forces, which were expected to lead this revolution. Defecting Czechoslovak Major General and top Warsaw Pact planner Jan Sejna recalled the long-term strategy towards Portugal: *"As party secretary in the Czechoslovak Ministry of Defense. I was also aware of the*

---

[52] Welles, Benjamin. "Lisbon 'Plays Up' Alabama Strife" New York Times May 28, 1961 page 38.

[53] Welles, Benjamin. "Tie to Red China Hinted in Lisbon" New York Times January 12, 1962 page 2.

[54] Hoffman, Paul. "Kind Words for Peking" New York Times December 8, 1962 page 12.

[55] "Taiwan's Office in Macao Is Shut Down by Portugal" New York Times March 13, 1965 page 2.

[56] Szulc, Tad. "Salazar Rules Out Automatic Support Of NATO by Lisbon" New York Times March 24, 1966 page 1.

[57] "Lisbon to Expand Trade With Reds" New York Times February 12, 1966 page 3.

Soviet long-term plan for Portugal which envisages the establishment of a 'progressive democratic government' under communist control by 1976-77. According to the Soviets the existing state and security apparatus could be smashed only by 'progressive' military forces, it was therefore essential for the PCP to penetrate the armed forces. This analysis was incorporated into the overall Warsaw Pact strategic plan which grouped Portugal with Italy. Greece and Turkey as the weakest links in NATO. The plan envisaged, however, that Portugal should not withdraw from NATO immediately after the collapse of the old regime, because continued membership would provide the Warsaw Pact with intelligence sources in NATO, disrupt the workings of the NATO organization, and contribute to the de facto dissolution of NATO. This process would be assisted in due course by the arrival in power of the Italian Communist Party. Within Portugal, continued adherence to NATO would still fears of the Portuguese bourgeoisie, remove any pretext for intervention by the United States and win time for the PCP to consolidate its hold on the armed forces and bureaucracy."[58]

When the leftist-reformist Armed Forces Movement (AFM) under General Spinola took power in 1974, the communists and their far-left allies were hard at work to consolidate a totalitarian dictatorship. Such a regime was opposed to the ultimate social-democratic goals of General Spinola and his supporters. The chief of the Portuguese COPCON security forces General de Carvalho threatened Portuguese anti-communists when he stated "*In the short term I think we will have to herd them into the bullring.*" General de Carvalho threatened that the AFM would carry out a "*very hard repression…We cannot have a revolution by entirely peaceful means.*"[59]

The waves of political persecution started in earnest after the AFM took power. In certain respects, these measures mimicked the hardcore fascist authoritarianism of the New State. In September 1974, the AFM banned the Portuguese Nationalist Party, the Progressive Party, the Liberal Party, and the Christian Democrat Party. Groups of Portuguese Communists and Army troops prevented anti-communist demonstrations. In November 1974, the Communists and other leftist-extremists sacked the offices of the Center Democratic Party. In January 1975, the AFM decreed that the Portuguese Communist Party would control the labor unions. Sensing the turn towards communist totalitarianism, President Spinola fled Portugal in March 1975. After General Spinola's departure, a Supreme Revolutionary Council took control of the AFM. In May 1975, the Socialist Party newspaper Republica was seized by Communist Party printers and taken over by the Army. In July 1975, the AFM moved to a one-party state by creating "*people's committees.*" Hence, the Socialists resigned from the AFM.[60]

The Soviets and Cubans also penetrated the AFM junta. The Portuguese AFM received $38 million in 1974 from the KGB and several top Portuguese military junta were Soviet agents and collaborators with the DGI of Cuba.[61] Not unsurprisingly, the AFM regime also assisted international revolutionary pro-Soviet and pro-Cuban forces in Africa and Latin America. In the spring of 1975, the AFM government in Portugal established ties with the South American leftist terrorist coordinating committee called the JCR. The JCR maintained a headquarters that was

---

[58] "Statement Describes Soviet Portugal Plans" The Sun (Lowell Mass.) May 16, 1975 page 5.

[59] "Portugal; To the Bullring" The Economist August 2, 1975 page 49.

[60] "Soldiers Don't Let Go" Economist July 19, 1975 page 10.

[61] Moss, Robert. The Collapse of Democracy (Abacus 1977) page 290.

camped in various militia units on the Tagus River with Portuguese armed leftists and foreigners that consisted of Cuban troops, Uruguayan Tupamaros, and Chilean leftists.[62]

The AFM also turned over a number of Portugal's colonies over to communist forces. By 1974-1975, Sao Tome e Principe became independent of Portugal and was turned over to the communists of the Movement for the Liberation of Sao Tome e Principe (MLSTP). On Soviet orders 1,000-1,500 Angolan troops were sent under the command of Cuban and Soviet officers. The AFM of Portugal handed power over to the MLSTP whose leaders were trained in East Germany or took orders from the USSR. Others were members of the Portuguese Communist Party.[63]

In Angola, the MPLA victory was aided by Portuguese Communists and the extreme left wing element in the AFM government. Portuguese soldiers also occasionally aided communist MPLA forces in the battles against the rival socialists of the FNLA in 1975. Portuguese troops and MPLA armored units participated in an assault on FNLA installations in Luanda.[64]

The Armed Forces Movement (AFM) government in Lisbon ordered its troops stationed in Mozambique to assume defensive operations. AFM committees in Mozambique independent of the national government refused to replenish weapons supplies during the decolonization process. The security forces of the communist Front for the Liberation of Mozambique (Frelimo) created a plan in Tanzania to arrest anti-Frelimo opposition. Portugal reportedly aided the Frelimo communists. Students were enticed to return from foreign countries and were arrested at the airports by Frelimo militants and the Portuguese. Portuguese secret police arrested anti-Frelimo activists at the country's airports and handed them over to Frelimo. Portuguese Nationalist Party (PCN) members were dispatched to Frelimo military barracks.[65]

Spain Under General Francisco Franco (1946-1975)

In order to comprehend the collectivism and fascism of General Francisco Franco and the FET/Falange, one must explore its historical antecedent in Spain in the form of the proto-fascist government of Jose Antonio Primo De Rivera. Both exhibited an organic nationalism that theoretically unified the social classes, opposed Marxism-Leninism, and heavily intervened in the economy. Such policies were reflective of the personal political ideology of Primo De Rivera himself. De Rivera opposed classical liberal, free market economics as principles that were contrary to nationalism and the strong state. For example, he noted in a speech in March 1935 that *"Property, in the sense that we have been hitherto regarding it, is coming to its end. The masses, who to a great extent are right, and who moreover have the power, are going to put paid to it, by peaceful means or by violence."* In September 1935, De Rivera noted that *"Capital...is an economic instrument which must serve the entire economy, and hence may not be an instrument for the advantage and privilege of the few who have had the good luck to get in first."* In a speech titled Spain and Barbarism (March 1935), De Rivera noted that *"Property is not capital: capital is an economic tool, and as a tool it must be put to the service of the economic*

---

[62] Sterling, Claire. The Terror Network (Penguin Group USA Incorporated 1983)

[63] Crozier, Brian. The Rise and Fall of the Soviet Empire (Forum 1999) page 344.

[64] Greig, Ian. The Communist Challenge to Africa (Foreign Affairs Publishing Co., 1977) pages 217-230.

[65] Cabrita, Joao. Mozambique: The Tortuous Road to Democracy (Palgrave Macmillan Limited, 2000)

whole, not the personal wellbeing of any one person. The reservoirs of capital should be like the reservoirs of water; not constructed so that one or two people may hold regattas on the surface, but so that the flow of rivers may be regulated and the hydro-electric plants may be driven." De Rivera noted in New Light in Spain (May 1934) that *"Liberalism is the mockery of the unfortunate. It proclaims marvelous rights: freedom of thought, freedom to propagate ideas, freedom of work...But these rights are mere luxuries for the favoured ones of fortune. The poor, in a Liberal regime, may not be bludgeoned into working; but they are starved out. The isolated workman, possessed of every sort of right on paper, has to choose between dying of starvation and accepting the terms the capitalist offers him, however hard they may be. Under the Liberal system the cruel irony could be seen of men and women working themselves to skeletons, twelve hours a day, for a miserable wage, and yet being assured by the law that they were 'free' men and women."*[66]

Some influential rightist-nationalists also supported the social reforms and interventionism that were enacted by Primo De Rivera. Primo De Rivera's Minister of Finance Calvo Sotelo believed that social reform would stave off a leftist, class-based revolution in Spain. He found that the programs of the Primo De Rivera government were sabotaged by the *"obstinate passivity of the conservative classes."* Sotelo observed that the tax reform and anti-evasion programs were viewed as *"Bolshevism"* by the landowners. In response, he also viewed the landowners and bankers as *"men of narrow vision."*[67] Specifically, in early 1926, Sotelo decreed the imposition of massive taxes on *"incomes and profits"* and the prosecution of tax evaders. The financial and industrial capitalist classes protested these measures and consequently, they were dropped.[68]

Like General Franco and the FET/Falange, Primo De Rivera also appealed to the Left to support his collectivist-fascist reform programs in the field of labor relations and a corporative state. Primo's Minister of the Interior Martinez Anido favored the *Sindicatos Libres*. Furthermore, the government approved the existence of a pliant *Union General de Trabajadores* (UGT). The regime of Primo De Rivera also enacted a corporative labor code. Wage disputes were settled by mixed committees called *comites parltarios,* which were composed of employers and unions. UGT officials became government bureaucrats who served in the *comites parltarios*.[69] The reformist elements within the UGT and Workers' Socialist Party of Spain (PSOE) paved the way for the acceptance of Primo's corporatist policies by elements of the Left. UGT officials occupied positions within the National Corporatist Organization, as well as many technical and administrative agencies. The 1926 Labor Code was written with the help of UGT

---

[66] Jose Antonio Primo De Rivera: Anthology of Speeches and Quotes (Ediciones Prensa del Movimiento Madrid 1950) Accessed From: http://archive.org/stream/JoseAntonioPrimoDeRivera-AnthologyOfSpeechesAndQuotes/JoseAntonioPrimoDeRivera-AnthologyOfSpeechesAndQuotes_djvu.txt

[67] Carr, Raymond. Modern Spain, 1875-1980 (Oxford University Press, 1980) page 109.

[68] Lieberman, Sima. The Contemporary Spanish Economy: A Historical Perspective (Routledge, 2013) pages 141-143.

[69] Lieberman, Sima. The Contemporary Spanish Economy: A Historical Perspective (Routledge, 2013) pages 141-143.

representatives.[70] Hence, Primo De Rivera's Popular Union and the PSOE became major pillars of the fascist dictatorship.[71]

The regime's relations with private industry and landowners varied widely. On the one hand, J. Fontana and J. Nadal cautioned that *"One should also not be misled by the appearances of state intervention in the economy, and by the fiction of the corporative state. It is true that immense number of bodies were created-committees, boards, councils-which gave the impression of controlling everything."* Reportedly, big business elites populated state economic agencies and used them to protect their respective industries. Primo De Rivera's government built roads, repaired and constructed railroads, and developed irrigation and rural electrification programs. The government also provided assistance and protection for industrial enterprises. In 1928, semi-public banks such as the *Banco Exterior de Espana* were formed by the government to finance trade with South America. The state intervened in order to rescue the coal, lead, and resin industries. The government also attempted to create a national car industry and to finance the home-grown cotton industry. State monopolies were created to eliminate foreign interests in Spain. The *Compania Arrendataria del Monopolio del Petroleo, S.A.* (CAMPSA) was created in order for the Primo De Rivera government to appropriate most of the profits of Standard Oil and Shell, which maintained operations in Spain. In 1927, the monopoly for the distribution of oil was granted to a Spanish government-owned company. It was clear that the Primo regime severely restricted the control of foreign capital over the Spanish economy.[72]

Business groups were also represented in the corporative bodies, including the Council of the National Economy and regulatory commissions which controlled prices and markets. Businessmen also supported the protectionist and interventionist policies of the government. However, industrialists, bankers, and landowners expressed concern about the economic effects of massive government spending programs, state corruption, and favoritism in government contracts. Businessmen also opposed the excessive state regulation of social affairs and compulsory membership in the Joint Committees.[73] Not unsurprisingly, Primo De Rivera's interventions turned the Catalan bourgeoisie against his rule.[74]

One of the main battlefields between communist and fascist-style collectivists occurred during the Spanish Civil War. By the beginning of the late 1930s, the Spanish leftist Republicans built a government that became closely aligned with the Soviet Union. Aspects of Republican political and economic policies moved leftwards to state ownership of property, repression of rightists and other non-communists, and subordination to Moscow. Both Franco and the communist-dominated Republicans:
1) Looked to foreign totalitarian states as models.
2) Espoused economic and political collectivism.

---

[70] Berger, Stefan and Compston, Hugh. Policy Concertation and Social Partnership in Western Europe (Berghahn Books, 2002) pages 256-257.

[71] Lieberman, Sima. The Contemporary Spanish Economy: A Historical Perspective (Routledge, 2013) pages 141-143.

[72] Ibid, pages 141-143.

[73] Berger, Stefan and Compston, Hugh. Policy Concertation and Social Partnership in Western Europe (Berghahn Books, 2002) pages 256-257.

[74] Lieberman, Sima. The Contemporary Spanish Economy: A Historical Perspective (Routledge, 2013) pages 141-143.

3) Utilized the otherwise reviled international business community to gain valuable technology, funds, and war-related materials.

4) Constructed police states which utilized terror and other mass human rights violations.

The Republicans engaged in capitalist-style trading in order to raise hard currency for the war effort. In the summer of 1938, Republican authorities in Barcelona sold silver to private French and Belgian firms. From the summer of 1938 to January 1939, the Republicans raised $5 million in foreign currency for the war effort. In May and July 1938, secret provisions of the Republican government made it possible for the Ministry of Finance and Economy to legally mobilize all resources to raise foreign currency. The population was forced to turn over all gold, silver, bullion, jewels, and foreign assets to the Republican government. Private deposits in the Bank of Spain were expropriated, along with funds from the Reparations Fund. The Reparations Fund was financed from the proceeds of assets and properties confiscated from the alleged enemies of the Republicans. Old gold coins that were not sold to companies in Paris or Moscow were also deposited in the Bank of Spain. Until November 1938, these transactions generated $9 million in foreign currency. The Republican government also conducted business with private Swiss and French firms. In late 1938 and early 1939, remittances of precious metals from Catalonia to Paris netted the Republicans at least another $2 million. In 1938, the leftist, pro-Soviet Republican Prime Minister Negrin negotiated a credit of $75-100 million dollars with the USSR. Spain paid for this credit with bartered mercury, salt, lead, potassium, citric fruits, almonds, certain ships, and a small volume of gold. The Republicans also exported $7 million worth of goods such as lead, oranges, lemons, olive oil, peanuts, almonds, potassium chloride, tartaric acid, cork, and textiles. The National Subscription was used by the Republicans to channel gold coins, watches, charms, jewelry, and other valuables to raise foreign currency estimated to be worth one million pounds; six million francs; $500,000 US dollars; 2 million lira; and 5 million escudos.[75] The Spanish Republicans used the Soviet banking system and its branches in the United States and Europe to move funds to purchase goods and weapons.[76]

The wartime Spanish Republican governments also centralized the management of the private economy in the hands of the state. Part of this policy was rooted in the pro-Soviet socialist ideology of the successive Republican governments in Madrid. The Spanish Republicans also applied a practical reasoning for the imposition of state socialist policies. Quite simply, the Republicans needed to get their hands on as much wealth as possible to fund the war effort. It was believed that liberal capitalist methods were not up to the task in mobilizing the Spanish war effort. Minister of Finance (and future Prime Minister) Juan Negrin mobilized the financial wealth in the Republican zones to finance the war effort. Spain centralized and extended government control over its banks. Wartime government powers also granted the Spanish government to right to appropriate private wealth. The government also impounded the holdings of gold bullion, precious metals, and jewelry owned by individuals, private banks, and corporations in an effort to build up foreign exchange holdings. The government also encouraged private businessmen to export textiles, fruits, and nuts abroad in an effort to earn foreign

---

[75] Preston, Paul. Revolution and War in Spain, 1931-1939 (Routledge, 2012) pages 267-272.

[76] Seidman, Michael. Republic of Egos: A Social History of the Spanish Civil War (University of Wisconsin Press, 2002) page 46.

currency.[77] In 1938, the *Tribunales Especiales de Guardia* judged numerous cases of alleged infractions of the price control regulations. Special courts defended the consumers in the Republic against the *"greedy merchants and speculators."*[78]

The Republican state also used industrial chaos in the factories to seize control of the plants themselves. In August 1936, the Republican Minister of Industry and Commerce Placido Alvarez Buylla decreed that abandoned private enterprises were to be taken over by the state. By September 1936, the Giral government appointed state advisers to electric power companies and created a Board of Electricity to intervene in technical and administrative affairs. Outright communization policies were to be avoided, lest such experiments hamper production for the war effort. The Spanish Communist Party (PCE) Secretary Jose Diaz noted this in regard to what he termed the *"premature experiments in collectivization and socialization"* in Spain: *"If in the beginning these experiments were justified by the fact that big industrialists and landlords had abandoned their factories and estates and that it was necessary to continue production, later on they were not…At first it was understandable that the workers should take possession of the abandoned factories in order to continue production at all costs…I repeat that this was understandable and we are not going to censure it…But today when there is a government of the Popular Front in which all the forces engaged in the fight against fascism are represented such things are not only inadvisable but they have an opposite from that intended. Today we must coordinate production rapidly and intensify it under a single direction so as to provision the front and the rear with everything they need…To rush into these premature experiments in collectivization and socialization when the war was still undecided and at a time when the internal enemy aided by foreign fascism is violently attacking our positions and endangering the future of our country is absurd and is tantamount to aiding the enemy."* The Left Republican Councilor of Finance in the Regional Government testified that he used the worker's finances in collectivized properties *"to capture control of the collectives."* Finance Minister Juan Negrin told Louis Fischer *"When the war broke out working men's committees often Anarchist took over the factories…They paid themselves in wages everything they took from sales. Now they have no money. They are coming to me for running expenses and for raw materials. We will take advantage of their plight to gain control of the factories."* The official Communist <u>History of the Civil War and Revolution</u> concluded that *"There arose in the Spanish economy a very special kind of state capitalism. It was not the kind of state capitalism utilized or manipulated by the financial oligarchy. It was a state capitalism in which control was exercised through the representatives of the Popular Front parties which assured no small influence to the working class. The Giral government despite its limitations carried out revolutionary measures that until that time no bourgeois government in Spain had undertaken. And one can only speak of it with respect and admiration."*[79]

The Soviets rebuilt the Spanish regular police force and placed Communists in top positions. The Soviet NKVD opened its own prisons in Spain and carried out assassinations and launched flying raids. In 1937, the Soviets helped Spain developed SIM for counter-espionage

---

77 Jackson, Gabriel. <u>Juan Negrín: Physiologist, Socialist and Spanish Republican War Leader</u> (Sussex Academic Press, 2010) pages 50-51.

78 Seidman, Michael. <u>Republic of Egos: A Social History of the Spanish Civil War</u> (University of Wisconsin Press, 2002) page 167.

79 Bolloten, Burnett. <u>The Spanish Civil War: Revolution and Counterrevolution</u> (University of North Carolina Press, 1991) pages 222-223.

and became a part of the Soviet apparatus. SIM used Soviet techniques of barbaric physical torture and sensory and disorientation techniques against its prisoners. In the eyes of some observers, terror and collectivism were the common threads that united the Franco forces and the communists. Hilton Kramer noted that *"The evidence is unmistakable that by 1937 the Spanish 'Red' Republic had more in common with Franco's territories in Spain or with the authoritarian regime after his victory…"* One Anarchist militant noted *"Whether Negrin won with his communist cohorts or Franco won with his Italians and Germans the results would be the same for us."*[80]

Also, the system of Soviet-style privileges also trickled down into Spanish society under the Republic. In 1937, the communist-dominated Madrid Writers' Congress took place in Republican-ruled Spain. Stephen Spender noted that he and other leftist and communist writers who attended this Congress were *"treated like princes or ministers…riding in Rolls-Royces, banqueted, feted, sung and danced to…"*[81]

The Soviets also played a tremendous role in supporting and even controlling the Spanish Republican government, army, and secret police forces. Soviet commercial fronts in the West such as the *Narodny* Bank in London and the Paris-based *Banque Commerciale pour l'Europe* channeled funds between the Spanish Republicans and the Stalin dictatorship. The French Communists (PCF) founded a shipping company France-Navigation to ferry goods between the USSR and Spain.[82] The USSR exported weapons to the Spanish armed forces starting in October 1936. Weapons delivered included 6 English howitzers with 6000 shells, 240 German grenade launchers and 100,000 grenades, and 20,362 rifles with 7 million rounds of ammunition. Other ships transported 50 Soviet-built T-26 tanks and 40 armored cars. In total, the Soviets delivered 806 planes, 362 tanks, and 1,555 artillery pieces to the Spanish Communists and Republicans. Fighter aircraft was also acquired from France, Czechoslovakia, the United States, Great Britain, and The Netherlands. COMINTERN agents were instrumental in handling these purchases. The Soviets also built several aircraft factories which repaired or built bombers and fighters. Moscow also dispatched at least 1,123 troops, pilots, and tank operators to serve alongside the Republicans.[83]

The dictatorship of General Francisco Franco took complete power in Spain in 1939, with the massive assistance of the Axis Powers. During the period 1939 to 1945, Spain was officially a neutral power in World War II. However, the reality clearly illustrated that Spain under Franco tilted solidly in the camp of Nazi Germany and Fascist Italy. Franco's Spain was characterized by a highly interventionist totalitarian state that constantly meddled and competed with a cowed private sector and the general population. The Falange and other pro-Franco political forces were unified into an umbrella, mass political organization called the FET.

One of the misinterpretations of the Spanish Civil War peddled by the Western and American Left was the prevailing notion that Franco and his Nationalists represented a *"right wing"* or *"conservative"* phenomenon. Nothing could be further from the truth. Franco and his comrades represented a fascist form of collectivism that was equal to the Left in its hostility to

---

[80] Kramer, Hilton. New Criterion (Simon and Schuster, 1988) page 17.

[81] Johnson, Paul. Modern Times (Harper Collins Publishers 1983) page 337.

[82] Payne, Stanley G. The Spanish Civil War, the Soviet Union, and Communism (Yale University Press 2008) pages 151-152.

[83] Kowalsky, Daniel. Stalin and the Spanish Civil War (Columbia University Press) Accessed From: http://www.gutenberg-e.org/kod01/frames/fkod18.html

free market capitalism. In fact, the Falangists sought to absorb the Communists. Hamilton wrote in his 1943 book <u>Appeasement's Child</u> *"Many extreme Leftists in fact had joined the Phalanx."* Cardozo described the Falangists as a force *"...little different from the Socialists they have been fighting."*[84] In 1938, Falange official Fernandez Cuesta reported that his organization contained *"many former Socialists and Communists."*[85] In 1937, a Falangist official named Hellida noted to Fascist Italian correspondents that the goal of the movement was to capture the communist masses, kill their leaders, and incorporate these converted Reds into the Falangist National Militia.[86]

Top Nazis even expressed second thoughts about their backing of the Falangists and Franco. Hitler believed that the captured leftist Republican and Spanish Communist POWs possessed genuine socialist revolutionary attitudes. In 1943, Hitler remarked to Albert Speer that *"You know my opinion of Franco... We ought to keep these Red Spaniards on the back burner... They're lost to democracy, and to that reactionary crew round Franco too... I believe you to the letter, Speer, that they were impressive people. I must say, in general, that during the civil war the idealism was not on Franco's side; it was to be found among the Reds ... one of these days we'll be able to make use of them... The whole thing will start all over again. But with us on the opposite side."* Hitler also ordered the bestowal of special privileges to Spanish Republican POWs in Nazi custody.[87]

Even in the early days of the Franco/Falangist insurrection, capitalism was denounced. The Franco/Falangist provisional military government asserted its power over businessmen in the territories under Nationalist control. During the Civil War of the 1930s, Nationalist commanders threatened stiff sanctions on capitalists who refused to honor the social legislation of the Republican period. Early in the Civil War, Nationalist newspapers threatened employers to conform and provide financial contributions to Franco.[88]

Even Franco himself concluded that capitalism would not be restored in the event of a Nationalist victory. In 1936, Franco stated *"Do not believe that the army is defending capitalism. It is fighting for the people, including all workers, who will enjoy full rights of citizenship but who must realize that rights also entails duties."*[89] Franco's 1936 manifesto declared that *"We repudiate the capitalistic system which does not provide necessaries for the masses and places the people in the position of misery and desperation."*[90]

[84] Walker, Bruce. "Leftist Mythology of the Spanish Civil War" <u>American Thinker</u> July 17, 2011 Accessed From:
http://www.americanthinker.com/2011/07/leftist_mythology_of_the_spanish_civil_war.html
[85] Callender, Harold. "Wheat is Exported From Franco Spain" <u>New York Times</u> May 1, 1938 page 28.
[86] Payne, Stanley G. <u>Falange: A History of Spanish Fascism</u> (Stanford University Press, 1961) page 126.
[87] Speer, Albert. <u>Spandau: The Secret Diary</u> (Weidenfeld & Nicholson, 2000) page 167.
[88] Payne, Stanley G. <u>Fascism in Spain 1923-1977</u> (University of Wisconsin Press, 1999) pages 182-183.
[89] "Insurgents Name Franco Dictator in an Army Regime" <u>New York Times</u> October 2, 1936 page 1.
[90] Kluckhohn, Frank L. "Spanish Fascists Doom Capitalism" <u>New York Times</u> September 7, 1936 page 2.

The founder of a fascist-minded journal under the control of the syndicalist leader Ledesma Ramos received funding from the Falange and the German Labor Front. The German Labor Front justified its support for funding Ramos' journal in a letter which stated *"This journal will pillory the destructive influence of English capital in Spain. It will discredit English capitalism in the Peninsula to the advantage of Nazi trade."*[91]

In 1938, the Franco zone government issued a Charter of Labor that outlined the policy of class cooperation and a repudiation of liberal capitalism and communism. In 1938, the Carto del Trabajo noted that the Spanish state was a *"totalitarian instrument in the service of the integrity of the Patria"* and denounced *"liberal capitalism"* and *"Marxist materialism."*[92] The 1938 Charter of Labor was considered by the Nationalists *"a reaction against liberal capitalism and Marxism."* A system of *"vertical syndicates"* was created to control the economy and social relations, thus ensuring social peace.[93] Falangist Fernandez Cuesta noted that the *"syndicalist state"* will *"govern the national economy through syndicates. When employer and worker come in conflict the state will intervene and have the last word."*[94]

A questionnaire sent to Falange officials in 1938 addressed various political, social, and economic issues. In respect to economic policy, Fernandez Cuesta specifically stated that *"We repudiate that conception of the capitalist system which takes no account of the needs of the people, dehumanizes private property, and agglomerates workers in shapeless masses, propitious to misery and despair."*[95] Foss and Gerahty predicted that Franco Spain *"...will be in essence a Socialist State."*[96] Franco also remarked that *"I want Labour to be protected in every way against the abuses of Capitalism."*[97]

Despite the opposition to capitalism by Franco and the Falangists, American multinational corporations poured aid and strategic goods into the hands of the Nationalists. The United States provided some trade credits to Franco's zones. In April and August 1939, one million pounds was provided by the *Societe de Banque Suisse* to the Franco-held zones. Foreign businessmen in Britain and the United States also provided fuel, trucks, and other goods to the Franco forces.[98] The German Nazis, Italian Fascists, Portuguese banks (under the quasi-fascist

---

[91] Burns, Emile. The Nazi Conspiracy in Spain (Victor Gollancz London 1937) Accessed From: http://archive.org/stream/TheNaziConspiracyInSpain/TheNaziConspiracyInSpain_djvu.txt

[92] Payne, Stanley G. Fascism in Spain 1923-1977 (University of Wisconsin Press, 1999) page 298.

[93] "Spirit of Crusade a Spur to Rebels" New York Times April 12, 1938 page 4.

[94] Callender, Harold. "Wheat is Exported from Franco Spain" New York Times May 1, 1938 page 28.

[95] Carney, William P. "If Franco Triumphs-What?" New York Times January 9, 1938 page E5.

[96] Walker, Bruce. "Leftist Mythology of the Spanish Civil War" American Thinker July 17, 2011 Accessed From: http://www.americanthinker.com/2011/07/leftist_mythology_of_the_spanish_civil_war.html

[97] Walker, Bruce. "Leftist Mythology of the Spanish Civil War" American Thinker July 17, 2011 Accessed From: http://www.americanthinker.com/2011/07/leftist_mythology_of_the_spanish_civil_war.html

[98] Preston, Paul. Revolution and War in Spain, 1931-1939 (Routledge, 2012) pages 271-272, 278-279.

Salazar regime), General Motors, and Texas Oil Company all provided funds to Franco.[99] During the Spanish Civil War, the Nationalists exported wheat to Nazi Germany, Fascist Italy, and Salazar's Portugal.[100] Standard Oil supplied oil to the Franco forces during the Spanish Civil War. Ford Motor Company, Studebaker, and General Motors exported 12,000 trucks to Franco's troops. DuPont exported 40,000 chemical bombs via Nazi Germany to Franco in an effort to circumvent the Neutrality Act. It should be no surprise that in 1945, the Spanish Under-Secretary for the Ministry of Foreign Affairs Jose Maria Doussinague noted that *"without American petroleum and American trucks and American credit, we could have never won the civil war."*[101] Despite Franco's tilt towards the Axis Powers, multinational companies in the United States continued to trade with Spain. In 1939 and 1940, the Texas Oil Company exported oil to Franco's Spain via tankers. By 1942, the United States continued to trade with Franco's Spain on a *"cash and carry basis."*[102]

The Nazis also engaged in economic penetration of the Franco-held zones during the Civil War. The German propaganda organs cast their exploitation of Spanish resources as being part of their fight against capitalism. A Nazi government corporation called ROWAK was formed in October 1936 to purchase Spanish raw materials through another Nazi state-owned holding company called HISMA. Henceforth, the import-export trade between Spain and Germany was controlled through the Nazi state corporations HISMA and ROWAK.[103]

Despite protestations of neutrality, Franco's Spain was also solidly aligned with the Axis Powers almost until the end of World War II. Thousands of German *Reichswehr* troops were secretly transported to Fascist Italy and Franco-held Spanish Morocco between April and July 1936. The troops and their officers were disguised as tourists. The Nazi General Wilhelm von Faupel organized these troops to *"rise Spain to her old glory"* and to *"repudiate the Capitalist system which overlooks the needs of the masses."*

Furthermore, Franco's Spain became an ally in the Nazi effort to subvert Latin America through the encirclement of the United States by unfriendly, fascist governments. In April 1939, the *Reichswehr* accepted General von Faupel's recommendation that Spanish FET members be trained by the Gestapo to fulfill Axis goals in Latin America. Special schools for Spaniards were established in Hamburg, Bremen, Hanover, and Vienna. These Spanish FET agents were trained by Germans in the arts of sabotage, espionage, radio, secret codes, map-making, microphotography and allied subjects. These trainees were then enrolled in the Spanish Army Intelligence Service (SIM). SIM worked under the direction of the Gestapo. SIM agents dispatched to Latin America received orders from Gestapo and Japanese *Kempetai* officers. During the summer of 1941, the workload of the SIM agents stationed in Latin America increased after most of the German Embassies were closed in Latin America. Spanish Embassies

---

[99] Seidman, Michael. Republic of Egos: A Social History of the Spanish Civil War (University of Wisconsin Press, 2002) page 46.

[100] Ibid, page 95.

[101] Beevor, Antony. The Battle for Spain: The Spanish Civil War, 1936-1939 (Penguin 2006) page 138.

[102] Stanton, Sean. "The Myth of Spanish Neutrality: US Foreign Relations with Spain 1939-1941" Accessed From: http://www.drake.edu/media/departmentsoffices/dussj/2013-2011documents/SpanishNeutralityStanton.pdf

[103] Whealey, Robert H. Hitler And Spain: The Nazi Role in the Spanish Civil War, 1936-1939 (University Press of Kentucky, 2004) page 79.

in Latin America served as liaison points between the SIM, Gestapo, and the Spanish Foreign Ministry. Spanish ships would drop off SIM agents in Latin America. The number of SIM agents in Mexico and Guatemala alone numbered 1,000.[104]

Spanish workers were also dispatched to Nazi Germany. Heavy industries, such as the steel mills in Vizcaya, fertilizer plants, and silk firms produced goods for the German war machine. These factories operated under the control of German supervisors. Spanish heavy industries also came under the control of Nazi-controlled *"private"* companies such as IG Farben. Spanish artillery attacked British and American planes near Gibralter. German *Luftwaffe* planes bombed Allied shipping from bases in Majorca.[105] German Army officers frequented bars and other social establishments in Bilbao and Madrid. *Lufthansa* operated an office in Spain and maintained flights between Stuttgart, Madrid, Barcelona, and Lisbon.[106] In May 1942, the Nazis directed the foreign cells of the Spanish Falange to:

1) Stimulate disturbances and the creation of border complications.
2) Provoke disputes between pro-communists and anti-communists.
3) Provoke American intervention in order to inflame anti-American sentiments in Spain and Latin America.
4) Coordinate military movements on the orders of Nazi Germany.
5) Cooperate with Spanish and Falangist agencies (e.g. cultural groups, the *Auxilio Social*, and news bureaus) with German agents in Latin America and the United States.

In early 1942, Himmler helped reorganize the Spanish *Seguridad* (Security) on the Nazi model, with the input from the Nazi *Ibero-Amerikanische Institut*. The Falange's intelligence service (Information Service of the FET/JONS) maintained stations at the ports of Seville, Vigo, and Bilbao. These ports funneled Falangist agents into foreign countries. Himmler encouraged the Department for Foreigners in the *Seguridad* to monitor foreign Jews and Allied nationals resident in Spain. Spanish *Seguridad* agents were dispatched to Latin America, the United States, France, and England, where they awaited orders from Spanish Consulates. The *Seguridad* were advised by a number of *Abwehr* and Nazi Security Service (SD) agents. The *Wehrmacht* dispatched councilors to advise the Spanish Army. German Gestapo offices were located in Vigo, Madrid, and Tangier. The Gestapo advised and collaborated with the *Seguridad* and SIM.[107]

Even in the last years of World War II, Franco Spain continued its tilt towards the Axis Powers. In 1944, the radical Falangists demonstrated against the British and Americans. An FET official noted to the German Embassy counselor in mid-1944 that National Socialism was more like a west European nationalist form of Bolshevism. As of 1944, Spanish intelligence still

---

[104] Chase, Allen. Falange-The Secret Axis Army in the Americas (Putnam 1943) Accessed From: http://spitfirelist.com/books/falange-the-secret-axis-army-in-the-americas/
[105] Plenn, Abel. Wind in the Olive Trees: Spain from the Inside (Boni & Gaer New York 1946) Accessed From: https://archive.org/stream/windintheolivetr011564mbp/windintheolivetr011564mbp_djvu.txt
[106] Hamilton, Thomas J. Appeasement's Child: The Franco Regime in Spain (Knopf 1943) Accessed From: https://archive.org/services/borrow/appeasementschil00hami
[107] Office of Strategic Services. "Analysis of Certain Reports About the Spanish Secret Service and Their Relations with the Germans" August 15, 1944 Accessed From: http://cryptome.org/0005/spain-spies-1944.pdf

cooperated with the Germans. In October 1944, the Spanish transferred Western-made penicillin to Nazi Germany. In 1944, the Spanish press portrayed Nazi institutions and the German war effort in a positive light. As of 1944, the pro-Nazi Falangist Jesus Suevos served as a liaison with the fascist PPF in France. Even in 1945, the state-controlled Spanish press still carried pro-Nazi reporting.[108]

The rhetoric which emanated from the Falangist press and the Franco regime mirrored the anti-capitalist, anti-communist and fascistic themes that spewed from Berlin, Rome, and Tokyo. The book Reivindicaciones de Espana, written by FET Council member Jose M. Areilza and the fascist-minded international law professor Fernando M. Castiella denounced the *"decadent and worm eaten structure of the British and French empires which were stuffed with wealth, rotten in their moral fibre, unwilling to consent to an indispensable social adjustment, and shut up within frenetic egotism…"*[109] In 1940, Serrano Suner remarked in an interview with the Volkischer Beobachter that the European conflict was directed against *"the capitalism of the great democracies."*[110] In April 1943, the FET declared that *"the war of Spain like that of today was a civil war in the European and universal sense, a war between fascism and antifascism. On one side, Masons, democrats, liberals, communists, and anarchists; on the other side Spain, Italy, and Germany. On a much vaster scale this situation is repeated today."*[111] A Falangist intellectual Lain Entralgo noted that *"there is much discussion of cultural unity within the New Order, and this European culture at once old and renewed is justly that which is defended with the assault against the Marxist materialism of the East and against the capitalist materialism of the West…Our duty as Spaniards is without doubt within the ranks of that proclaimed newborn New Order."*[112] The FET magazine Fotos published an article which emphasized the unity between Nazi and Spanish institutions. In May 1943, Haz observed that the world war was a conflict between *"capitalist nations and proletarian nations."*[113]

Similar to the Axis Powers, businessmen and landowners in Spain were regimented by the Franco/Falangist dictatorship. Massive regulations, taxation, and cronyism pervaded the government's administration of factories, banks, and farmlands. The book Olive Trees: Spain from the Inside reported that *"Thanks to his faithful cooperation with the Falange's network of Syndicates, and the labyrinthine Fiscalías de Tasas, or internal revenue bureaus…Spanish commerce and industry had reached an all-time high--in inefficiency and graft…trade and manufacturing throughout Spain--from the smallest wine shops of Andalucia to some of the most important metallurgical plants of the Basque region or the largest textile factories in Cataluna-- were so rigidly controlled by government regulations, and so closely supervised by Falange and other officials, that no business could survive unless the owners were Falangists in good standing. In lieu of this, a responsible Falangist had to be brought into the business as a silent partner whose sole job was to cut away the mass of government regulations, and deliberately*

---

[108] Payne, Stanley G. Fascism in Spain 1923-1977 (University of Wisconsin Press, 1999) page 397.

[109] Hamilton, Thomas J. Appeasement's Child: The Franco Regime in Spain (Knopf 1943) Accessed From: https://archive.org/services/borrow/appeasementschil00hami

[110] Payne, Stanley G. The Franco Regime (University of Wisconsin Press, 2011) page 270.

[111] Payne, Stanley G. Fascism in Spain 1923-1977 (University of Wisconsin Press, 1999) page 390.

[112] Ibid, page 391.

[113] Ibid, page 396.

imposed red tape which constantly threatened to paralyze business operations." Government and FET officials levied fines, taxes, and mandated the redistribution of profits, which in turn, forced business establishments to shut down. The FET also controlled the distribution of raw materials and manufactured goods. One story noted told of "*the case of an acquaintance of mine, a dealer in oils and resins--once one of Spain's most flourishing industries--who had tried vainly for days to hold freight officials to their promise to deliver a shipment of resins which was being delayed in the local freight-yard. Instead of receiving his goods, he had gotten a heavy fine for failing to remove the supplies from the freight-yard!*" Shortages were rife in Spain as a result of massive exports of food and commodities to Nazi Germany. It was also reported that "*...there was the appalling economic stumbling-block of shortages which were created artificially by the Franco officialdom itself for the purpose of channeling production and distribution into a vast, official black-market.*"[114]

Industrialists such as Juan March, who originally supported Franco, turned against the regime on the account of strict government controls and regulations. Spanish businessmen reportedly commented during the late 1930s and early 1940s that "*The Falange is redder than the Republic.*"[115] The clash of big business interests versus the Falange/Franco regime stretched as far back as the Civil War years. In late 1937, a group of businessmen organized themselves into the *Junta Directiva Provisional de Fuerzas Economicas* to press the FET into adopting a more liberal economic policy. This recommendation was rebuffed by the writer Gonzalo Torrente Ballester, who was an FET intellectual that supported state control and interventionism.[116]

Businessmen complained that the Falange delayed the postwar economic recovery of Spain. It was noted that "*Enraged by the endless red tape and favoritism with which they have to contend, many of Spain's business men have been growling ever since 1940, at least, that 'this gang is redder than the Reds.'*" Commissions proliferated in Franco's Spain. They included the agencies that distributed food and other rationed items (the Spanish OPA), special courts which enforced rationing laws, and the Tribunals of Political Responsibilities. Private businesses were controlled by the Franco government. It was noted that "*Not a bottle of sherry could be exported or a ton of coal imported without a permit from the Ministry of Industry and Commerce.*" The import-export process took months for a business to undertake. The Foreign Money Institute approved allocations of foreign currency such as pounds, dollars, or pesos to firms that needed to import goods. A permit from the Ministry was required to open, repair, or expand a factory. Prices and wages were controlled by the government and private firms were ordered to operate at a loss. A government agency maintained a monopoly over wheat, while prices for all farm products were fixed by the Ministry of Agriculture. The Rationing Office distributed foods. In 1941, the Franco government took over the railroads. Tires and gasoline were rationed for trucks

---

[114] Plenn, Abel. Wind in the Olive Trees: Spain from the Inside (Boni & Gaer New York 1946) Accessed From:
https://archive.org/stream/windintheolivetr011564mbp/windintheolivetr011564mbp_djvu.txt
[115] Ibid.
[116] Payne, Stanley G. Fascism in Spain 1923-1977 (University of Wisconsin Press, 1999) pages 396-397.

and automobiles. Car imports were also regulated by the state. The Ministry of Marine controlled the shipping lines and its itineraries and cargoes.[117]

Businessmen who violated different laws and regulations were fined, imprisoned, or subjected to slave labor. In 1939, a war against profiteers was launched by Franco and Governor Luis Alarcon where heavy fines were imposed against offending businessmen. Some fines reached as high as $20,000.[118] The special courts sentenced 1,300 black market businessmen to labor battalions and fined them over $5.5 million between October 1940 and June 1941.[119]

The landowners were also regimented to produce for the good of the state. In 1937, Franco created the National Wheat Service to fix the prices and organized the production, distribution, and sale of wheat.[120] Arriba in 1940 warned landowners that were *"indifferent to the mission of Spain"* must *"come within the orbit of our plans…the privileged classes of Spain know what is their duty before the urgent work of the revolution. The countryside despite the happy owners and big estates will die for the Spain of Franco and its Falange."*[121] In November 1939, the National Wheat Service ordered landowners to surrender 661 pounds of wheat to the state.[122]

Falangist, Franco government, and foreign diplomatic officials enjoyed privileges while the rest of the population experienced shortages and privations. The book Wind in the Olive Trees: Spain from the Inside reported that *"The Spanish people could have borne their naked misery and suffering with less resentment and smoldering fury, and perhaps more of that patience which they had shown toward the conditions of extreme poverty that had been one of Spain's cruelest burdens for centuries, had it not been for the prevalence of such crass practices as permitting vast quantities of expensive cakes and other pastries to be manufactured and brazenly placed in show-windows at the same time the people were told to believe that the scarcity of bread was due to a flour shortage. Worst of all was the flagrant display of abundance and general good-living in which officials and friends of the regime, and their families, often indulged publicly."* One taxi driver in Madrid exclaimed in frustration that *"There is plenty of eating going on in Spain, even if we do not eat."* Hotels, bars, restaurants, and cabarets in Madrid were filled with privileged Falange officials, government officials, their *"harlots and hangers-on,"* and foreign diplomats and their clerks. They gorged themselves on fine wine and food and listened to music.[123]

The Franco government operated special government commissaries for the Falange and the Army to procure their food. In 1941, the Falange established its own separate rationing

---

[117]Hamilton, Thomas J. Appeasement's Child: The Franco Regime in Spain (Knopf 1943) Accessed From: https://archive.org/services/borrow/appeasementschil00hami

[118] "Madrid Fines Fail to Cut High Prices" New York Times May 15, 1939 page 4.

[119]Hamilton, Thomas J. Appeasement's Child: The Franco Regime in Spain (Knopf 1943) Accessed From: https://archive.org/services/borrow/appeasementschil00hami

[120] Callender, Harold. "Wheat is Exported from Franco Spain" New York Times May 1, 1938 page 28.

[121] Hamilton, T.J. "Land Reclamation Decreed in Spain" New York Times January 27, 1940 page 4.

[122] "Spain Requisitions Wheat" New York Times November 3, 1939 page 7.

[123] Plenn, Abel. Wind in the Olive Trees: Spain from the Inside (Boni & Gaer New York 1946) Accessed From: https://archive.org/stream/windintheolivetr011564mbp/windintheolivetr011564mbp_djvu.txt

system for its members and officers. The diplomatic corps were given a special monthly quota of sugar, potatoes, coffee, rice, lentils, and other staple foods. Diplomats could also purchase meat from the same government butcher shop that supplied Franco and Serrano Suner and other high level officials. The wealthy classes also received their properties back and were able to afford rationed and unrationed goods. Axis diplomats were given the best cuts of meat at a special price discount.[124]

The leadership and its press organs reinforced Spain's commitment against capitalism, government by checks and balances, and even the privileges of the aristocracy. Journalism was nationalized by the state, as a measure to rescue newspapers *"from the servitude to capitalism or to revolution or Marxism."*[125] In 1940, the Falangist newspaper <u>Arriba</u> complained that *"a certain foreign frivolous attitude of good taste...invaded certain sections of our society that take imbecile pleasure in scandalizing patient and sensitive Spaniards with the example of their distinguished manner of living on the edge of the profound tragedy that has come to our native land at the end of two centuries of decadence."* The newspaper <u>ABC</u> charged that the wealthy classes manipulated tariffs, hence *"there existed among us a veritable plutocratic masonry"* that made more money keeping Spain a *"colony."*[126] Franco stated before an audience of Falangists in 1941 that the enemies of Spain included *"materialist Reds...frivolous bourgeoisie...(and) foreign influenced aristocrats."*[127]

In December 1942, Franco stated *"Spain's way of thinking cannot go back to the 19th Century, accursed by so many false conceptions. It is necessary for Spaniards to abandon the old liberal prejudices and take a survey of Europe in order to analyze contemporary history...All contemporary events show us we are witnessing the end of one era and the beginnings of another; that the liberal world is going down a victim to its own errors and with it are disappearing commercial imperialism, financial capitalism, and mass unemployment. The happiness promised by the French Revolution became nothing but barter business, competition, low wages, and mass insecurity...Those are mistaken who dream of the establishment of democratic liberal systems in Western Europe, bordering on Russian communism. Those err who speculate on liberal peace agreements or a bourgeois solution."*[128]

In 1943, the Spanish periodical <u>Espanol</u> stated *"At present the operations against the legitimate regime are being launched in the name of nationalism, capitalism, monarchism, conservatism, and Christian liberalism. All these groups, in league with the Reds in a half-baked alliance, fear the Falange and its unified leadership because it represents a revolutionary menace."* The newspaper even alleged that the Falange never *"hated the Reds,"* even during the Spanish Civil War.[129] In 1943, Franco noted that the *"liberal capitalist"* system was disappearing and *"neither the desire for liberty of colonial peoples nor the tremendous sums which the struggle consumes nor the incalculable destruction, nor the spirit of rebellion of the*

---

[124]Hamilton, Thomas J. <u>Appeasement's Child: The Franco Regime in Spain</u> (Knopf 1943) Accessed From: https://archive.org/services/borrow/appeasementschil00hami

[125] "New Press Decree Issued by Rebels" <u>New York Times</u> May 14, 1938 page 6.

[126] "Useful Life Urged on Rich Spaniards" <u>New York Times</u> January 5, 1940 page 8.

[127] "General Franco's Outburst" <u>Times (London)</u> July 19, 1941

[128] "Address by Generalissimo Franco" <u>New York Times</u> December 9, 1942 page 4.

[129] Reston, James B. "Opposition to Franco Gains; Madrid Paper Sounds Alarm" <u>New York Times</u> October 6, 1943 page 1.

masses against social injustices makes the return of such a system possible."[130] At a meeting of the Falange, Franco noted in 1943 that *"the liberal regime is the regime of exploitation; the regime of injustice, because justice is like the sword. Justice has no place in it…This regime deals with men as though they were chattels.*"[131]

After World War II, many of the institutions and practices of this interventionist and highly intrusive state were retained by Franco and his allies. Franco also re-ignited some foreign policy positions that were explicitly opposed to the interests of the United States and even conflicted with Madrid's official anti-communist stance. Much of this stemmed from the influence of the Falange/FET, who retained a bitterness against the United States and Britain that was leftover from the World War II period. This resulted in closer relations with communist Cuba. Spanish state-owned and private enterprises also sought to profit from commerce with the communist world. Despite Franco's qualms about radical anti-Semitism and his resistance to appeals to collaborate in the Final Solution, the official Spanish press hurled insults against the Jews and later the State of Israel. By the 1950s, Spain could be counted upon as being an ally to radical Arab socialist states and a steadfast member of the anti-Zionist camp. Such positions also stemmed from the influences of the pro-Nazi Falangist elements in the FET, along with traditional Catholic anti-Semitism that was periodically present in Spain since the late 1400s.

Even after the defeat of the Axis Powers in 1945, Spain continued to host conferences that networked different neo-fascist and Nazi groups from all over Europe. By the end of the late 1960s, these neo-Nazi conferences also hosted delegations from the ardently pro-Soviet, Marxist-oriented PLO. In March 1950, Portuguese and Spanish Falangist/FET representatives attended a meeting of racial nationalists and neo-fascists in Rome. The Spanish Falange/FET also attended the Third Congress of European New Order coalition of neo-fascist parties in 1953. A Falangist representative named Albinana also attended another neo-fascist congress that was held in December 1953.[132]

In April 1969, the New European Order held its 10th Congress in Franco's Spain where at least 100 neo-Nazis, ex-SS officers, and Al Fatah PLO leaders met.[133] General Franco gave his official support to this meeting, which was held mainly to support the cause of the PLO. The conference leaders agreed to supply ex-Nazi military instructors to the PLO.[134] Two SS officers named Erich Altern (former regional leader of the Gestapo Jewish Affairs Section in Galicia and Willi Berner (former SS officer in Mauthausan concentration camp and the *Waffen SS Brandenberg* Division) trained PLO terrorists in Basra (located in Baathist Socialist Iraq and PLO-dominated Lebanon, respectively.[135] Slogans abounded at this conference which stated: *"Long Live the Glorious Palestinian Fighters Against Imperialzionism."* A prolific number of anti-Jewish and anti-Israel books such as the Protocols of Zion and The Enemy of Man were distributed at this meeting.[136]

---

[130] "Franco Holds Way Open for Monarchy" New York Times July 18, 1943 page 22.

[131] "General Franco Attacks Democracy" Times (London) May 5, 1943

[132] Alan, Ray. "Spanish Anti-Semitism Today" Commentary Magazine August 1964 Accessed From: http://www.commentarymagazine.com/article/spanish-anti-semitism-today/

[133] Coogan, Kevin. Dreamer of the Day (Autonomedia, 1999) pages 543-544.

[134] Sterling, Claire. The Terror Network (Holt, Rinehart, and Winston, 1981) pages 114-115.

[135] McForan, Desmond. The World Held Hostage (Oak-Tree Books, 1986) pages 95-96.

[136] Sterling, Claire. The Terror Network (Holt, Rinehart, and Winston, 1981) pages 114-115.

In the 1950s, reports trickled out of Spain which pointed to occasional trade between Madrid and the communist bloc. In some cases, exports from the Soviet bloc even served to crush strikes. In July 1951, Spain sold refined copper to the Soviet Union through Egyptian middlemen.[137] During the 1957 strike by Asturian miners, Poland shipped coal to Franco's Spain, which broke apart the labor unrest.[138] These transactions were more than likely motivated by the communist bloc's need for Western-made goods and hard currencies that could be funneled through Spain.

However, by the early 1960s, Spain's opening to the communist world took on an additional, ideological dimension. In 1962, the Vice Secretary of the Falange/FET Fernando Herrero Tejedor noted that communist systems have become "*very differentiated*" with "*national communist*" systems developing outside China and the Soviet Union. He advocated "*new postures and adequate actions*" to meet the challenges of "*neo-Marxism and neo-capitalism.*" Tejedor noted that Spain was taking a "*fourth position*" in the East-West conflict. He favorably observed that liberal capitalism absorbed many socialist techniques, thus transforming itself into what was termed neo-capitalism.[139] Another report confirmed that a faction of the FET/Falange reportedly desired a diplomatic rapprochement with the USSR.

Trade relations between Spain and the communist world became steadier by the end of the late 1960s. For example, Spain purchased oil seeds from the USSR via West German firms.[140] In 1961, Spain shipped synthetic fibers to the Soviet Union in exchange for oil. The state-owned INI concern Fefasa shipped synthetic fibers to the USSR. The trading company *Latino Maris* served as the agent for this particular commercial transaction between Franco's Spain and the Soviet Union. In 1960, Spain shipped citrus products to the USSR in exchange for mostly cellulose products.[141]

In the 1960s, Spain expanded commercial relations with communist Romania, Poland, Hungary, Czechoslovakia, and Bulgaria. At the same time, a small delegation from TASS and the Soviet merchant marine were also stationed in Madrid. In 1972, a Soviet-Spanish reciprocal trade treaty was signed. Under the terms of this treaty, Spain would export citrus fruits, wines, ships, agricultural products, shoes, and traffic lights to the USSR. The Soviets would then export oil, timber, machine tools, and other industrial goods to Spain. The value of this two-way commerce totaled $30 million per year.[142]

Much to Washington's chagrin, Franco's Spain developed very close economic relations with Castro's Cuba. This partially stemmed from the mutual Hispanic affinities and anti-Americanism of both leaders. For example, General Franco informed his Ambassador to Cuba

---

[137] Sulzberger, C.L. "Spain is Reported Selling to Soviet" New York Times July 23, 1951 page 6.

[138] Carl Boggs and David Plotke. Politics of Eurocommunism (South End Press 1980) page 108.

[139] Hoffman, Paul. "Spain Urged to be Flexible on Reds" New York Times October 29, 1962 page 15.

[140] Hoffman, Paul. "Spain is Weighing Ties with Soviet and Neutralists" New York Times August 12, 1963 page 1.

[141] "Spain Is Increasing Her Barter Trade With the Red Bloc" New York Times June 25, 1961 page 22.

[142] Giniger, Henry. "Moscow and Madrid Sign a Trade Pact" New York Times September 16, 1972 page 5.

Jose Miro Cardena to *"tell Fidel to give hell to the Americans."*[143] Trade levels between Cuba and Spain increased from $8.4 million in 1962 to $30.8 million in 1963. In early 1964, the total trade between Cuba and Spain totaled $17 million.[144] In 1964, two-way trade between Cuba and Spain increased by leaps and bounds to a grand total of $97 million.[145]

Iberia Airlines also maintained flights between Havana and Madrid. Spain sold agricultural machinery, electrical equipment, light machinery, food, and consumer goods to Cuba. Spanish shipyards built 20 vessels for export to Cuba. Spain also purchased tobacco, sugar, and some raw materials from Cuba. The United States quietly expressed concerns that NATO members would transship sensitive goods through Spain for re-export to Cuba.[146] Apparently, even Spain even served as a *"pit stop"* for a *"garden variety"* of leftists, communists, and subversives in transit to Cuba. Two planeloads of leftist African, Asian, and Latin American officials and groups departed from Madrid in transit to the Tri-Continental Conference that was held in Cuba.[147]

Even by the early 1970s, communist countries seemingly threw off international proletarian and anti-fascist solidarity in favor of profits derived from trade with Franco's Spain. One of the leaders of the Spanish Communist Party wryly admitted in 1971 that *"The Polish communist government is helping Franco to fight against the miners—a rather peculiar way of understanding proletarian internationalism."*[148]

The Franco regime also clung to anti-Jewish prejudices since it took power in 1939. In May 1939, Franco condemned the *"Judaic spirit which brings about the alliance of capitalism and Marxism."* Blue Division[149] propaganda exhorted *"Your family names are democracy, Marxism, and plutocracy but your baptismal name is without doubt Judaism."* Since 1945, Franco indulged in anti-Zionist propaganda and applauded Arab efforts to destroy Israel. Franco desired to succeed Mussolini as the *"protector of Islam"* in an effort to break the boycott of Spain by the Western democracies in the 1940s. Franco flirted with the Arab League during the 1940s and the 1950s. In 1964, the Spanish Minister of Information Fraga Iribarne visited Egypt and praised *"the similarity between Egypt's revolution and Spain's."* Shortly thereafter, Egypt and Spain concluded press and television agreements. Falangist propaganda also portrayed Israel as a nation of hardnosed atheists, Marxists, and capitalists. Not surprisingly, Franco withheld diplomatic relations with Israel.[150]

Various political scientists in the West and even Falangists admitted that they represented the forces of collectivism and even the Left. The corporate globalists in the Council on Foreign

---

[143] Geyer, Georgie Anne. "Fidel and Franco" The Daily Record (Ellensburg Washington) August 3, 1992 page 4.

[144] Middleton, Drew. "Spain Increasing Cuban Trade Despite U.S. Pleas for Blockade" New York Times September 28, 1964 page 8.

[145] Szulc, Tad. "Anti-Red Spain is Helping Cuba" New York Times December 30, 1965 page 4.

[146] Middleton, Drew. "Spain Increasing Cuban Trade Despite U.S. Pleas for Blockade" New York Times September 28, 1964 page 8.

[147] Szulc, Tad. "Anti-Red Spain is Helping Cuba" New York Times December 30, 1965 page 4.

[148] Radio Free Europe Research: Poland Radio Free Europe, 1971 page 36.

[149] The Spanish Blue Division were volunteer Falangist troops who fought against the Soviets alongside Nazi forces.

[150] Alan, Ray. "Spanish Anti-Semitism Today" Commentary Magazine August 1964 Accessed From: http://www.commentarymagazine.com/article/spanish-anti-semitism-today/

Relations (CFR) noted in their 1950 Political Handbook of the World that the Falange was a party of the Left and not the Right. It should also be pointed out that many alumni and active members of the CFR supported the American engagement of the Franco dictatorship.[151] The Falangist official Jose Luis de Arrese noted in 1947 that *"In Spain the worst opponent of Falangism has always been the man of the Right."*[152] In 1968, one Falangist student revealed that *"I feel far closer to the communists and anarchists than I do to the leaders of the Movement."*[153]

Even in the postwar period, the Franco regime continued its heavily interventionist and fascist-socialist policies directed at the Spanish economy. In 1939 and 1940, various laws for the protection of national industry were promulgated by Franco which led to the creation of the Institute for National Industry (INI). The purpose of the INI was to stimulate and create heavy and productive industries. Thus, a large number of state-owned enterprises and bureaucracies proliferated in Franco's Spain.[154]

Such observations were not lost on various scholars who were specialists on the history and economy of Spain. Shubert observed that *"The unprecedented breadth of state intervention in the economy which took place after the Civil War was clearly ideological, following both Nazi and Fascist models and the indigenous interventionism of the Primo de Rivera regime. Agriculture was controlled through fixed prices and marketing boards. The Instituto Nacional de Industria, INI, symbolized the new place of the state in the industrial and service sectors. Despite the reorientation of economic policy towards liberalism at the end of the 1950s, the Spanish state retained a prominent role in economic life. The National Wheat Board remained an imposing institution, while the INI has kept its fingers in an astounding range of pies: 'from golf clubs to cars, from iron and steel to luxury hotels, from technologically sophisticated ships to the products of artisans.'"*[155]

By the end of the late 1950s, elements of the Franco government realized that the excessively socialist-fascist policies of Spain distorted the economy and exacerbated poverty and corruption. Many of these *"reformist"* bureaucrats sought to preserve the Franco dictatorship and were themselves opposed to unrestrained liberal capitalism and free market forces in general. These officials and experts who led the efforts to streamline the Spanish economy in the late 1950s and early 1960s belonged to a cultic Catholic faction called *Opus Dei*. Arango noted that ***"In the place of a free market economy, the Opus Dei technocrats borrowed a scheme that had worked successfully in France and adapted it to Spain: indicative planning, a cooperative effort between the state and private enterprise. The government set out the general scheme, which private enterprise was free to either follow or ignore***. *Following the plan brought great benefits, however, including tax advantages, accelerated depreciation, special lines of credit, and subsidies. To encourage private investment in areas that the planners considered in need of development, the government designated certain national regions as Economic Poles and*

---

[151] Walker, Bruce. "Leftist Mythology of the Spanish Civil War" American Thinker July 17, 2011 Accessed From:
http://www.americanthinker.com/2011/07/leftist_mythology_of_the_spanish_civil_war.html

[152] Payne, Stanley G. Falange: A History of Spanish Fascism (Stanford University Press 1961) page 244.

[153] Eder, Richard. "Radicals Splitting Falange in Spain" New York Times December 1, 1968 page 2.

[154] Payne, Stanley G. The Franco Regime (University of Wisconsin Press 2011) pages 250-251.

[155] Shubert, Adrian. A Social History of Modern Spain (Routledge 2003) page 251.

granted special benefits to private firms willing to operate within them. Development Poles were established in regions where a certain amount of industrialization already existed. Industrial Promotion Poles were created in regions with no or very little industrialization. And Poles of Industrial Decongestion (Polígonos de Decongesción Industrial) were established to relieve the pressure built up in cities like Barcelona and Madrid...the activities of the INI were curtailed and coordinated with the overall development plans. The INI was to concentrate on risky, long-range activities: providing aid for private firms in temporary financial difficulty until the firms were again stable and protecting infant industries until they were strong enough to compete on their own. "[156]

Lieberman confirmed many of Arango's points when she wrote that "***Some economic historians appear to believe that the remarkable performance of the Spanish economy in the 1960s was due either to Spain's gradual adoption of a free market system, and/or to the indicative economic planning put into effect by the government of 1962. Nothing could be further from the truth. Men such as Gregorio Lopez Bravo and Laureano Lopez Rodo, the head of the Planning Commission, had no intention of abandoning dirigisme and the power it gave to those in charge of the management of the economy. They clearly realized that rapid progress to a relatively free market system could bring disastrous political consequences for them. In the end, they opted neither for a free market economy nor for a rationally planned economy in the sense that indicative planning should be used to achieve greater economic and technological efficiency. They favoured instead the establishment of a partnership between the managers of large private firms and themselves. The philosophy adopted was to work out a 'marriage' between a group of select private entrepreneurs and high-ranking government officials***.*" In other words, it appeared that the Spanish ministers in charge of the economy during the period of the late 1950s and early 1960s weaved crony capitalism together with continued doses of technocratic central planning.

Lieberman also wrote that "***Although Gregorio López Bravo advocated an increase in the relative importance of the private sector in the economy, he was not a champion of the free market system. He wanted a managed economy and supported the discretionary powers of public administrators***. *His views were well expressed by the language of Point 2 of Article 4 of the Law 194/1963 which provided that 'Government will evaluate the insufficiency of private initiative and the opportunity to supplement it with public activity, among other instances when the former will not achieve in a determined sector the objectives defined for it, in an indicative way, by the Plan of Economic and Social Development.' The scope of administrative discretion was widened by the assertion that 'government will evaluate the insufficiency of private initiative.'*"[157] During this time period, other government policies confirmed that Spain did not move in a truly free market, competitive direction. For example, the Bank of Spain was nationalized by the Bank Reform Law of 1962. The Bank supervised the private financial institutions in Spain, carried out state monetary policies, and supervised the foreign exchange holdings in partnership with the Directorate General for Foreign Transactions.[158]

---

[156] Arango, E. Ramon. Spain: Democracy Regained (Westview Press 1996) pages 240-241.

[157] Lieberman, Sima. Growth and Crisis in the Spanish Economy, 1940-93 (Routledge 2005) pages 112-116.

[158] "Spain: A Country Study" Accessed From: http://rs6.loc.gov/cgi-bin/query/D?cstdy:2:./temp/~frd_TsGH::

Despite the "*reforms*" of the late 1950s and early 1960s, the number of state agencies and INI-owned enterprises expanded, rather than decreased. Throughout the 1960s and 1970s, the INI expanded its ownership of enterprises. INI took partial or full control of enterprises such as HISPANOIL, the steel mills of UNINSA, and the coal mining enterprise HUNOSA. Lieberman noted that "*Government dirigisme grew stronger in the latter part of the 1960s. Critics denounced the expanding governmental interventionism as being inconsistent with the major goals of the economic reformers of 1959 and incompatible with the 1962 recommendations of the IBRD. The Minister of Industry remained indifferent to these assertions.*"[159] In 1974, the Franco government decided that the INI would dominate the steel, iron, and petrochemical industries in Spain. INI heavily invested in the Spanish electronics and aircraft manufacturing sectors.[160] In 1975, the INI included 76% of shipbuilding, 64% of trucks built, 50% of the coal mined, 67% of aluminum, 58% of the iron, 45% of steel produced, 46% of cars produced, 37% of oil refined, and 23% of electricity produced.[161] By the end of 1975, the INI directly participated in 59 companies. INI also directly owned 16 companies and had a stake in 200 other firms. It provided 10% of Spain's gross industrial product and employed 4% of the total work force.[162]

Franco and his fellow FET officials and Ministers denounced liberal, free market capitalism with the fervor equal to any leftwing militant. Such denunciations continued well into the 1960s and even crept into the political discourse of Franco's Spain of the 1970s. In 1949, Franco exhorted in a speech that "*we hate this contemptible capitalism and liberalism and all that they represent.*"[163] At the state-owned SEAT factory, Franco confirmed in 1949 that "*We reject capitalism as much as Marxism.*"[164] In rhetoric reminiscent of the Falangist press of the 1930s, Franco stated in 1950 that "*The easy going ways and the neglect of planning and direction that are the basis of the life of the liberal political societies are incompatible with progress and improvement in the older nations.*"[165]

Initially, Franco was uncomfortable with the "*reformist*" suggestions of some of his technocratic-minded ministers in 1959. As a matter of ideological conviction, he was comfortable with the statist-mercantilist policies of the Falangist/FET dictatorship. Franco indicated his support for a statist economy in the late 1950s when he authored a memorandum which stated: "*The interest of the nation, the common good, and the will of the Spanish people require above all a transformation of the capitalist system, acceleration of economic progress, a more just distribution of wealth, social justice, transformation and modernization of credit, and the modernization of many basic elements of production. The fact that the state nationalizes*

---

[159] Lieberman, Sima. Growth and Crisis in the Spanish Economy, 1940-93 (Routledge 2005) pages 112-116.

[160] "Spain: A Country Study" Accessed From: http://rs6.loc.gov/cgi-bin/query/r?frd/cstdy:@field(DOCID+es0093)

[161] Payne, Stanley G. The Franco Regime (University of Wisconsin Press 2011) page 475.

[162] Harrison, Joseph. An Economic History of Spain (Manchester University Press, 1978) pages 161-163.

[163] "US Loan is Assailed by Pamphlet in Spain" New York Times November 20, 1950 page 5.

[164] Payne, Stanley G. The Franco Regime (University of Wisconsin Press 2011) page 392.

[165] Brewer, Sam Pope. "Franco Predicts Doubled Income" New York Times June 4, 1950 page 15.

certain industries and services is criticized as socialism when this is accepted in many countries who are considered liberal but adopt this from socialism as good and proper."[166]

Into the 1960s, Franco continued his pseudo-leftist ideological attacks on the concepts of limited government and free market economics. In 1961, Franco attacked liberalism, capitalism, and democracy in general. He praised "*organic democracy*" and predicted that the West with its "*party politics*" would be headed to the dustbin.[167] In 1962, Franco denounced "*liberal capitalism*" as a system where "*individuals are exploited.*"[168] In a 1962 article, the Spanish newspaper ABC denounced the materialism, greed, decadence, mismanagement, cowardice, and cruelty of the bourgeoisie in article titled "*Hypocrisy.*"[169] In 1963, radicals in the Falange denounced the "*capitalist oligarchy*" in public speeches.[170] In 1964, Franco stated that "*the old political parties and the worn out liberal capitalist systems*" would not allow Spain to meet the future challenges.[171]

Even in the last days of the Franco dictatorship, excessively statist and interventionist economic policies were held in high esteem by the government. The Falangist/FET official Fernandez Miranda noted in 1971 that Spain needed "*an integrating national socialism*" and that "*the only authentically effective attitude in the face of Marxism is a radical and profound national socialism that carries to its consequences the national revolution, the revolution of the Movement, and the achievement of social justice.*" Industrialization, state welfare programs, and full employment were praised during this period by the Falangists.[172] Another Spanish Francoist official named Senor Fraga Iribarne stated in 1975 that "*monopolistic and privileged situations which have grown up in the present state of capitalism require correction if a real equilibrium of power is to be achieved.*" He also supported "*a strong public sector*" in an economy balanced with private enterprise.[173]

Businessmen continued to gripe about the unfair competition which stemmed from the well-funded state enterprises and subsidized "*private*" firms; the massive number of government controls and regulations; the corporative measures; and the hostile propaganda against capitalism, the bourgeoisie, and liberalism. Sulzberger reported that businessmen in Spain complained "*that they are stifled by too much government intervention, unnecessary controls, red tape, connected with permits covering almost every type of transaction; that the spirit of private enterprise is being sapped.*" Businessmen also pointed out that they were forced to compete with companies funded or owned by INI. They charged that INI favored certain political favorites and established a multitude of government enterprises. Spanish farmers resented the orders of the government which dictated the specific crops they could grow, the

---

[166] Payne, Stanley G. The Franco Regime (University of Wisconsin Press 2011) page 470.

[167] Welles, Benjamin. "Franco Condemns Western Policies" New York Times June 4, 1961 page 1.

[168] Hoffman, Paul. "Franco Promises Fair Share to All" New York Times September 19, 1962 page 11.

[169] Welles, Benjamin. "US is Disturbed by Spanish Press" New York Times January 21, 1962 page 27.

[170] Hoffman, Paul. "Falange Faction Asks Labor Gains" New York Times May 24, 1963 page 9.

[171] "Appeal to Nation by General Franco" Times (London) December 31, 1964

[172] Payne, Stanley G. The Franco Regime (University of Wisconsin Press 2011) pages 549-550.

[173] Wigg, Richard. "Senor Fraga Outlines His Vision for New Spain" Times (London) October 31, 1975

price levels, and the mandatory quotas for delivery to the state.[174] Even the institutions of American capitalism and government continued to support the fascistic, interventionist economy in Spain. For example, an American loan disbursed in 1950 to Spain was worth $62.5 million. The loan was reportedly distributed to industries associated with the INI.[175]

Government threats lodged against private landowners, industrialists, and other businessmen were not unknown in postwar Spain. In 1951, Franco denounced food profiteers and speculators.[176] In December 1953, Spain threatened its farmers with fines if they refused to turn in their quota of wheat to the government.[177] Such punitive threats, taxes, and fines levied against the wealthy and entrepreneurial classes in Spain continued even in the later years of the Franco dictatorship. In 1967, the Franco government raised taxes on the wealthy based on their tangible, visible signs of material luxuries. Government assessors were dispatched to review real and intangible properties and assets possessed by the wealthy: real estate, rents paid or received, travel/sporting/social activities, number of maids and chauffeurs, and possessions (cars, aircraft, yachts, and race horses).[178] In 1970, the Count of Motrico was an example of the growing sector of conservative property owning classes in Spain who opposed Franco's dictatorship. Manu called for a more limited government. The Count of Motrico was fined 600 pounds for his opposition to Franco.[179]

Chile Under General Augusto Pinochet (1973-1989)

Before General Augusto Pinochet Ugarte seized power in a military *coup* on September 11, 1973, Chile was a country beset in chaos, massive economic decline, and infiltration by the communists. President Salvador Allende Gossens took power in 1970 via parliamentary maneuvers and established an increasingly authoritarian communist-type state. The economy suffered the suffocating blows of full-scale socialist policies, which was replete with rationing, price controls, and outright nationalization of private enterprises. Some American corporate investments, such as the properties owned by ITT and Anaconda Copper, were also nationalized by the Allende government. During Allende's tenure, large swathes of the Chilean Left coalesced into the Popular Unity (UP) coalition. Allende's party, the Socialists, possessed hegemony in the UP coalition. Cubans, Soviets, and other communist bloc personnel trickled into Chile to help train Allende's intelligence services and paramilitary gang of thugs known as the Group of Personal Friends (GAP).

Despite my critiques of Pinochet, it is important to discuss the extensive communist, Soviet, and Cuban contacts of Allende himself and his government. This helped set the stage where the military sincerely saw the need to stave off the violence of an increasingly totalitarian Chile. Allende himself was a hardline Marxist who masqueraded as a "*democratic socialist*." In

---

[174] Sulzberger, C.L. "Poverty Scourges Spanish Economy" New York Times February 9, 1951 page 5.

[175] Brewer, Sam Pope. "Spaniards View US Loan as a Big Boost for Franco" New York Times September 3, 1950 page 70.

[176] "Franco Assails Food Profiteers" New York Times March 29, 1951 page 9.

[177] "Stiff Penalties Set for Farmers in Spain" New York Times December 29, 1950 page 8.

[178] Szulc, Tad. "Madrid Widening Taxes on the Rich" New York Times December 31, 1967 page 10.

[179] "Monied Men Deserting Franco" Times (London) July 1, 1970

1953, Allende praised Stalin, who according to the future Chilean president, *"was a banner of creativity, of humanism and an edifying picture of peace and heroism! Everything he did, he did in service of the people. Our father Stalin has died but in remembering his example our affection for him will cause our arms to grow strong towards building a grand tomorrow-- to insure a future in memory of his grand example!"*[180]

Allende also had every intention to turn Chile into a base for Cuban-style communist revolution in South America. During his 1970 presidential campaign, Allende declared that *"Cuba in the Caribbean and a Socialist Chile in the Southern Cone will make the revolution in Latin America."* Allende headed the Chilean Socialist delegation to the 1966 Tri-Continental Conference in Havana Cuba. Thereafter, Socialist Party of Chile militants were trained in Cuba. As the Vice President of the World Peace Council, Allende himself visited the Soviet Union in 1954.[181] The Soviets always desired a foothold in South America as a means of communizing that continent. Soviet Peace Committee and high level Communist Party official defector Michael Voslensky noted that *"It has long been remarked in Moscow that because of its geographical position that thin strip of territory stretching from north to south along the western border of Argentina would be an ideal base for a communist partisan movement in the countries of South America."*[182]

From the start, Allende practiced strategic deception during the election of 1970 and in its relations with the United States. The system of parliamentarism and free elections was viewed as a means to an end, according to Allende. In a conversation with the French Marxist journalist Regis Debray, Allende admitted that he viewed the democratic electoral process *"as a simple tactical necessity to gain power."*[183]

However, once in power, Allende and his comrades promoted violent revolution in Chile. In January 1971, Allende's Minister Carlos Altamirano noted *"We're following the example of the Cuban Revolution and counting on the support of her militant internationalism...represented by Fidel Castro and Che Guevara. Armed conflict in continental terms remains as relevant today as ever!"* Salvador Allende proclaimed *"Hear me loud and clear! We will employ revolutionary violence!"* An Allende governmental ally, Oscar Guillermo Garreton noted that *"In the final analysis only armed conflict will decide who is the victor! Without the complete destruction of the bourgeois character of the state we cannot march on the path of Socialism! The class struggle always entails armed conflict. Understand me, the global strategy is always accomplished through arms!"* Allende's Deputy Economic Minister, Sergio Ramos, stated in mid-1973 that *"It's evident that the transition to socialism will first require a dictatorship of the proletariat."*[184]

---

[180] Fontova, Humberto. "Allende: The Untold Story" Frontpagemag.com December 14, 2006 Accessed From: http://www.frontpagemag.com/Articles/Printable.aspx?GUID=6FD2775C-F4FD-4414-A3E4-FF46B4B16505

[181] Meyer, Cord. Facing Reality: From World Federalism to the CIA (University Press of America, 1982) pages 175-177.

[182] Voslensky, Michael. Nomenklatura: The Soviet Ruling Class (Doubleday 1984) page 338.

[183] Skinner, Kiron K. Reagan's Path to Victory: The Shaping of Ronald Reagan's Vision (Simon and Schuster, 2004) page 135.

[184] Fontova, Humberto. "Allende: The Untold Story" Frontpagemag.com December 14, 2006 Accessed From: http://www.frontpagemag.com/Articles/Printable.aspx?GUID=6FD2775C-F4FD-4414-A3E4-FF46B4B16505

Plan Z was drawn up in August 1973. It was an effort by Allende's Popular Unity (UP), GAP, and communist infiltrated elements of the armed forces. These forces were projected to massacre anti-communists in the armed forces and *"to seize total power and impose the dictatorship of the proletariat against the action of part of the whole of the Armed Forces supported by civilian groups."* After anti-communist military officers were massacred, the UP and the communists would seize radio, television, and newspapers in an effort to inundate Chile with propaganda. Ultimately, Plan Z was the *"straw that broke the camel's back"* which pushed the anti-communist sectors of the Chilean military to depose Allende.[185]

Allende also fostered close relations with the Soviet Union. He noted that *"The Soviet Union is Chile's elder sister."*[186] In 1972 and 1973, Allende sought to work with the KGB to reorganize the Chilean intelligence apparatus and armed forces. Socialist and Communist personnel infiltrated the *Servicio de Investigaciones* and turned it into a ruthless instrument of Allende's regime. The Soviet KGB also provided thousands of dollars to Allende during his rule in order to influence the armed forces, intelligence services, and the political class. The Soviets also recommended that the Peruvian and Chilean armed forces establish liaisons.[187]

According to the smuggled documents of the Mitrokhin Archive, the KGB reported that it convinced Allende to *"understand the necessity of reorganising Chile's army and intelligence services, and of setting up a relationship between Chile's and the USSR's intelligence services."* The KGB provided Allende with $30,000 *"in order to solidify the trusted relations."* Allende appealed for Soviet funds through the KGB officer Svyatoslav Kuznetsov. The KGB subsidy for Allende's 1970 presidential campaign totaled $400,000. KGB Chairman Andropov stated that the KGB *"will carry out measures designed to promote the consolidation of Allende's victory and his election to the post of President of the country."* The KGB reported that Allende *"stated his willingness to co-operate on a confidential basis and provide any necessary assistance, since he considered himself a friend of the Soviet Union."* In mid-1973, the Soviets approved the delivery of weapons, such as artillery and tanks to the Chilean Army. After Allende was *"elected"* in 1970, the Soviets suggested the reorganization of the Chilean military and intelligence services to Allende. The Soviets also recommended that the Chilean intelligence service establish contacts with the KGB. Allende agreed to implement the suggestions made by the Soviets. After September 1973, the KGB launched *Operation Toucan*, which created and disseminated disinformation that linked the CIA with the overthrow of Allende and his subsequent death.[188]

Military personnel from North Vietnam, Cuba, and North Korea trained Allende's paramilitary gang called the Group of Personal Friends (GAP). The GAP numbered 200 troops. Their weapons were imported from Czechoslovakia and the USSR.[189] The Cubans also played an important role in advising Allende's intelligence and paramilitary services of *coup* attempts and

---

[185] Labin, Suzanne. Chile: The Crime of Resistance (Foreign Affairs Pub. Co., 1982) pages 162-164.

[186] Labin, Suzanne. Chile: The Crime of Resistance (Foreign Affairs Pub. Co., 1982) page 190.

[187] Mitrokhin, Vassili and Andrew, Christopher. The World Was Going Our Way (Basic Books, 2005) pages 70-84.

[188] Billingsley, Lloyd. "Chile Con Commies" Frontpagemag.com January 24, 2006 Accessed From: http://archive.frontpagemag.com/readArticle.aspx?ARTID=5818

[189] Labin, Suzanne. Chile: The Crime of Resistance (Foreign Affairs Pub. Co., 1982) pages 88-89.

its enemies. The Cuban intelligence service (DGI) trained the GAP, while their Embassy in Santiago totaled 150 diplomats/spies.[190] Since September 1970, the Cubans also cooperated with the official Chilean intelligence services.[191] In August 1973, a declassified Chilean document recounted the visit of two Cuban Communist Party Central Committee officials Carlos Rafael Rodriguez and Manuel Piniero to Allende's government: *I am sending you two confidential agents under the pretext of discussing the non-aligned countries with you. In reality I would like them to examine with you the domestic situation in Chile and the dangers that the putschists represent for the revolution…The most important thing is to warn the enemy that there are forces ready and fully armed to go into action against him…Let my two envoys know all the points on which we can collaborate with you.*[192]

From 1970 to 1971, flights of Chile's state-owned airline LAN transported arms for Allende from Cuba. When the head of the Criminal Investigation Department Coco Paredes returned from one of his many trips to Cuba, Chilean customs inspected 13 crates. Paredes and Allende claimed they contained consumer goods, but documents later revealed that they carried MP-40 machine guns, anti-tank missiles, heavy machine guns, and ammunition and spare parts.[193] Chilean Army intelligence also alleged in early 1973 that thousands of Soviet, Cuban, East German, and Czechoslovak troops were located in the Cerillas industrial suburb. These forces were armed with Czechoslovak-made weapons.[194] By September 1973, Chile hosted officers of the Cuban Special Forces and Americas Department. They included the legendary agents Antonio De La Guardia and Manuel Pineiro. High ranking KGB officers were also present in Chile, such as Viktor Efremov, Vasili Stepanov and Nikolai Kotchanov.[195] Moscow also played an economic role in Chile. Most of Chile's copper exports were transported by the Soviet-owned Baltic Steamships. Soviet technicians were also given access to Chile's industrial secrets.[196]

Allende's Socialist Party and later his government (1970-1973) engaged in the drug trade to undermine the United States and to garner hard currency. Robert Workman of the National Defense University stated that a DEA intelligence report recounted a meeting (held in 1961) of high-ranking Cuban officials. The meeting participants included the *revolutionary leader and President of the National Bank of Cuba, Che Guevara, Captain Moises Crespo of the Cuban secret police, and Dr. Salvador Allende, a Senator and future Marxist President from Chile, to discuss establishing a cocaine trafficking network.*[197] The Chilean cocaine trade with the United States was supervised by criminal mafia groups. Their agents utilized double bottom suitcases and female couriers. The smugglers were part of the financial and political apparatus of the

---

[190] Ibid, page 192.

[191] Harmer, Tanya. Allende's Chile and the Inter-American Cold War (University of North Carolina Press, 2011) pages 54-55.

[192] Labin, Suzanne. Chile: The Crime of Resistance (Foreign Affairs Pub. Co., 1982) page 191.

[193] Ibid, pages 92-94.

[194] Ibid, page 190.

[195] Fontova, Humberto. "Allende: The Untold Story" Frontpagemag.com December 14, 2006 Accessed From: http://www.frontpagemag.com/Articles/Printable.aspx?GUID=6FD2775C-F4FD-4414-A3E4-FF46B4B16505

[196] Labin, Suzanne. Chile: The Crime of Resistance (Foreign Affairs Pub. Co., 1982) page 190.

[197] Douglass, Joseph D. Red Cocaine (Edward Harle, Limited, 1999) Accessed From: http://www.usa-anti-communist.net/Perestroika-4books/Douglass_Joseph_Red_Cocaine.pdf

Popular Unity (UP) government of Allende. The cocaine was grown in labs owned by the Communist Party of Chile. The *Linea Aerea Nacional Chile* also transported cocaine to the United States and was protected by the Chilean police. Drugs were also smuggled through Mexico. One Popular Unity activist named Maria Isabel Jarmane admitted her desire to smuggle drugs in order to "*poison many US imperialists.*" Drugs were also transported through Cuba in official containers that belonged to Chilean state agencies such as the *Banco Central.* The drugs were then exchanged for arms, which were then dispatched to Chilean leftists and to Popular Unity activists. Drugs were also sent to other Latin American countries via Allende's Chile. This activity was part of the Allende government's plan for the "*exportation of the revolution.*" The Chilean cocaine producers were protected by Marxists within the Department of Investigations. Examples of Marxist moles that were embedded in the Department of Investigations included people such as Eduardo Paredes. The Popular Unity regime of Allende used the profits from the drug traffic to purchase black market arms from dealers in American cities. These weapons were then shipped to Latin American Marxists. The profits from Allende's drug trade were also utilized to fund subversive activities in the United States and to corrupt youth as a tool to defeat America.[198]

The Allende regime also stoked international opposition to American multinational corporations which invested in the Third World. In May 1973, an international trade union conference was organized by the *Central Unica de Trabajadores* (CUT) and held in Santiago. It was attended by representatives from sixty-five countries. The participants strategized on the best methods to harrass multinational corporations. The multinationals were characterized as "*An instrument of U.S., Western European and Japanese monopoly capital, to intensify the exploitation of the workers, impinging on their economic rights and worsen their working conditions, employment and wages.*" The conference resolved "*to establish efficient forms of control over multinational corporations, especially in the field of employment and workers' benefits, wage policies, and respect for the advances in trade union rights won by the workers, and the right of nations to force multinational groups to reinvest profits in those countries from which such profits are derived, or to nationalize such concerns; the right of every nation to dispose of its natural resources (as it sees fit), and to create the bases for independent economic development, free of all interference on the part of multinationals.*"[199] Allende and his comrades hypocritically maintained trading links with American multinationals and even imported weapons from the United States to beef up the Chilean armed forces. As a loyal Marxist-Leninist, Allende knew that he could strategically utilize the greed of American businessmen to help sustain his Marxist dictatorship and salvage political legitimacy in Washington.

At the Chilean Socialist Party Congress in January 1971, General Secretary, Carlos Altamirano, publicly declared that Uruguayan and Brazilian revolutionaries would "*always*" receive asylum and support from their "*comrades in arms*" in Chile. In a meeting with Soviet bloc leaders (May 1971), Foreign Minister Clodomiro Almeyda noted that the Chileans explored the possibility of exchanges between Argentina's military forces. The Chileans and their Soviet

---

[198] "The Theory and Practice of Communism Part 5: Marxism Imposed on Chile-Allende Regime" Committee on Internal Security November 15, 1973

[199] "International Trade Union Conference" Chile Economic News May 15, 1973 Accessed From: http://www.virtual.vietnam.ttu.edu/cgi-bin/starfetch.exe?5u47Kdz2bFa1co.we7fTz7OzFy@N3j95g58EVbrrsbj1urhKtAUvW@2pJvRJs jiJtMRgkVT1H@snhIaHlBybbsgvLg5bv@xOnefhHJsju7A/14511516019.pdf

bloc counterparts hoped that such exchanges with the Argentine Armed Forces would isolate its pro-American right-wing members. The ultimate result would be a takeover of Argentina by radical Peronists or Communists.[200]

The Allende regime and some of its leftist allies also actively wooed the Chilean military and national police in an effort to win their support. Allende ally and Communist Party boss Luis Corvalan noted in early 1971 that the Chilean "*army is not invulnerable to the new winds blowing in Latin America and penetrating everywhere. It is not a body alien to the nation, in the service of antinational interests. It must be won to the cause of progress in Chile and not pushed to the other side of the barricades.*"[201] Allende himself noted that "*Not for nothing is the motto of the Carabinieros 'Order and Fatherland.' Order, based on moral authority, in the correct carrying out of duties, which in no way implies the negation of hierarchy. In fact you have a sense of discipline and hierarchy which grows on the conception that this government has of social discipline and the use of public force.*"[202]

Another carrot that Allende used to entice the Chilean military to support his regime were material privileges. Allende increased the military's budget and gave the officers a large stake in the management of the state-owned corporations. Senior military officers were appointed to the boards of some 40 state enterprises and research institutions, including the mines.[203]

The Allende regime and its political allies also called for intense production and labor discipline from Chile's workers. This foreshadowed the highly authoritarian controls on labor imposed by General Pinochet after his *coup* in September 1973. Communist union leader Luis Figuero stated April 1972 that: "*Participation must be expressed NOT in the ownership of the firm's property by their workers, but in an effective and active role in management and planning.*" Figuero also called for an organized drive for greater productivity and "*voluntary work.*"[204] Cuban dictator Fidel Castro lectured the workers at the Chuquicamata mine that "*a hundred tone less per day means a loss of $36 million a year.*"[205]

Allende and his Popular Unity dictatorship also employed elements of the military, police, and gangs to crush labor strikes. It appeared that Cuban communist dictator Fidel Castro also leaned on Allende to crush labor unrest. In November 1971, Fidel Castro visited Chile and labeled striking miners "*demagogues.*"[206] In August 1972, shopkeepers clashed with police in Santiago, while Communist elements of the Chilean police attacked leftist MIR agitators outside Santiago and killed five peasants.[207] In September 1972 Allende called for "*social peace*" in cooperation with the commander of the Chilean Army and restored some of the old factory

---

[200] Harmer, Tanya. Allende's Chile and the Inter-American Cold War (University of North Carolina Press, 2011) pages 97 and 111.

[201] Lewis, Tom. "Chile: The State and Revolution" ISR Issue 6 Winter 1999 Accessed From: http://www.isreview.org/issues/06/chile.shtml

[202] Ibid.

[203] "The Illusion of a 'Democratic' Army" World Revolution April 17, 1973 Accessed From: http://www.the-spark.net/csart224.html

[204] "From the archives of Marxism: lessons of the 1973 coup in Chile" December 12, 2006 Accessed From: http://www.wsws.org/articles/2006/dec2006/chil-d12.shtml

[205] "The irresistible fall of Allende" December 30, 2004 Accessed From: http://en.internationalism.org/wr/268_chile.htm

[206] Ibid.

[207] Ibid.

bosses in plants in northern Chile.[208] When the workers at the El Teniente Copper Mines went on strike from April to June 1973 as a result of Allende's wage freezes, they were attacked by the regime. Allende requested that the miners accept sacrifice *"for the general good."* The miners refused and Allende called the strikers *"fascists"* and *"traitors."* Corvalan noted that *"We continue to support the absolutely professional character of the armed institutions. Their enemies are not among the ranks of the people but in the reactionary camp."*[209] The Allende regime repressed the striking copper miners and placed the industrial areas under martial law in early 1973. Allende legalized military searches of factories and workplaces and disbanded workers' self-defense militias. He brought three top generals into his cabinet.[210] After returning from a trip to the USSR, Allende attacked the striking copper miners in January 1973 as *"real monopoly bankers, asking for money for their pocket without any consideration for the situation in the country."* The striking copper miners at the El Teniente were repressed by Allende and the Communists using water cannons and tear gas. The province where the mine was located was placed under military control.[211] In the period from May to June 1973, the miners at El Teniente were repressed by Allende, who used 500 *carabineros* to attack the workers with tear gas and water cannon. When 4,000 striking miners marched to Santiago, they were repressed by riot police. The government smeared the workers as *"agents of fascism."* The Communist Party of Chile organized parades in Santiago, which called for the government to use a *"firm hand"* against the striking miners.[212]

Despite the anti-American foreign policy and anti-capitalist rhetoric of Allende and the Popular Unity, there was another side to Chilean foreign/trade policy during this time period. Chile under Allende was invariably willing to trade with the noncommunist world, including the United States. Chile would receive capital goods and technologies, along with increased political clout in Washington DC to combat the Nixon Administration's partial anti-Allende campaign. While the CIA helped fund opposition groups that fought Allende, the United States government and multinational companies continued to export goods and weapons to the Popular Unity regime. An internal Chilean Foreign Ministry memorandum predicted that both U.S. governmental and nongovernmental organizations would react to Chile's *"struggle against imperialism."* Fidel Castro strategically advised Allende to remain in the dollar area, maintain copper exports to the United States, and to retain Chile's membership in the Organization of American States (OAS). Orlando Letelier, a Chilean Socialist Party member who worked at the Inter-American Development Bank (IDB) also counseled Allende to exercise strategic caution in its relations with the United States. Letelier wrote the Socialist Party General Secretary, Aniceto Rodríguez, to urge Allende and the Popular Unity Party (UP) to formulate a coherent international strategy which stressed that confrontation with the United States was not inevitable. Letelier pointed out that the Nixon administration was faced with various *"internal problems"*

---

[208] Lewis, Tom. "Chile: The State and Revolution" ISR Issue 6 Winter 1999 Accessed From: http://www.isreview.org/issues/06/chile.shtml

[209] Ibid.

[210] Saavedra, Mauricio and Rees, Margaret. "The Lessons of Chile-30 Years On" September 17, 2003 Accessed From: http://www.wsws.org/articles/2003/sep2003/chil-s17.shtml

[211] "From the archives of Marxism: lessons of the 1973 coup in Chile" December 12, 2006 Accessed From: http://www.wsws.org/articles/2006/dec2006/chil-d12.shtml

[212] "The irresistible fall of Allende" December 30, 2004 Accessed From: http://en.internationalism.org/wr/268_chile.htm

and difficulties in the Middle East and Vietnam. Letelier noted that *"the tremendous criticism that Nixon's international policy is receiving daily in the North American congress, its attitude toward the Chilean situation will not be able to be of an openly aggressive character…. I think that faced with what is occurring in Peru and what is occurring in Bolivia, the (United States') position in respect to Chile will be to find a level of understanding and to avoid a situation of crisis. All this favors us."*[213] In December 1970, Allende called for *"healthy realism"* in foreign affairs because Chile was not ready to *"fight the giant."* Socialist Party leader Almeyda noted *"The only way to restrain our adversaries was to try and neutralize them, divide them, negotiate with them; to compromise and even retreat tactically in order to avoid collision or confrontation, which could only have a negative outcome for Chile."*[214]

In early 1971, the Chilean Foreign Ministry vowed to improve the image of the Allende regime within diverse sectors of the American public. The Popular Unity regime would coordinate its actions with the relevant Chilean institutions and financial sectors to ensure that the United States did not suspend military credits to Chile's armed forces. The Chileans also focused on improving their country's relations with other Latin American nations as a means of forming a *"front"* against the United States. The Chilean Foreign Ministry believed that the continued flow of military credits helped *"project an image of normality"* as a positive factor in US-Chilean relations.[215] Allende-era Chilean diplomats lobbied leftwing Democratic Senators such as Edward Kennedy (D-MA) to paint the Popular Unity (communist) regime with a positive brush. Allende and his comrades were confident that the United States would not seriously sever ties with Chile or cease trading relations. The ardent communist Chilean Ambassador to the United States Orlando Letelier wrote that *"Today it is not possible that a President of the United States can intervene in Latin America as President Johnson did in the Dominican Republic in 1965."* In 1972, Chilean diplomats in Washington were encouraged by the moves to détente by the Nixon Administration and Henry Kissinger. The Chilean diplomats rationalized: *"If we are reaching an agreement with the Soviet Union and with China…How are we not going to be able to reach an agreement with Chile?"* In 1972, Letelier also remarked that *"We are living in a moment of convergence and understanding between the United States and the socialist countries."*[216]

Contrary to popular belief, the United States did not enact a complete trade ban towards Allende's Chile. During the rule of Allende, Chile was able to acquire American-made goods through purchases by private entrepreneurs, Soviet, and Mexican intermediaries. Two former functionaries of the Allende regime also reported that American goods and spare parts were purchased from overseas subsidiaries of US companies in Europe and Latin America. The US government allowed Chilean industries to purchase goods for cash, including critical parts and equipment for the mining industry. For example, Ford Motor Company was requested to supply

---

[213] Harmer, Tanya. <u>Allende's Chile and the Inter-American Cold War</u> (University of North Carolina Press, 2011) pages 77-79.

[214] Ibid, page 79.

[215] Harmer, Tanya. <u>Allende's Chile and the Inter-American Cold War</u> (University of North Carolina Press, 2011) pages 97 and 111.

[216] Brands, Hal. "Latin America's Cold War" 2009 Accessed From: http://www.utexas.edu/lbj/archive/osap/uploads/file/Brands_Dissertation.pdf

parts to Chile with the backing of firm letters of credit.[217] As of October 1971, American oil and pharmaceutical companies continued to export goods to Allende's Chile. US multinational corporations such as RCA, Gillette, General Tire, and General Electric also traded with Chile.[218] In 1972, Allende purchased three airliners from Boeing, which was paid for in part by a $50 million credit from the Soviet Union.[219]

From 1971 to 1973, public aid from the American government totaled $7 million. Surplus food aid was also shipped to Allende's Chile. For example, American-made powdered milk allowed the Popular Unity (UP) government to supply free milk to schoolchildren.[220] Over $20 million of American economic assistance was sent to Allende from 1971 to 1973.[221]

The United States and the West also provided weapons and spare parts for the tanks and aircraft of the Chilean army. In 1972, the United States still sold the Chilean military equipment, including C-130 transport planes.[222] By 1973, Chile received military and economic aid from the United States, which totaled $21.4 million. Former US Ambassador Nathaniel Davis noted that Allende and his ministers *"requested and approved all credits, sales, training, and other military cooperation between Chile and the United States…the consistent thrust of President Allende's public and private posture was to support military cooperation and credit and to criticize us if we showed signs of cutting back."*[223] Allende's purchases of British and other Western European arms overshadowed US weapons.[224]

Cuba used Allende's Chile to circumvent the American embargo. Private Chilean corporations also provided a channel for Cuban purchases in various noncommunist countries. For example, Cuba purchased Californian strawberry seeds through a Chilean business surrogate. The seeds were then transshipped to Cuba for their famous Copelia ice creams.[225]

On September 11, 1973, the Chilean military led by anti-communist generals such as Augusto Pinochet, moved in a timely fashion to forestall a massacre of anti-Allende forces (Plan Z). Pinochet's army troops and the Chilean secret police (DINA) brutally suppressed the pro-Allende forces and leftwing terrorists through mass executions in sports stadiums and imprisonments. Many Chileans, even moderately leftwing parties such as the Christian Democrats, initially welcomed the takeover by the anti-communist elements in the military. They hoped, at long last, that the military under General Pinochet would restore the economy and

---

[217] Falcoff, Mark. <u>Modern Chile, 1970-1989: A Critical History</u> (Transaction Publishers 1989) page 225.

[218] Novitski, Joseph. "Marxist Chile After One Year" <u>New York Times</u> October 10, 1971 page F1.

[219] Falcoff, Mark. <u>Modern Chile, 1970-1989: A Critical History</u> (Transaction Publishers 1989) page 247.

[220] Ibid, pages 226-227.

[221] Ibid, pages 225-227.

[222] Szulcs. Tad. "U.S. Is Continuing Aid to the Chilean Armed Forces" <u>New York Times</u> December 9, 1972 page 12.

[223] Falcoff, Mark. <u>Modern Chile, 1970-1989: A Critical History</u> (Transaction Publishers 1989) page 226.

[224] Ibid, page 271.

[225] Harmer, Tanya. <u>Allende's Chile and the Inter-American Cold War</u> (University of North Carolina Press, 2011) page 134.

eventually hold free and fair elections. General Pinochet became the head of the new military junta that ruled Chile until 1989.

It should be pointed out that Pinochet himself was no believer in limited, liberal forms of governance. He specifically believed in an authoritarian state that demobilized many forms of independent political action. Pinochet lashed out at the old political elites for their selfish, anti-national sentiments, whose vices ultimately paved the way for a communist takeover. In 1975, Pinochet complained bitterly that *"The politicians wanted us to clean the house (and) let them occupy it again."* In 1979, Pinochet also stated that *"We are not a vacuum cleaner that swept out Marxism to give back power to those Mr. Politicians."* Pinochet also lashed out against *"partisan oligarchs"* and *"privileged minorities"* within the civilian elites. Pinochet imposed a *"recess"* on all political parties, including conservative groups.[226] Pinochet even declared his preference for a new, quasi-fascist, authoritarian ideology for the Chilean state: *"Our duty is to give form to a new democracy that will be authoritarian, protected, integrating, technically modern, and with authentic social participation."* He stated further that *"the classic liberal state, naive and spineless"* must be replaced with one willing to use *"use strong and vigorous authority."*[227]

Pinochet modeled himself and his rule after the nationalist, collectivist dictator of Chile during the 1830s, Diego Portales. It was observed that *"Portales disdained partisan politics and believed that the best government was an 'impersonal' semi-dictatorship with limited concessions to popular representation."* It was observed that *"Pinochet's studied emulation of Portales was evident in the calls for discipline, efficiency, and the 'principle of authority' that peppered his speeches. He posed for official photographs with an oil portrait of Portales behind his shoulder, named the regime's principal office building in his honor, and encouraged the cult of a 'Portalian ethos' among his aides.'"*[228] Grugel elaborated that *"**As well as authoritarian, Portales appears to have been anti-oligarchical, anti-militaristic, and party to state intervention in the economy**."*[229]

During Pinochet's tenure of power, policies were enacted to place Chile's economy on a partially free market path. There was much division on how far the Pinochet government should go in transforming the Chilean economy from Marxist slavery to a free market system. Most military officers and allies of the regime did not desire a full transformation of Chile into a free enterprise system. Some military officers even desired an increase in state controls over the economy and little or no privatizations of state-owned enterprises. Ideology was the chief motivation for these officers, who distrusted liberal capitalism as much as communism. Many of the *"free market"* advocates were not the advocates of pure *laissez faire*. Instead, they believed that the government should *"guide"* the process of privatization and the economy in general. The so-called *"free market"* technocrats were more than willing to use government agencies such as the state planning agency (ODEPLAN), the National Planning Office, the Central Bank, and the

---

[226] Constable, Pamela. <u>A Nation of Enemies: Chile under Pinochet</u> (W. W. Norton & Company, 1993) page 69.

[227] Ibid, page 71.

[228] Ibid, page 70.

[229] Grugel, Jean. "Nationalist Movements and Fascist Ideology in Chile" <u>Bulletin of Latin American Research</u> Volume 4, Number 2 1985 Accessed From: http://pics3441.upmf-grenoble.fr/articles/auth/nationalist_movements_and_fascist_ideology.pdf

Ministry of Finance to fulfill their goals.[230] However, it is fair to say that these *"free market"* elements desired a general de-regulation, de-bureaucratization, and de-nationalization of the economy, which in turn would jumpstart Chile's path to prosperity. Most military factions in the Pinochet dictatorship also valued certain state-owned enterprises for the profits generated for government coffers. Furthermore, much of the government (including Pinochet himself), also opposed the denationalization of certain enterprises on the grounds of national security. In July 1981, Pinochet noted that *"there are no plans to sell CODELCO, the post office, or the state bank because these are state enterprises and the state must carry out its subsidiary role."*[231] The Pinochet regime and some of its advisers (such as law Professor Jaime Guzman) supported corporative economic policies during its early days. Professor Guzman's social and economic model was that of fascist Spain under the iron rule of General Franco. The secret police (DINA), elements of the army (General Gustavo Leigh), and the neo-fascist *Patria y Libertad* movement opposed the shift to the partial economic liberalism by the Pinochet regime.[232] Various neo-fascist forces, while anti-communist and anti-Allende, actively opposed all privatization measures and were just as totalitarian as Allende and the Communists. They believed in a collectivism that highlighted the supremacy of race in all state matters.

David Felix noted that *"virtually the entire banking system was taken over by the government in an attempt to salvage the economy, leading some to describe the transition from Allende to Pinochet as 'a transition from utopian to scientific socialism, since the means of production are ending up in the hands of the state' or 'the Chicago Road to socialism.'"* It was also noted that the London Economist Intelligence Unit noted that *"the believer in free markets, President Pinochet, had a more comprehensive grip on the 'controlling heights of the economy' than President Allende had dared dream of."*[233]

It was observed that *"General Luis Danus, the head of CORFO[234], supported the privatization process, but some senior officers believed that strategic industries should remain in state hands. In 1979, the economic planners tried to sell off the state copper-mining consortium, which they viewed as an unmanageable 'monster.' But its vice-president, Colonel Gastón Fréz, argued that to abandon this critical commodity to private whims was 'antipatriotic,' and threatened to resign from the army. Pinochet quickly ordered his aides to leave the monster intact."* By 1980, the Chilean government owned 23 strategic industries, such as mining, energy, and communications. It was observed that *"the state continued to control about 75 percent of*

[230] Drake, Paul W. and Jaksic, Ivan. The Struggle for Democracy in Chile (University of Nebraska Press, 1995) page 56.

[231] "Pinochet on Terrorism, Economy, Other Issues" Santiago Chile Domestic Service July 14, 1981

[232] Drake, Paul W. and Jaksic, Ivan. The Struggle for Democracy in Chile (University of Nebraska Press, 1995) pages 44-46.

[233] Chomsky, Noam. Year 501 (South End Press, 1993) Accessed From: http://books.zcommunications.org/chomsky/year/year-c07-s15.html

[234] CORFO was the state corporation that managed various government-owned economic sectors. It was created during leftist government of the 1930s and was retained by the Pinochet dictatorship to guide the economy, including the *"privatization"* process.

national production. Indeed, while the Chicago Boys' aggressive efforts drastically reduced the government's property and payroll, it still wielded more economic power than in 1965."[235]

Some conservatives, independents, and libertarians were not snowed by the euphoric propaganda that Chile was on the fast track to pure free enterprise. The Hoover Institution observed that *"It is often said and widely believed that Pinochet's economic reforms eliminated any significant role of the state in the economy. The claim is that he introduced a neoliberal model, that is, raw, savage capitalism of the kind attributed to Chile in the nineteenth century. The facts are otherwise. Chile's largest industry and biggest foreign-exchange earner by far is copper, which was nationalized in the late 1960s and early 1970s and has remained so ever since. Domestic banks were deregulated in the late 1970s but reregulated with vigor in the early 1980s…Major state expenditures for direct action social programs targeted to the poorest of the poor were initiated in the middle 1980s, not after 1990…"*[236] Indeed, the Pinochet regime was proud of its record on the expansion of certain social welfare programs for the poor and even conscripted the rhetoric of the Left to justify the existence of such government services. In May 1981, Pinochet noted that the extension of family allowances to needy children under the age of 5 as being a part of the *"true spirit of social justice proposed by the government."*[237]

Mark Falcoff reported that under Pinochet *"…in many ways, the government is stronger than ever. It exercises complete control over the armed forces and police, and possesses the capacity to establish strict limits to judicial independence or academic freedom. Moreover, since the collapse of private Chilean banks in 1982, the government has assumed their obligations, and in so doing, acquired a de facto control of Chilean industry to which Allende aspired but never achieved. The difference is that Pinochet's 'socialism' is wholly informal and at least theoretically reversible-in the unlikely event that the debtors can find a way to retire their loans. Meanwhile, generals active and retired are sitting on the governing boards of major credit institutions, and are therefore able to influence the conduct of key Chilean enterprises, including newspapers and other forms of mass media. Thus the notion-widespread in conservative circles in the United States-that Chile has become in some way a showcase for free enterprise is somewhat wide off the mark."*[238]

<u>Reason</u> magazine reported that *"The biggest danger, according to several of the team members, comes from the large state-owned corporations. Currently run by military officers, they provide shells for government interference in the economy that may expand again when Pinochet is no longer in power. The overall economic picture is gratifying, although it is not the utopian free market that it sounds after a litany of deregulated industries and privatized businesses. Chile still has its share of regulation, and many of the free-market measures have been introduced only after prolonged struggle and negotiation between the Economic Team and other government elements, such as some military officers who favor government regulation of almost every sector. One retired officer explains that the military mentality naturally favors government interference. For them, the government has always been the source of everything,*

[235] Constable, Pamela. <u>A Nation of Enemies: Chile under Pinochet</u> (W. W. Norton & Company, 1993) page 189.
[236] Packenham, Robert A. and Ratliff, William. "What Pinochet Did for Chile" <u>Hoover Digest</u> January 30, 2007 Accessed From: http://www.hoover.org/publications/hoover-digest/article/5882
[237] "President Pinochet Gives Labor Day Address" <u>Santiago Chile Domestic Service</u> May 1, 1981
[238] Falcoff, Mark. "Coming Crisis in Chile" <u>Policy Review</u> Fall 1985 page 20.

from policy to supplies to salaries, and they see no reason why that should be different for the rest of the country. So the criticism can be leveled that Chile still has an enormous state-owned mining sector, government-regulated utilities, and a many-tentacled bureaucracy that inhabits dozens of downtown Santiago buildings and generates piles of paperwork and bureaucratic delays."[239]

Reason magazine noted that *"While Pinochet says he still supports the market model, tariffs have been boosted to 20 percent from the previous uniform rate of 10 percent; on selected goods, tariffs have gone even higher. Other moves away from the free-market program include a plan to send state managers into bankrupt companies and the temporary fixing of interest rates this past January. Pinochet has started public-works programs such as road building; like higher tariffs, these may serve mainly to muster support for the regime. Economic freedom is now being traded away in the name of pragmatism, and with the effect of buying time for the generals. It seems more likely that the same bayonets that once backed the free market will now be used to back state meddling in the private sector. The change would not be as great as the old free-market label implies. Chile was never a model free market, whatever that may be. The claim to economic distinction came from the sharp differences between Allende socialism and the plan the Chicago boys were able to negotiate with the military. State spending dropped from more than half of yearly GNP under Allende to a quarter of GNP under Pinochet but a quarter is still a hefty fraction. Chile was never whole-hearted in its acceptance of laissez-faire policies and had parted reluctantly in the first place with industries regarded as 'strategic' by influential generals. Even when the Chicago boys were at their height, the state owned 19 of the largest companies in Chile, including the copper mines, which accounted for more than 40 percent of exports in 1980, the last boom year.*"[240]

The former chief economist for the Coalition for a Prosperous America Ian Fletcher noted that *"One of the hidden stories of Chile is the conflict within the Pinochet regime between the notorious free market 'Chicago boys' and their right-wing opponents in the military government who leaned, like militarist regimes from General Park's Korea to General Franco's Spain, towards authoritarian developmentalism and disliked free markets.*"[241]

Tulchin observed that the *"notion that Chile, under Pinochet, institutionalized a laissez faire economy is a myth; the 'low' social expenditure is another. In fact, government expenditures in Chile are still relatively large. Fiscal expenditures are 30 percent of GDP, much higher than in most other Latin American countries. If the rest of public sector expenditures are considered, for instance the value added by large state enterprises (CODELCO and ENAP) and social security, the share of the public sector in the economy is easily among the highest of any country with a market economy with a degree of economic development similar to Chile's. The Junta has approved, or is considering the approval of, COLs that will establish or enlarge the autonomization of state institutions, such as the armed forces, the Central Bank, and the state*

[239] Rosett, Claudia. "Chile's Economic Revolution An eye-opening, first-hand look at the world's most radical attempt at economic decontrol" Reason Magazine April 1982 pages 32-39.

[240] Rosett, Claudia. "Was it the Free Market that Failed in Chile?" Reason Magazine August 1983 pages 41-43.

[241] Fletcher, Ian. Free Trade Does Not Work (U.S. Business & Industry Council, 2010) Accessed From: http://www.freetradedoesntwork.com/samples/Notes_bibliography_index.pdf

copper corporation, CODELCO. These institutions will be directed by unremovable authorities chosen by the current military government and unaccountable to elected representatives."[242] In the face of all the above-mentioned information, Spooner quite reasonably concluded that *"...the economic changes brought about by the Chicago Boys never produced a completely free market economic system in Chile."*

One of the most infamous cases of military resistance to privatization occurred when the free market civilian economists urged the denationalization of CODELCO, to no avail. One observer noted that CODELCO was the *"military's cash cow"* and therefore not on the agenda to be privatized.[243] In fact, Pinochet signed a decree in September 1975 that merged the copper mines into one large state owned enterprise CODELCO and also created the Chilean Copper Commission that will advise the Mining Ministry, Central Bank, and the Foreign Investment Committee.[244] In January 1987, Mining Minister Samuel Lira Ovalle noted that CODELCO and the National Mining Enterprise (ENAMI) would not be privatized because *"of the relevant role it plays in the national economy."*[245]

Teichman also observed that *"The military, through Pinochet, continued to exercise enormous influence over the resurrected market reform process, particularly in privatization. The privatization of the firms intervened by the government as a consequence of the financial crisis was carried out in 1985-86... Even with Pinochet's assistance, however, resistance was still strong and the task was not an easy one."*[246] In November 1981, Pinochet warned that the government intervention into private banks was designed *"to protect the less affluent sectors. He who breaks the rules will be punished here."* The government intervened (took over) eight private banks in Chile.[247]

Sometimes, private enterprises were even nationalized under Pinochet due to economic distress or national security reasons. Chilean Vice President General Javier Palacios stated in April 1974 that CORFO *"will not return the bank shares for any reason."* When questioned about the formation of joint companies with foreign firms, General Palacios noted that CORFO did *"not want to mortgage Chile with foreign companies."* General Palacios noted that CORFO *"will remain with one or two enterprises in each sector in order to guide and regulate the market."*[248] In May 1974, CORFO reportedly established 6 new industries for the production of fertilizers, rayon, potassium nitrate, and detergents.[249] In November 1975, the Chilean National Tire Industry (INSA) was nationalized by Pinochet and absorbed into CORFO, in light of

---

[242] Tulchin, Joseph S. From Dictatorship to Democracy: Rebuilding Political Consensus in Chile (Lynne Rienner Publishers 1991) pages 34 and 63.

[243] Spooner, Mary Helen. Soldiers in a Narrow Land (University of California Press, 1999) page 182.

[244] "New Corporation to Manage Five Mines" Buenos Aires LATIN September 8, 1975

[245] "Copper Enterprises to Remain Under State Control" Santiago Radio Chilena January 28, 1987

[246] Teichman, Judith A. The Politics of Freeing Markets in Latin America: Chile, Argentina, and Mexico (University of North Carolina Press, 2001) page 83.

[247] "Government Takes Control of 8 Banking Institutions" Paris AFP November 3, 1981

[248] "CORFO Will Not Return Bank Shares Says General Palacios" Santiago Chile La Patria April 30, 1974

[249] "New CORFO Industries" Santiago Chile Radio Portales May 20, 1974

allegedly illegal foreign currency transactions and bankruptcy.[250] Even after 1986, state-owned corporations such as CORFO and ENAP were not privatized. Between 1983 and 1989, the number of state-owned enterprises in Chile was reduced only by three.[251]

It also appeared that the Pinochet regime's economic ideology rejected *laissez-faire* capitalism as much as any type of socialism or communism. Instead, the dictatorship favored a massive dose of denationalization and deregulation that was balanced with corporative social policies, some government-owned enterprises, and some state controls over the private sector. On September 17, 1973, Pinochet remarked to Paris-based Radio Luxemburg reporters that *"the Junta de Gobierno does not wish to go back on social gains. On the contrary, it wants to direct all social advances through legal channels, not illegal ones."* Also in September 1973, General Gustavo Leigh noted that the military junta would push private firms to have the *"workers share in the profits of enterprises."* A statement by the Chilean junta noted that *"the military Government will not be a return to the past, near or remote. The workers have waged long and difficult battles in defense of their legitimate interests. The Armed Forces are part of this noble people and never will betray those who, like themselves, join forces to return Chile to the place that history has reserved for it…Chilean worker, the Armed Forces respect your rights. The participation of the workers in the management of large firms will cease to be a slogan and a pretext through which a caste of leaders obtains an absurd 'total power.' No one needs to have fear who mistakenly had confidence in traitors who offered 'a new fatherland,' and only gave them hunger, hatred, beatings and injustice. Only national unity will save Chile from self-destruction and will rescue its people from the degradation to which communism had reduced it. The Government will demonstrate with deeds its concept of sharing in management of firms. The workers will return to their work and trade union activities without fear, complexes or grudges in a united struggle for a common destiny of greatness and liberty."*[252]

In May 1974, President Pinochet rejected economic liberalism and socialism in his speeches regarding the Social Statute of Enterprises: *"The Social Statute of Enterprises will regulate the operation of Chilean enterprises. The statute imposes the necessity of first remembering that an enterprise exists to provide goods and services which the community as a whole requires. Therefore the company does not exist solely for the interest of its investors and its workers and cannot be the exclusive business of some of them in particular because both investors and workers must realize that there is a greater interest which is above them: the social nature which it should insure…With the Social Statute of Enterprises we will correct the great socialist error which ignores the goals of the individual who joins a company and sacrifices himself in the pursuit of the social goal in a totalitarian manner as well as the liberal error which sacrifices the social goal for the sake of the private interest and profit of the investor."*[253] In January 1975, General Leigh revealed the Social Statute of the Enterprise stipulated that workers wanted *"To take part in management…To obtain security, recognition and identity; and to participate in the results…These three objectives can be obtained without the workers necessarily being owners of the enterprise in which they work."* The Social Statute was passed in

---

[250] "Government Expropriates National Tire Industry" <u>Madrid EFE</u> November 28, 1975

[251] Teichman, Judith A. <u>The Politics of Freeing Markets in Latin America: Chile, Argentina, and Mexico</u> (University of North Carolina Press, 2001) page 83.

[252] Alexander, Robert Jackson. <u>The Tragedy of Chile</u> (Greenwood Press, 1978) pages 342-343.

[253] "General Pinochet Addresses Workers on May Day" <u>Santiago Chile Radio Portales</u> May 2, 1974

May 1975. It stipulated that workers' representatives to be placed on the boards of directors and the subsequent creation of an Enterprise Council.[254]

Alexander wrote that the Pinochet regime was divided over the role that the state would take in regulating the labor unions: *"...the government itself had not yet fully made up its mind as to the labor movement's future. One element in the regime favored some kind of 'corporativist' regime for labor-management relations, in which collective bargaining would for practical purposes be outlawed; the role of whatever workers' organizations that would be permitted would be to 'cooperate' with the government and employers' groups in establishing working conditions. Other elements wanted a return to collective bargaining, but some of them wanted less government support of unions and involvement in the collective bargaining process than had been customary in Chile. Virtually all of the government leaders dreamed of 'depoliticizing' the labor movement."*[255]

Alexander also revealed that the University of Chicago-educated economists did not exclude interventionism in the Chilean economy: *"The only part of the economy that was not subjected to the free operation of the market was wages. These were strictly controlled by the government, and the tendency consistently was to have the increase in wages lag far behind the increase in the price level...The only sectors in which the free market or its equivalent was not applied were those of labor and bank credit. Wages were rigidly controlled, and although the government periodically enacted substantial wage rises, these lagged far behind the increase in the cost of living...Bank credit, in conformity with the 'monetarist' philosophy of the Chicago Boys, was kept under very close control, which results I shall note later in this chapter."*[256]

Air Force Commander in Chief and Junta Member General Gustavo Leigh warned in April 1974 that *"We are not afraid of those sectors; they are very small. If one observes the work that has been done-the economic crime and anti-monopoly law, the measure to take family allowances equal-one will realize that the junta is not acting for the extreme right, is not acting for 'the Piranhas,' and is not favoring the wealthier classes."*[257]

In May 1976, Labor Minister Sergio Fernandez noted that *"the government seeks to harmonize progress with social justice and an accelerated development of our economy."* He noted that *"the goal of the government is the general well-being the true concept of which differs from both liberal capitalism and totalitarian collectivism."*[258]

In May 1976, Pinochet noted that the concepts of Left and Right should not exist in Chile: *"I wish to sincerely state that this government is working exclusively for the benefit of Chileans without taking into account either rightist or leftist tendencies...it is also our desire that all Chilean workers have social peace and the peace to enable them to carry out their tasks and not have as in years gone by the permanent pressure of political parties or political factions."*[259]

In May 1977, Chilean Labor Minister Sergio Fernandez endorsed government-mandated labor-capital harmony: *"The government does not wish to persecute anyone. It is guided by a*

---

[254] Alexander, Robert Jackson. The Tragedy of Chile (Greenwood Press, 1978) pages 438-442.

[255] Ibid, page 435.

[256] Ibid, page 399.

[257] "Leigh Comments in Interview" Santiago Chile Ercilla April 17-23, 1974

[258] "Labor Minister Delivers May Day Address to Workers" Chile Domestic Service May 1, 1976

[259] "Pinochet Addresses Labor Leaders at May Day Event" Santiago Chile Domestic Service May 1, 1976

spirit of concord and harmony in resolving social problems. But those who think that this will permit them to mock the workers' rights as occurred in the past are greatly mistaken. With the same energy with which the government today fights demagogy and populism it will continue to apply the full weight of its legal authority to punish any abuse of workers' rights by any employer.[260]

In May 1978, Labor Minister Vasco Costa Ramirez noted that "*worker and businessman are two components of a single relationship and that one without the other cannot exist…*" He noted that "*the subsidiary role of the state is not an end in itself but a means to promote the common good with the state intervening anytime it feels that a segment of the production sector deviates from the objective of serving this common good.*"[261]

Even in the 1980s, purist concepts of liberal capitalism were still rejected by the Pinochet regime and many of its officials and ideologists. In April 1984, Chilean Minister of Economy Modesto Collados noted that he would choose "*a social market economy. I believe this is the best system for the Western world at this time. It is neither capitalist nor socialist.*" Collados elaborated that this meant "*no to (Milton) Friedman and Marx.*"[262]

Pinochet noted in May 1984 that "*workers were exploited for the benefit of selfish political interests and in which demagogy prevailed in labor relations.*" He noted that "*to maintain harmonious labor relations those laws that regulate labor must be upheld.*" Pinochet also proposed to create "*special labor courts so that workers may have access to a more expeditious and simplified justice to handle labor issues.*" He also ordered employers to pay workers "*indemnization payments*" in accordance with "*unjustified firing regulations.*" Pinochet also created the National Employment Commission to reduce unemployment and work with the state sector to create productive jobs. Pinochet stated that the government wanted to "*achieve material progress and social justice.*"[263]

Despite the support of some prominent "*free traders*" such as Dr. Milton Friedman, the Pinochet dictatorship embarked on predatory trade policies directed at the American market. The chief motivation for Chilean dumping in the American market appeared to be commercial. The chief culprit was the state-owned copper company CODELCO, which dumped copper into the American market, which impaired our domestic copper industry. American copper producers accused the Chilean government of subsidizing copper exports to the United States. They complained that CODELCO dumped copper in the American market, thus generating unemployment. They also contended that American copper companies could not compete with CODELCO's subsidized prices. Chilean Treasury Minister Luis Escobar Cerda complained to the US Chamber of Commerce in Chile that "*It concerns us that the United States speaks to us of economic freedom while on the other hand they threaten us with market restrictions.*"[264]

In February 1984, Chilean Mining Minister Samuel Lira noted that "*We are going to advocate that from the socio-political point of view, a leading country in free trade such as the United States cannot establish a protectionist measure of this nature.*" Lira also revealed that CODELCO hired a team of lawyers to defend Chile before the International Trade Commission

---

[260] "Labor Minister Announces New Reforms at Ceremony" <u>Santiago Chile Domestic Services</u> May 1, 1977

[261] "Labor Minister Addresses May Day Rally" <u>Santiago Chile Domestic Service</u> May 1, 1978

[262] "Economy Minister Interviewed on Economic Policy" <u>Santiago El Mercurio</u> April 8, 1984

[263] "Pinochet Addresses Nation on Labor Day" <u>Santiago Domestic Service</u> May 1, 1984

[264] "Treasury Minister Raps US Copper Protectionism" <u>Rome IPS</u> May 16, 1984

(ITC).[265] Chile's complaints were very similar to that of Red China, who also accused the United States of engaging in protectionism and violating the principles of *"free trade"* when it sought to tepidly assert its national interests.

Other more extreme forces within the Chilean nationalist camp desired a reversal of any privatization and deregulation of the economy. They included the various neo-Nazi and neo-fascist parties in Chile. While they welcomed the overthrow of Allende, groups like the Chilean Nazis, the *Patria y Libertad*, and the *Avanzado Nacional* became disillusioned with Pinochet because they believed that his regime sold out to foreign multinational companies and economic liberalism. The Chilean neo-Nazis noted in 1987 that *"We are neither international socialists nor Marxists, nor are we capitalists. We are neither with the bourgeoisie or with the economic liberalism, nor are we with international socialism, that is, Marxism."* They also noted that *"The true Chilean national socialists cannot support the system of super-capitalism which has been established in Chile during the last fourteen years."*[266]

According to the Nationalist Manifesto written by Paul Rodriguez in 1971, the *Patria y Libertad* movement supported a corporative economy, nationalism, anti-capitalism, anti-imperialism, and anti-communism. The *Patria y Libertad* movement supported the notions that the *"State was the integrator who seek to build a society united by national values, to promote national cohesion over ideologies, and economic interests…an authoritarian government that restores the principle of order and authority…a people with collective responsibility and social discipline…a youth program, attracting a nationalist project of building a new state…an integrated company, replacing the capitalist enterprise by a company to the workers, we are for employee participation in company profits, which implies a change in economic policy in Chile instituting a system of social market economy that stimulates the creative spirit of the Chilean private initiative and competition without monopolies or distortion, while ensuring the effective application of the common good of the State…(and) a functioning democracy, eradicating traditional parties for new forms of popular representation, through labor unions (unions), professionals, technicians, students, and other organizations conducting Chile Chileans ensuring their active participation the state."*[267] It should be noted that the CIA backed the *Patria y Libertad* (along with more liberal-minded Christian Democrats and labor unions) as a powerful force to fight Allende and his group of pro-Cuban Marxists. Naturally, the CIA did not seem to consider that the possible end-result of funding the *Patria y Libertad* movement would be the potential creation of an anti-American fascist regime in Chile.

Deutsch noted that elements of the *Patria y Libertad* movement formed the *Avanzada Nacional* in 1983 as a *"pro-Pinochet movement and backed by the secret police. The smallest and most extreme of the rightist parties, it favored economic nationalism and increased authoritarianism."*[268] According to Coplin and O'Leary, the *Avanzada Nacional* *"openly*

---

[265] "Minister Concerned About US Copper Policy" Santiago Radio Cooperative February 22, 1984

[266] Etchepare, Jaime Antonio and Stewart, Hamish I. "Nazism in Chile" Journal of Contemporary History Volume 30 Number 4 October 1995 Accessed From: http://pics3441.upmf-grenoble.fr/articles/auth/nazism_in_chile.pdf

[267] "Frente Nacionalista Patria y Libertad" Accessed From: http://es.wikipedia.org/wiki/Frente_Nacionalista_Patria_y_Libertad

[268] Sandra McGee Deutsch. Las Derechas: The Extreme Right in Argentina, Brazil, and Chile (Stanford University Press, 1999) page 320.

criticized the free market policies of the Chilean economic team, favoring more statist of corporatist economic strategies."[269]

Interestingly, Chile under Pinochet continued diplomatic and trade ties with a number of communist countries that had previously backed Allende. Some like East Germany even supported pro-Allende forces in exile while simultaneously trading with the Pinochet regime. Isabel Diez reported in May 1987 in La Segunda that *"Business is business and is more powerful than ideologies. This is proven by the trade figures between Chile and the Communist countries."*[270] Pinochet's Chile maintained trade and diplomatic relations with Romania, Red China, and Yugoslavia.[271] Chile also maintained lesser trade relations with Poland, Czechoslovakia, Cuba, Albania, Bulgaria, and Hungary.[272]

Pinochet himself was unaware or unwilling to question the validity of the Sino-Soviet *"split"* and thus believed that Beijing also opposed the interests of the USSR. However, as my book Golitsyn Vindicated?: A Second Look at "Splits" in the Communist World During the Cold War revealed, the Sino-Soviet *"split"* was, at best, vastly exaggerated by the United States or worse, a calculated deception to fool the West into thinking that the communist bloc weakened. Trade relations were deepened between the two countries as a result of the alleged Sino-Soviet *"split."*[273] Chile was even willing to forsake any anti-communist alliance with Taiwan for the sake of commerce and an illusory anti-Soviet alliance with Beijing. The Pinochet regime rejected an offer to accept a Nationalist Chinese ambassador and instead chose to recognize the Communist Chinese. In September 1973, China in turn recognized the Pinochet regime.[274]

Trade between China and Chile totaled $130 million in 1986 and consisted of shipments of machinery, textile products, medicines, household items to Chile. Chile shipped copper, fish meal, wood, wine, cellulose, and salt peter to China.[275] Much of this trade was conducted between Chilean state-owned enterprises and Red Chinese communist corporations. Trade between Red China and Chile commenced under the Allende regime and continued in earnest under Pinochet. In March 1976, China and Chile negotiated a loan worth over $100 million to purchase Chinese products. As of March 1976, Chile sold copper and nitrate to Red China.[276] In October 1978, Chile proposed to sell 90,000 tons of copper to China over a 3 year period. This agreement was concluded between CODELCO and the Chinese Mining and Metal Export-Import Corporation.[277] In April 1979, a Chilean trade delegation led by Roberto Kelly Vasquez met with the Red Chinese Minister of Foreign Trade Li Qiang. A trade agreement was inked for a $10 million credit for China to purchase Chilean goods. The National Banks of Chile and China also agreed to open representative offices in Beijing and Santiago.[278]

---

[269] William D. Coplin, Michael K. O'Leary. The 1989 political risk yearbook: South America Issue 3 (Political Risk Services, 1990) page B-3.

[270] Diez, Isabel. "La Segunda Daily Reports on Trade With Socialist Countries" May 4, 1987

[271] Geldenhuys, Deon. Isolated States (Cambridge University Press, 1990) page 157.

[272] Diez, Isabel. "La Segunda Daily Reports on Trade With Socialist Countries" May 4, 1987

[273] Geldenhuys, Deon. Isolated States (Cambridge University Press, 1990) page 157.

[274] "Chile to Negotiate $100 Million Loan PRC" Paris AFP March 11, 1976

[275] Diez, Isabel. "La Segunda Daily Reports on Trade With Socialist Countries" May 4, 1987

[276] "Chile to Negotiate $100 Million Loan PRC" Paris AFP March 11, 1976

[277] "Copper to PRC" Santiago Chile Domestic Service October 6, 1978

[278] "Visitors to China; Chilean Minister of Economy" AFP in English April 21, 1979

Chile's trade with China increased from $12 million (1975) to over $28 million in 1977. Chinese exports to Chile included goods such as tea, alarm clocks, bandages, dressings, vegetable extracts, cotton, and toys. Chile exported fishmeal, wool, apples, grapes, saltpeter, copper, and chemical compounds to Red China.[279]

In October 1985, the eighth PRC-Chilean economic and trade commission inked an agreement for the Chilean purchase of Chinese oil and the purchase of Chilean copper by Beijing. The Chilean and Chinese state-owned enterprises involved in this trade were CODELCO (Chile), the China International Trade Investment Corporation (CITIC), ENAP (National Petroleum Enterprise) and the Chinese National Chemicals Import and Export Corporation (SINOCHEM). The Chilean National Electric Power Corporation (ENDESA) also purchased generators from Red China.[280] In June 1985, the Chilean National Oil Enterprise inked an agreement with Red China to import 100,000 tons of oil.[281] In August 1986, the Chilean Ambassador to Red China Benjamin Opazo Brull noted that his country exported copper, salt peter, fishmeal, and mining and marine products to China. The Red Chinese supplied handicrafts, petroleum, machinery, and equipment to Chile.[282]

By the mid-1980s, Chilean firms even commenced joint venture agreements with Red Chinese communist companies. In November 1986, Chile and Red China set up a joint venture for the construction and administration of copper pipe, iodine, and copper sheet/tubing/wiring, factories.[283] In April 1987, Chinese State Councilor Fang Yi met with the President of CODELCO Rolando Ramos Munos. Subsequently, a joint venture was created between CODELCO and the Number 2 Beijing Copper Pipe Factory. The joint venture was supposed to produce 5,000 to 10,000 tons of red copper pipes per year.[284]

Even more amazing was the fact that the Soviets quietly conducted trade with the Pinochet dictatorship, despite Moscow's support for leftwing terrorists and the Communist Party of Chile. In 1974, the Soviet-owned Narodny Bank in London and the Banque Commerciale pour l'Europe du Nord negotiated repayment terms with the Pinochet regime for loans disbursed to the Allende dictatorship. The economic affairs director of the Foreign Ministry Andres Concha noted that Chilean exports to the USSR totaled $20 million per year. In 1978, there were rumors that the USSR purchased Chilean molybdenum.[285] The Austrian news agency APA reported that the Soviets sold 55 assault vehicles to the Pinochet regime. This was originally reported by Charles Levinson of the International Federation of Chemical and Energy Workers.[286] In 1986 Chilean-Yugoslav trade totaled over $33 million. The Yugoslav Consul to Chile Nikola Magdic justified Yugoslavia's trade with Pinochet's Chile when he stated that "*We*

[279] "Chile-Trade" Radio Nacional de Chile January 31, 1979

[280] "Chile; Trade with China" El Mercurio October 29, 1985

[281] "Chile; Oil Imports From China" Santiago home service June 25, 1985

[282] "Chile; Trade Surplus with China" La Tercera de la Hora August 19, 1986

[283] "Chile; Planned Co-Operation with China in Industrial Plant Construction" BBC Summary of World Broadcasts November 25, 1986

[284] "Fang Yi Greets First Sino-Chilean Joint Venture" Xinhua April 13, 1987

[285] Economist Foreign Report Issues 1614-1661 1980 page 32.

[286] "USSR Reportedly Sends 55 Assault Vehicles to Chile" Buenos Aires TELAM November 23, 1978

are basically a socialist country but we are outside the blocs. We belong to the Non-Aligned Movement. "[287]

Another surprising trading relationship between a communist country and the Pinochet regime was the case of East Germany. East Berlin provided safe houses, funding, and training to the deposed Allende forces and Chilean leftwing terrorists. However, this did not deter official East German-Chilean trade and quasi-diplomatic relations. East German–Chilean trade totaled over $26 million in 1986. Chile imported East German steel products, machinery, synthetic fabric, and vials. Chileans such as Rafael Silva represented the East German textile firm *Kombinaten Textima* in Chile itself.[288] By the end of 1977, East Germany bought $200 million worth of Chilean copper.[289] In 1979, two-way trade between East Germany and Chile totaled over $7.5 million.[290] In June 1980, it was reported that Chile and East Germany agreed to set up commercial offices in East Berlin and Santiago. These East German-Chilean negotiations were conducted through the Romanian Embassy in Santiago.[291] The East German trade office operated out of the Finnish Embassy in Santiago. It was headed by Eugen Kraut.[292]

The Chileans were also led to believe that the hardline Communist dictatorship of Nicolae Ceausescu represented an allegedly "*independent*" form of Marxism-Leninism. However, as my book Golitsyn Vindicated?: A Second Look at "Splits" in the Communist World During the Cold War revealed, Romania under Ceausescu was still allied with the Soviet Union and international communism. Bucharest's *"independent"* streak was an effort to gull the West into providing trade and high technology goods. Unfortunately, it appeared that even Pinochet's Chile fell into this trap. Under the Pinochet regime, the Romanian Embassy was upgraded.[293] Romanian-Chilean trade totaled over $13 million. The Romanian communists shipped machinery, chemicals, medicines, bearings to Chile. Chile shipped copper, timber, and fish meal to Romania.[294] In June 1979, the Romanian Deputy Minister of Mines, Petroleum and Geology visited Chile to discuss cooperation in the production of mineral products.[295] In November 1982, Andres Concha, Director-General for Economic Affairs of the Chilean Foreign Ministry explored different methods to expand the trade and marketing of Chilean products in Romania. The Chileans also sought to use their trade ties with Romania to export their products to other European communist countries and the Middle East.[296] In November 1988, the fifth session of the Romanian-Chilean joint economic commission concluded an agreement to enhance cooperation in the field of heavy industries.[297]

Even in the field of weapons transfers, Pinochet occasionally jettisoned his anti-communist ideology for profits. In August 1987, it was reported that Pinochet's Chile was able

---

[287] Diez, Isabel. "La Segunda Daily Reports on Trade With Socialist Countries" May 4, 1987

[288] Ibid.

[289] "USSR Reportedly Sends 55 Assault Vehicles to Chile" Buenos Aires TELAM November 23, 1978

[290] "GDR-Chilean commercial ties" BBC Summary of World Broadcasts June 16, 1980

[291] Ibid.

[292] Economist Foreign Report Issues 1614-1661 1980 page 32.

[293] Ibid.

[294] Diez, Isabel. "La Segunda Daily Reports on Trade With Socialist Countries" May 4, 1987

[295] "Romania; Chile G Fulea" Santiago de Chile home service June 7, 1979

[296] "Chile: 2nd Session of Joint Commission" Santiago home service November 11, 1982

[297] "Chile 5th session of joint commission" Romanian Press Agency November 10, 1988

to procure spare parts for their F-5 fighter-bombers through communist Vietnam. An American observer reported that *"For sources of spare parts, the Chileans have found a few places around the world where they can buy some specialty items…They bought stuff in South Korea, in Vietnam. They've had the attitude, 'we don't care where it comes from.'"*[298] Sometimes, the Chilean arms trade resulted in the bolstering of Latin American communist forces. As of October 1987, the Sandinista Communist regime purchased cluster bombs from Noriega's Panama and Pinochet's Chile. These cluster bombs were dropped by Sandinista Air Force planes on FDN and ARDE rebel positions. The Panamanians purchased cluster bombs on behalf of the Sandinistas from the Chilean corporation Ferrimar. These bombs were dropped by the Sandinistas from Soviet-made AN-26 transport planes that were retrofitted as bombers.[299]

Argentina Under the Military Junta (1976-1983)

In order to understand the background of the Argentine rightist dictatorships of the 1970s and early 1980s, once must explore the background of the Peron and Ongania regimes. In Argentina, Colonel Juan Peron and other extreme nationalist, fascist-minded officers took control beginning in 1943. Peron's dictatorial government imposed many collectivistic-fascistic economic policies in the 1940s until his overthrow in 1955. The press was heavily controlled, while opposition media was suppressed. The Catholic Church was also repressed as an allegedly oligarchic and reactionary institution. The economy was rigidly controlled by a panoply of socialist and fascist laws and social engineering projects. Peron established the state-owned export trade monopoly, the Institute for the Promotion of Trade (IAPI) which broke the influence of the landowners, meat-packing firms, and the grain companies. The nationalized Central Bank channeled credits to manufacturers and implemented exchange controls. The Ministry of Labor and Social Welfare approved large wage increases from 1946 to 1948. During his first two years as president, Peron nationalized railroads and telephones. The Peron government also seized control of the labor union, the CGT and opposition was suppressed by regime thugs nicknamed the *decamisidos* (*"shirtless ones"*).[300]

The Nazis, Italian Fascists, and various European fascist collaborators all sought refuge in Peron's Argentina and provided all manner of advice and support to their new patrons. From 1943 to 1945, the Argentine regime leaned towards the Axis. Argentina only declared war on Germany in 1945, when the Reich was in the midst of certain defeat. Officials who served the old Axis Powers in Europe became ideological and policy mentors to Peron and his minions. Several Italian Fascists and German Nazis worked with the Peron regime. Italian General Mario Roata worked for Peron in the *Casa Rosada*; former Italian Minister of Agriculture Eduardo Moroni received a 6,000 peso per month job with the Argentine *Banco Central de la Republica Argentina*; Austrian Nazi Fritz Mandl transferred his industrial empire to Argentina and worked with Peronist officials in developing the Five Year Plan; Ludwig Freude served as a personal secretary to Peron; Dr. H. Theiss, F. Adam, H. Richner, and J. Paescht were former Gestapo officers who advised the Argentine Federal Police Force; Jose Figuerola was a Spanish Falangist

---

[298] "U.S. Parts Embargo Grounds Chilean Air Force F-5 Fleet" <u>Aviation Week & Space Technology</u> August 24, 1987 page 73.

[299] Goshko, John M. "U.S. Says Chile, Panama Help to Arm Nicaragua; Contras Reportedly Target of Cluster Bombs" <u>The Washington Post</u> October 28, 1987 page A23.

[300] Rock, David. <u>Authoritarian Argentina</u> (University of California Press, 1993) page 160.

who served as an economic adviser to Peron. He helped Peron draw up the Five Year Plan.[301] Until 1949, Spain's fascist dictator General Francisco Franco and Peron maintained close ties. Argentina provided loans for Spain to purchase cattle. The Franco regime publicized slogans such as *"What Marshall Won't Give Us, Peron Will"* and *"Franco and Peron are the World's Best Friends."*[302]

The Peron dictatorship made many outward proclamations of friendship to American officials and businessmen. Beneath the surface, Peron and his comrades admitted that they exploited the United States for valuable technologies and trade relationships. Such trade and the political legitimacy derived from such commerce propped up the dictatorship in Argentina and boosted its revolutionary ambitions in Latin America. This was similar to the two-tracked game the Nazis, Fascists, and Bolsheviks played with the Western business classes: smiles to their faces and curses and subversion behind their backs. The defecting Polish Communist diplomat Romould Spasowski reported that Peron told him of a meeting where the American Ambassador gave the Argentine dictator a gold 20 dollar piece. Peron responded to the US Ambassador: *"I was taking that twenty dollars because any money used to counteract American imperialism is good money."*[303] In 1946, Peron implicitly noted that his regime could play upon the greed of American businessmen to support his regime: *"Stay with me and don't worry. You will see that when the smoke all clears away the Yankees will be down here with satchels trying to get orders from us."*[304] When Peron later allied himself closely with the Soviets during the early 1970s, he told KGB Second Department officer Vladimir Tolstikov not to be deceived by his public proclamations of *"friendship toward the United States...If one is not in the position to defeat the enemy, then one must try to deceive him."*[305]

American and British businessmen and politicians all lobbied for trade with both Peron dictatorships (1943-1955 and 1973-1976), despite the rampant populist-fascist anti-capitalism and massive economic interventions by the Argentine state. In 1946, Truman sent George Messersmith as ambassador to Buenos Aires. He took a soft line towards Peron, insisting that it was not a dictatorship. He slammed the embassy door shut to the anti-Peronists. An influx of American businessmen flooded Argentina *"who thought they saw profits to be made in Peron's economic development program."* Examples included shipbuilder Andrew Jackson Higgins and George E. Allen. Higgins attended Peron's inauguration in 1946 and was a staunch defender of the regime, while Allen closed a business deal with Ricardo Staudte, who was accused of being Argentina's number two Nazi. Messersmith's successor, James, was even more of a Peron apologist and defender. In 1949, Argentina exported $66 million goods to the United States in the first nine months and $153 million during the same period in 1948. The United States sold $100 million in the first nine months of 1949, as opposed to $318 million in the same period during 1948. In 1950, the US Export-Import Bank provided *"private"* Argentine banks with a loan of $153 million. An element of the State Department opposed anti-Peronist American

---

[301] Alexander, Robert J. <u>The Peron Era</u> (Russell & Russell, 1965) pages 225-227.

[302] Ibid, pages 171-173.

[303] Spasowski, Romuald. <u>The Liberation of One</u> (Harcourt Brace Jovanovich, 1986) pages 318-320.

[304] Alexander, Robert J. <u>The Peron Era</u> (Russell & Russell, 1965) pages 205-216.

[305] Mitrokhin, Vasili and Andrew, Christopher. <u>The World Was Going Our Way: The KGB and the Battle for The Third World</u> (Basic Books, 2005) pages 98-101.

officials such as Spruille Braden and supported closer relations with Argentina.[306] In 1953, Peron received a group of 11 American businessmen headed by John Arnold, general manager in Argentina of the National City Bank of New York. Arnold was convinced that trade relations and friendship would continue between Peron and American business.[307] In the early and mid-1970s, multinational corporations maintained a preference for the Peron dictatorship over his communist rivals: *"Better a lower profit rate than the People's Revolutionary Army (a Cuban and Libyan backed Trotskyite Communist terrorist group)."*[308] Just as in Germany and Italy, the capitalist classes were forced to choose between the lesser of the two threatening forms of collectivism. In the final analysis, both Peronism and Communism proved to be injurious to the business community and individual freedom.

Despite the anti-British rhetoric of the Peron dictatorship, London became a major trading partner with Argentina. The United States also continued military support to the virulently anti-American Peron regime. In late 1948, one hundred Argentine officers trained in the United States. Britain sold Lincoln bombers and 100 Gloucester Meteor jet fighters to Argentina.[309] As late as 1954, the British and Argentina inked trade agreements where meat would be exchanged for coal, oil, iron, steel, chemicals, drugs, machinery, textiles, hardware, ceramics, and other products.[310]

During the second Peron dictatorship (1973-1976), there were attempts by the more fascistic elements of the Peronist camp to split the Western capitalist camp into countries that were representative of the Latino *"race"* versus the allies of the American imperialists. Minister of Social Welfare Lopez Rega noted in February 1975 that *"Not all the big industries which find themselves affected are industries belonging to great imperialist capitalism; on the contrary they are European industries which have agreements, from very populous countries such as Italy, France, Spain which is also the home of our race."*[311] Domestic private businessmen were ordered by the Peronist state to serve the national interest and eschew the exploitation of the workers. In November 1975, Chamber of Deputies President Nicasio Sanchez Toranzo noted that *"praised those capitalists who accept the rules of the game and do not come to the country to make profits at whatever the cost or sacrifices to our people. She did not praise multinational corporations. I want this clearly understood."*[312] Argentine Minister of Economy Antonio Cafiero noted in August 1975 that *"let me be well understood by the businessmen. Our philosophy is not based on resentment or hatred of profits or income returns. Not at all. We believe that with the mixed economy that Argentina is experiencing-with an ample state sector but with an even more ample private sector-the surplus must be the source of reinvestment, of innovation, and the source of more labor sources and resources. Within this context we will enforce a group of measures and controls in order for these objectives to be perfectly fulfilled."* Cafiero noted that *"income returns of enterprises to be conditioned to social means"* thus for

---

[306] Alexander, Robert J. The Peron Era (Russell & Russell, 1965) pages 205-216.

[307] "US Group Sees Peron" New York Times August 7, 1953 page 4.

[308] Veigel, Klaus Friedrich. Dictatorship, Democracy, and Globalization: Argentina and the Cost of Paralysis, 1973-2001 (Penn State Press, 2009) page 28.

[309] Alexander, Robert J. The Peron Era (Russell & Russell, 1965) page 119.

[310] Ibid, pages 178-179.

[311] "Lopez Rega Visits Province" Buenos Aires TELAM February 22, 1975

[312] "Chamber Speaker Proclaims Support for Peron" Buenos Aires TELAM November 5, 1975

private firms to *"fulfill their social function."* He supported the notion that *"capital had to be at the service of the economy and the economy at the service of man."*[313]

The Soviets and their puppet Argentine Communist Party maintained topsy-turvy relations with the Peron dictatorship. While Peron's fascism was anti-communist, a common anti-Americanism united Argentina and the Soviet Union on various political, strategic, and economic issues. Soviet Ambassador to Argentina Rezanov noted that Peron's anti-US ideology was useful for the Soviets and the bloc countries. He stated: *"You see Peron understands that the Soviet Union is his ally against America. The other socialist countries too."*[314]

Trade was increased between the Soviet Union, its allies in Eastern Europe, and Peron's Argentina. The Soviets and Argentina also negotiated a trade agreement in 1953 where Argentina exported hides, tanning materials, and wools to the USSR in exchange for Soviet-made oil drilling equipment, coal mining, and agricultural machinery.[315] In 1951, Hungary exchanged $19 million of Argentine farm products for Hungarian-made equipment.[316]

Expressions of communist solidarity with the Peronist fascists also cropped up in the 1950s. In 1953, the Peronist press praised Stalin upon his death. Peron himself cabled Nicolai Shvernik of the Presidium his sympathy: *"Please accept my sincere condolences on the loss of the eminent statesman Marshal Joseph Stalin."*[317] The Communist Party of Argentina pledged support for Peron's second Five Year Plan. Since August 1946, the communists noted that its policy was the *"strengthening the workers and the popular sector supporting Peron."* The communists supported Peron's appeal for support for the Five Year Plan because of the *"economic situation of the country and the systematic plots of the oligarchy at the service of imperialism."*[318]

In his years in exile, Peronist forces were funded by the communist world as a means of consolidating and maintaining links with the anti-American front in Latin America. In 1971, Juan Peron, in exile in Franco's Spain, approached Romania communist dictator President Nicolae Ceausescu for financial assistance for his movement within the Argentine CGT and for his luxurious living in Madrid in fascist Spain. A diplomatic pouch was used to transport the Romanian cash to Peron in Madrid. This money funded the mobilization of Peron's labor unions for a return to power.[319]

Isabel Peron was a confidential contact of the KGB while serving as Vice President and President of Argentina. A KGB confidential agent who was a Peronist Deputy was authorized to contact Juan Peron in Franco's Spain. This agent sounded out Peron on *"establishing unofficial contacts with Soviet representatives"* while he was President. Vladimir Tolstikov, the Head of the KGB Second Department, contacted Isabel Peron. In July 1973, Peron received the support of the Communist Party of Argentina (CPA) in his electoral campaign despite purges of Marxists from the Peronist movement. Peron claimed to Tolstikov that *"his concept of justicialismo or a*

---

[313] "Cafiero Outlines Economic Policy; Devalues Peso" <u>Buenos Aires Domestic Service</u> August 26, 1975

[314] Spasowski, Romuald. <u>The Liberation of One</u> (Harcourt Brace Jovanovich, 1986) pages 318-320.

[315] "Soviet Toasts Peron Men" <u>New York Times</u> April 18, 1953 page 9.

[316] "Peron, Hungary to Step Up Trade" <u>New York Times</u> July 6, 1951 page 3.

[317] "Peron Cables Sympathy" <u>New York Times</u> March 17, 1953 page 5.

[318] "Reds Pledge Aid to Peron" <u>New York Times</u> December 13, 1952 page 2.

[319] Pacepa, Ion Mihai. <u>Red Horizons</u> (Regnery Publishing 1990) page 78.

society based on fairness differed little from socialism…the transformation of society proceeds harmoniously and in stages changing the social structure gradually and not subjecting it to a radical break which causes great disruption and economic ruin."[320]

Tolstikov also had discussions with Peronist Minister of Economy Jose Gelbard, who was a confidential contact of the KGB since 1970. KGB files reported that Fidel Castro stated that Gelbard was a communist who helped fund the CPA. Gelbard also held meetings in the homes of various businessmen with the KGB resident Vasili Muravyev. In December 1973, Tolstikov reported to Moscow Centre that Gelbard *"was in favor of strengthening political and economic relations with the USSR…He believes that cooperation with the USSR in the fields of hydroelectric energy, petrochemicals, shipbuilding, and fishing will help put an end to Argentina's dependence on the US and will reinforce progressive tendencies in government policy."* In May 1974, Gelbard led a massive Argentine trade delegation to the Soviet bloc to personally meet with Brezhnev, Kosygin, and Podgorny. The USSR provided Argentina with $600 million in credits, while the Warsaw Pact nations provided another $350 million in credits.[321]

CPA General Secretary Arnedo Alvarez noted that the presence of a Soviet trade mission in Argentina would reinforce Peron's links with *"democratic forces."* Radio Moscow praised Argentina for *"having shown other countries in South America how to strengthen their independence and how to free themselves from the shackles of the multinational companies."*[322]

Even the virulently anti-communist, neo-fascist Peronist Minister of Social Welfare Jose Lopez Rega admired various leftist and communist states. Lopez Rega admired communist North Korea and Qaddafi's Libya, opposed political parties, and supported the imposition of fascist totalitarianism in Argentina.[323] He also was involved in stimulating trade relations between anti-US Arab dictatorships and Argentina during the 1970s. In early 1974, Lopez Rega signed a trade deal with Qaddafi where 3 million tons of Libyan oil were exchanged for an Argentine oil refinery, Ika Renault jeeps, and a vehicle assembly plant.[324] In February 1976, another Argentine trade mission visited Libya. Lopez Rega noted that Peron identified with the pro-Soviet, anti-American Qaddafi regime in Libya. In March 1976, a Libyan mission visited Argentina. That same month, the Peronist Revolutionary Legion released the following statement from Party headquarters: *"We must be members of the Third World, whose bases are Argentina and Libya. We clearly are against Free Masonry, Zionism, and international societies. We must immediately abandon all ties with Israel."* *"Students"* from Syria, Libya, Algeria, Egypt, and Lebanon were present in Argentina. The Cinema Committee of the Third World showed anti-Israeli films from Baathist Socialist Syria and war-torn Lebanon. One such film was titled Palestine, Another Vietnam, which was viewed at the University of Buenos Aires.[325]

---

[320] Mitrokhin, Vasili and Andrew, Christopher. The World Was Going Our Way: The KGB and the Battle for The Third World (Basic Books, 2005) pages 98-101.

[321] Ibid.

[322] Ibid.

[323] McGuire, James W. Peronism Without Peron: Unions, Parties, and Democracy in Argentina (Stanford University Press, 1997) page 166.

[324] Veigel, Klaus Friedrich. Dictatorship, Democracy, and Globalization: Argentina and the Cost of Paralysis, 1973-2001 (Penn State Press, 2009) pages 29-30.

[325] "Latin America-Argentina-Domestic Affairs" Accessed From: http://www.ajcarchives.org/AJC_DATA/Files/1976_8_LatinAmerica.pdf

Argentina issued annual loans of $200 million to Cuba for the purchase of motor vehicles and light machinery from Argentine factories. Many of these Argentine factories were subsidiaries of the American multinational companies General Motors, Ford, and Chrysler.[326]

The Peron dictatorship also sought to export its fascist ideology to other fellow South American republics. Peron hailed the the 1943 fascist Bolivian revolution of General Gualberto Villarroel. He exclaimed to Argentine War Minister Edelmiro Farrell: *"We have just triumphed in Bolivia."*[327] In 1947, Lucio M. Moreno Quintana a greater Argentine Republic on the model of the Third Reich: *"The Argentine Republic must come to include not only the territory within its present boundaries but also the Republics of Uruguay, Paraguay, Bolivia and the southern part of Brazil."* This speech was reprinted in the Peronist-controlled University of Buenos Aires bulletin.[328] The secret proclamation of the Argentine General Officers' Union of May 1943 noted that *"Hitler's struggle in peace and war will be our guide. Our first step will be to make alliances. We already have Paraguay and next we will have Bolivia and Chile. With Argentina, Paraguay, Bolivia and Chile united in a single bloc it will be easy to put pressure on Uruguay. Then the five allied nations will have no trouble in attracting Brazil, given its form of government and the large concentrations of Germans existing there. Once Brazil has fallen the American continent will be ours..."*[329] Even during the 1970s, Peron was still committed to a united, anti-imperialistic, and fascist Latin America. Peron declared that *"the year 2000 will find us united or dominated."*[330]

Peron placed CGT Labor Attaches in each embassy and legation in Latin America. Second rank Peronist labor leaders were trained at a special school in Buenos Aires in the effort to export Peronism. The labor attaché in Chile wooed both warring factions of the Confederation of Workers of Chile. The Argentine Embassy in Colombia offered students industrial scholarships and institutes. Pedro Otero, the Labor Attaché in the Argentine Embassy, ingratiated himself with the unions, federations, and the Colombian Confederation of Labor (CTC) by offering these forces scholarships and training in Argentina. They also influenced the officials of the Colombian Social Security System. In Peru, the Labor Attaché became very friendly with the Independent Trade Union Committee, which consisted of ex-communists and ex-Apristas. In 1948, a military dictatorship in Peru took power and favored the Independent Trade Union Committee. The Argentine Labor Attaché helped frame the new social legislation of the Peruvian dictatorship. Peruvian trade unionists were bribed, enticed, and persuaded to visit the Argentine Embassy for all-expenses paid trips and training at the Trade Union School. Peronist agents were trained at this School for the exportation of his doctrine to other countries of Latin America.[331]

Despite the continued trade with American multinational companies, the second Peron dictatorship engaged in interventionist policies directed at domestic and foreign businesses. In 1974, the Peron regime enacted the Law on Economic Subversion to prosecute corrupt

---

[326] Veigel, Klaus Friedrich. Dictatorship, Democracy, and Globalization: Argentina and the Cost of Paralysis, 1973-2001 (Penn State Press, 2009) pages 29-30.

[327] Alexander, Robert J. The Peron Era (Russell & Russell, 1965) page 196.

[328] Ibid, page 186.

[329] Gutierrez, Alberto Ostria. The Tragedy of Bolivia a People Crucified (Prestige Book Company, 1958) page 135.

[330] Veigel, Klaus Friedrich. Dictatorship, Democracy, and Globalization: Argentina and the Cost of Paralysis, 1973-2001 (Penn State Press, 2009) pages 29-30.

[331] Alexander, Robert J. The Peron Era (Russell & Russell, 1965) pages 187-195.

businessmen and bankers.[332] In 1974, the Argentine government nationalized foreign banks such as the subsidiaries of Chase, Morgan, First National City Bank, and Deltec Swift.[333]

Various fascist elements supported a corporative reorganization of the Argentine economy which rejected liberal capitalism and communism. The Peronist Social Pact was heralded as a new model for a corporatist society which conciliated labor and capital and controlled the "*private*" economy. In August 1974, Air Force Commander Brigadier General Hector Luis Fautario noted that the Social Pact "*between the state and working and business forces*" rejected "*the extremisms of the class struggles on the one hand and of the false liberty of laissez faire on the other hand.*" He supported the notion of "*a nation which will be politically independent from ruling imperialisms and which will maintain a truly national socio-economic doctrine as the proper alternative in the face of international Marxism and capitalism.*"[334] In May 1974, President Peron that the Social Pact was a unique experiment which did not "*exist in capitalist countries since these countries try to avoid the joint activity of these three factors (businessmen, workers, and the state). It does not exist in communist countries either because state capitalism does not tolerate pacts of this type.*"[335]

In December 1974, Juan Queralto, a top leader of the Nationalist Liberating Alliance, noted that "*Trotskyism, liberal capitalism, the capitalism of the multinational firms, Zionism and all the interests into which the world was divided in Yalta are conspiring against the present Argentine political process.*" He noted that "*Argentina needs a substantial economic reorganization; the house must be put in order together with moral order.*"[336] A draft of President Peron's 1976 National Plan determined that "*Our future Argentine model society must thoroughly respond to the concept of an organized community...The ideal solution must avoid the two dangers: suffocating collectivism and dehumanizing individualism.*" Peron noted that this society would be based on what he termed "*Social Democracy.*' Peron described this new system as "*social in that it tries to balance the right of the individual with that of the community.*" He noted that the armed force would "*participate in the process for national liberation against all forms of internal or external imperialism.*"[337] Lopez Rega noted in February 1975 that "*Solutions should be found through the joint efforts of the workers, the labor union organizations and the employers of the provincial governments and the national executive branch.*"[338]

Free market economics were vigorously denounced by all Peronist factions, whether neo-fascist or pro-Marxist. In November 1974, a communiqué of the Justicialist National Militants noted that "*Liberalism in no way means the people's sovereignty but rather that of oligarchic bourgeoisie which it serves.*" It also noted that "*the liberal capitalism on which Balbin's obsolete party is based in contrary to the country...is completely against natural social order*

---

[332] "Argentine lawmakers defeat Duhalde" BBC News May 24, 2002 Accessed From: http://news.bbc.co.uk/2/hi/business/2005983.stm

[333] Veigel, Klaus Friedrich. Dictatorship, Democracy, and Globalization: Argentina and the Cost of Paralysis, 1973-2001 (Penn State Press, 2009) pages 29-30.

[334] "Air Force Commander Makes Air Day Speech" Buenos Aires La Opinion August 11, 1974

[335] "Peron Meets ILO Delegation, Discusses Social Pact" Buenos Aires TELAM May 30, 1974

[336] "Nationalist Alliance Leader Queralto Interviewed" Buenos Aires TELAM December 30, 1974

[337] "General Peron's National Plan Draft Published" Buenos Aires CLARIN January 7, 1976

[338] "Lopez Rega Visits Province" Buenos Aires TELAM February 22, 1975

and…was imposed on us by the arms of foreign imperialism…"[339] In September 1975, Minister of Labor Carlos Federico Ruekauf noted to the CGT that "*The liberal doctrine supported by bayonets is only good for destroying a policy and not for forming the basis for one. This is the liberal line which speaks of nationalism and then transfers the national enterprises to capitalism. This is the liberal line which speaks of production and then eliminates job sources.*" He also noted "*The heirs of those subservient tools of the multinationals still want to teach us Peronists how to govern. And we tell them that we respond only and exclusively to the mandate of the people based on the doctrine that Peron taught us.*"[340]

In 1966, General Juan Carlos Ongania took over in a military *coup*. His dictatorship renounced most of the tenets of Peronism, supported a firm anti-communist program, and an alliance with the United States. The Ongania regime was split between the fascist-minded nationalists, technocratic statists, and free market champions. Guillermo O'Donnell observed that the paternalists were "*Reluctant to accept capitalism, profit, and big corporations…they believed that in the long run these could be superseded by a less prosaic and selfish social system.*" The nationalists rejected "*'communism' as well as of 'liberal,' 'individualistic,' and internationalist patterns of capitalist growth. The nation they wished to construct required a strong state apparatus, more active economically than the one envisioned by the paternalists and better disposed to repress in good conscience. The size and predominantly foreign character of big business evoked the hostility of the nationalists, who saw in the 'national entrepreneurs' the political and economic base for a nationalist version of capitalism. Moreover, the nationalists hoped—with clearly fascist overtones—to combine corporatism and the authoritarian mobilization of the pueblo, by means of a movement, not a party, that they would control from the government.*"

Ongania and his ideologists supported aspects of corporative social and economic policy. The 1966 "*Argentine Revolution*" announced that it would "*modernize*" the country and eliminate the evils of the 1955-1966 period, which was rife with inflation, sluggish economic growth, acute social conflict, corruption, "*sectoral egoism,*" "*subversion,*" "*lack of faith*" and the absence of "*spiritual cohesion*" among Argentines, and the "*inorganic,*" "*unrepresentative*" character of civilian organizations. The military would restore "*order*" in Argentine society and encourage "*genuine representativeness*" of the "*basic organizations of the community.*" The "*social stage*" of the Revolution would support distributive justice and "*structural transformations.*" The "*political stage*" of the Revolution would set up "*genuinely representative organizations of the community.*" The "*economic stage*" of the Revolution would restore discipline within the economy and repair the damage from demagogic economic policies. The Revolution saw politics as the "*division of the Argentines.*" In December 1966, Ongania noted in La Nacion that "*One day political parties will have to be replaced by other organizations, equally political, based on a revitalized community, based on ideals rather than biases, and loyal to the Nation before the group.*" Minister of the Interior Martinez Paz noted that "*political parties encouraged the division of the people and, comfortable in the pretense of a purely formal and sterile legality, established (polarized) choices as a system.*" In November 1966, Martinez Paz also noted in La Nacion that "*the expression of special interests that did not coincide with the national interest…and constituted a struggle among factions artificially crystallized around*

---

[339] "Justicialist Communique Attacks UCR Bloc Move on Ottalagano" Buenos Aires TELAM November 19, 1974

[340] "Minister Addresses CGT on Labor Policy" Buenos Aires TELAM September 2, 1975

ideological banners." The nationalists supported a "*just equilibrium*" among social classes. It was noted that "*...the paternalists tried to distance themselves from the dominant classes, aware that they had to gain their support but convinced that these classes had to be tightly controlled in order to achieve a society more balanced and more concerned with distributive justice than any the dominant classes were willing to tolerate.*" In October 1966, Ongania noted in La Nacion that "*It is necessary to give preference to the organization of the state...to place a high priority on organizing the state such that this takes precedence over the other one that must also be organized, which is the community.*" In 1968, the Ongania government supported the notion of the "*organic amalgamation of the state with the organized community.*" Ongania noted in a July 1967 issue of La Nacion that "*We know what politics consists of: a party platform and an electoral agenda, after which everything goes on as before, with the lie of long-unpracticed democracy...Democracy should not be confused with the mechanical and obligatory act of voting, nor with the now dissolved political parties.*" Ongania also noted in that same year that the purpose of his regime was the "*spiritual process of reconstructing the unity of the Nation, (which requires that) conflict between interests and sectors be subordinated to a common idea, the ideal we all share.*" In March 1967, the regime noted in La Razon that "*...the government has made explicit its firm commitment to maintaining the principle of authority. It does not flaunt itself as the victor, nor does it propose that any sector should bear the weight of its victory. It simply insists on fulfilling its political and economic plans, and will resist any pressure that stands in the way of its adopting the measures required by the common good, regardless of the social sector from which such pressures might arise.*"

While the government clearly sought a more active role for the private sector in the economy, public policy was not entirely devoid of state controls. It was observed that the "*the paternalists' view of the state apparatus as responsible for controlling 'excessive profits' and 'sectoral egoism.'*" In December 1967, Ongania noted that "*The Revolution dissolved political parties but refrained from intervening in other organs of the community, in the belief that (such organs) would find internally the strength to recommit themselves to the service of the country. Business as well as labor organizations must exert themselves so that we may achieve our goal of bringing the government close to the community and governing with it. It is our hope that the organs of the community will be restructured...with men representative of the new era the country seeks to enter, and that the basic organs of the community will acquire a weight and strength they lack today...No group or sector shall abuse the whole.*" The Ongania government developed state agencies which indirectly managed aspects of the economy. They included the National Council on Development (CONADE), the National Security Council (CONASE), the National Council on Science and Technology (CONACYT), the Armed Forces General Staff, and the Secretariat of Information (SIDE). Labor-management relations were also subjected to state control. The Ongania regime discouraged strikes through the Law of Mandatory Arbitration of August 1966. Ongania noted that "*it is the intention of this government that industry remains in the hands of industrialists, and not in those of the state.*" In August 1966, the metal workers' and the textile workers' unions found that the government intervened on their behalf to achieve a "*just solution*" which left their employers perturbed with the Ongania regime. Yet the Ongania government also enacted price controls in response to union complaints of price increases. The government also imposed penalties against what the regime termed "*unscrupulous businessmen."* The Regulation of Supply Law of November 1966 increased government controls of prices and the penalties imposed on businessmen who violated these rules.[341]

In the midst of political upheaval and economic dislocations, the dictatorship of President Isabel Peron was overthrown in 1976 by the Argentine military. A succession of generals became the presidents of Argentina. They sought to allegedly reverse the excessive collectivism present in the Argentine economy and mop up the communist terrorists of the People's Revolutionary Army and the left-wing Peronists called the Monteneros. Buenos Aires' relations with the communist world and domestic economic policies sharply conflicted with the anti-communist, capitalistic image projected by the Argentine military leaders. The large majority of Argentine officers were collectivist economic nationalists who retained many positions within government agencies and state-owned enterprises. During the 1970s and 1980s, even the most committed proponents of *"privatization"* in Argentina were careful to point out that they opposed unrestrained free market capitalism and called for a continued government role in planning the economy. Others were as committed as the Left and the Peronists in expanding the public sector and the number of government-owned companies. The Argentines also maintained trade and political relations with the very communist nations they ideologically opposed. The Argentine military leaders maintained close ties with the communist world on the account of

1) Traditional economic relationships between Argentina and the communist bloc.
2) Pressure from the big business lobby for profitable trade relations with the Soviets.
3) Aggravation over American support for Britain's occupation of the Falkland (Malvinas) Islands.
4) The presence of a long-standing anti-American nationalism present in the officer corps of the armed forces.

All of these points will be examined in some detail in this chapter. In May 1976, the supposedly *"free market"* oriented Argentine Economy Minister Jose Martinez de Hoz *"ruled out the possibility of returning to the liberalism of the 19th Century and reiterated that private enterprise should be the basis of the economy. He said the state should plan, set priorities and coordinate but it is weakened when it involves itself in fields which naturally belong to the private sector..."*[342] As previously mentioned, other Argentine generals were staunch supporters of an increase in government intervention into the economy. Chirot wrote that *"Some of the military still preferred Nazism and many of those tortured report having seen pictures of Hitler posted on the walls. Some of the military seemed to want an open capitalist economy and justified their murderous activities as the only way to bring back an open market. Others were devout Catholics who disliked open market capitalism almost as much as they disliked communism and who insisted on extending not decreasing state control over industry."*[343] One high ranking, extreme nationalist, Catholic traditionalist figure in the military dictatorship was Admiral Emilio Massera. Massera was the former Argentine Naval Commander in Chief and former junta member and head of the Party for Social Democracy. He rejected liberal capitalism and communism. In November 1981, Admiral Massera noted that *"We believe in private property but insist that it must have a social function as the Church says...We consider ourselves*

---

[341] O'Donnell, Guillermo. <u>Bureaucratic Authoritarianism: Argentina 1966-1973 in Comparative Perspective</u>. Berkeley: University of California Press, 1988 Accessed From: http://publishing.cdlib.org/ucpressebooks/view?docId=ft4v19n9n2;chunk.id=0;doc.view=print

[342] "Main Features of Economy Program Noted" <u>Paris AFP</u> May 9, 1976

[343] Chirot, Daniel. <u>Modern Tyrants</u> (Simon and Schuster 1994) page 285.

to be as far away from Marxist collectivism as we are from capitalist materialism. Social democracy calls on the state to supervise without interfering."[344] In February 1982, Admiral Massera admitted his *"total opposition to any form of privatization of strategic natural resources...We proclaim that plans such as the one we are objecting to are not only against the nation's major interests but they also expressly violate the basic documents of the national reorganization process."* Massera predicted that *"when the republic is ruled by its true representatives...(we) will sponsor the total repeal of privatizations and the restoration of the companies to their lawful owners which are the nation and its people."* Massera asserted that the armed forces *"will not allow themselves to be deceived by the prophets of liberalism and of monetarism...(for) in this case privatization is a synonym for surrender."*[345]

The Argentine military President General Jorge Videla established a Ministry of Planning, which coordinated various economic and intellectual sectors to develop a *"national reconstruction plan."* After examining such policies in detail, the classical liberal economist Hans Sennholz concluded that *"It would be difficult to distinguish the Videla plan of reconstruction from similar plans designed by Juan Peron, or for that matter, by any dictator anywhere in the world. It provides for more government planning, more ministries, more bureaus and bureaucrats, and more government power over the lives of individuals. His thought and language are those of Caesars who lack all understanding of the nature of freedom and a free society and who have lost all respect for humanity. Even those who passionately attacked world communism because of its atheism embraced the ideas of the Communist Manifesto and the program of the Communist International."* Sennholz reported that the Argentine military generals *"believe in every point of the Communist Manifesto. When I interviewed the commanding general of the War Academy for senior officers, in April, 1982, he promptly rejected the suggestion of elementary courses in market economics and the private property order on grounds that 'both sides must always be presented.' In short, he felt at sea without mainstream economics, which is socialist, Peronist, and Marxist."*[346] Statist-nationalists were also present in the military dictatorship in Argentina. The Videla regime appointed Nationalists to the Supreme Court, the Ministries of Education and Justice, the Central Bank, and the universities in 1976.[347] The Nationalist presence in these agencies would theoretically have a profoundly negative impact on the power of business and capitalism in Argentine society. Furthermore, the Supreme Court and the Ministry of Justice could overturn business-friendly policies, while the Central Bank could exercise strong control over the private banking community. To be clear, the Nationalists were anti-communists who nevertheless supported heavy amounts of economic interventionism as a means to develop and modernize the economy; strike a blow at *laissez-faire* capitalism; and to combat class divisions that could be potentially exploited by the Left.

Point 5 of the so-called military-led Process of National Reorganization (PRN) supported economic notions where *"...the State maintains control over areas vital to security and development."* Deborah Norden commented that the PRN supported *"capitalism, but with a more*

---

[344] "Former Junta Member Massera Criticizes Regime" <u>Buenos Aires Herald</u> November 5, 1981

[345] "Massera's Party Objects to Privatizations" <u>Buenos Aires Noticias Argentinas</u> February 13, 1982

[346] Sennholz, Hans F. "Argentina on the Brink" <u>The Freeman</u> December 1982 pages 720 and 725.

[347] Rock, David. <u>Authoritarian Argentina</u> (University of California Press, 1993) page 227.

nationalist thrust." Norden also noted that *"A subtle tension between liberalism (free market policies and a close alliance to the West) and the army's more common nationalist tendencies pervaded the plan."* The PRN also supported *"fruitful work"* and *"an adequate sense of social justice"* for the general population in Argentina. The junta saw the need to hitch the workers and middle classes to the political wagon of the military regimes of General Videla and his successors. Such goals were predicated on continued state interventionism into the economy and the private business community.[348]

Arceneaux also concluded that *"The Proceso economy was a militarized economy, in that military officers administered nearly every public sector business and army officers were placed in most large businesses and banks as supervisors."* It was also noted that *"...the number of failed businesses absorbed by the state outstripped the number of state businesses privatized by the state so that state involvement in the economy during the Proceso actually increased."*[349]

Lewis observed that the size and scope of the public sector bureaucracy actually increased during the military dictatorship, despite rhetorical support for the contrary: *"Martinez de Hoz had only modest success in tackling this governmental leviathan. By the end of 1980, he had managed to trim the bureaucracy by about 200,000 and the state enterprises by around 103,000. It had not been an easy fight because at first he found, like all his predecessors, that firing employees in one part of the government only led to personnel increases in other areas. During the first few months of the new regime, 7,228 people were cut from the payroll, but at the same time 7,874 others were hired, resulting in a net gain of 646."* Public sector wage increases crept up from 9.5% to 13% of the GDP by 1980. Under the military regime, businesses engaged in tax evasion, which was justified by private entrepreneurs on the grounds that they believed that the government was too large and that more revenues would only encourage growth in the size and scope of the bureaucracy. The Argentine military chiefs forbade Martinez De Hoz from increasing the prices of essential public services.

Public works cost the military regime about $40 billion between 1976 and 1980. The military insisted on the development of projects such as hydroelectric power plants, a suspension bridge across the Parana River, the opening of new iron mines in Patagonia, and nuclear power stations for national defense purposes. The Argentine military also forbade the closure of state enterprises such as the Rio Turbio coal mines on the grounds of national defense and economic nationalism. Since 1978, Argentina placed first amongst Latin American countries in military spending. The Argentine military government opposed any efforts to break up or privatize state-owned enterprises such as the armaments company Fabricaciones Militares, Fabricaciones Militares incurred losses of over $600 million in 1980. The military also refused to privatize the state-owned fuel and steel companies SOMISA and YPF on the grounds of national security. Other state-owned enterprises continued to be subsidized by the military regime, such as ENTEL, Gas del Estado, Agua & Energia, the railroads, the merchant fleet, and Aerolineas Argentinas. Lewis elaborated on the military's motivation to resist increased privatization of state enterprises during the 1970s and early 1980s. This book noted that *"For the most part, the military resisted the idea of privatization. Efficiency was only one factor they considered. National security dictated that certain kinds of production and services had to be guaranteed. It*

[348] Norden, Deborah L. Military Rebellion in Argentina: Between Coups and Consolidation (University of Nebraska Press, 1996) page 55.
[349] Arceneaux, Craig L. Bounded missions: military regimes and democratization in the Southern Cone (Penn State Press, 2001) pages 132 and 135.

also indicated a need for developing the poorer regions of the interior, which might be done through locating branches of the state enterprises there. Finally, the armed services were worried that a high rate of unemployment might create opportunities for the guerrilla Left to infiltrate the labor movement; therefore, the military put a higher priority on maintaining full employment than on reducing economic costs. Indeed, they even insisted in some cases on adding to the state enterprise sector. In 1979 they forced the government to purchase the Swiss-owned Compania Italo-Argentina de Electricidad for $93 million, and in 1980 they forced the acquisition of Austral, a private airline company servicing the interior of the country. Also, in 1979-80 there were several bankruptcies that required the government to take over the management of those companies. All of that wiped out any gains made from the sale of other enterprises."[350]

Based on the evidence mentioned in the previous pages, it was no small wonder that top government officials admitted that the Argentine economy did not display the hallmarks of a true free enterprise economy. In June 1982, Economy Minister Roberto Alemann noted that *"If the situation is viewed from the standpoint of extreme liberalism the people will say that we have a state directed plan in force."*[351] Former Argentine Economy Minister Alvaro Alsogaray noted in August 1976 that *"...liberals have not been involved in policy-making and neither is there a free economy."* Incidentally, he was an adherent of the free market economics.[352]

Throughout the reign of the military dictatorship in Argentina, trade relations with the Soviets, Cubans, and other like-minded nations were maintained and even expanded. This was yet another holdover from the Peronist era. Mitrokhin and Andrew noted that after General Videla took over *"Moscow did its best to salvage what it could of the Argentinean connection...The Soviet delegation at the United Nations went to the extraordinary lengths of vetoing American attempts to secure UN condemnation of the regime's appalling human rights record...In 1980 80% of Argentina's grain exports went to the Soviet Union."*[353] Laurence Birns, director of the leftist Council on Hemispheric Affairs, noted in respect to the close Argentine-Soviet relations that *"What we may be seeing is one of the most eccentric alliances in history (between) the two most opportunistic nations in the world today."*[354]

A document issued by the Communist Party of Argentina (PCA) leadership in 1980 stated *"only one aspect of national economy has been protected from the generalized crisis, trade with the Soviet Union and the socialist countries."* The PCA offered critical support for the military dictatorship. It criticized the regime's domestic economic policies and supporting its foreign economic policies. The PCA official Fernando Nadra outlined the *"progressive aspects"* of the military regime's foreign policy, which included:

1) The trade and economic cooperation with the USSR.
2) Participation in the Non-Aligned Movement.

---

[350] Lewis, Paul H. The Crisis of Argentine Capitalism (University of North Carolina Press, 1992) pages 452-456

[351] "Alemann Discusses Economic Policies, Rumors" Buenos Aires TELAM June 1, 1982

[352] "Alsogaray Hits Gradualist Economic Policy" Buenos Aires Herald August 23, 1976

[353] Mitrokhin, Vasili and Andrew, Christopher. The World Was Going Our Way: The KGB and the Battle for The Third World (Basic Books, 2005) pages 98-101.

[354] Stuart, Peter C. "Argentine bonanza in sale of wheat to hungry Soviets" Christian Science Monitor April 22, 1980 page 4.

3) A refusal to join the American-led grain embargo.[355]

In 1980, Argentina became the Soviet Union's biggest grain supplier. Soviet-Argentine trade totaled $1.8 billion in the period 1979 and 1980. As of June 1981, the Argentines exported heavy amounts of grain and beef to the USSR and Cuba. Since January 1981, the USSR imported 12 million tons of grain and at least 150,000 tons of beef.[356]

As of April 1982, Argentina purchased 75% of Soviet grain exports. The Argentines also signed a trade agreement with the USSR where Argentine krill was exchanged for Soviet-made machine tools, oil exploration equipment, and nuclear fuel.[357]

The Cubans also increased their trade relations with the military junta. The Argentines and Cubans re-activated a science and technology agreement that provided Cuba with Argentine-made products, such as 300 trucks.[358] As of May 1982, Argentine-built Ford Falcons served as taxis and official cars in communist Cuba. Also, the Argentine Ford subsidiary shipped $2 billion worth of trucks to Cuba.[359] In September 1981, Jose Courard, the president of Ford Argentina, noted that negotiations for the export to Cuba of *"several thousand Ford vehicles"* were almost completed.[360]

Aside from existing commercial relationships and business pressure, the Argentine generals also clung to anti-US attitudes that stemmed from as far back as the early 1940s. High ranking military personalities from the 1940s such as General Ramirez and Colonel Peron leaned towards the Axis Powers out of resentment of the power of the United States. They viewed Germany and Italy as positive examples of national development and modernization in the face of communism and Anglo-Saxon capitalism. Daniel Southerland reported that anti-Yankee sentiments amongst the Argentine officer corps *"...goes back to World War II, when US officials accused high-ranking Argentine officers of being pro-Nazi...They accused the US of interfering in Argentina's internal affairs."*[361]

Although the Argentines remained dependent on the United States for its armaments, Buenos Aires opened military relations with the Soviets. In August 1979, a Soviet military mission headed by Lt. Gen. Ivan Yakovich Braiko visited Argentina to *"promote the strengthening of the ties between our countries."* Braiko spoke of *"the fraternal and positive development"* of ties between the training centers of the Soviet Union and Argentina.[362] An Argentine military mission led by General Jose Montes visited the USSR in 1979. They toured Soviet military academies in Moscow, Leningrad and Kiev and held talks with Defense Ministry officials. The Soviets even kowtowed to the political interests of Argentina. This resulted from

[355] Vacs, Alfredo Cesar. Discreet Partners: Argentina and the USSR Since 1917 (University of Pittsburgh Press 1984) pages 99-100.
[356] "The Soviets find trade partners on the right" Business Week June 29, 1981 page 64.
[357] Kinzer, Stephen. "Argentines Report Increasing Soviet Support" Boston Globe April 13, 1982
[358] Handler, Bruce. "Say Cuba Offers Argentina Weapons for Falklands War" The Associated Press June 6, 1982
[359] Bohning, Don. "Cubans Court Argentines With Care, Trying to Reverse Bad Blood in Region" Miami Herald May 7, 1982
[360] "Ford-Cuba Pact Near" The New York Times September 9, 1981 page D2.
[361] Southerland, Daniel. "Global isolation prods Argentina closer to USSR" Christian Science Monitor April 13, 1982 page 1.
[362] Belnap, David F. "Argentina Warms Up to Soviets As Ties With U.S. Cool Off" Washington Post August 28, 1979

the desire to maintain the mutually beneficial trade relations between the two nations. After a walkout by the Argentine delegation in August 1979, the Soviets apologized for the screening of a Swedish film that was critical of the military regime in Buenos Aires. Commerce trumped ideology in the eyes of the Argentine junta and the Soviet leadership.[363]

One area where the interests of the communists became linked with the Argentine military dictatorship was the conflict over the Falklands (Malvinas) Islands. In 1982, British forces occupied the Falklands (Malvinas) and the Reagan Administration threw its support behind London and Prime Minister Thatcher. The Soviets, Cubans, the Sandinistas, and the Argentine Communist Party (PCA) sensed a potential opening to stoke anti-American emotions amongst the Argentine military elites and nationalists. Henceforth, Moscow and Havana hoped that Buenos Aires would become more ideologically and economically linked with international communism.

The Argentine military junta engaged in subversive espionage and propaganda actions against the United States during the conflict over the Falklands. In May 1982, two Argentine Air Force officials attached to the Argentine Embassy in Washington DC attempted to buy spare parts for A-4 Skyhawk fighter bombers from a California-based dealer. These parts included external fuel tanks which would have extended the flight range of these planes, thus giving them the projection power to strike British Navy vessels and aircraft. Sympathetic Latin American businessmen assisted Argentina in evading US military sanctions. Colonel Ruben A. Corradetti, the Argentine Embassy official in charge of Air Force purchases in the United States appealed to US businessmen when he stated *"We need your help…I know at the moment it is close to impossible. People are afraid…We don't want to go to Russia, (but) if I go to other places it is because I need it very badly."*[364] In November 1982, it was reported that British Lance Corporal Philip Aldridge visited the Soviet Embassy and provided information that was believed to have been passed to the Argentines.[365] Delegations of Argentine labor and political officials traveled abroad in so-called *"truth squads"* to propagandize the point of view of the military junta.[366]

Taking a leaf from Cuban and Sandinista political warfare operations, the Argentine Communists (PCA) sought to assist the military junta through the establishment of solidarity committees within Argentina and abroad. Also, the Soviets and the military dictatorship also facilitated the convening of an international conference to support Argentina's claim to the Falklands (Malvinas). In June 1982, it was reported that the Central Committee of the Communist Party of Argentina supported *"the concentration of all national efforts to defeat Anglo-Yankee imperialism…Argentina's national struggle has developed into a struggle of the Latin American countries against imperialism."* It was also reported that the Communist Party of Argentina *"proposes to organize the people's participation by setting up committees for the defence of sovereignty, to support the soldiers fighting at the front and prevent any attempted coups in the service of foreign monopolies."*[367]

---

[363] "Argentina: to Russia with love" Latin America Political Report September 21, 1979 page 293

[364] Pichirallo, Joe. "U.S. Intervened Against Key Sale" Washington Post May 30, 1982

[365] Popeski, Ronald. "Two more spy trials in Britain" United Press International November 29, 1982

[366] Kinzer, Stephen. "Argentines Report Increasing Soviet Support" Boston Globe April 13, 1982

[367] "CP of Argentina to Set Up 'Committees for the Defence of Sovereignty'" BBC Summary of World Broadcasts June 3, 1982

In August 1982, the Soviet news agency TASS reported that an "*international conference for the restoration of Argentine sovereignty over the Malvinas and for peace in the South Atlantic and in the world*" was held in Buenos Aires under the auspices of the military government. The conference approved the "*Buenos Aires Declaration*," which expressed full support for the Argentine invasion of the Falklands. TASS supported the "*struggle of the Argentine people against the British colonial rule in the islands.*" TASS reported that "*The participants in the international forum expressed solidarity with the Argentine people and came out for the elimination of colonialism, against economic and military aggression, against the arms race, for banning nuclear and other weapons of mass destruction and for detente. They said that sub-regional organs should be established in Latin America to replace the ineffective Organization of American States and the Inter-American Treaty of Reciprocal Assistance which are being used by the USA for strengthening its domination on the continent.*" TASS also reported that "*the conference expressed solidarity with the Palestinian people and denounced Israel's aggression. The participants criticized Washington's aggressive policy in Central America and voiced support for the peoples of Cuba, Nicaragua, El Salvador and other countries of the region.*"[368]

In another report, Buenos Aires radio noted in August 1982 that "*political, trade union and intellectual representatives of 13 countries*" supported Argentina's control of the Falkland Islands in a conference. The conference also supported the notion that the Atlantic Ocean should become a "*zone of peace.*" Buenos Aires radio also reported that "*the British also intended to establish (ports) as part of a project for the exploitation of natural resources of part of the Argentine.*"[369] A Cuban representative named Severo Aguirre del Cristo also was in attendance at the "*international conference for reaffirmation of Argentine sovereignty over the Malvinas in Buenos Aires*" noted on Havana radio that the purpose of the conference was "*to continue through other means the struggle of Argentina and Latin America to assure the sovereignty of that sister nation over the Malvinas which, there is no doubt, belong to Argentina…The struggle, far from over, is now much wider. There is genuine national indignation for the way it ended…This blow against Argentina was the product of the ferocious policy of Yankee imperialism, interested in using the Malvinas for the construction of a military base.*"[370]

The PCA and the Soviets also sought to cripple public opinion in Britain regarding its intervention in the Falklands (Malvinas). In May 1982, Moscow radio reported that "*The progressive public of Great Britain resolutely condemns the course being taken by the British government towards escalation of armed conflict with Argentina. As McLennan, General Secretary of the Communist Party of Great Britain stressed, the Anglo-Argentine conflict over the Falkland (Malvinas) Islands should be settled by means of talks. The Scottish Confederation of Ship-building and Engineering Unions has called for an immediate cease-fire in the South Atlantic. The trade union council of the town of Doncaster has put forward the same*

---

[368] "Buenos Aires Conference on Falklands: 'Against British Colonial Rule'" TASS August 17, 1982

[369] "Conference's 'ratification' of Argentine claim to Falkland" Buenos Aires radio August 18, 1982

[370] "Cuban interest in Argentina's claim to the Falklands" BBC Summary of World Broadcasts August 27, 1982

demand. "[371] By May 1982, the Committee for Peace in the South Atlantic was formed in Portsmouth Britain, which was the location of an English Naval base. The Committee adopted a resolution which called upon the Thatcher government to "*reject the use of force and seek a peaceful solution without pre- conditions through the UN.*" The British Trades Union Congress (TUC) and the International Department of the British Communist Party opposed the British war with Argentina. The Communists called for "*all progressive forces to work towards a settlement of the conflict by means of talks.*" Activists in London, Leeds, Glasgow, Edinburgh, Nottingham and other towns intended to stage antiwar demonstrations against the British government and military forces.[372]

The PCA also assisted the military dictatorship even before the war over the Falklands. The PCA was relatively unharmed by the Argentine military's purge of political parties, especially those on the Left.[373] As of July 1981, the Argentine military regime tolerated the PCA because it was useful in Buenos Aires' relations with the USSR. Party members were middlemen in Soviet-Argentine trade.[374] As of April 1982, Argentine Communists continued to assist the military regime in setting up massive trade deals with the Soviets. The Communists remained the middlemen between the military dictatorship and the USSR in these deals.[375]

Even some of the Latin American communist terrorist movements also displayed their political solidarity with the Argentine junta's claim on the Falklands. The Christian Anti-Communist Crusade observed that "*The war between Argentina and England over the Falkland Islands, or the Malvinas, as the Argentineans call them, has produced profound changes in both the external and internal policies of Argentina. Externally, it has led to reconciliation between Argentina and Cuba and to a closer relationship between Argentina and the Soviet Union. Internally it may lead to a new surge of activity by the guerrilla forces of the communists and leftwing Peronists. Our Argentinean correspondent writes that the Montoneros now want to fight for their fatherland, and the government is facing a difficult dilemma in deciding whether to accept their help.*"[376] A communiqué of the General Command of the Salvadoran Farabundo Marti National Liberation Front (FMLN) asserted its support for the Argentine military conquest of the Falklands: "*In spite of everything about General Galtieri's regime, this is an hour to give consideration to his national and international conduct. Only in this manner can he victoriously complete the patriotic gesture he has made before the British Empire and its allies.*"[377]

The open Soviet propaganda organs also viciously attacked the United States and Great Britain during the conflict over the Falklands. Radio Moscow broadcasts to Argentina denounced "*British aggression.*" TASS radio commentator Yuri Kornilov stated that "*these bellicose*

---

[371] "Other Reports on the Falklands Crisis; Progressive British public 'condemns' government course" Moscow home service May 15, 1982

[372] "British Organizations for Peace in South Atlantic Call for Talks" TASS May 24, 1982

[373] Mitrokhin, Vasili and Andrew, Christopher. The World Was Going Our Way: The KGB and the Battle for The Third World (Basic Books, 2005) pages 98-101.

[374] Schumacher, Edward. "Argentina and Soviet Are No Longer Just Business Partners" The New York Times July 12, 1981 page 4.

[375] Whitley, Andrew. "Threat to play the Soviet card" Financial Times April 15, 1982 page 5.

[376] Schwarz Report August 1, 1982 Accessed From: http://www.schwarzreport.org/Newsletters/1982/august1,82.htm

[377] "El Salvador: FMLN support for Argentina" BBC Summary of World Broadcasts April 24, 1982

actions, in which London's ruling circles behave as if they are living not in the 20th century but in the 18th century and as if Britain still rules the world, create an immediate threat to international peace and security." The Soviets also asserted that American mediation of the conflict served more as "*a messenger for the British neocolonialists.*"[378]

Nationalist elements within the military junta's governmental apparatus appropriated pseudo-leftist rhetoric to attack the West during the Falklands conflict. Even the triumphs of communist revolutions were praised by Buenos Aires. In 1982, the nationalist-minded Foreign Minister Nicanor Costa Mendez stated "*I cannot ignore the fact that countries such as Algeria, India, Cuba, Vietnam, and others fought long liberation struggles for their full rights to an independent life.*"[379] In June 1982, Foreign Minister Costa Mendez also remarked that Buenos Aires' efforts to conquer the Falklands were similar to "*the struggles of Algeria, India, Cuba and Vietnam, among others, to gain their independence.*" Mendez denounced "*the aggression of Great Britain and the aid it is receiving from the United States.*" He also opposed the presence of the American Naval base in Guantanamo Bay, Cuba, as "*a typical colonialist act.*"[380] Mendez called Cuba "*the pride of the Caribbean.*"[381]

Even cooperation agreements with the United States were severed during this period. In May 1982, the Argentine military government announced its withdrawal from the Inter-American Defense Board.[382] The Argentines also reportedly withdrew their advisers from assisting anti-Sandinista rebels and anti-communist forces in El Salvador.[383]

The Soviets also sought to increase the scope of their overtures to the Argentines during the Falklands conflict. Moscow sought to use the explosive nationalism in Argentina to increase the chasm between Washington and Buenos Aires. Reportedly, the Soviet Ambassador in Buenos Aires visited the Deputy Foreign Minister Enrique Ros with an offer to supply the Argentine military with weapons during the Falklands conflict with Britain. The Soviet Ambassador then visited the military junta leader, General Leopoldo Galtieri. The Soviets offered to supply these weapons through a third party such as Libya. The Soviets requested that:

1) The Argentines withdraw their military personnel from Central America.
2) The Argentines abstain from all votes in the UN that opposed the USSR.
3) The USSR would be allowed to build a fishery in the Argentine port of Ushuaia.
4) The cessation of support for the fascist government in Bolivia.

The Argentines refused the Soviet offer, in light of their anti-communism.[384] However, this did not mean that Moscow and Havana did not provide intelligence, military, and political support to the Argentine military junta led by General Galtieri. Soviet technicians reportedly

---

[378] Kinzer, Stephen. "Argentines Report Increasing Soviet Support" Boston Globe April 13, 1982

[379] "Courting the Third World" Times (London) June 5, 1982 page 4.

[380] Kinzer, Stephen. "Anti-American Feeling Is On Rise in Argentina" Boston Globe June 5, 1982

[381] Riding, Alan. "Havana Exploits Falkland Dispute" The New York Times June 7, 1982 page A7.

[382] "Argentina's withdrawal from Inter-American Defence Board" BBC Summary of World Broadcasts May 27, 1982

[383] Diehl, Jackson. "Argentine Army Reportedly Says Anti-Nicaragua Efforts at an End" The Washington Post December 18, 1982 page A16.

[384] Wilson, Andrew. "Soviets offered to help Argentina during Falklands conflict, book says" The Globe and Mail (Canada) March 3, 1984

upgraded Argentine radar systems.[385] The Soviets supplied intelligence and material support to Argentina via Cuba during the 1982 Falklands war. The Soviets passed signals intelligence (SIGINT), communications intelligence (COMINT), and electronic intelligence (ELINT) to Argentina.[386]

As of April 1982, it was reported that the Soviet spy ship Akademik Knipovich was berthed at the Argentine naval base at Ushuaia. Soviet long-range Tupolev TU-142 reconnaissance planes flew from Cuba and monitored British radio communications.[387] As of April 1982, the Soviets provided the Argentines with satellite data and intercepts of British radio communications.[388]

Various radical Third World states served as intermediaries for the Soviets to ship weapons to Argentina. In December 1982, it was reported that British forces captured about 100 Soviet-made SA-7 SAMs that were provided to Argentine forces on the Falkland Islands. These SAMs reportedly were provided by the Soviets through Peru and Libya.[389] The Libyans sent missiles, mortars, mines and machine guns to Argentina.[390] In 1982, it was reported that Boeing 707 jetliners owned by the state-owned airline Aerolineas Argentinas ferried missiles from Baathist Socialist Iraq and Qaddafi's Libya to Argentina.[391]

In September 1982, Galtieri recalled that the flow of weapons and aid from other Latin American countries, Libya and other Third World countries would have sustained the Argentine war effort against Britain. Galtieri admitted that Libya sent five transport planes that were loaded with *"very valuable elements"* for the prosecution of the war. Galtieri elaborated that Libya *"sent five Boeing airliners loaded with different materials, with very valuable elements, without our having asked for or offered to buy anything, and without any economic or political obligation involved."* Reportedly, the Libyans sent French-made Exocet missiles to Argentina. Galtieri also reported that Argentina's *"Latin American brothers"* and the Non-Aligned Nations backed Buenos Aires in its war with Britain.[392]

In May 1982, President Galtieri proclaimed his ideological solidarity to Qaddafi: *"The struggle of our people for liberation urgently requires today the solidarity of the spiritual forces which are alone capable of confronting the heretical imperialism and materialism which is destroying our civilization. In the name of the Argentine nation I greet through Your Excellency the Libyan people who know how to wage the battle of faith and belief, how to save the religious*

---

[385] Handler, Bruce. "Say Cuba Offers Argentina Weapons for Falklands War" The Associated Press June 6, 1982

[386] Copley, Gregory. "The Falklands War: Update" Defense & Foreign Affairs May, 1982 page 6.

[387] Blanche, Ed. "International News" The Associated Press April 15, 1982

[388] Hoffman, Fred S. "U.S. Says Soviets Supplying Naval Intelligence to Argentina" The Associated Press April 13, 1982

[389] "Argentines Had Soviet Missiles in Falklands" Aviation Week & Space Technology December 6, 1982 page 126.

[390] "Argentina asked Libya for war aid, report says" The Globe and Mail (Canada) January 8, 1987

[391] Diehl, Jackson and Hornblower, Margot. "Argentina Said to Obtain New Arms" Washington Post June 10, 1982

[392] "Galtieri Muses on What-If's on Falkland War" The New York Times September 16, 1982 page A11.

and spiritual values and the morals of Islamic society from certain destruction…I express to you our admiration for your great revolution which, inspired by the glorious Koran and the sound Islamic religion, has been able to fulfill its national will and complete the serious task which Providence had wished - to be the lasting example and model for the whole Arab world and all the free peoples of the world…Our state has suffered from the treacherous and cunning aggression of heretical colonialist forces which are hostile to the values of Christianity, which Your Excellency knows very well. I want to thank you for your sincere and brave attitude towards the unjust war to which we are subjected and whose ordeals we suffer; we are confident that our steadfastness and struggle share the same meaning and values as the holy jihad in Islam."[393]

In May 1982, Tripoli-based Voice of the Arab Homeland indicated its support for President Galtieri in his struggle against *"heretical imperialism and materialism."* Galtieri noted that the Libya was a *"lasting example and model for the whole Arab world and for all the free peoples of the world."*[394] In May 1982, Qaddafi noted in a broadcast by the Tripoli-based Voice of the Arab Homeland that Argentina would defeat Great Britain who tried to *"impose obsolete colonialist concepts on the south."*[395]

Fidel Castro's Cuba also provided support to the regime of General Galtieri out of mutual anti-Yankee sentiments. It was reported in May 1982 that Cuban IL-62 transport planes delivered advanced Soviet military electronic equipment to Argentina. The cargo included *"highly sophisticated Soviet electronic surveillance gear, antisubmarine hunter-killer gear and electronic jamming equipment."*[396] Also, Cuban transport planes loaded with officials met with the Argentine military government in Buenos Aires.[397] It was reported in May 1982 that Cuban Ambassador Emilio Aragones Navarro was the most frequent visitor to the Argentine Foreign Ministry building. Cuban Ambassador Aragones exhorted that *"We all ought to be fighting and I, personally, would like to be in the Malvinas…The cause of the Malvinas is the cause of Cuba, of Latin America, and of the Third World."* While visiting Paris, Cuban Vice-President Carlos Rafael Rodriguez remarked that Cuba was ready to provide massive assistance, including weapons to Argentina.[398] In June 1982, the Argentine newspaper Clarin also reported that Cuba offered its military assistance to Argentina in its conflict with Britain. This offer was made to Foreign Minister Nicanor Costa Mendez and General Hector Iglesias, the secretary-general of the presidency.[399]

In the waning days of the Falklands conflict, the Sandinistas also conducted an about face towards the Galtieri regime and supported Buenos Aires. Offers of economic and military

---

[393] "Galtieri's Message to Qadhafi" Tripoli Voice of the Arab Homeland May 29, 1982

[394] "Galtieri's message to Qadhafi" BBC Summary of World Broadcasts May 29, 1982

[395] "Qadhafi's message to Galtieri on Argentina's National Day" BBC Summary of World Broadcasts May 28, 1982

[396] Reppert, Barton. "U.S. Worried About Argentine-Soviet Arms Link" The Associated Press May 11, 1982

[397] Copley, Gregory. "The Falklands War: Update" Defense & Foreign Affairs May, 1982 page 6.

[398] Goodsell, James Nelson. "Falklands crisis: Cuba replaces US as Argentina's best friend" Christian Science Monitor May 11, 1982 page 5.

[399] Handler, Bruce. "Say Cuba Offers Argentina Weapons for Falklands War" The Associated Press June 6, 1982

cooperation were also extended by the Sandinistas to the Argentine militarists. The Sandinista Foreign Minister Miguel d'Escoto noted in June 1982 that *"the anti-imperialist sentiments of Latin America have reached levels never previously achieved"* as a result of the British-Argentine war over the Falklands. Argentina also offered 7,000 tons of wheat to the Sandinistas to help overcome food shortages in Nicaragua.[400] By December 1982, the Argentine military regime signed a trade agreement with the Sandinista communist regime in Nicaragua. A Sandinista delegation visited Argentina and signed a trade agreement which offered financing for Argentine exports to Nicaragua. The Argentines also backed Nicaragua's efforts for a seat on the UN Security Council.[401] In November 1982, the Argentines reportedly provided a $15 million credit to the Sandinista government in Nicaragua for the purchase of capital goods and manufactured products.[402] Sandinista Deputy Foreign Minister Victor Hugo Tinoco noted in June 1982 that *"Nicaragua is ready to send any help that Argentina asks us to, including troops…The United States is now sitting on the bench of the accused because, being a member of the Organization of American States and the Inter-American Treaty of Mutual Assistance, it gave its support to the English."*[403] On another occasion, Tinoco remarked that *"Our country is disposed to cooperate in the military field with the Argentine cause of recovering the Falklands. In any case, the Argentines will have the last word about accepting this offer."*[404] One Argentine official viewed their poor relations with the Sandinistas *"as a closed chapter, something that happened in the past…I think they are anxious to rebuild relations with Argentina. They see themselves as under a serious threat from the United States, a tightening ring, and they would like to have the support of Latin American countries."*[405] In 1983, the succession of military dictatorships collapsed and freer forms of government reigned in Buenos Aires for much of the 1980s.

Bolivia Under Generals Barrientos, Banzer, Garcia-Meza

In order to comprehend the public policies and ideological background of the dictatorships of Generals Barrientos, Banzer, and Garcia-Meza, one must explore the Bolivian quasi-fascist regimes from the 1930s to the 1950s. Starting in the 1930s, Bolivia turned to a fascistic form of government and economic structure. In mid-May 1936, Colonels David Toro and German Busch took power and established a regime based on the fascistic concept of what they termed *"Military Socialism."* Elements of this government outwardly praised the Third Reich and Fascist Italy. Toro's ambassador to Germany expressed admiration for German National Socialism while Minister of Defense Oscar Moscoso also sympathized with the Nazis.

---

[400] Riding, Alan. "Havana Exploits Falkland Dispute" The New York Times June 7, 1982 page A7.

[401] Diehl, Jackson. "Argentine Army Reportedly Says Anti-Nicaragua Efforts at an End" The Washington Post December 18, 1982 page A16.

[402] "Argentine loan to Nicaragua" BBC Summary of World Broadcasts November 12, 1982

[403] Maltes, Juan. "Left-wing junta offers aid to Argentina, including troops" The Associated Press June 4, 1982

[404] Bonilla, Oswaldo. "Nicaragua offers military aid to Argentina" United Press International June 5, 1982

[405] Diehl, Jackson. "Argentine Army Reportedly Says Anti-Nicaragua Efforts at an End" The Washington Post December 18, 1982 page A16.

Toro officially announced that the military dictatorship would be based on what he termed *"state socialism"* and the authoritarian *"right of the State"* as opposed to individualism. On other occasions, the Toro regime called itself a *"syndicalist state."* Toro declared himself *"in favor of a corporative state"* and for a *"regime of trade-union association identified with the organs of power and political representation."* One regime theorist noted that *"...the National State, as the definitive successor to the oligarchic State prior to the Chaco War, would replace class conflicts by a division of productive functions, in which contradictions would give way to integration within a development project directed by the State."*

Both the Toro and Busch governments actively intervened in the Bolivian economy. The Toro government was also supported by labor and by the Legion of Chaco War Veterans (LEC). The LEC formed the *Frente Unico Socialista* which called for *"authoritarian Nationalism."* Toro created state-controlled *"functional syndicates"* which controlled the economy. The functional syndicates were supported by the Bolivian Socialist Party, which urged them to adopt anti-communism. When the *"functional syndicates"* proved a failure, Toro attempted to create a *"state socialist party."* The Toro dictatorship also supported or even imposed compulsory union membership for all workers; the creation of a corporative state; a social security system; and state-subsidized food stores. Despite the anti-communism of the Toro regime, its Ministry of Labor was also infiltrated by self-proclaimed Marxists. The Ministers of Foreign Affairs and Haciendas were members of the Socialist Party who favored the imposition of a corporative state. The state also controlled the labor union movement through a corporative arrangement of worker and employers' associations. The Toro regime also decreed mandatory work for all Bolivians. All citizens were ordered to possess employment papers (*carnet de trabajo*). If citizens lacked these documents, they would be declared *"unemployed"* by the authorities and conscripted into forced labor brigades.

A regime theorist opined that *"State socialism, far from abolishing the principle of private property, would limit itself to modernizing it, giving it the content of a social function."* Busch nationalized the Central Bank. The Toro dictatorship also issued laws which curbed speculation and limited concessions for foreign multinationals. A state-owned Mining Bank was also established. Standard Oil properties were nationalized in 1937, while a state-owned enterprise called *Yacimientos Petrofileros Fiscales* Bolivianos (YPFB- Bolivian State Oil Deposits) was created.

By the early 1940s, the quasi-fascist/socialist National Revolutionary Movement (MNR) increased its power and developed its collectivist platform. The MNR preached a revolutionary anti-capitalist, anti-Jewish line which tilted towards the Axis Powers. MNR theorist Cuadros Quiroga denounced the *"sinister figure of the Jew Mauricio Hochschild...the pontiff of palace machinations."* In the *"Principles and Action of the National Revolutionary Movement"* (1942), the false democracy of the foreign interests and the exploitation of pseudo-socialism were denounced. The MNR also specifically excoriated *"as antinational any possible relationship of the international political parties and the maneuvers of Judaism."* The MNR also supported the *"absolute prohibition of Jewish immigration, as well as any other immigration not having productive efficacy."* The MNR platform also endorsed a Nazi-like collectivism as its core ideology. The platform called for the *"solidarity of Bolivians to defend the collective interest and the common good before the individual interest."*

In December 1943, the fascist *Razon de Patria* (RADEPA) and MNR took power in Bolivia and was led by Major Gualberto Villaroel. Various pro-Axis military officers and intellectuals populated the new regime. During the 1930s, RADEPA members were dispatched to Fascist Italy for training during the period of *"military socialism."* In January 1944, one government adviser named Dr. German Quiroga Galdo called for Bolivia to join the Axis. Pro-government forces in RADEPA kidnapped the Bolivian-Jewish tin baron Mauricio Hochschild and held him hostage for several weeks. Once Hochschild was released, he fled into exile. RADEPA forces also executed ten anti-Villaroel politicians and military officers in November 1944. The regime also imposed foreign exchange controls and recognized state controlled labor unions.[406]

President Villaroel maintained very close ties with Argentina, which was under the rule of a fascistic military dictatorship. MNR bigwig and Minister of Economics Paz Estenssoro noted his support for the fascist Ramirez government. In 1943, Estenssoro noted in an interview with a journalist for the magazine <u>Ahora</u> that *"If Argentina's example is followed in other South American countries, if they interpret it fully and correctly, it may well be that this date which the Argentines consider exclusively theirs will come to be celebrated as the day of economic emancipation for all Latin America."*[407] In May 1946, President Villarroel's aide-de-camp, Captain Ricardo Cardona, provided Peron with a proposed a plan for a *"Lima-La Paz-Asunción-Buenos Aires bloc"* where Argentina would serve *"as an elder sister."*[408] The Peron regime sent several planeloads of Argentine police advisers and large amounts of propaganda materials to the Bolivian MNR regime. The Bolivian MNR regime mimicked the rhetoric of the Peronists in their denunciation of *"oligarchs, reactionaries, plutocrats, traitors."*[409]

By 1951, the forces of the MNR took power again and were led by Estenssoro. It militantly opposed classical liberalism and conservatism in politics and the economy. The Minister of Foreign Affairs noted in an April 1954 speech at the Municipal Theatre in La Paz that *"Liberalism liquidated conservatism politically, but not economically…It let the conservatives keep economic power in their hands. This was a great mistake: those who retain economic power will one day recover political power."*[410]

Like the Nazis and Peronists, the MNR dictatorship happily accepted aid and trade from their ideological enemy in Washington DC. While the MNR opposed liberal capitalism and foreign multinationals, they also realized that the survival of its dictatorship was of paramount importance. Similar to their Nazi, Argentine, and Soviet counterparts, the Bolivian Foreign Service became an instrument for the MNR to deceive the United States and to extract as much aid and trade concessions as possible. All Bolivian diplomats were required to be MNR members. Furthermore, an armed MNR party cell called the *Maria Barzola* was set up in the Ministry of Foreign Affairs.[411] Gutierrez noted that *"The United States was unquestionably acting from the highest humanitarian motives when it heeded the Bolivian appeal for aid but by giving it to the MNR regime rather than to the people direct it only helped to keep the party in power. The foodstuffs thus acquired by the regime gave it a powerful weapon, for it could*

---

[406] Anti-capitalism or anti-imperialism? Interwar authoritarian and fascist sources of a reactionary ideology: The case of the Bolivian MNR Accessed From: http://libcom.org/files/The%20case%20of%20the%20Bolivian%20MNR.pdf

[407] Gutierrez, Alberto Ostria. <u>The Tragedy of Bolivia a People Crucified</u> (Prestige Book Company, 1958) page 134.

[408] Ibid, page 135.

[409] Ibid, page 136.

[410] Ibid, page 189.

[411] Ibid, page 178.

withhold them from anyone who did not present a party card. The result was that people joined the party in order not to die of hunger and membership rose to nearly two million. The receipt of foodstuffs also enabled the regime to save much-needed foreign exchange which it could then use to strengthen its position. "[412] President Estenssoro admitted to AP correspondent Richard Massock that "*Without United States aid my Government would not have survived.*"[413] Juan Lechin Oquendo admitted that the MNR regime still despised the United States and practiced deception when extracting trade and aid concessions: "*We are anti-imperialists but we use the imperialist countries in order to survive.*"[414]

The Americans also provided political cover for the MNR. United States Assistant Secretary of State Henry Holland praised the so-called "*national revolution*" of the MNR in Bolivia. In 1954 and 1955, Holland visited Bolivia and was accorded a hero's welcome. Holland's motorcade in La Paz was greeted by officially-organized worker and student demonstrations. Holland was received by the pro-government and communist officials of the COB union. Bolivia was also granted an Export-Import Bank loan of $40 million. Bolivia continued to sell the US tin and received economic aid from Washington after the MNR revolution in 1952. The Bolivian Ambassador to the United States told a Kiwanis Club gathering in New York that "*Bolivia's situation today is worse than it was before the arrival of the Spaniards four hundred years ago…My country desperately needs funds…Unless we obtain a long-term contract with the United States for the purchase of tin, hunger and economic paralysis will aggravate the chaotic situation of our unfortunate people.*"[415]

In 1964, General Rene Barrientos took over Bolivia and established a military dictatorship. It took a strong position against communism and suppressed leftist terrorism in that country. Bolivia's foreign policy was strongly aligned with that of the United States. The Barrientos regime established a system of strong economic controls, welcomed American multinational companies, and smashed independent labor organizations. Barrientos glossed over his authoritarianism with a populist and even pseudo-leftist veneer. In 1966, Barrientos and peasant leaders signed "*the Military-Peasant Pact.*" The Pact proclaimed that "*The Armed Forces will make sure that the conquests achieved by the majority classes are respected, such as the Agrarian Reform, basic education, union rights, and others…*"[416]

Barrientos took on various titles while he was the fascist dictator of Bolivia. They included: the Condor of the Andean Skies; Creator of the Second Republic; Paladin of Social Democracy; Restorer of Faith in the National Revolution; and the General of the People. Barrientos noted that "*I am a man of the Christian left-nationalist in economics, democratic in doctrine. But this democracy is just, active, belligerent, dynamic and profoundly revolutionary because I am seeking only social justice and the happiness of the peasant, worker and middle class majority; in sum, the happiness of the people.*"[417] Barrientos claimed that his government

---

[412] Ibid, page 198.

[413] Ibid, page 198.

[414] Ibid, pages 177-179.

[415] Ibid, pages 177-179.

[416] Alexander, Robert J. A history of organized labor in Bolivia (Greenwood Publishing Group, 2005) page 132.

[417] Dunkerley, James. Barrientos and Debray: All Gone or More to Come? Institute of Latin American Studies Occasional Papers Number 2 Accessed From: http://sas-space.sas.ac.uk/3403/1/B58_-_Barrientos_and_Debray_all_Gone_or_More_to_Come.pdf

represented the ideology of the neofascist/socialist National Revolutionary Movement (MNR) and National Revolution of 1952. It condemned the *"excesses"* in the MNR dictatorship of President Paz Estenssaro. In a speech in November 1965, Barrientos told a group of peasants that *"We never threw the Bolivian Revolution aside; we would never change it for anything…We made a revolution within the revolution…We achieved the restoration of the revolution."*[418] Barrientos noted that *"The MNR, in its first period of government carried out fundamental reforms which were applauded by all…But along with the farsighted measures, the MNR also made some gross errors that caused loss of prestige and precipitated the fall of the MNR in November 1964…All the great objectives of the National Revolution had been betrayed…the social and revolutionary content of the April 9th revolution was dissipated…The revolution of 1952 will now take a new road of honesty, of order, of peace, and of social justice such as that which the people demanded on November 4, 1964."*[419] Barrientos organized a populist-sounding new party, the *Movimiento Popular Cristiano* (MPC), which formed a pro-government coalition called the *Freute de la Revolucion Boliviana* (FRB).[420]

Despite the official anti-communist policies, the Barrientos regime was highly interventionist in the area of the economy. This stemmed from the political traditions of various Bolivian collectivist-military regimes such as Villaroel, Busch, Estenssaro, and other proponents of *"Military Socialism."* Barrientos also sought to rationalize the state economy in Bolivia as a means of not abolishing government companies, but to make them more efficient. Barrientos suppressed labor unions and political parties.[421] The state-owned mining corporation COMIBOL was reorganized and placed under the control of a military director. The new director announced rationalization measures which resulted in layoffs and salary reductions.[422] The Labor Code was weighted to favor employers, while political organizing by labor unions was forbidden. The Barrientos regime implemented an investment plan that favored the developed of certain manufacturing sectors. This plan was carried out by the newly created Institute for the Promotion of Investment.[423] Eduardo A. Gamarra and James Malloy noted that *"General Barrientos attempted to follow the same state-capitalist strategy of the Paz government without the burden of labor."*[424] However, there were indications that Barrientos was contemplating a purge of the old politicians, wealthy classes, and labor leaders in order to create a fascist state. In May 1969,

---

[418] Mobley, Billy M. <u>Bolivia: Search for Stability</u> March 2, 1972 US Army War College Accessed From: <u>http://www.dtic.mil/cgi-bin/GetTRDoc?Location=U2&doc=GetTRDoc.pdf&AD=AD0912757</u>

[419] Mobley, Billy M. <u>Bolivia: Search for Stability</u> March 2, 1972 US Army War College Accessed From: <u>http://www.dtic.mil/cgi-bin/GetTRDoc?Location=U2&doc=GetTRDoc.pdf&AD=AD0912757</u>

[420] Ibid.

[421] Dunkerley, James. <u>Barrientos and Debray: All Gone or More to Come?</u> Institute of Latin American Studies Occasional Papers Number 2 Accessed From: <u>http://sas-space.sas.ac.uk/3403/1/B58_-_Barrientos_and_Debray_all_Gone_or_More_to_Come.pdf</u>

[422] Mobley, Billy M. <u>Bolivia: Search for Stability</u> March 2, 1972 US Army War College Accessed From: <u>http://www.dtic.mil/cgi-bin/GetTRDoc?Location=U2&doc=GetTRDoc.pdf&AD=AD0912757</u>

[423] Ibid.

[424] Guillermo Camacho. <u>Bolivian Forever: Celebrating an Extraordinary Heritage and an Unforgettable People</u> (AuthorHouse, 2011) page 60.

rumors abounded in Bolivia that Barrientos would declare himself dictator, nationalize many big businesses, and kill hundreds of political and labor union leaders.[425]

Barrientos was overthrown and replaced by a socialist-oriented military regime. The Soviets established ties with the anti-imperialist and socialist dictatorship of Generals Ovando Candia and Jose Torres. He nationalized American companies and took no action when US offices were broken into by leftist rioters. The General Secretary of the Bolivian Communist Party Jorge Kolle Cueto reported to the KGB Resident in La Paz Igor Sholokhov that Torres is *"taking steps to involve the Left in cooperation with the government"* and offered to help the communists build paramilitary groups to oppress the Right. KGB Chairman Yuri Andropov reported to Soviet dictator Leonid Brezhnev that President Torres sought to establish *"multifaceted cooperation with the USSR."* When General Banzer launched his coup in 1971, the Bolivian army found Soviet and Czech arms caches.[426] Hence, the communist threat to Bolivia was real and the military acted accordingly to prevent their country from becoming another Cuba or Chile.

In 1971, General Hugo Banzer seized power and overthrew the pro-Soviet, leftist dictatorship of Ovando Torres. Despite being painted as yet another *"right wing"* dictator, Banzer actually expanded the size and scope of the state in the economy and adhered to a collectivist ideology that rejected liberal capitalism and communism. Once again, this was in keeping with the Bolivian political traditions dating as far back as the mid-1930s. Banzer believed that the collective needs of the nation and the state were superior to the needs of the individual. Banzer noted that *"No longer are we trying to maintain things as they were, to assume the defense of a public order which protects privileged or unjust situations. The order which should be conserved is that which benefits the collectivity."*[427] Banzer noted in January 1974 that *"We hope to build a fraternal and communitarian society based on security."* Banzer's new society would not be *"included within the scope of an insensitive and orthodox capitalism or totalitarian and dehumanized communism."* Banzer felt that *"cooperatives…will introduce the concept of communitarian society."*[428]

Banzer's economic program strongly recognized the role of private enterprise in sustaining the Bolivian economy. However, Banzer also confirmed the strong role of the government in regulating the private sector and even supported the strengthening of the state sector. The values of the free market were explicitly rejected by Banzer. He noted in January 1974 that *"The state will be directly in charge of the strategic sectors of the economy and will act by itself or through mixed societies in those fields in which private initiative cannot operate…Private enterprise must identify itself with the national objectives, with the people and their rights and needs. In this age in which the great fortunes lessen the feelings of men and constitute a monument to egoism, wealth per se is not justified."*[429]

---

[425] Guillermo Lora. A History of the Bolivian Labour Movement 1848-1971 (Cambridge University Press, 2009) page 357.

[426] Andrew, Christopher and Mitrokhin, Vasili. The World Was Going Our Way (Basic Books 2006) page 65.

[427]Loveman, Brian. The Politics of Anti-Politics (Rowman & Littlefield 1997) pages 221-222.

[428] "President Banzer Delivers New Year's Eve Speech" La Paz Domestic Service January 1, 1974

[429] Ibid.

In May 1975, Banzer noted that *"the nationalist government seeks to create a basis for a reality which will be neither an exploiting and insensitive capitalism nor a totalitarian inhuman and atheistic extremism. Our objective is a fundamentally humanist, communitarian, cooperative and Christian society."*[430] In July 1976, Banzer noted that *"the world is divided into two factions, communism and capitalism which in fact reflect European thought and are being formulated unilaterally...In general terms nationalism presents development of backward and dependent countries as the only way to strengthen their sovereignty, change their structures, and create a just and constantly improving social order."*[431] Banzer noted in a March 1976 speech that *"Our government is building a new society; a society midway between exploiting capitalism and totalitarian and atheist extremism; a cooperative and communal society in which God, the family, and the fatherland will be worshipped."*[432] Radio La Plata in Bolivia reported in July 1976 that President Banzer stated that *"capitalism has sought to expand using political methods and even economic and military pressure...neither capitalism nor communism has solved the problems of man, but they are not the only alternative...nationalism is a road left to the developing nations."*[433] Banzer also noted that *"My government offers freedom and a guarantee to private initiative...But this freedom under no circumstances should be the source of privileges or unbearable discriminations. No sector by itself should be superior or be above the fatherland. Let those who export capital in order to strengthen and subsidize foreign economies or those who amass fortunes which offend the general poverty understand that they will receive no protection from the state and they are warned either to fill a social function or give way to the progressive enterprise."*[434]

Unsurprisingly, some elements of the organized Left and communists were attracted to Banzer's nationalistic collectivism which took an ideological stand in opposition to liberal capitalism. Some members of the Marxist-Leninist Party of the Revolutionary Left (PIR) supported Banzer and even entered the government.[435]

The public sector grew under Banzer. By 1978, the number of governmental institutions totaled 200: 21 central agencies; 89 decentralized agencies; 60 state-owned or mixed enterprises; 9 regional corporations; and 9 municipal corporations. They constituted 33% of GDP, 13% of employment, and 59% of exports, and 70% percent of national investment. Government-owned enterprises during the Banzer period included COMIBOL, YPFB, ENAF, SIDERSA, BAMIN, CBF, and the state railways and airlines.[436]

---

[430] "Banzer in Labor Day Message Reiterates Social Policy Goals" La Paz Domestic Service May 1, 1975

[431] "Banzer Closes National Mineworkers Conference" La Paz Radio Cruz del Sur Network July 20, 1976

[432] "Banzer Warns of Extremism in Santa Cruz Speech" La Paz Domestic Service March 18, 1976

[433] "Report on Agreements" Sucre Radio La Plata July 21, 1976

[434] "President Banzer Delivers New Year's Eve Speech" La Paz Domestic Service January 1, 1974

[435] Sachs, Jeffrey D. "Developing Country Debt and Economic Performance, Volume 2: The Country Studies -- Argentina, Bolivia, Brazil, Mexico" National Bureau of Economic Research, (University of Chicago Press, 1990) page 182.

[436] Morales, Waltraud Queiser. Bolivia: Land of Struggle (Westview Press, 1992) pages 143-145.

Business elites in Banzer's Bolivia expressed concerns about the growth of government-owned enterprises and the general statist direction of economic policy in general. Leaders inside the Bolivian Confederation of Private Enterprises (CEPB) expressed concerns about the proliferation of state-owned companies and the displacement of private sector. Bolivian business was particularly disturbed by the creation of the COFADENA, which was an army-owned corporation. A pro-Banzer businessman stated *"The left has always said that the bourgeoisie controlled the Banzer government. This was not the case. While there were businessmen in the government we did not realize our private interests. You had someone like Jaime Quiroga who was minister of finance and an associate of a medium mining firm and yet he was the one who put taxes on the sector."* Another CEPB leader recalled that Banzer threatened him after publishing criticisms in the press: *"Look next time you publish something like that I'm going to throw you out the country."*[437]

By 1978, Banzer's dictatorship was overthrown and a civilian government took over. However, the Bolivian military overthrew the civilian regime and replaced it with another fascist dictatorship led by General Luis Garcia-Meza. When General Garcia-Meza took power in a military coup in 1980, the government jumpstarted the old nationalist-collectivist rhetoric. The principle of state interventionism and dirigisme was upheld by the new dictatorship. In July 1980, Garcia-Meza stated over Radio Nueva America that *"the government of national reconstruction clearly advocated the participation of workers, with equal social justice, within the framework of Bolivian humane principles…We advocate a social market economy and a mixed economy in which the essential task of the state is harmonized with the private sector."* Furthermore, Garcia-Meza advocated *"workers' participation in the main state enterprises."*[438]

The dictatorship of Garcia-Meza weaved an extreme nationalism, a vaguely leftish-sounding populism, and a fascist corporative vision for the future Bolivia. Garcia-Meza believed that *"Our political and institutional action therefore springs from ideas and from nationalist, democratic, anti-imperialistic and very deep popular practices."* He called for *"a New Bolivian idea of democracy and a new economy that will be at the service of man, the homeless and the poverty stricken."* Garcia-Meza supported *"the structural notion of social solidarity which binds together the Bolivian people in a national doctrine, a broad social doctrine which has the virtue of being an incentive for social mobilization toward change and revolution."* He also supported *"social and distributive justice within the framework of a Bolivian humanism."* This economy would be *"aimed at motivating the people into playing the leading role in national liberation."* Garcia-Meza supported *"liberation through social justice and popular participation in state affairs."* Meza felt that his regime were *"agents and advocates of new social guidelines aimed at the activation of a broad front of national classes interested in liberation and institutional harmony which implies civilian-military agreement for the reconstruction of the fatherland."*[439]

In August 1980, Garcia-Meza noted that the goal for state enterprises was to generate more income for the government's social programs: *"we must take into account that increased production will necessarily result in larger profit margins which will justify and back our*

---

[437] Malloy, James M. and Conaghan, Catherine M. Unsettling Statecraft (University of Pittsburgh Press, 1995) pages 67-68.

[438] "The situation in Bolivia" BBC Summary of World Broadcasts July 24, 1980

[439] "Garcia Meza Discusses Junta Ideology, Policies" La Paz El Diario July 23, 1980

requests of a social nature."[440] In September 1980, Garcia-Meza noted that his government desired the modernization of the operation of the state-owned enterprises and laid down *"social functions"* (i.e. controls) to private companies. Garcia-Meza urged the government *"to modernize and reorganize the national production system particularly public enterprises and provide adequate guarantees to private enterprises in accordance with their social function."*[441] On another occasion, Garcia-Meza called for the *"opening of the market for private investments under conditions beneficial to the nation."*[442]

The Garcia-Meza regime explicitly rejected communism and imperialism (i.e. the United States) and declared itself in the camp of a collectivist-fascist economic nationalism. In September 1980, Garcia-Meza noted to a peasants' meeting that he was seeking to *"resurrect national institutions, eradicating imperialist penetration and Marxist alienation, seeking the give the nation a personality of its own."*[443] Garcia-Meza confirmed in 1981 that *"economic independence"* would be partially achieved by Bolivia freeing itself from *"pressures and impositions from the centers of world power who try to impose new forms of colonialism on the countries which produce strategic, primary products such as is the case of Bolivia."*[444] In August 1980, Garcia-Meza noted in his National Day speech that *"I must emphatically point out that the armed forces national reconstruction government will promote a political process destined to change the economic, social and political system of the country, which means that we will eradicate our historic condition as an underdeveloped country which depends on and is tied to the interests of imperialism..."*[445] By June 1981, Garcia-Meza noted that the universities *"had become sectarian trenches of foreign ideas, alien to our national character"* and *"political forums for imperialist interests."*[446]

While ideologically opposing communism, the Garcia-Meza dictatorship also sought to set itself apart from strict adherence to the foreign policy goals of the United States. In August 1980, Garcia-Meza noted that *"we express a clear and full repudiation of international extremism and of greedy imperialisms, since our project is based on the greatest values of humanism and revolutionary nationalism."*[447] Garcia-Meza also noted that *"neocolonialism is responsible for the frustrations of our people."* Garcia-Meza urged the creation of *"a new world economic order to protect the poor nations from the contradictory interests of the rich*

---

[440] "Garcia Meza Addresses Nation on Independence Day" La Paz Domestic Service August 6, 1980

[441] "President Garcia Meza Outlines Government Policies" La Paz Radio Illimani Network September 18, 1980

[442] Ibid.

[443] "Garcia Meza Urges Hard Work to Fight Economic Blockade" Buenos Aires TELAM September 7, 1980

[444] Loveman, Brian. The Politics of Anti-Politics (Rowman & Littlefield 1997) pages 224-225.

[445] "Bolivian President's National Day speech to the nation" BBC Summary of World Broadcasts August 9, 1980

[446] "Around the World; Bolivia Reopens Colleges Closed Since 1980 Coup" The New York Times June 16, 1981 page A5.

[447] "Garcia Meza Addresses Nation on Independence Day" La Paz Domestic Service August 6, 1980

countries. "[448] In June 1982, Garcia-Meza struck an almost leftist note when he stated that the *"present national economic crisis can only be overcome through the efforts and toil of all Bolivians…We must avoid dependence on the capitalist world. They are only interested in our natural resources, renewable and nonrenewable for their war-mongering projects.* "[449]

The Garcia-Meza dictatorship and its supporters also harassed the American Embassy and its diplomats in response to Washington's criticisms of Bolivia's human rights violations and cocaine trafficking. In June 1980, the Garcia-Meza government was sharply critical of US Ambassador Marvin Weissman. A signed letter from the Bolivian National Security Council Secretary General General Augusto Calderon noted *"We are sure that the colonialist attitude of the State Department is not a reflection of the actual feelings of the people of the United States, whom we recognize as generous, valiant and full of friendship.* "[450] As of June 1980, the walls along the streets of La Paz were spray painted with slogans that denounced the American Ambassador. These offensive slogans dubbed the Ambassador a *"cocaine dealer,"* a *"pig,"* and a *"lackey of the toothy Carter."* Fascist-minded Bolivian parties and pro-regime workers' organizations held protests outside the US Embassy.[451] By August 1980, Garcia-Meza ordered paramilitary gangs to wreck the American consulate and firebomb the Bolivian-American Center in Santa Cruz de la Sierra.[452]

Garcia-Meza also intensely resented American accusations which implicated the Bolivian military in the cocaine trade. He stated that Bolivia *"rejects the infamous international campaign launched against Bolivia by pro-imperialist extremism which not only claims the perpetuation of genocide, but also offensively accuses us of having ties with the international drug trafficking mafia whose headquarters is certainly not in poor countries but which is part of the colonial system that oppresses the peoples.* "[453]

The Western and American-style political system and *"bourgeois"* political values were rejected by Garcia-Meza and his government. Garcia-Meza remarked *"In Bolivia we can speak no more of liberal democracy with the political parties shut down and proscribed when social movements tend to dissolve the multitude of small political factions which have been obstacles to the political activity of recent times."* The democracy to be installed was supposed to be *"organic"* and *"republican"* which *"permits the active and real participation of the popular sectors of the country, of the peasants who, even today, still live outside the national decision-making process."* The democracy was to be based on *"social justice"* and *"the humanization of labor and capital"* and not through *"elites who gained their status through inheritance or fortune."* Garcia-Meza also stated that *"liberal and bourgeois democracy should give way to a*

---

[448] "President Garcia Meza Outlines Government Policies" La Paz Radio Illimani Network September 18, 1980

[449] "Garcia Meza: Quagmire" La Paz Cadena Panamericana June 25, 1982

[450] Olmos, Harold. "Bolivian Armed Forces Critical of U.S. Ambassador" The Associated Press June 6, 1980

[451] Hoge, Warren. "General Garcia Meza" The New York Times June 16, 1980 page A2.

[452] Hoge, Warren. "Man in the News; Bolivian General With Iron Fist: Luis Meza Tejada" The New York Times August 13, 1980 page A12.

[453] "President Garcia Meza Outlines Government Policies" La Paz Radio Illimani Network September 18, 1980

democracy…where the political, economic, and social decisions are not made by miniscule minorities…"[454]

On several occasions, Garcia-Meza also hailed the Bolivian political and economic tradition of "*Military Socialism.*" In August 1980, Garcia-Meza reflected: "*Long and difficult was the path that led to the Bolivian revolution that was started by the governments headed by David Toro and German Busch. The first of these nationalized the oil industry that was in the hands of foreign consortium and the latter adopted basic measures that forced the powerful mining sector to contribute to the national economy with the foreign currency from its mineral exports. The decisive step of the Bolivian revolution was taken by Gualberto Villarroel who on December 20, 1943 issued important measures to improve the peasants' and the living conditions of mineworkers. Villarroel had to confront strong opposition from both rightist and leftist sectors. He failed in his objectives and was killed.*"[455]

In a speech on the National Radio Network, Garcia-Meza noted in July 1980 that "*The current revolutionary action and the nature of this government of national reconstruction are based on the rich traditional doctrines that started with the military socialism of President David Toro (1936), which merged with the nationalist and anti-oligarchic doctrine of President German Busch (1937-1939) and was enriched by the blood of martyr President Gualberto Villaroel (1943-1946) finally becoming a vivid reality with the popular blossoming of the national revolution whose formation and development was frustrated by the early demise of President Rene Barrientos (1966-1969).*"[456]

On the surface, one of the most unexpected features of the Garcia-Meza regime was its willingness to cautiously open up trade and political relations with the Soviet Union and its allies. While the Bolivian regime was strongly anti-communist and violently fought the Left, Garcia-Meza sought to spite the United States for opposing his government. This was to be achieved by cautiously improving relations with Moscow. Both the Soviets and Bolivians were also united in their opposition to liberal capitalism and American imperialism. Hence, these ideological commonalities could have potentially served as a point of agreement between the two countries. Garcia-Meza also noted that "*the armed forces government of national reconstruction is interested in increasing relations with socialist countries whose experience in making changes from starting points of similar backwardness will be very useful for a country like Bolivia, irrespective of political or ideological positions.*"[457] In September 1980, Soviet Charge D'Affairs Anatoly Koslov commented to Bolivian Under-Secretary of Foreign Relations that "*We do not need to act specially regarding the takeover by the current Bolivian government…We maintain relations with states and with the governments of these states. This is appropriate in international practice.*"[458] Garcia-Meza himself asserted in September 1980 that the Bolivian

---

[454]Loveman, Brian. The Politics of Anti-Politics (Rowman & Littlefield 1997) pages 224-225.

[455] "Garcia Meza Addresses Nation on Independence Day" La Paz Domestic Service August 6, 1980

[456] "Garcia Meza Discusses Junta Ideology, Policies" La Paz El Diario July 23, 1980

[457] "President Garcia Meza Outlines Government Policies" La Paz Radio Illimani Network September 18, 1980

[458] "Soviet Charge D'Affairs Confirms Establishment of Relations" Buenos Aires LATIN September 20, 1980

government did not fear communism and announced that he would accept aid from the USSR.[459] The USSR also offered Garcia-Meza assistance. Fernando Bedoya Ballivian recalled: *"General Garcia Meza told us not to accept it but also not to refuse it because if the Carter Administration doesn't change its position, we will talk to everybody."*[460] Simply stated, the prospect of a drastic improvement in Bolivian-Soviet relations was a *"Sword of Damocles"* that La Paz dangled over the head of Washington. By 1981, steps were taken to re-open and improve trade relations between Moscow and La Paz. In July 1981, Bolivian Minister for Foreign Affairs Mario Rolon Anaya reported that the Bolivian Ambassador to the Soviet Union Javier Murillo de la Rocha and the Soviet Minister of Trade signed an economic cooperation agreement.[461] In March 1981, the Bolivian State Mining Corporation (COMIBOL) negotiated with the Soviet firm *Machinexport* to retool the plant.[462]

Unfortunately, there were a number of countries that were willing to break the international trade embargo imposed on Bolivia. This struggle was framed by the Bolivian government as a conflict with American economic imperialism versus a popular-based nationalism. In July 1980, Garcia-Meza urged unity between the Bolivian people and the armed forced to form *"a great national unity front to fight foreign dependence"* over Radio Nueva America.[463] In August 1980, Garcia-Meza noted that Bolivia would not *"bow to imperialism"* and vowed to neutralize the international blockade.[464] Fernando Bedoya Ballivian, the head of the *Banco Nacional de Bolivia* and a principal backer and longtime friend of General Garcia-Meza, stated that *"We hope that your Government will understand that the blockade of this Government is going to be very bad for your Government as well as ours…Everyone's going to be with us, Brazil, Argentina, Uruguay, Paraguay and Chile, and they will help us."* Argentina, Brazil, Israel, and South Africa were Bolivia's top trade partners during the Garcia-Meza period. Argentina, Brazil, Egypt, Israel, Taiwan, Paraguay, Uruguay, and South Africa were the only nations which accorded diplomatic recognition to the Garcia-Meza regime.[465]

The collectivist-nationalist rhetoric and ideological statements of Garcia-Meza and his junta were translated into action in the field of the economy. Massive state interventionism was the order of the day in the Bolivian economy. In July 1981, the Garcia-Meza regime imposed controls on foreign currency transactions. Bolivian businessmen needed to gain the approval of the state-owned Central Bank to:

1) Accept foreign loans.
2) Apply for letters of credit to import foreign-made goods.
3) Purchase American dollars and other foreign currencies.

---

[459] "Garcia Meza Comments on Communism, Soviet Aid" <u>Buenos Aires TELAM</u> September 23, 1980

[460] Hoge, Warren. "Bolivia Regime Looks to its Friends to Help Foil US" <u>The New York Times</u> August 6, 1980 page A2.

[461] "Soviet-Bolivian financial agreement" <u>Radio Illimani, La Paz</u> July 10, 1981

[462] "Bolivian fuming plant suffers new setbacks" <u>Metals Week</u> March 2, 1981 page 2.

[463] "The situation in Bolivia" <u>BBC Summary of World Broadcasts</u> July 24, 1980

[464] "Garcia Meza Affirms Defiance of Economic Blockade" <u>Buenos Aires LATIN</u> August 2, 1980

[465] Hoge, Warren. "Bolivia Regime Looks to its Friends to Help Foil US" <u>The New York Times</u> August 6, 1980 page A2.

The Garcia-Meza regime justified the imposition of this law on the grounds that foreign governments and bankers engaged in an *"international conspiracy"* to *"systematically blockade"* the disbursement of foreign credits to the Bolivian government.[466]

Garcia-Meza sought to simultaneously retain and rationalize the operations of state-owned enterprises. In some cases, these *"reforms"* actually expanded the number of state agencies and sought to prevent *"profiteering."* In June 1981, the Garcia-Meza government proposed changes in the mining codes through national political planning agency (CONAL) and the Ministry of Mining and Metallurgy. The purpose for these proposed policy changes was to rescue the industry out of its *"frank state of crisis and decadence."* The government recommended that vast state-owned lands that were rich with minerals be opened to the mining industries. CONAL cautioned that the government should prevent *"excessive accumulation of large reserves in the hands of a few entrepreneurs."* A high-level Garcia-Meza regime official observed in an interview with the American publication Metals Week that his government had no intention to denationalize the mining industry. This official also noted that the Garcia-Meza government supported the formation of a centralized marketing corporation for the sale and distribution of commodities. This proposal was opposed by the Bolivian private sector.[467] The business community naturally expressed concerns about the political and economic controls imposed by the Garcia-Meza regime. One CEPB leader recalled: *"The Confederation first met in a group of very important entrepreneurs who saw that there were great problems with Garcia Meza-problems of trying to do things in ways that were not suitable for members of the private sector, problems of human rights, economic problems."*[468]

The Garcia-Meza dictatorship also sought to portray itself as an ally of the workers and peasants in Bolivia. In July 1980, Garcia Meza stated that *"the objectives and purposes of the armed forces are to achieve national welfare and preferably for the national majorities, for the brother peasants, for the brother workers and various sectors of the country."*[469] In July 1980, General Garcia-Meza noted before an audience of mineworkers *"that the objectives of the armed forces were to achieve national welfare preferably for the national majorities - the brother peasants and workers."* Garcia-Meza tried *"to make the brother miners understand that the armed forces are not their enemies; their enemies are those who foster foreign ideas."*[470] The government also sought to construct a corporative state backed by generous programs for social welfare and worker protections. Garcia-Meza also called for *"a social pact"* that would provide full employment to workers, minimum wages, *"the orderly functioning of worker-employer relations,"* and housing, health, and social welfare programs.[471]

Meanwhile, independent labor unions were smashed by the Garcia-Meza regime on the grounds that they were dominated by the communists. In August 1980, Garcia-Meza decreed the imposition of corporative controls on labor-management relations. He noted that labor leaders

---

[466] Enders, John. "Bolivia Imposes Foreign Currency Controls" The Associated Press July 31, 1981

[467] "Bolivia considering mining policy revisions" Metals Week June 1, 1981 page 8.

[468] Malloy, James M. and Conaghan, Catherine M. Unsettling Statecraft (University of Pittsburgh Press, 1995) page 90.

[469] "Garcia Meza Seeks Reconciliation With Workers" Buenos Aires TELAM July 25, 1980

[470] "The situation in Bolivia" BBC Summary of World Broadcasts July 26, 1980

[471] "President Garcia Meza Outlines Government Policies" La Paz Radio Illimani Network September 18, 1980

would be elected at the workplace level, with the ultimate approval of the Ministry of Labor. Candidates were to be of *"high moral character, have three years seniority, and have had no prior experience as a labour representative."*[472] Labor was also regimented by Decree Number 17536 of July 1980. This government decree created the "*Patriotic Service to the State,"* which imposed compulsory labor on all classes of the population.[473]

Given its fascist ideology, Bolivia unsurprisingly became a haven for some of the worst and infamous Nazi war criminals. One such criminal thug was SS officer Klaus Barbie, the monstrous *"Butcher of Lyon."* Criminals such as Barbie were unrepentant about their socialist-collectivist and racialist beliefs. Barbie charged the Carter administration and "*international capitalist interests"* of interfering with Garcia-Meza's radical nationalist programs. Barbie also admitted that he advised the Bolivian Ministry of the Interior. The Interior Ministry controlled the secret police of Bolivia under Garcia-Meza. The Minister of the Interior Luis Arce Gomez was knee-deep in cocaine trafficking.[474] While resident in Bolivia, Barbie fondly recalled that he expounded on the old Nazi *"battle against American capitalism and against Communism."*[475]

Klaus Barbie was a partner in the state-owned *Transmartima* shipping line. This enterprise was involved in arms smuggling and developed close relations with the Bolivian military. He also created internment camps for General Hugo Banzer and was also involved in drug smuggling.[476] Barbie also taught *"some of our good National Socialist ideas"* to workers at a sawmill he managed in Bolivia. In fact, Barbie personally treated work injuries that were sustained by Bolivian workers. He recalled that this close connection with his workers "*really impressed them. They never forgot it and I never had any problems."*[477]

Various fascist-minded groups cooperated with the Banzer and Garcia-Meza despotisms. After all, the Banzer and Garcia-Meza regimes fulfilled many of the ideological and practical programs of fascist-minded groups such as the Bolivian Socialist Phalange (FSB) and the Nationalist Centre (CEN) .The FSB was founded in 1937. It advocated Bolivian nationalism, a form of state socialism, and an anti-bourgeois revolutionary outlook. Its goal was a *"New Bolivian State."* It was opposed to both the Right and "*leftist anarchy."* The FSB opposed capitalism as a *"system of usury"* and communism for its *"class struggle."* The program of the *"New Bolivian State"* asserted that the new government would be "*an integral organism that based on the will of being of a Nation, will subordinate the personal interests, of group or classes, to the supreme interest of Bolivianidad."* The Socialism of the FSB consisted of the ideals of social justice, class solidarity, and the "*harmonization of the productive factor with the social factor."* The FSB opposed the class warfare of Marxism and the "*liberal plutocracies."* The FSB Economic Program supported the nationalization of strategic, productive industries and

---

[472] "Appointment of labour representatives in Bolivia" <u>BBC Summary of World Broadcasts</u> August 21, 1980

[473] "Report on the Situation of Human Rights in the Republic of Bolivia" July 1, 1985 Accessed From: http://www.cidh.org/countryrep/Bolivia81eng/chap.5.htm#B.

[474] Magnus Linklater, Isabel Hilton, Neal Ascherson. <u>The Nazi legacy: Klaus Barbie and the international fascist connection</u> (Henry Holt 1985) page 296.

[475] Robert Wilson, James Osborne, Klaus Barbie. <u>The confessions of Klaus Barbie, the Butcher of Lyon</u> (Arsenal Editions, 1984) page 167.

[476] Robbins, Christopher. <u>Test of courage: the Michel Thomas story</u> (Simon and Schuster, 1999) pages 307-308.

[477] Bower, Tom. <u>Klaus Barbie, Butcher of Lyons</u> (M. Joseph, 1984) page 183.

a form of socialist economy which opposed class struggle. The FSB supported private investment in other sectors of the economy and the concept of mixed companies. On the foreign policy front, the FSB opposed all forms of imperialism and sought the development of a Latin American power bloc. By 1987, the FSB reserved a special hostility to North American imperialism and capitalist dominance of the world.[478]

The radical nationalist CEN was formed around 1978. It subsequently supported the 1980 fascist takeover by Garcia-Meza. The CEN rejected both *"liberal democratic bourgeois capitalism"* and *"Marxist scientific socialism."* The CEN supported economic nationalism and autarky.[479] The extreme nationalist groups in Bolivia and the Garcia-Meza regime also occasionally linked up with European neo-fascists in an effort to forge international solidarity. In 1979, Stefano del Chiae visited officials of the FSB and MNR in Bolivia. He described the 1980 Garcia-Meza takeover as *"A revolution in which the people's role was extensive and widespread, the peasants' league, housewives' league and consumers' league, the hauliers, the free trade union and upwards of 50% of the miners backed the coup."* Del Chiae recollected that he received a request to provide consultations to the Garcia-Meza dictatorship. He recalled: *"I called upon the collaboration of some 20 FSB and MNR comrades and saw to it that some personnel from the MIR were added to them."* One extreme nationalist/fascist tract noted that *"Support for the new regime in Bolivia amounts to embarking on a fight for a third way between Marxist socialism and multi-national capitalism."*[480]

Lastly, the Garcia-Meza regime attempted to launch an international propaganda campaign to counter the foreign criticisms of the Bolivian government. Diplomats were conscripted to lead the effort to whitewash the image and atrocities of the Garcia-Meza government. In August 1980, the Press and Information Minister ordered the Bolivian Embassies *"to deny false information about Bolivia released by some biased press organizations."*[481]

The Dominican Republic Under General Rafael Trujillo (1930-1961)

General Rafael Trujillo took power in the Dominican Republic by 1930 and established a ruthless, corrupt fascistic dictatorship. He took power in the wake of political instability that arose from weak governments and American occupations. Trujillo was anti-communist, closely aligned with the United States, and clearly opposed to the free market and limited government. Trujillo often ruled the Dominican Republic through various puppet presidents and sometimes directly. He ran the country as a personal fiefdom and garnered many economic benefits. In a style reminiscent of Stalin and Hitler, Trujillo developed a far-reaching cult of personality where he became known as The Benefactor. In 1961, Trujillo was overthrown in a military coup and was replaced with a more democratically-minded anti-communist government. There were reports that the CIA had a hand in the overthrow of Trujillo.

---

[478] "Bolivian Socialist Phalange" Accessed From: http://www.myetymology.com/encyclopedia/Bolivian_Socialist_phalange.html

[479] Ciarán Ó Maoláin. The radical right: a world directory (Longman, 1987) page 36.

[480] "Stefano Delle Chiaie in Bolivia—Notes on the memoirs of Stefano Delle Chiaie by Paul Sharkey" Accessed From: http://www.christiebooks.com/ChristieBooksWP/2013/02/stefano-delle-chiaie-in-bolivia-notes-on-the-memoirs-of-stefano-delle-chiaie-by-paul-sharkey/

[481] "Bolivia" BBC Summary of World Broadcasts August 29, 1980

Trujillo and his cronies established the Dominican Party, which served as a mass mobilization tool and propaganda instrument for Trujillo's rule. The Dominican Party had as its motto "*Rectitude, Liberty, Work, Morality.*" All government employees were required to join it, while 80% of the electorate joined it. Its founder declared that the purpose of the Party was to "*create mass subordination to the principle of authority.*" The Dominican Party demanded contributions from businessmen and engaged in its own profitable enterprises. In 1957, its investments totaled $6 million. Many welfare benefits and state charities were managed by the Party, who also provided large quantities of milk, shoes, cement, and building materials to the poor.[482]

Even at the height of the Dominican Republic's alliance with the United States, the Trujillo regime also explicitly opposed the functioning of the free market. Trujillo supported an economy based on "*suitable wages*" and a "*planned and coordinated economy.*" He dubbed this the "*Dominican Revolution*" whose hallmark was "*solidarity for the achievement of progress…all progress to be effective must be harmonious.*" Trujillo also noted that "*the observance of present day world events teaches us that political democracy cannot be made workable if it is not founded upon economic democracy.*"[483]

In the early Trujillo years, the government press explicitly opposed capitalism. Listin Diario urged that Trujillo's land reforms should meet "*collective and private needs.*" It also stated "*That infliction of degenerate capitalism which has cost humanity so many rivers of blood and so many tears, the latifundiam, is being fought and steadily overcome.*"[484] La Opinion asserted that pre-Trujillo governments prevented crackdowns on the mistreatment of sugar estate workers and their families. La Opinion believed that such inaction was "*due to the fear of confronting powerful capitalist entities.*"[485]

There were even occasions where Trujillo supporters sincerely painted the Dominican dictator as a socialist. One pro-Trujillo politician indicated that the Dominican dictator achieved true "*Socialism*" in the Dominican Republic which was opposed to "*biased class Socialism.*" Trujillo's labor and social legislation and regulations were described as "*far-reaching, humane and fundamentally Christian legislation…of a Socialist pattern.*"[486]

Trujillo established a state-controlled economy where state corporations and agencies existed side by side with private enterprises. The private sector in the Dominican Republic was closely controlled and looted by the Trujillo regime. The economic policy of the Trujillo dictatorship was motivated by fattening its own bank accounts and property portfolios, which was in turn, overlaid with the veneer of nationalist collectivism. Trujillo, his family members, and cronies directly owned a plethora of companies that served as their personal piggy bank. Betances wrote "*When Trujillo took control of the Dominican government in 1930, he was already a wealthy man, but he was not the representative of a national bourgeoisie. Instead, he led a political movement that consolidated national political institutions and used them to spearhead a process of capital accumulation that provided a solid economic foundation for a new economic elite. The formation of this Trujillist elite began with a process of accumulation*

---

[482] Wiarda, Howard J. Dictatorship and Development (University of Florida Press, 1968) pages 75-79.
[483] Ibid, pages 97-101.
[484] Turits, Richard Lee. Foundations of Despotism (Stanford University Press, 2004) page 136.
[485] Ibid, page 94.
[486] Nanita, Abelardo. Trujillo: the biography of a great leader (Vantage Press, 1957) pages 67-69.

directed by the state that expropriated traditional elites and rural and urban producers -in sum, most of the economically active population. " Laws were enacted under Trujillo which created a government monopoly on basic consumer goods such as milk, salt, beef, oil, cigarettes, and shoes. Food producers, craftsmen, and businessmen were required to pay a regressive income tax to the state. Exporters were selectively granted permits by the Trujillo government. Trujillo also purchase and sold state-owned companies based on their profitability. State funds and infrastructure were also used for Trujillo's *"private"* business operations. The new economic elite were concentrated among Trujillo's cronies and family members. These pro-Trujillo elites competed against the more established Dominican entrepreneurs. Trujillo monopolized control of the sugar industry and used leftist language to attack the private sugar producers when the Dominican dictator intended to confiscate these sugar plantations. In the 1940s and 1950s, Trujillo launched a government-led import substitution program to develop industries in the textile, chemical fertilizer, cement, sacks and cord, rubber products, and metal products industries. Betances observed that *"Industrialization policy exempted investors from local taxes and allowed them to import duty-free all the machinery they needed to initiate their industrial activities. In exchange they were to promote import substitution, generate hard currency, create employment, bring new technologies to the country, and, of course, advance national industrial development...Trujillo's economic development model had, however, some important limitations: it was highly concentrated in the hands of the dictator; markedly dependent on U.S. technology, investments, and advice on production decisions; and extremely vulnerable to sudden changes in the world market prices of raw materials and agricultural products."*

Betances observed that the size and scope of government agencies and bureaucracies vastly increased under Trujillo: *"The government bureaucracy and Congress played key roles in concentrating political power. Despite the virtual absence of economic growth during the 1930s, Trujillo orchestrated the rapid expansion of the government, creating ten new institutions, including the Internal Revenues Agency, the Ministry of Telecommunications, the Ministry of Public Health, the Ministry of Industry and Commerce, a Land Court, and others in the 1930s. During the 1940s he created seven more, including a nationally controlled customs receivership, a government-sponsored credit union, the Reserve Bank, and the Central Bank. The creation of these institutions led to an expansion in government employment as the number of middle-level technical workers and professional administrators went from 5,579 in 1935 to 12,168 in 1950 and to 23,190 in 1960. The bureaucrats functioned with disciplined loyalty to one individual -- Trujillo. As he had with the military, he chose bureaucrats for loyalty rather than efficiency, placed his relatives in key positions, and shuffled personnel so that no one would accumulate sufficient power to undermine him."*[487]

Ornes noted that the Trujillo state closely controlled the Dominican economy and business community: *"The Government intervenes from start to finish in the process of establishing a new enterprise in the country. If the project is considered 'satisfactory' to Trujillo himself or those of his associates whom he has put in charge of that operation, the matter is referred to the proper Government authorities and a contract is signed between the company and the State specifying taxes, tariff exonerations, extent of the investment and other pertinent points. As a result, practically all of the principal industrial enterprises now in operation within the country have been established by Trujillo himself or by people in partnership with him. A few*

---

[487] Betances, Emilio. State and Society in the Dominican Republic (Westview Press, 1995) pages 100-107.

have been started by the Government itself and later, if proven profitable, turned over to private interests, usually those in which 'the Big One' has his hand." Ornes also wrote *"Unable to free themselves from government controls, Dominican businessmen are at the mercy of Trujillo's caprices. The Benefactor can make or destroy them and knowing it they show, like the rest of the Dominicans, insecurity and timidity in their everyday doings."*[488]

A pro-Trujillo publication admitted the scope of government control over the Dominican economy: *"There are few countries in the world where commercial and industrial activity is so thoroughly blended and coordinated with Government. That, of course, could be both an asset and a liability...It might even be said that with good government relations no foreign firm loses money in the Dominican Republic."*[489]

Ornes wrote *"Through an extreme protection of certain articles, taxes encouraged the growth of a series of Trujillo-owned monopolies. Last but not least, they were a fool-proof instrument of terror, adroitly exploited to keep in line the wealthy classes. Fear of additional taxation, coupled with visits by Treasury agents, has been the favorite method of keeping in check businessmen and wealthy farmers."* When businessmen raised the prices of their goods in late 1934 and 1935, the Trujillo government arrested them. The government intimidated employers when they printed a warning in the newspaper Listin Diario which threatened them for any expressions of disloyalty voiced by employees or relatives. When a match factory in Puerto Plata shut down, Trujillo announced to the press that the government would *"not permit the stoppage of any industry"* and that if the owners could not keep them running, the state would take charge and give them an *"efficient, honest and economical administration."*[490]

Businessmen were forced to join the Dominican Party and depended on Trujillo's government for passports, business licenses, and import and export permits. Wealthy enterprises were also forced to share their profits to Trujillo's family and friends. Foreign firms had to seek permission from Trujillo to employ Dominican nationals.[491]

Trujillo took over the government-owned salt and tobacco monopolies and became the country's largest cattle rancher. His enterprises were also given preference for the export of sugar, coffee, beef, rice, sisal, cacao, coconuts, and wood. Trujillo opened a pasteurizing plant and controlled the slaughterhouse industry. Trujillo's shares in the sugar industry totaled $120 million. After 1945, Trujillo owned the Ozama Construction Company, shipyards, dry docks, and two shipping lines. He also controlled the two airlines and motor vehicle distributors. He also controlled the Bank of Agricultural and Industrial Credit, which provided funds to private businesses.[492] The Trujillo family established monopolies and forced independent businessmen to accept partial or full Trujillist control over their enterprises. Businessmen were required to become members of the Dominican Party. They were also heavily taxed, while quotas were established on imported materials. Such measures benefited Trujillo's enterprises to the detriment of independent businesses. The government also purchased the electric and telephone companies in 1955 and attacked American-owned sugar companies in 1954.[493]

---

[488] Ornes, German E. Trujillo: Little Caesar of the Caribbean (Nelson, 1958) pages 163-165.
[489] Ibid, pages 65-66.
[490] Ibid, pages 238-239.
[491] Wiarda, Howard J. Dictatorship and Development (University of Florida Press, 1968) pages 97-101.
[492] Ibid, pages 84-85.
[493] Galindez, Jesus de. The Era of Trujillo (University of Arizona Press, 1973) pages 178-181.

The Trujillo regime also engaged in pressure tactics to force the old elites to accept regime figures as equals. Trujillo also forced his election and re-election to the elite Club Union, which rejected him in earlier times.[494] Trujillo also forced the Union Club to admit his military and political cronies. Eventually, Trujillo forcibly dissolved that group. Trujillo bitterly resented the landed elites in the Dominican Republic. A new aristocracy developed under Trujillo which included high government officials, military men, family members, and friends of the regime. The Trujillo elites sent their children to the best boarding schools in the United States and Europe; possessed luxury homes replete with servants; and spent massive sums of money on cars, art, and fancy clothes.[495]

The Trujillo regime also strictly controlled the Dominican working class and labor unions. In 1951, the Trujillo Code of Labor was implemented, while the Dominican Confederation of Labor continued to be controlled by the government. The governors of each province were the president of each labor federation. Some of the early leftist labor leaders cooperated with Trujillo and became officials in the Confederation of Labor. In 1955, a congress of workers was called to proclaim Trujillo as *"Protector of the Dominican Working Class."*[496]

Trujillo also mimicked the communist world in maintaining a large stable of propagandists and lobbyists in the United States. Trujillo maintained fifty-four consulates in the United States to cement friendly ties with American business and political interests. These consulates planted stories with friendly American journalists in order to propagandize the notion that the Dominican Republic was an anti-communist republic and a vital supplier of sugar to the US market. Bernard Diederich reported that Trujillo spent over $6 million during the 1950s for the dissemination of propaganda in the United States. Dominican agents and diplomats killed dissidents within the United States. Not unsurprisingly, these brutal and bold assassination operations strained the American relationship with Trujillo.[497]

Equally sinister was Trujillo's blackmail and manipulation of American Congressmen and Senators. Such operations mirrored the efforts of the communists and Nazis in gaining support amongst influential Americans. Even when the Trujillo regime moved to the Left by 1960, the same anti-communist politicians blamed the United States for forcing the Dominican Republic to gravitate towards the Soviets and Cubans. The Dominican Consul in New York Arturo Espaillat reported that *"An ordinary run-of-the-mill Representative would cost $5,000 or less. A few House Committee Chairmen could be had for about three times that much, depending on the committee. Senators came higher, of course."* Prominent American citizens were secretly photographed with Dominican prostitutes during all-expense-paid visits to Ciudad Trujillo.[498] Trujillo had many supporters among conservative, Southern Democratic Congressman whose districts contained large agribusiness interests. Trujillo bribed a number of these Congressmen. The Dominican Minister of the Interior General Arturo Espaillat noted that *"Many of the North American Congressmen were provided with female companionship during their visits to the Dominican Republic. Senator Ellender entered into a relationship with one of Trujillo's*

---

[494] Ibid, pages 178-181.

[495] Wiarda, Howard J. Dictatorship and Development (University of Florida Press, 1968) pages 97-101.

[496] Galindez, Jesus de. The Era of Trujillo (University of Arizona Press, 1973) pages 155-157.

[497] Hall, Michael R. Sugar and Power in the Dominican Republic: Eisenhower, Kennedy and the Trujillo (Greenwood Publishing Group, 2000) pages 85-86.

[498] Ibid, page 52.

prostitutes, who was promptly dispatched to the Dominican embassy in Washington so that she might be more accessible to the Senator."[499] Senator Allen Ellender (D-Louisiana) remarked that "*What Latin America needs is more dictators like Trujillo.*" Senator James Eastland (D-Mississippi) noted that "*I wish there was a Trujillo in every country in Central and South America.*" Congressman Harold Cooley (D-NC) was instrumental in providing Trujillo with an extra sugar quota. Cooley and family traveled to the Dominican Republic and were lodged at at the luxury Jaragua Hotel, the Boca Chica seaside resort, and the Hamaca Beach Club. All expenses were paid for by the Trujillo regime. Other pro-Trujillo Congressmen included Democratic Majority Leader John McCormack (D-Massachusetts), Don Jackson (R-California), Tom Abernathy (D-Mississippi), and Gardner Withrow (Progressive Party-Wisconsin).[500]

As the Eisenhower and Kennedy Administrations became aggravated by Trujillo's tyranny and corruption, the Benefactor commenced an open shift to the Left. This was reflected in the rhetoric of the state-controlled media and revisions in the foreign policy of the Trujillo regime. To be sure, the Trujillo dictatorship always adhered to a collectivist economic and political ideology which criticized liberal capitalism. Hence, the final to the Left was not an ideological quantum leap or a logical inconsistency for the Trujillo dictatorship. In fact, one could argue that such a shift to a pro-Cuban, pro-Soviet, and anti-American position was consistent with the political culture and domestic collectivism of the Trujillo dictatorship. In response, the Eisenhower Administration reduced a portion of the Dominican Republic's sugar export quota to the United States. Extremist sections of the Dominican press and radio opposed "*North American imperialists,*" "*Yankee imperialism,*" and "*United States monopolies.*"[501] The Trujillist Radio Caribe also subscribed to bulletins from the Soviet news agency TASS.[502] Radio Caribe unequivocally supported Trujillo and opposed the Catholic Church and "*Yankee imperialists.*"[503] These measures reflected the ever-present anti-US elements of the ruling Dominican Party.[504] Anti-American demonstrations also became ever-present in the Dominican political scene. In May 1960, anti-US Dominican demonstrators carried signs condemning "*Yankee racial discrimination*" and "*The interventionist conduct of Ambassador Joseph Farland-Former FBI Agent.*"[505]

The radical anti-American elements of the Dominican state-owned press actually claimed that Trujillo represented one of the first outposts of Marxist-style socialism in Latin America. The Dominican radio claimed that Trujillismo was "*the vanguard of Socialism.*" The newspaper Radio Caribe stated: "*Today for the first time on the American continent and thanks to the Cuban revolution of Fidel Castro, the day of the workers, is being celebrated in Cuba with all the dimensions of the Red Square of Moscow. And this represents a big slap in the face of the*

---

[499] Ibid, page 98.

[500] Pearson, Drew. "Merry Go Round Release" March 4, 1961 Accessed From: http://dspace.wrlc.org/doc/bitstream/2041/48982/b17f02-0304zdisplay.pdf

[501] "Dominican Regime Silent" New York Times August 27, 1960 page 4.

[502] Lissner, Will. "Dominicans Calm After OAS Move" New York Times August 25, 1960 page 16.

[503] Frankel, Max. "Castro and Trujillo Call Truce, Diplomats in Caribbean Believe" New York Times January 5, 1961 page 13.

[504] Lissner, Will. "Dominicans Calm After OAS Move" New York Times August 25, 1960 page 16.

[505] "US May Replace Dominican Envoy" New York Times May 25, 1960 page 7.

Yankees who had never wanted to allow any movement directed toward the realization of popular aspirations. All this is old in the Dominican Republic. When the Socialist movement began taking on strength in the Soviet Union placing the people's interest above that of privileged minorities, imperialism and colonialism, in this nation of the Caribbean, in this proud and dignified Dominican Republic, a system of government devoted to vindication of national life, to protection of the worker and peasant was already in full swing. The great social revolution which lifted the Republic from disorder and poverty had already started because under the motto of social dignity which this day of the worker represents in the most advanced nations of the world, the doctrine of the Trujjillismo had already been instituted."[506]

Santo Domingo started to forge a concrete political, economic, and military relationship with the Soviet Union, Cuba, and possibly East Germany. In August 1960, two Soviet trade representatives visited the Dominican Republic to sell industrial goods and raw materials. Some of Trujillo's more anti-American advisers suggested that the government negotiate with these Soviet representatives.[507] Dominican Col. John Abbes Garcia visited the USSR and Czechoslovakia in late 1960 to solicit communist bloc support for Trujillo.[508] In late 1960, Cuban and Dominican officials met in eastern Cuba; the Dominican side consisted of John Abbes, former intelligence chief for Trujillo and General Arturo Espaillat.[509] In the wake of these overtures to Cuba, Ernesto *"Che"* Guevara stated that Trujillo was *"now our friend."*[510] In January 1961, 25 East German missile experts were reportedly stationed in the Dominican Republic. They allegedly worked with Dominican military officers on guided missile tests.[511] In that year, pro-American, anti-communist military officers overthrew Trujillo. However, the Dominican Republic's experience with free government and markets were shaky during the early and mid-1960s.

Haiti Under Presidents Francois and Jean-Claude Duvalier (1957-1986)

Haiti was long a country that was animated by a fierce nationalism against the French which culminated in an anti-colonial revolution. Independent Haiti was also characterized by a class-and-racial based division between the black masses and the mulatto elites. However, by the 1940s, there were political efforts to reverse this trend. By 1957, Dr. Francois Duvalier ran for the office of president of Haiti on a platform which allegedly sought to empower the oppressed black workers and peasants in Haiti. During his campaign, Duvalier and his supporters blended pseudo-Marxist rhetoric with racialism. In the 1956-1957 election campaigns, Duvalier called for the improvement of the conditions of the *"exploited masses"* and lambasted the pro-American President Paul Magloire as a regime of *"reactionary conservatism"* and *"a system of slavery."*

---

[506] Newman, Joseph. "Pact ties Castro, Trujillo in drive to save Socialism" Globe Gazette Mason City Iowa May 31, 1961 page 17.

[507] Lissner, Will. "Dominicans Calm After OAS Move" New York Times August 25, 1960 page 16.

[508] Szulc, Tad. "A Dominican Bid to Moscow Seen" New York Times May 15, 1961 page 13.

[509] Frankel, Max. "Castro and Trujillo Call Truce, Diplomats in Caribbean Believe" New York Times January 5, 1961 page 13.

[510] Kihss, Peter. "News Held a Day" New York Times June 1, 1961 page 1.

[511] "German Reds Said to Aid Dominicans on Missiles" New York Times January 20, 1961 page 8.

Duvalier attacked "*false negative liberalism*" and supported "*economic democracy.*" He also assailed the "*forces of money*" and "*financial interests*" in Haiti. Duvalier also stated: "*It is necessary to march now towards the suppression of economic inequalities.*"[512]

After Duvalier was elected in 1957, Haiti became a totalitarian dictatorship. He built a secret police force officially known as the Volunteers for National Security (VSN) and nicknamed the *Tontons Macoute*. All political parties were suppressed and Duvalier became President-for-Life in 1964. Duvalier's propagandists portrayed his dictatorship as a progressive, nationalist, and revolutionary alternative. Leftist-sounding language was also used to portray the Duvalier government as favorable to the interests of the working masses and opposed to the capitalists. Antoine Herard, the director general of the Haiti Tourist Office in Chicago noted: "*Duvalier is not a dictator. He is a man who is working for the true people and has against him all those who used to exploit the people since independence. The French priests and the rightists keep the people down and exploited. That is why they are against the people. You have good democracy and bad democracy. You have a dictatorship in the United States. You are not free in the United States. You have the dictatorship of Wall Street, that is a kind of dictatorship. You have a dictatorship of the press trusts. You have a dictatorship of the labor unions because I am in Chicago and I know.*" He later compared the VSN with the FBI.[513]

As of 1963, Duvalier's government denounced "*Yankee capitalists*" and "*North American imperialists.*" Duvalierist Raymond Moise noted that "*When it becomes necessary to turn the cannons against the capitalists and imperialists we will be the second to do it.*" There were concerns amongst the Haitian middle and upper classes that the government would proclaim a "*Socialist Republic of Haiti.*"[514] In 1963, Duvalier staged May Day demonstrations where his minions carried signs which demanded "*social justice.*" Duvalier himself lambasted "*the foreigners and anti-nationalists.*" Broadcasts extolled the "*Duvalier revolution.*"[515] In 1963, Haitian Cabinet Ministers indulged in an anti-US campaign which also opposed the upper classes. The United States and the Haitian upper classes were blamed for the nation's woes and threatened with the bloody prospect of slaughter by machete-wielding Haitians.[516] Duvalierist Hermann Louis Charles noted that the Duvalier revolution favored "*a better distribution of national wealth.*" The Duvalier regime also blatantly supported the repression of opposition and clung to social revolutionary views. Duvalier himself observed that his government was revolutionary and that "*revolutions must be total, radical, inflexible.*" In 1967, Duvalierist Gerard Daumec created the Breviaire d'une revolution which was a Maoist-style collection of Duvalier's sayings. Jean M. Fourcand in 1964 authored the Catechisme de la revolution which stated that one of its so-called "*sacraments*" was "*instituted by the people's army, the civil militia, and the Haitian people…to crush with grenades, mortars, Mausers, bazookas, flame throwers, and other weapons enemies of the state.*"[517]

---

[512] Nicholls, David. From Dessalines to Duvalier: Race Colour, and National Independence in Haiti (Rutgers University Press, 1996) pages 210-211.

[513] Dubois, Jules. "Haitian Communists Aided by Dictator" Hartford Courant February 5, 1962 page 1.

[514] Hendrin, Hal. "Nobody Wants Duvalier's Republic" Miami News May 9, 1963

[515] Szulc, Tad. "Haiti Marks May Day" New York Times May 2, 1963 page 12.

[516] "Duvalier Men Score US in Haiti Rallies" New York Times April 24, 1963 page 9.

[517] Nicholls, David. From Dessalines to Duvalier: Race Colour, and National Independence in Haiti (Rutgers University Press, 1996) pages 236 and 233.

After Francois Duvalier died in 1971, his son Jean-Claude became the new President-for-Life of Haiti. Although he tried to give a *"reformist"* veneer to his government, Jean-Claude continued the basic authoritarianism that was always the hallmark of Duvalier family rule. The pseudo-leftist and populist rhetoric also continued to emanate from the Palace. In January 1975, Duvalier noted that the *"economic revolution I have promised to carry out even at the risk of my life continues irreversibly."* He issued a hypocritical warning to *"bourgeois and middle class Haitians"* that *"we must live as citizens of the Third World; that is we must house, feed, dress, and move ourselves with austerity without ostentation and undue luxuries which constitutes an affront to the misery of the poor who make up the majority of the country."*[518] In April 1977, Duvalier proclaimed the need for changes in *"old and obsolete Haitian structures."*[519] In April 1977, Duvalier noted that oppositionists who fled to the United States were *"alienated from national life"* and noted that monopolies in areas such as energy and telecommunications were converted to state enterprises.[520] Duvalier also announced the imposition of price controls and a *"decisive"* turn for his *"economic revolution"* in the year 1979. He reaffirmed the continuation of the *"liberation process within the limits of peace and security for all."*[521]

Even anti-Duvalier priests were painted as corrupt and capitalistic. In March 1983, the Duvalier newspaper <u>Le Nouveau Monde</u> criticized *"speculating priests"* and *"some members of the Haitian clergy"* and their benefits which served *"to pay for costly vehicles, trips abroad every three months, or simply to keep expensive mistresses."* The newspaper praised the Pope for pointing out that Duvalier wanted to *"establish a society based on political liberty, social justice, and prosperity."*[522]

By the early 1960s, concerns were expressed by Haitian and American anti-communists that Duvalier would turn towards Moscow and Havana. During the Kennedy Administration, Duvalier's human rights violations, totalitarianism, anti-US propaganda, and corruption were criticized. Indications at the time pointed to the possibility that Duvalier would allow communist Cuba to establish military bases in Haiti. In 1963, the Dominican Republic charged that Duvalier offered Castro military bases in Haiti.[523]

Haitian anti-communists and American journalists also reported that Duvalier's dictatorship retained the services of domestic and French Communists. Former President Magloire charged that Duvalier *"knows his rule is doomed to destruction and as a last ditch stand will declare the Haitian Republic a Socialist State on either May 15 or May 22. Duvalier and the misguided intellectuals in his cabinet have no idea that by proclaiming Haiti a socialist country that they are taking the first step in the direction of communism much in the same manner as Cuba did...some time ago a paper which will be used as the framework of Haiti's new socialist government."* The move towards a Haitian Socialist State was prepared by Duvalierist/Communist officials such as Jacques Fourcand, Minister of Welfare; Dr. Herve Boyer Minister of Finance; and Clovis Desinor Minister of Commerce.[524]

---

[518] "Duvalier Calls on Haitians to Practice Austerity" <u>Paris AFP</u> January 3, 1975

[519] "Duvalier Seeks Changes in Haiti's Obsolete Structures" <u>Paris AFP</u> April 7, 1977

[520] "Duvalier in Address Scores Foreign Intervention" <u>Paris AFP</u> April 23, 1977

[521] "President Duvalier Announces More Dynamic Foreign Policy" <u>Paris AFP</u> January 3, 1979

[522] "Government Newspaper Criticizes Pope, Clergy" <u>Paris AFP</u> March 11, 1983

[523] "Says Duvalier Dickering For A Deal With Castro" <u>The Salina Journal</u> April 30, 1963 page 1.

[524] "Haiti Seen in Red Bloc" <u>New York Times</u> May 13, 1963 page 10.

American Ambassador to Haiti Raymond Thurston reported that *"Duvalier has Reds or pro-Reds in high government positions and some of them have Communist records. I do not believe Duvalier himself is a Communist, but he finds it useful to throw them in our face, and so far be seems so have them under control. We also know the Communists here maintain links with Castro's Communists in Cuba and with the international Communist base in Mexico. Although we do not feel all this represents an immediate threat, the longer it goes on the better is the chance the Commies will get control. And when Duvalier finally goes — by whatever means— there could be a Castro type takeover from the top."* Some reports indicated that there were as many as 30 known communists in key government positions, many of them trained in Moscow. At least two of these communists were in Duvalier's cabinet. They included Finance Minister Herve Boyer and Information Minister Paul Blanchet. Boyer was expelled from France in 1953 for Communist activity. Ambassador Thurston also noted that active Communists also agitated amongst university youths and some industrial labor unions.[525] French Communist Party members who served in prominent government positions during the Duvalier regime included Paul Blanchet, Secretary of Information and Coordination; Herve Boyer Minister of Finance, and Roger Gaillard.[526]

During the early 1960s, trade relations between the Communist Bloc and Haiti were established in an effort to spite the United States and on the account of the mutual ideological anti-Americanism of the Reds and Duvalier. In 1963, it was reported that Duvalier maintained relations with communist countries. During this period, the communist bloc exported to textiles to Haiti. Cultural and economic relations with Poland were solidified in the early 1960s.[527]

By the Johnson and Nixon Administrations, the relationship between Haiti and the United States was repaired. However, the Duvalier regime did continue to adhere to an anti-Western political culture and sought to maintain some credibility in the Non-Aligned Movement. In January 1979, Duvalier announced a *"policy of more dynamic opening toward the Third World countries."*[528] In February 1976, Duvalier refused to support the anti-Soviet/anti-Cuban UNITA forces in Angola. Furthermore, President Duvalier felt that *"An African solution should be found to the Angola problem and the big powers should withdraw from that battleground."*[529] In December 1976, the dean of Cuban journalists Elio Constantin reported a possible thaw in Cuban-Haitian relations. At that time, Radio Havana suppressed criticisms of Duvalier. Duvalier also suppressed the entry of anti-Castro elements from Cuba.[530]

Similar to their communist rivals, the Duvalierist state sought to kill oppositionists abroad and drum up support from Haitian exiles. In 1965, Haitian Consul General Rudolpho Baboun returned to Haiti in order to avoid facing Federal charges in Miami for illegally exporting arms to Haiti. Paul was given funds and full power by Minister of the Interior Roger Lafontant to wreck the anti-Duvalier opposition in Florida. As of April 1984, Haiti's top diplomat in Florida Alexandre Paul masterminded a terror and intimidation campaign against

---

[525] Boyce, Richard. "Duvalier Rule in Haiti Gives Reds a Chance" The Albuquerque Tribune October 6, 1962 page A4.

[526] Dubois, Jules. "Haitian Communists Aided by Dictator" Hartford Courant February 5, 1962 page 1.

[527] "Haitian Economy Weathers Crisis" New York Times July 15, 1963 page 5.

[528] "President Duvalier Announces More Dynamic Foreign Policy" Paris AFP January 3, 1979

[529] "Duvalier Refuses to Support Angola's UNITA" Paris AFP February 25, 1976

[530] "Relations with Cuba May Be Thawing Out, Says Observers" Paris AFP December 13, 1976

Haitian exiles. Paul established a cell of the *Tontons Macoutes* in Miami. Paul's agents firebombed the Haitian-American Community Association of Dade (HACAD) in 1982. Other *Macoute* agents attacked and firebombed Haitian-American businessmen and opposition radio stations in Florida.[531]

The Duvalier regime also utilized Soviet-style Potemkin village tours to spruce up the dictatorship's image within international public opinion. Businessman Lucien Rigaud was imprisoned by the *Ton Ton Macoutes*. The International Red Cross visited the National Penitentiary where Rigaud was imprisoned. It was purposely cleaned up where meal tables were decorated with tablecloths and flowers. Sheets were provided to the beds and the unhealthy political prisoners were hidden, while healthy ones were displayed to the Red Cross. Once the Red Cross left, the tablecloths, flowers, and sheets were removed and the sick political prisoners were taken out of hiding.[532]

The Haitian workforce was brutally controlled by the Duvalierist state. Despite its pro-worker and pseudo-leftist rhetoric, independent labor organizations were brutally suppressed and banned by law. The 1961 Labor Code of Haiti supported "*harmonization of labor and capital*" and "*social justice*," while defining work as "*manual*" and "*mental.*" The Labor Code was to be "*the true instrument of liberation of the worker and consolidation of democracy in Haiti.*"[533] In reality, the Labor Code controlled the Haitian working and peasant classes.

The few remaining labor unions in Haiti were arms of the Duvalierist state. The *Association des Chauffeurs Guides d'Haiti* (ACGH) was a pro-Duvalierist labor union in Haiti. It was established under the control of President Francois Duvalier, who provided the owner-driver members a monopoly of transport for all tourists. The ACGH lost this monopoly under policies enacted by the Ministry of Tourism in 1978. The organization owned its own garage and ran a school for 400 children near its headquarters.[534] Their personnel gathered around the journal Panorama.[535]

The Duvalier regime also terrorized and controlled the private sector in Haiti, along with increasing the number of state agencies and enterprises. Greed and ideology appeared to be the chief motivations for the intrusions of the Duvalier regime into the Haitian economy. The Duvalier regime was suspicious of the largely mulatto business and professional elites from the position of class and racial basis. Furthermore, Duvalier and his cronies sought to use the state's resources and agencies to line their own pockets. Naturally, the business community largely opposed Duvalier. The *Macoutes* forced businesses to remain open during labor strikes. The Duvalier regime oppressed the mulatto elites, while favoring the Syrian-Lebanese business community.[536]

---

[531] Wallace, Richard. "Haitian Consul Apparently Ousted From Post" Miami Herald February 19, 1986

[532] Rawls, Wendell. "Baby Doc's Haitian Terror" New York Times May 14, 1978 page SM4.

[533] Duvalier, Francois. "Code Du Travail Francois Duvalier" Accessed From: http://www.archive.org/stream/codedutravailfra00hait/codedutravailfra00hait_djvu.txt

[534] Gerald Michael Greenfield and Sheldon L. Maram. Latin American Labor Organizations (Greenwood Press, 1987) pages 452-453.

[535] Nicholls, David. From Dessalines to Duvalier: Race Colour, and National Independence in Haiti (Rutgers University Press, 1996) pages 217-220.

[536] Ibid, pages 217-220.

Extortion of the capitalists also occurred during the Duvalier dictatorship. In 1962, Duvalier launched a program of *"economic liberation"* of Haiti where workers would contribute money and taxes raised.[537] By 1962, Duvalier formed the National Restoration Movement, which squeezed businessmen of funds that were earmarked for national development schemes. New road toll fees, excises of consumer goods, payroll taxes, and the business levy were all channeled to *"liberation bonds."*[538]

Under Dr. Francois and Jean-Claude Duvalier, the number of government-owned companies expanded and became cash cows. Starting in 1979, the Duvalierist state purchased or established five large enterprises in the following sectors: soybean oil, wheat flour, sugar (two firms) and cement. None of these ever became profitable from a business or national point of view, but all yielded big profits for the Duvaliers and their cronies. The Duvalier regime also siphoned funds from the Finance Ministry, the tobacco monopoly, the state lottery, the government gambling commission, the wheat flour company, the telephone company, the electricity company, the cement plant, the government credit bank, and the tax administration.[539] The book Haiti: A Country Study noted that *"Despite irregularities in the allocation of funds under the François Duvalier regime, government revenues traditionally equaled, or surpassed, budget outlays, technically yielding balanced budgets. Jean-Claude Duvalier's unprecedented intervention in the economy in the 1980s, however, broke this tradition. The public sector under Duvalier established, or expanded, its ownership of an international fishing fleet, a flour mill, a cement company, a vegetable-oil processing plant, and two sugar factories. Duvalierist officials based these investment decisions primarily on the amount of personal profit that would accrue to themselves, to Duvalier, and to the rest of his coterie."* The state-owned enterprises were poorly managed and racked up deficits of 10.6% of the GDP. The *Regie du Tabac* (Tobacco Administration) was an important source of government revenue for the Duvaliers.[540] By 1986, Duvalier was overthrown and Haiti was ruled by a succession of military and civilian leaders, along with even a quasi-Marxist government.

Paraguay Under General Alfredo Stroessner (1954-1989)

In 1954, General Alfredo Stroessner seized power in a *coup d'état* and ruled as a highly authoritarian, quasi-fascist manner. Stroessner's dictatorship was strongly anti-communist, collectivist, and nationalist. Stroessner ruled through the anti-liberal, collectivist-oriented Colorado Party. It aligned itself with the United States during much of the Cold War and was one of the handfuls of anti-communist dictatorships which maintained few ties with any Red state. The only exception was Paraguay's diplomatic relations with Yugoslavia, which was depicted by Stroessner and the Colorado Party as an independent and pragmatic communist country.[541] It was possible that the relationship between communist Yugoslavia and quasi-fascist Paraguay covered issues such as covert trade or the exchange of leftists jailed by Stroessner. Furthermore, it was

---

[537] "Duvalier Launches Development Drive" New York Times January 11, 1962 page 14.

[538] Eder, Richard. "Haiti Is Defiant in Face of Reduction in U.S. Aid" New York Times October 2, 1962 page 17.

[539] Blomqvist, H.C. The Distorted Economy (Palgrave 2002) page 241.

[540] "Haiti: A Country Study" Accessed From: http://memory.loc.gov/cgi-bin/query/D?cstdy:2:./temp/~frd_0IsX::

[541] Geldenhuys, Deon. Isolated States (Cambridge University Press, 1990) page 80.

also possible that the Yugoslav connection could have been used by Asunscion to serve as an intermediary in covert relations with a nation like Cuba. In 1989, the Stroessner regime was overthrown and the path to freer forms of government was charted.

One of the modern forerunners of Stroessner's dictatorship was the regime of Higinio Morinigo. Morinigo clearly believed in the fascist variant of totalitarianism. In December 1940, Morinigo noted over state radio that "*We shall labour for the unity of the Paraguayan nation...The system of government by parties should be replaced by government for the nation...Hence we reject Liberalism, the product of the 19th Century...We stand, above all, for the intervention of the state in the economic field and especially in the relations of capital and labor.*" He endorsed a state based on the principles of "*Order, Hierarchy, and Discipline.*" All concessions and public services were to be owned by the state, while the government was to be free of any domination by foreign capital. The workers were also to be freed of exploitation by domestic capitalists, while class conflict was to be suppressed. Dissidents were interned in a penal colony on the island of Pena Hermosa.[542] Army officers swore an oath of loyalty to President Morinigo which proclaimed in part that "*the system of liberal individualism has been the principal cause of political anarchy, economic misery, and material backwardness of the nation.*" Professional politicians were repressed by the state, since they allegedly posed a threat to the New Nationalist Revolutionary Order.[543]

Morinigo tilted towards the Axis Powers. He refused to crack down on Nazi German activities in his country. Morinigo tolerated pro-Axis officers within the Army, refused to deport German Nazi nationals, and allowed local branches of Axis-owned companies to conduct business with the Paraguayan government. Early in the war, Vichy France maintained a military mission in Paraguay. The Paraguayan officer class viewed National Socialism and Fascism as viable alternative to weak liberal governments and economics and blamed Western imperialists for the nation's problems. The pro-government newspapers and radio were flooded with pro-Axis opinions.[544]

In the postwar years, the Colorado Party assumed the mantle of supporting collectivistic nationalism, while the Liberal Party supported classical individualism and limited government. The Liberal Party in Paraguay favored individualism and strong property rights, while the Colorado Party favored state control over people and property. At the 1947 Convention of the Colorados, Natalico Gonzalez remarked that he believed that "*The state, servant of the free man, should intervene in the social and economic life of the nation in order to prevent abuses by private interests and to promote the general welfare but without prejudice to anyone.*"[545]

Ironically for an anti-communist regime, the Colorados and Stroessner praised the most socialistic or even communist-oriented leaders in Paraguay's history. For example, in 1962, Stroessner praised socialistic and dictatorial rulers such as Jose Gaspar Rodriguez de Francia, Carlos Antonio Lopez, and Marshal Solano. Meanwhile, the Paraguayan strongman denounced

---

[542] " Totalitarian Ideas Taking shape In Paraguay" The Singapore Free Press and Mercantile Advertiser May 6, 1941 page 4.

[543] Loveman, Brian. For La Patria: Politics and the Armed Forces in Latin America (Rowman & Littlefield Publishers, 2004) page 113.

[544] Frank O. Mora and Jerry Wilson Cooney. Paraguay and the United States: Distant Allies (University of Georgia Press, 2010) pages 114 and 102-103.

[545] Lewis, Paul H. Paraguay Under Stroessner (University of North Carolina Press, 1980) page 148.

Liberal Capt. Benigno Ferreira, who was referred to as "*that Legionnaire sergeant who destroyed our country.*"[546] Throughout his rule, Stroessner criticized the Liberals, Communists, and the foreign press while enumerating on his achievements in public works. Stroessner continued to praise the socialistic and dictatorial leaders in Paraguay's past, such as Carlos Antonio Lopez, Marshal Solano Lopez, and General Bernardino Caballero.[547]

Despite leftist propaganda, the Stroessner dictatorship refused to ideologically adhere to free market economics. The economic philosophy of the Stroessner regime was outlined in various editorials in the Colorado Party journal Patria. The regime supported "*economic liberty*" as opposed to "*orthodox economic liberalism.*" The concept of "*economic liberty*" mandated that the private sector had to serve the interests of the nation above selfish desire. The private sector was encouraged to organize associations and cooperate with the government in constructing unselfish policies for national benefit. Intervention would be necessary when the private sector became too selfish, greedy, and exploitative, or failing to develop the nation as deemed by the state. In the eyes of Stroessner and the Colorado Party's ideologists, "*orthodox economic liberalism*" meant the selfish exploitation of the nation's resources and people, disregard for national and social objectives, and conservative rugged individualism ("*egoisme*").[548]

The regime also adhered to a state-led development strategy which supported state capitalism and corporative labor-capital relations. These policies sought to modernize Paraguay and fight the evils of communism and laissez-faire liberalism. In June 1974, Stroessner noted that "*I am glad to repeat that my government of which the powerful Colorado Party is an integral part is harmoniously encouraging economic activity in the country in which capital and labor, the businessmen, the worker, the agricultural producer join in the great task of building a vigorous nation.*"[549] In May 1977, Stroessner noted that "*Development will be promoted on the basis of overall programs based on principles of social justice aimed at securing a life compatible with human dignity for everyone.*"[550] In December 1980, President Stroessner remarked that his government would always "*support the private initiatives which aim at the common good.*"[551]

While businessmen appreciated the government's support for private enterprise and opposition to domestic communism, they disliked the collectivist rhetoric and massive state interventions into the economy. Businessmen were critical of government economic planning, the expansion of the size and scope of the government bureaucracy, and political favoritism for selected private companies.[552] Stroessner established public utilities, ports, merchant marine, railroads, and three airline companies. Many of these enterprises were governed by military officers. Two other profitable state enterprises were the Paraguayan Alcohol Administration and the Paraguayan Meat Corporation. The National Development Bank provided money to people

---

[546] Ibid, page 147.

[547] Ibid, page 106.

[548] Pincus, Joseph. The Economy of Paraguay (Praeger, 1968) pages 14-15.

[549] "President Stroessner Addresses Businessmen on Development" Ascunsion Domestic Service June 11, 1974

[550] "Stroessner Interviewed on National Economic Plan" Ascunsion ABC Color May 13, 1977

[551] "President Stroessner Addresses Nation at Year's End" Asuncion Domestic Service December 24, 1980

[552] Lewis, Paul H. Paraguay Under Stroessner (University of North Carolina Press, 1980) page 156.

in good standing with the Colorado Party. Other companies established by the state included steel, cement, ship repair, furniture making, quarrying, lumber, and the raising of cattle.[553] Much foreign debt was owed because of these state owned enterprises, such as INC (national cement company) and ACEPAR (the national steel company). Gifts of state-owned land were doled out to Stroessner's cronies.[554] Stroessner himself played a large role in regulating Paraguay's economy and promoting investments and exports. The government controlled prices, wages, banking, and insurance in Paraguay. Certain farm products such as sugar and meat received price supports, subsidies, and market quotas from the Stroessner regime.[555]

While Paraguay maintained close relations with the United States, there was an anti-American element within the Colorado Party. Colorado Party orthodoxy preached that the Paraguayan Liberals were the tools of unnamed colonialists and foreign interests. Naturally, these outside colonialists and imperialists were clearly the United States and its liberal, constitutional ideology. Under the Carter and Reagan Administrations, Stroessner's authoritarianism and human rights violations were the targets of American criticism. Such condemnations only served to fan the flames of Colorado Party anti-Americanism. As of July 1978, approximately 300 students from the official Paraguay University Federation demonstrated outside the American Embassy. This demonstration was officially approved by the ruling Colorado Party. The demonstrators shouted and carried signs that stated "*Paraguay Si, Gringos No*" and "*Yankees Go Home.*"[556]

While Stroessner predicted an improved relationship with the United States after Reagan became president, the opposite occurred. The American Embassy maintained relations with Paraguayan dissidents, which enraged the Stroessner regime. The United States was denounced by Stroessner and his Colorado Party as an imperialist power that intervened in Paraguay's internal affairs. Furthermore, Stroessner and his colleagues also mimicked the Left in painting the United States as a land of poverty, crime, and unemployment. In May 1985, Paraguay condemned the Reagan Administration's characterization of Stroessner's regime as that of "*entrenched military rule.*" The Colorado Party's newspaper Patria noted that this assertion was a "*rude mistake*" and claimed that Reagan was misinformed by "*his advisers in the Department of State, which has connections reaching as far as the U.S. Embassy in Asuncion.*"[557] In September 1987, the Paraguayan Foreign Relations Subsecretary Rodney Elpidio Acevedo stated that the United States displayed "*imperial arrogance*" in its relations with Stroessner.[558] President Stroessner in April 1986 noted that "*We do not have masses of very poor people begging for help to subsist. We do not have an alarming unemployment rate or the heavy burden of illiteracy. We do not have the dramas of some countries whose youth have surrendered to drugs and crime or the poison of extremist ideologies.*"[559] In January 1988, the Voz del Coloradismo noted that "*...during the sad days of the traitorous Liberalism that sold out the country we were not our own masters...Our economy and even the sacred land of our heroes was*

---

[553]Ibid, page 131.

[554] Roett, Riordan. Paraguay: The Personalist Legacy (Westview Press, 1991) pages 68-76.

[555] Ibid, pages 68-76.

[556] The Associated Press July 12, 1978

[557] "Stroessner Objects To Reagan's Description" The Associated Press May 9, 1985

[558] Seiferheld, Alfredo. "Government Says U.S. Shows 'Imperial Arrogance;' Ambassador 'Laughingstock'" The Associated Press September 24, 1987

[559] "Stroessner Addresses Opening of Congress" Asuncion Domestic Service April 1, 1986

mortgaged, rented, or sold to foreigners. " The Voz noted that *"The Liberals have been and continue to be pathetic beggars of colonialist and imperialist alms from their occasional masters."* The Voz also noted that the US Ambassador to Paraguay was *"the ambassador of hippies and drug traffickers…the ambassador from the country of free and accepted homosexuality, the ambassador from a country where his countrymen die from exposure to the cold and even hunger continues to consider Paraguay as a colony…"* The Voz also complained about the *"arrogant ambassador from an arrogant country."*[560]

Venezuela Under General Marcos Perez-Jimenez (1952-1958)

From 1952 to 1958, General Marcos Perez-Jimenez ruled Venezuela as an iron-fisted authoritarian who maintained tight political controls. He proclaimed a *"new Venezuelan nationalism"* which engendered a *"new national conscience."*[561] The Perez Jimenez regime also formulated the Nuevo Nacional Ideal (New National Ideal) as the ideology of the dictatorship. It was initially created by Laureano Vallenilla Lanz. His father was the theoretician of Democratic Caeserism, which postulated that Latin America was not ready for liberal democracy. Instead, Vallenilla Lanz and his father believed that Venezuela needed to adopt a paternalistic authoritarianism.[562] Perez-Jimenez confirmed his desire to affect major changes in Venezuela when he told Vallenilla *"I want to be a true revolutionary, the man who carries civilization to the entire nation. It does not matter if they call me a tyrant tomorrow, if a great work remains to defend me."*[563] This translated into ambitious state investment and even interventions into the Venezuelan economy. The regime undertook public works projects, steel works, and petrochemical plant, and housing for the working class.[564] The Social Assistance Fund was expanded and provided favorable mortgage and loans for the army personnel.[565]

One historian commented that Perez Jimenez's New National Ideal *"served as an ideological underpinning for the ambitious plans of state-run industry which was justified on the basis of national security imperatives."* Such developments included state-owned railroads, steel mills, petrochemical plants, and industrial development in Guayana. The development of a state-owned sector by the Perez-Jimenez dictatorship actually split the domestic Communist Party (PCV). PCV leader Salvador de la Plaza posed the following question to his comrades: why would a supposedly right-wing leader undertake such radical measures? Furthermore, De la Plaza opposed his comrades' disparagement of Perez Jimenez's plans for state-run industrial projects.[566]

---

[560] "Editorial on US Ambassador's Interference" Ascunsion Domestic Service January 21, 1988

[561] Kolb, Glen L. Democracy and Dictatorship in Venezuela (Connecticut College, 1974) page 152.

[562] Burggraaff, Winfield J. The Venezuelan Armed Forces in Politics (University of Missouri Press, 1972) pages 130-133.

[563] Ibid, pages 130-133.

[564] Ibid, pages 130-133.

[565] Ibid, pages 130-133.

[566] Ellner, Steve. "Venezuelan Revisionist Political History, 1908-1958: New Motives and Criteria for Analyzing the Past" Latin American Research Review Volume 30, Number 2 (1995), pages 106-107.

Private business in Venezuela also occasionally criticized the corruption and excessive state interventionism of the Perez-Jimenez dictatorship. In the Eighth Assembly of Fedecamaras (1954), the Chamber of Industrialists brought up the extent of state interventionism in the economy. They opined that the government agencies which carried out industrial and commercial duties would be efficiently handled by representatives of the private sector. The private sector was also uneasy of the prospect of a state-owned steel industry in 1952.[567]

Remarkably, the Perez-Jimenez regime also employed communists within his administration. The Perez-Jimenez regime employed known communists as puppet labor union leaders, police, National Security (SN) intelligence officers, and organizers for the regime's official party, known as the FEI.[568]

Perez Jimenez wanted to create a pliable national labor confederation to control and propagandize the working class. In 1952, a First National Convention of Independent Unions was held under the supervision of the Ministry of Interior. The outcome was the creation of MOSIT. MOSIT was headed by an ex-communist named Rafael Garcia. A headquarters for the MOSIT and Trade Union Houses were built by the state. In 1955, MOSIT became the National Confederation of Workers and became an affiliate of Peron's Latin America trade union federation ATLAS.[569] MOSIT also maintained SN officers in disguise. Furthermore, the hands of the Perez-Jimenez regime reached into the operations of the multinational corporations that invested in Venezuela. The regime and MOSIT negotiated with the American oil companies for workers' contracts.[570] MOSIT received support from the Ministry of Labor during collective bargaining agreements. MOSIT head Rafael Garcia insisted that the Perez Jimenez regime was pro-worker. Garcia cited the creation of the *Casa Sindical*, housing projects, and economic development plans as evidence of Perez-Jimenez's pro-labor disposition.[571]

Perez-Jimenez also embarked on a public relations (PR) campaign to attract further American investment into Venezuela and to increase the favorable international view of his dictatorship. In the summer of 1953, Perez Jimenez ordered Venezuelan consuls in the United States to attract foreign investment. In 1953 and 1954, many American businessmen, tourists, and journalists returned to the United States with glowing tales of Perez Jimenez's rule. They met with Venezuelan government officials, wealthy businessmen, and bankers who regaled the American visitors with tales of *"efficiency, order, and progress."* The American visitors were dazzled by the shops bulging with imported goods, Cadillacs, luxury buildings, and the charm of officials.[572] By 1958, the Perez Jimenez regime was overthrown and Venezuela experienced a transition to social democracy, which lasted until 1999.

---

[567] Sonntag, Heinz R. "The State and Industrialization in Venezuela" Latin American Perspectives Autumn, 1985 pages 92-93.

[568] Alexander, Robert Jackson. Romulo Betancourt and the Transformation of Venezuela (Transaction Books 1982) page 346.

[569] Alexander, Robert J. The Venezuelan Democratic Revolution (Rutgers University Press, 1964) page 46.

[570] Kolb, Glen L. Democracy and Dictatorship in Venezuela (Connecticut College, 1974) pages 129-132.

[571] Alexander, Robert Jackson. Romulo Betancourt and the Transformation of Venezuela (Transaction Books 1982) pages 337-338.

[572] Kolb, Glen L. Democracy and Dictatorship in Venezuela (Connecticut College, 1974) pages 129-132.

Cuba Under Sgt. Fulgencio Batista

Another bête noire of the American progressive Left was Sgt. Fulgencio Batista, who was the authoritarian Cuban President during much of the 1930s and 1950s. Much of the pro-Castro Left, the American Communists, anti-communist liberals, and New Leftists viewed Batista as an autocratic ruler that was the mere puppet of domestic oligarchs, American multinational companies, and criminal racketeers. While Batista was ideologically hostile to communism and was betrayed by the Eisenhower Administration, the former Cuban dictator did adhere to a collectivist ideology out of a sincere desire to "*reform*" his country and to foster economic development. Heavy state controls and participation also allowed Batista and his political allies to use Cuba as their personal piggy bank in various corruption schemes. Batista promised under the slogan "*peace, prosperity, and employment*" as a "*democratic dictator*" as he called himself. Batista sought to win the support of middle and working class Cubans, the armed forces, the American government, and multinational corporations.[573]

Batista's speeches and printed propaganda confirmed the Cuban President's populist and corporative agenda. He noted that "*A constructive nationalism requires the elimination of illiteracy, healing the moral wounds of social inequality, and provision for the basic physical and educational needs of underprivileged children and of the aged poor.*"[574] Batista noted that "*We would have to diversify our production and through progressive industrialization of the nation, free ourselves from the dependency of foreigners.*"[575] Batista noted after his 1952 coup that he would "*revive the light of peace… and restore the government to work for all. The ambitions and selfishness (of the past regime) have upset this beautiful aspiration, but now there is hope that it may become a reality… Here I am again, with risk to my life, to stop this chaos and anarchy…We are neither here as simple, ambitious, and egotistical politicians, nor as militants who want to impose our rules and interests ahead of the people. We are for Cuba, for its progress, for justice, for liberty and our country.*"[576] Batista noted that he wanted to create an "*organic democracy*" where "*efficient and rigorous intervention by the state.*"[577]

Batista rationalized his support for a rent control law by stating that "*Government has worked for your benefit… For us, it is worthwhile, because we know we are ruling the right way, doing work by the way of the people, and in the service of the nation*" Batista also noted that he

---

[573] Skwiot, Christine. <u>The Purposes of Paradise: U.S. Tourism and Empire in Cuba and Hawaii</u> (University of Pennsylvania Press 2012) page 158.

[574] Batista, Fulgencio. <u>Growth and Decline of the Cuban Republic</u> (Devin-Adair, 1964) page 110.

[575] Ibid, page 146.

[576] McGuigan, Michael P. "Fulgencio Batista's Economic Policies, 1952 – 1958" (2012) Open Access Dissertations Paper 834 Accessed From: http://scholarlyrepository.miami.edu/oa_dissertations/834

[577] Whitney, Robert. <u>State and Revolution in Cuba: Mass Mobilization and Political Change, 1920-1940</u> (UNC Press Books, 2001) page 158.

supported *"social justice."* He reminded farmers of his land reforms in 1937 and the existing rent control laws.[578]

The Cuban government of Batista also heavily promoted the idea of the corporative state where the government would supervise the relations between capital and labor in an effort to bridge class divisions. He viewed this as part of the battle against communism. Batista remarked that *"We only ask for everybody's cooperation to consolidate our movement so that we have the essential power, only what is absolutely necessary, to govern by the will of the people, and for the sake of the people… for the progress of the people, unity of the workers, security of industry, harmony between capital and labor, thank you. Salud! Salud!"*[579] In July 1936, Batista supported *"a renovated democracy under which there should be discipline of the masses and of institutions so that we can establish a progressive state. We want to teach the masses that capital and labor both are necessary and should cooperate."*[580]

Batista noted that *"One of the most disturbed classes on the island is labor…In my opinion the rights of labor must be protected, but equal protection must be extended to capital. One cannot take rights away from either. The only equitable basis is an arrangement that will permit both to operate peacefully and with benefit to themselves and the nation. The economic situation of the island cannot improve when labor and capital are in eternal strife. We greatly need the influx of foreign capital but on the other hand no exploitation of the working classes should be permitted."* Batista noted that capitalists had the right to earn *"just"* profits. He noted that the Cuban government *"has paramount interest in balancing national wealth not in destroying it. We can neither create nor consolidate an all absorbing capitalist system nor an anarchical, unfruitful collectivism."*[581] Perhaps even more surprising to Leftists and conservative, limited government anti-communists was Batista's admissions that he represented socialism. Batista remarked that he could be described as a *"progressive Socialist"* since he divided socialism into two categories: *"one means anarchy, and the other functions under the discipline of the government."*[582]

Batista also sought to co-opt elements of organized labor in Cuba as a means of solidifying mass support for his populist and authoritarian program. Most notable was the support given by labor leaders like Eusebio Mujal to Batista's regime. Mujal noted that radical leftist and communist unionists such as Lazaro Pena wanted to control the Cuban Confederation of Labor (CTC). Mujal and his supporters felt that the communist-dominated elements of the CTC desired a *"repeat in Havana (of) a 'Bogatazo'…that an inhuman struggle might take place between the workers and the armed forces, and that seemed the best field for anti-Cuban and anti-American agitation. But he (Pena) was mistaken. Cuba found the Government headed by General Batista and the CTC in an attitude of nationalistic and revolutionary understanding and*

---

[578] McGuigan, Michael P. "Fulgencio Batista's Economic Policies, 1952 – 1958" (2012) Open Access Dissertations Paper 834 Accessed From: http://scholarlyrepository.miami.edu/oa_dissertations/834

[579] Ibid.

[580] McGillivray, Gillian. Blazing Cane: Sugar Communities, Class, and State Formation in Cuba, 1868–1959 (Duke University Press, 2009) page 232.

[581] Whitney, Robert. State and Revolution in Cuba: Mass Mobilization and Political Change, 1920-1940 (UNC Press Books, 2001) pages 128-130.

[582] Farber, Samuel. Revolution and reaction in Cuba, 1933-1960: a political sociology from Machado to Castro (Wesleyan University Press, 1976) page 81.

rapidly, without giving any time to our common enemy, Communism, our hands were clasped." Batista also established cooperation with the Sugar Workers Federation (FNTA).[583]

The Batista regime also developed a myriad of social welfare programs that actually improved life for average Cubans. He expanded the functions and scope and size of the National Corporation for Public Welfare (CNAP), which was originally formed in 1936.[584] Perhaps on the downside, Batista instituted a personal income tax, along with taxes on capital, corporate income, and real estate.[585]

Batista also established new bureaucratic agencies and enterprises during the 1950s in an effort to improve the standard of living and the industrial base in Cuba. They were also avenues for the regime and its cronies to line their pockets. In January 1955, Batista changed the name of the Economy Board (formed in 1943) to the National Economic Council (CNE) to formulate plans for the coordination and regulation of the Cuban economy to achieve high employment, production, and government revenues.[586] Law 1038 of 1953 expanded Cuban industry and acquired 39 plants with over 6,800 workers.[587] By 1958, the state-owned Agricultural and Industrial Development (BANFAIC) loaned over $146 million 148 borrowers.[588] In August 1953, the government created the National Finance Corporation which regulated the development of national wealth through public investment projects.[589] Batista developed the Bank for Social and Economic Development (BANDES) in 1954. It was used to develop tourism and industry as its stated goal.[590] Much of the money from BANDES was channeled to public works. Funds from BANDES eventually were also used to personally enrich members of the regime. Loans from BANDES and other state-owned development banks were also used by the Batista dictatorship to control private businesses. Private companies were forced to take Batista and his cronies as business partners. One nationalist-minded business executive noted "*I was never a Batistiano by heart, but due to my perhaps excessive business ambitions I must confess that I was a Batistiano by convenience.*"[591]

Michael McGuigan observed that "*To many Cubans, the FNC, FHA, BANFAIC, new public works and construction were merely symbolic, and never felt any real impact from them. Certainly the programs created new jobs, but so far they had a small impact on chronic unemployment. Real private sector economic expansion without government assistance was generally non-existent during the past two years under Batista's programs. In addition, some Cubans viewed the government development banks as only mechanisms to support crony*

---

[583] McGuigan, Michael P. "Fulgencio Batista's Economic Policies, 1952 – 1958" (2012) Open Access Dissertations Paper 834 Accessed From: http://scholarlyrepository.miami.edu/oa_dissertations/834

[584] Batista, Fulgencio. Growth and Decline of the Cuban Republic (Devin-Adair, 1964) page 110.

[585] Ibid, page 124.

[586] Ibid, page 127.

[587] Ibid.

[588] Ibid, page 145.

[589] Ibid.

[590] Skwiot, Christine. The Purposes of Paradise: U.S. Tourism and Empire in Cuba and Hawaii (University of Pennsylvania Press 2012) page 158.

[591] Houchang E. Chehabi and Juan J. Linz. Sultanistic Regimes (JHU Press, 1998) pages 124-125.

capitalism, whereby a small circle of stakeholders got rich from public funds as the majority of the population suffered in poverty. The general features of crony capitalism existed in Cuba when Batista took over in 1952. These included monopoly and quasi-monopoly economics characterized by privileged access to state-owned enterprises; favoritism in the awarding of government contracts; a distributive system at the expense of privatization expansion and free market competition; and exclusive access to credit and capital."[592]

The Batista dictatorship also utilized armed police, intelligence, and paramilitary forces to maintain order and stamp out communist subversion by the 26th of July Movement led by Fidel Castro. Some of the pro-Batista forces were outright gangs that even had leftist origins. After all, Batista maintained the image as a progressive reformer who believed in a form of socialism. The Socialist Revolutionary Movement (MSR) was led by Rolando Masferrer, who was a former Cuban Communist and fighter in the International Brigades of the Spanish Civil War. Mansferrer and other members of the MSR were communists who became stalwart Batista supporters by the 1950s.[593]

Fidel Castro and his fellow militants in the 26th of July Movement launched a war to overthrow the Batista regime in 1953. Many militants desired mere social reforms, while much of the leadership of the 26th of July Movement covertly desired a communist dictatorship that was hostile to the United States. Castro stated in a letter to confidante Celia Sanchez that *"I have sworn to myself that Americans are going to pay dearly for what they are doing. When this war is over, a much wider and bigger war will begin for me, the war I am going to wage against them. I realize that is going to be my true destiny."*[594]

The Soviets and their allies maintained very secret relations with elements of the 26th of July Movement. The worst of the accusations by the Cuban and American anti-communist communities were proven correct. According to former American Communist Nathaniel Weyl, a former close collaborator with Fidel Castro noted that *"Once, Carlos Rafael Rodriguez, an active member of the Communist party in Cuba, arrived with a dozen men loaded with money. It came to $800,000 and Fidel hugged him and shouted 'Now we're ready to win the war.'"* Reportedly, that same Cuban source informed Weyl that Raul Castro traveled to the Soviet Union and thence Red China to fight alongside Mao's Red Army during the Korean War. Raul gained practical military experience as a result of fighting alongside the PLA.

Raul Castro's units also received Soviet and Czechoslovakian-made weapons during the latter stages of the Cuban Civil War against Batista. This was confirmed by the authoritative publication Intelligence Digest. Raul also was allegedly trained at the Anti-Col (Anti-Colonialism) School for international cadres in Melnik Czechoslovakia. Raul also reportedly traveled to Moscow and met with high-level Soviet Communist Boris Ponomarev.[595]

[592] McGuigan, Michael P. "Fulgencio Batista's Economic Policies, 1952 – 1958" (2012) Open Access Dissertations Paper 834 Accessed From: http://scholarlyrepository.miami.edu/oa_dissertations/834
[593] Thomas, Hugh. Cuba: A History (Penguin UK 2013)
[594] Betancourt, Ernesto F. "Is Castro Preparing for a Gotterdammerung?" CubaNet November 9, 1999 Accessed From: http://www.cubanet.org/opi/11099902.htm
[595] Weyl, Nathaniel. Red Star Over Cuba (Devin-Adair, 1960) pages 94-95 and 141.

While in Mexico, Fidel Castro and other members of the 26th of July Movement turned to KGB contacts to procure firearms from the Soviet Union. The Soviets provided weapons to Castro's guerrillas that were absolutely untraceable, which would prevent American suspicion.[596]

The nucleus of the Cuban communist movement also proved to be Soviet assets early on. The underground of the communist Popular Socialist Party (PSP) of Cuba penetrated the Batista intelligence services and penetrated Communist Party of the USA (CPUSA) front groups in the US. Many PSP agents were also trained by the KGB. They were soon absorbed into the Castro intelligence apparatus. The Rebel Army also developed an intelligence service in the later stages of the struggle against Batista, which then became the Cuban intelligence service of Fidel Castro (G-2, later the DGI).[597]

Even open communist sources admitted by the end of the late 1950s their support for the Castro rebellion. A 1959 pamphlet of the American Communist Party wrote of the *"strong contingent of party members and sympathizers (which) belonged to the rebel forces" and the 'mass actions' in support of Castro organized by the Cuban C.P."* In April 1959, Politburo member Carlos Rafael Rodriguez bragged that *"We the Cuban Communists have done our part in the Cuban revolution to overthrow the bloody tyranny of Batista which served as the instrument of imperialistic interests and was supported by imperialism."*[598]

The leadership of the 26th of July Movement clearly saw the need to deceive the Cuban people and the Americans by hiding and even denying their communist ideology. Castro himself admitted that he lied to the West in the late 1950s and 1960, when he presented himself and the Cuban Revolution as an effort to merely restore the Cuban Constitution of 1940.

During Castro's infamous admission that he was a Marxist-Leninist in December 1961, he also noted his movement's strategy of deceiving the Cuban public: *"If, while we were on Turquino Peak (in the Sierra Maestra of Eastern Oriente Province), at a time when we were 'cautro gatos' (a Cuban idiomatic expression meaning, when we were nothing), we had said 'we are Marxist-Leninists,' it is possible that we would never have been able to descend to the lowlands from Turquino Peak…So…we called it something else…We did not present that theme. We presented others which people were able to easily understand."*[599]

Castro declared to the French Le Figaro magazine: *"The United States wanted us to make a strategic and tactical error and proclaim a doctrine as a communist movement. In fact, I was a communist…I think that a good Marxist-Leninist would not have proclaimed a socialist revolution in the conditions that existed in Cuba in 1959. I think I was a good Marxist-Leninist in not doing that, and when we did not make known our underlying beliefs. What the United States wanted was to judge, to know what we thought, and we did not want to allow ourselves to be maneuvered or manipulated by it. I think it was an excellent thing that we did not proclaim the Marxist-Leninist or socialist nature of the revolution at the time."*[600] In a 1987 book review

---

[596] Magee, J.J. Indictment: For the Murder of John F. Kennedy (AuthorHouse 2013) page 32.

[597] Blight, James G. and Welch, David A. Intelligence and the Cuban Missile Crisis (Frank Cass Publishers England 1998) pages 90-119.

[598] Weyl, Nathaniel. Red Star Over Cuba (Devin Adair 1960) page 177.

[599] "Castro Declares He Was Communist in War Times" The Galveston Daily News December 23, 1961 page 1.

[600] Mauro, Ryan. "Liberating Cuba From Communism" Accessed From: http://www.hspig.org/phpbb/viewtopic.php?f=10&t=11127&view=previous&sid=3d5b3580e55f24a8b5601aba6a997429

entitled Cuba and Its Critics, Saul Landau noted that *"Fidel Castro in 1968 explained to me that he had become a Marxist from the very time that he read the Communist Manifesto in his student days, (emphasis added) and a Leninist from the period when he read Lenin while in prison on the Isle of Pines in 1954."*[601]

In order to fend off American intervention to support Batista or a non-dictatorial anti-communist alternative, Castro had to mobilize his assets in the United States and Cuba to transmit disinformation. High level Cuban Communists and left-extremist Fidelistas purposely crafted the image of the 26th of July Movement and the Castro regime as native revolutionaries committed to a healthy nationalism and social reform. Previously unpublished sources revealed this strategy. In 1954, Fidel Castro instructed his comrade Melba Hernandez that *"We cannot for a second abandon propaganda...Propaganda is vital—propaganda is the heart of our struggle."* Ernesto "Che" Guevara wrote in his diaries that *"Foreign reporters, preferably American, were much more valuable to us than any military victory. Much more valuable than rural recruits for our guerrilla force, were American media recruits to export our propaganda."*[602]

The biggest victory Castro and his comrades received was the US abandonment of Batista as a result of disinformation and propaganda that emanated from the State Department and elements within the American Embassy in Havana. Castro's sympathizers pressured the State Department and also infiltrated the Cuban exile community and Batista's Embassy in Washington. The reports of journalist Herbert Matthews played a huge role in delegitimizing the Batista dictatorship. Former US Ambassador to Cuba Arthur Gardner remarked in Congressional testimony that *"I feel it very strongly, that the State Department was influenced, first, by those stories by Herbert Matthews, and then it became kind of a fetish with them."* Ambassador Gardner also charged that the pro-Castro Assistant Secretary of State for Latin America Roy Rubottom had an arms shipment destined for the Batista army halted in the Port of New York.

Ambassador Earl E.T. Smith also testified that another pro-Castro State Department official, William Wieland, the Director of the Caribbean Division and Mexico, ordered the new ambassador to get briefed about Cuba by pro-Castro New York Times journalist Herbert L. Matthews. Ambassador Smith noted that the Batista regime was a corrupt authoritarian dictatorship, while Fidel Castro's forces ultimately represented communism. Smith testified that *"the Batista regime was disintegrating from within. It was becoming more corrupt, and as a result, was losing strength. The Castro forces themselves never won a military victory. The best military victory they ever won was through capturing Cuban guardhouses and military skirmishes, but they never actually won a military victory. The Batista government was overthrown because of the corruption, disintegration from within, and because of the United States and the various agencies of the United States who directly and indirectly aided the overthrow of the Batista government and brought into power Fidel Castro."* Smith specified that these American government agencies that were sympathetic to Castro included *"influential sources in the State Department, lower down echelons in the CIA. I would say representatives of the majority of the U.S. Government agencies which have anything to do with the Embassy."*

Smith also remarked that *"I would say that when we refused to sell arms to the Cuban Government and also by what I termed intervening by innuendo (which was persuading other*

---

[601] Diaz-Verson, Salvador. When Castro Became a Communist (Institute for U.S.-Cuba Relations 1997) Accessed From:http://www.latinamericanstudies.org/diaz-verson.htm

[602] Perdue, Jon B. The War of All the People: The Nexus of Latin American Radicalism and Middle Eastern Terrorism (Potomac Books, Inc., 2012) page 118.

friendly governments not to sell arms to Cuba) that these actions had a moral, psychological effect upon the Cuban armed forces which was demoralizing to the nth degree. The reverse, it built up the morale of the revolutionary forces. Obviously when we refused to sell arms to a friendly government, the existing government, the people of Cuba and the armed forces knew that the United States no longer would support Batista's government."

Smith also thought *"that Roy Rubottom was under terrific pressure from segments of the press, from certain Members of Congress, from the avalanche of Castro sympathizers and revolutionary sympathizers who daily descended upon the State Department, also their official representative, Betancourt, and Rubottom may have taken the line of least resistance."* Smith reported that the Chief of the Political Section, John Topping, and the Chief of the CIA Section at the American Embassy in Cuba provided encouragement to the Castro forces.

The Americans also cut off weapons shipments to the Cuban Army of Batista. The United States also refused to sell 15 training planes to Cuba under Batista. Also *"revolutionary sympathizers in New York and in Washington"* also brought pressure to bear on the State Department to halt a shipment of nearly 2,000 M-1 Garand rifles for the Cuban Army in March 1958. These rifles were paid for by the Batista regime and were still at the New York Docks ready to be shipped to Cuba.[603]

Brazil Under Military Rule (1964-1985)

In order to comprehend the rise of rightist-nationalist military rule in Brazil during the 1960s and 1970s, one must explore the quasi-fascist regime of General Getulio Vargas. Both Vargas and the post-1964 Brazilian military dictators believed in nationalism, state-led economic development, government regulation of the economy, and a strong anti-communism. Both were devoted to a corporatist social and economic arrangement. By the early 1930s, Vargas took over as a fascistic dictator in Brazil. He immediately increased the role of the government in the economy. Vargas created state-owned enterprises such as *Petrobras* (oil), *Vale* (mining), National Siderurgy Company (steel), National Alkalis Company (akalis), and National Motors Factory (cars). Starting in 1934, Vargas also decreed the creation of a corporative state where the social classes were reconciled. In 1937, Vargas declared the imposition of the *Estado Novo* (New State) in Brazil.[604]

Vargas maintained relations with both the Axis Powers and the United States. However, by the end of the 1930s, it appeared that Brazil would align itself with the Axis Powers on the account of the quasi-fascist and extreme nationalist ideology of Vargas. Between 1933 and 1938, Brazil exported massive amounts of cotton, cacao, and coffee to Nazi Germany. Under Vargas, the German Bank for South America established three hundred branches in Brazil. In 1937, the leftist revolutionary Jewish German refugee Olga Benario Prestes was deported to Nazi Germany.[605] The Italian airline LATI flew cargo in and out of Brazil. It was dubbed by a British intelligence officer as *"the biggest gap in the British economic blockade."* LATI ferried platinum, mica, diamonds, chemicals. Axis agents, diplomatic pouches, and propaganda between

---

[603] Committee on the Judiciary. Communist Threat to the United States Through the Caribbean GPO August 27, 1960 Accessed From: http://www.latinamericanstudies.org/us-cuba/gardner-smith.htm

[604] "Getulio Vargas" Accessed From: http://en.wikipedia.org/wiki/Get%C3%BAlio_Vargas

[605] Ibid.

Italy, Germany, and Brazil. The subsidairy of German *Lufthansa* in Brazil was Condor. Condor assisted Axis ships in breaking the British blockade. The Press Attache and Counselor at the German Embassy in Brazil was well-financed. It was responsible for funneling anti-US and pro-Nazi propaganda via sympathetic newspapers, radio broadcasts, and pamphlets.[606]

The Vargas regime also spewed fascistic, collectivist rhetoric which renounced liberal capitalism, sizable foreign investments, and limited government. In June 1939, President Vargas noted that *"We and all humanity are passing through a historical moment of great repercussions, resulting from a violent shifting of values. We are marching to a future different from the one we knew in the realm of economic, social, and political organization, and we feel that old systems and antiquated formulae have entered into decline. It is not, however, as die-hard pessimists and conservatives maintain, the end of civilization, but the tumultuous and fruitful beginning of a new era...Balanced economy no longer allows privileged classes to enjoy a monopoly of comfort and benefits...the State, therefore, should assume the obligation of organizing the productive forces, to provide the people with all that is necessary for the collective welfare...The era of improvident liberalism, sterile demagoguery, useless individualism, and disorder has passed."*[607] Even after Brazil declared war on Germany in August 1942, Minister of War Gaspar Dutra continued to speak of the danger of the *"voracious interests of foreign capitalism, allied to the imperialism of its governments, and the impatriotism of many of our countrymen..."*[608]

During the postwar era, Vargas' rhetoric moved steadily leftward. In December 1946, Vargas noted that *"old liberal capitalist democracy is in rapid decline"* while he supported *"socialist democracy...To that I belong. For this I will fight on behalf of the people."* In October 1945 Vargas declared that *"I was the victim of agents of international finance who intended to keep our country simply an exporting colony for raw materials and a purchaser of industrial goods."*[609]

One major fascist group which initially supported the Vargas dictatorship were the *Integralistas* led by Plinio Salgado. By the late 1930s, they were suppressed by the Vargas regime. The *Integralistas* supported state control of the press, theater, and radio *"which today favor international capitalism and Moscow agents."* The manifesto of the *Integralistas* also opposed *"the unrestrained individualism"* of capitalism and supported the enactment of more regulations to govern production and commerce to prevent what it viewed as harmful imbalances. Integralista founder Salgado noted in a pro-Vargas speech that 50,000 marchers were taking an opportunity to *"affirm their solidarity with the President of the Republic and the Armed Forces in their fight against communism and anarchial democracy, and to proclaim the principles of a new regime."* He also noted that the regime and the Integralistas fought against *"international capitalism, which acts against our economy, knifing us from time to time."*[610]

Integralista economics expert Miguel Reale identified three stages of capitalist development, which culminated with the advent of what he termed *"financial supercapitalism"* where the nation was a *"simple employee of the supranational-capitalist State, whose prime ministers were all almost of the Judaic race."* Salgado hoped that the *Integralistas* would free *"a*

---

[606] Dulles, John W.F. <u>Vargas of Brazil: A Political Biography</u> (University of Texas Press 2014)
[607] Ibid.
[608] Smallma, Shawn C. <u>Fear & Memory in the Brazilian Army and Society, 1889-1954</u> (University of North Carolina Press, 2002) page 73
[609] "Turn to the Left taken by Vargas" <u>The Milwaukee Journal</u> December 1, 1946 page 16.
[610] Dulles, John W.F. <u>Vargas of Brazil: A Political Biography</u> (University of Texas Press 2014)

proletarian Brazil from imperialist hands." Another *Integralista* theoretician Paulo Fleming castigated immoral and evil property owners as vile bourgeois and capitalist. However, such characters were condemned as individuals, not a social class.[611]

In 1964, the pro-communist regime of Joao Goulart was overthrown by elements of the Brazilian army in an effort to restore the economy. Furthermore, it also appeared that Goulart was about to implement an authoritarian regime of the Left. In 1961, the Brazilian Vice President Joao Goulart became the President of Brazil. He was formerly the Minister of Labor in the fascistic dictatorship of General Getulio Vargas. Goulart also visited the USSR and Red China in 1961 and started to impose leftwing policies in Brazil. Members of the business and professional classes became concerned about the direction of the country under President Goulart. He also allowed secret communists to penetrate key posts in agencies and even Ministries of the central government of Brazil. The most heavily infiltrated Ministry was that of Education. The approved textbooks for students contained Marxist propaganda. The government-subsidized National Student Union was dominated by the Communist Party. Its members traveled to Cuba and coordinated activities with other Latin American communist youth groups. The Brazilian Communist Party chief, Luis Carlos Prestes bluntly bragged that *"Seventeen of ours are in Congress."*[612]

Goulart eventually came out into the open and followed the example of Vargas by attempting to rule as a dictator. He tried to suspend the Brazilian Constitution and rule by executive decree. Goulart felt that the liberal political system was *"outmoded"* and urged basic changes in the Brazilian Constitution that favored increased dictatorial controls. He also signed decrees that illegally confiscated private property.[613] Brazilian Communist Party chief Luis Carlos Prestes bragged once again that *"We already have the power; we have now only to take over the government!" "Liquidation lists"* were drawn up for a purge of anti-communists and even lower ranking officers and soldiers in the Armed Forces were infiltrated by the Reds. Goulart also forcibly appointed communists to leadership positions in the labor unions. In September 1963, the army intercepted a shipment of weapons from Eastern Europe that were destined for pro-communist forces. American assistance via the Alliance for Progress program was embezzled by the Goulart government. Goulart and his cronies were also very corrupt and possessed plantations with a size of almost 3000 square miles. Regime officials were also provided with advance knowledge on changes in government policies such as exchange rates. Goulart's allies then profited tremendously from this knowledge. Goulart's agents, the military, and the Bank of Brazil also harassed independent newspapers that criticized the regime and its communist allies.[614] These specific political moves galvanized opposition from the business community, noncommunist labor unions, and the military. Goulart was overthrown in 1964 and the military promised to restore the economy and political system in a non-Marxist direction Despite popular perceptions that the new Brazilian regime was *"right wing,"* the rhetoric and actions of this government was anything but conservative or oriented towards a free market economy. The official government party was the National Renewal Alliance (ARENA), which

---

[611] Sandra McGee Deutsch. <u>Las Derechas: The Extreme Right in Argentina, Brazil, and Chile, 1890-1939</u> (Stanford University Press, 1999) pages 269-270.

[612] Methvin, Eugene. <u>The Riot Makers</u> (Arlington House 1970) pages 508-514.

[613] Ibid, pages 508-514.

[614] Hall, Clarence W. "The Country That Saved Itself" <u>Reader's Digest</u> November 1964 pages 2-10.

held power during the tenure of the military dictatorship. It appeared that the Brazilian government moved from pro-communist leftism to fascism in 1964. The military government tried to represent itself as representative of the mainstream middle. The first President of the Brazilian military regime was General Castelo Branco. Branco stated from the start that the new order did not represent the ideologies of the Left or Right: *"The extreme right is reactionary; the extreme left is subversive. Brazil must steer an honest middle course."* Shortly after the 1964, various large landowners and industrialists pressed President Branco for various favors. He reputedly retorted: *"The answer to the evils of the extreme left does not lie in the birth of a reactionary right."* The government urged that every Brazilian needed to *"subordinate selfish interests to the good of the nation."*[615]

Other regime officials and subsequent military rulers in the 1960s and 1970s confirmed their opposition to limited government of checks and balances and free market economics. Instead, a government-guided capitalist economy and a social welfare state were supported by the succession of military rulers in Brazil during the 1960s and 1970s. General Jose Maria de Andrade Serpa of Brazil concluded that *"economic and political liberalism in outdated. Democracy must not be allowed to run along a suicidal path; the fight against communism and corruption must not be interrupted."*[616] President Medici stated in 1972: *"The revolutionary state will last as long as it takes to implant the political, administrative, judicial, social and economic structures capable of raising all Brazilians to a minimum level of well being."*[617] ARENA leader Petronio Portela noted in March 1976 that *"the world economic crisis did not lead the country astray and did not turn the country from its political goals of social justice."* He also supported the government's program of *"development which increases wealth, benefits everyone, transforms society with a profound humanistic feeling, helping people of all classes and providing them with the means for participation."* Portela noted that *"modern capitalism is being consolidated in the country without disregarding the national foundation it must have."*[618] In certain respects, the military dictatorships continued the highly interventionist tendencies leftover from the Vargas and Goulart regimes. Labor was heavily controlled by the new state. In Brazil, all finances and elections in the unions were controlled by the Ministry of Labor.[619] The Medici regime expanded social welfare programs and increased wages for private and public sector employees.[620] When private sector wages increased, the government immediately decreed in August 1965 that it would regulate the wages of workers in private companies. Controls on prices were also attempted. At first, the Castelo Branco government attempted voluntary price controls through tax and credit rewards for companies who followed the *"suggestions"* of the regime.[621] Few firms followed these voluntary price guidelines. In 1967, Minister of Planning

---

[615] Ibid, pages 22-24.

[616] Arceneaux, Craig L. Bounded missions: military regimes and democratization in the Southern Cone (Penn State Press, 2001) page 175.

[617] Sloan, John W. Public policy in Latin America: a comparative survey (University of Pittsburgh Press 1984) page 215.

[618] "Portela Comments on Economy, Human rights" Rio de Janeiro Jornal Do Brasil March 18, 1976

[619] Skidmore, Thomas. The Politics of Military Rule in Brazil (Oxford University Press, 1988) page 35.

[620] Ibid, page 144.

[621] Ibid, page 35.

Antonio Delfim Netto enacted price controls which required all price hikes undertaken by the private sector to be approved by the government. The Inter-Ministerial Price Council was formed in 1968 to help enforce and formulate these price controls. One historian concluded that *"this resort to price control interestingly enough was hardly what businessmen had envisaged when they supported the 1964 revolution."* This historian also noted *"The Brazilian revolutionaries product of a revolt against an alleged statist threat from the left, were now embracing their own dirigisme: indefinite wage control."*[622]

Some historians and reporters even argued that the supposedly *"right wing"* dictatorship maintained and even expanded the role of the state in the economy. A historian noted that *"one of the ablest defenders of the Campos policies during the Castelo Branco era never tired of baiting leftists over the fact that it was supposedly right wing government that was rescuing the state sector of the economy."*[623] In 1969, Brazilian Senator Joao Calmon stated *"In Brazil 70 percent of existing investments is in government controlled sectors, from which one conclusion might be drawn: There is a numerical difference of only 30 percent in this sector between Brazil and the Soviet Union."* By 1974, state enterprises in Brazil controlled the steel, mining, petroleum, petrochemicals, energy, and some transportation sectors.[624] In Brazil, state ownership or intervention in the economy during the mid-1970s reached a level comparable to Allende's Chile or Peron's Argentina. Some Brazilian government officials defended this state intervention as a means of protecting investments against foreign multinationals.[625] ARENA Party Congressman Jose Machado called for the state takeover of the importation of agricultural products, the nationalization of the biggest foreign-controlled utility company, and a state monopoly on iron ore.[626]

Furthermore, it was no surprise that the Brazilian business community complained about these heavy statist policies and the collectivism of the military dictatorship. Sometimes these complaints led these businessmen and their media allies in jail or harassed by the regime. In 1965, Brazilian private businessmen complained that the new military government imposed price controls, wages, taxes, utility rates, and public payrolls under the rubric of controlling inflation. The business community also requested that the Brazilian government slash public payrolls.[627] Businessmen opposed credit policies, import controls, and price controls that were imposed by the military regime. Private business also complained about the *"enormous presence of the state in the economy."* Their rallying cry was *"desestatizar-denationalize."* In 1979, eight prominent Sao Paulo industrialists signed a petition urging a return to democracy.[628] Jose Barreto Filho of the Sao Paulo Chamber of Commerce noted *"Private enterprise in Brazil sees its future*

---

[622] Ibid, pages 67-70.

[623] Ibid, page 330.

[624] Hovey, Graham. "Capitalism, Brazil-Style" New York Times July 3, 1974 page 31.

[625] Kandell, Jonathan. "Brazil Moves Toward State Capitalism" New York Times September 12, 1976 page 119.

[626] Kandell, Jonathan. "Brazilians Voice Growing Fear Of Dominance by Multinationals" New York Times January 26, 1976 page 35.

[627] De Onis, Juan. "Controls Vexing Brazil Industry" New York Times December 29, 1965 page 39.

[628] Skidmore, Thomas. The Politics of Military Rule in Brazil (Oxford University Press, 1988) page 201.

threatened by the declarations of certain figures in national politics. "[629] A newspaper columnist Jose Celso de Macedo Soares Guimaraes was jailed in 1976 for criticizing the government's intervention in the economy.[630] O Estado de Sao Paulo noted in an editorial: "*Why not admit that we are confronting one of the gravest threats Brazilian society has ever faced? During these last 10 years we have verified a real escalation of statism without precedent in the history of the country and comparable only to socialist states.*" Directors of these enterprises had luxury houses, fine cars, high salaries, swimming pools, large expense accounts, and secure positions. The Minister of Commerce and Industry Severo Gomes justified the state's heavy presence in the economy as a means of keeping the multinational companies in check.[631]

Despite the pronounced ideological anti-communism of the Brazilian military dictatorship, trade with the communist world was maintained and even increased. This was due to the desire to maintain overseas markets for Brazilian exports and to maintain a non-aligned image in respect to East-West relations. In July 1981, a delegation of Brazilian businessmen and government officials led by Planning Minister Antonio Delfim Netto visited the USSR to sign a barter trade agreement that exchanged Brazilian agricultural products for machinery and oil from the Soviets. In 1980, the Brazilians exported $370 million worth of goods to the USSR and imported $31 million worth of Soviet goods. A Brazilian trade official commented that "*At one time the Soviets wanted to deal only with North American multinationals…But now they are more open-minded.*" Several Brazilian companies, such as Coque e Alcool de Madeira do Brasil (COALBRA), purchased Soviet technology for use in the development of alternative sources of energy. These purchases were financed through a consortium of COMECON banks. The Brazilians also increased their soybean exports to the Soviets. A Brazilian official also noted that "*We take their machines just to help balance the trade.*"[632]

Nicaragua Under Presidents Somoza (1936-1979)

Despite assertions of many American anti-communists, the dictatorships of President Anastasio Somoza Garcia and his son Anastasio Somoza Debayle did not represent legitimate or even actual examples of free enterprise and limited government. On a positive note, the reality was that the Somoza regimes represented a consistent anti-communist position that was friendly towards American political interests in the Hemisphere. Internally, the Somozas represented a solid break from political and economic liberalism and large step in the direction of centralization of the state and the vast expansion of state interventionism in the economy. Somoza had his army of apologists within the United States, even when it appeared that President Carter was hell-bent on abandoning him to the communist and Cuban-supported Sandinistas. According to Somoza and Jack Cox, "*Nicaragua was a free country with progress and patriotism, and its system of government, election laws, free enterprise, and even mode of*

[629] Kandell, Jonathan. "Brazilians Voice Growing Fear Of Dominance by Multinationals" New York Times January 26, 1976 page 35.

[630] Kandell, Jonathan. "Brazil Will Try a Right-Wing Writer" New York Times July 18, 1976 page 3.

[631] Kandell, Jonathan. "Brazil Regime Widening State Economic Control" New York Times April 11, 1976 page 1.

[632] "The Soviets find trade partners on the right" Business Week June 29, 1981 page 64.

wearing apparel were modeled after the U.S., and Carter was able to destroy it all, starting with inaccurate slander about Human Rights."[633]

While the Somoza family financially benefited enormously from these interventions in the Nicaraguan economy, they were also motivated by a set ideological framework. The ideology of Somoza and his political movement, the Nationalist Liberal Party (PLN), was predicated on collectivism, anti-communism, a controlled economy based on private enterprise, friendship towards the United States, and class cooperation. The updated Nicaraguan Liberalism eschewed undiluted individualism and embraced elements of a fascistic collectivism. Horacio Espinoza made a speech at the Ateneo Militar (Military Club) of Managua in July 1935 which redefined Nicaraguan liberalism. Espinoza castigated classical economic and political liberalism which he considered out of date in a world dominated by collectivism. Espinoza noted that Nicaraguan liberalism needed to break with the past and embrace policies that achieved tangible results for the Nicaraguan masses such as social justice. Espinoza felt that the government should control the capitalist system through a system that he termed as "*moderate state socialism.*" A Somocista campaign card dated from mid-1935 was titled "*Por que soy Somocista?*" The card outlined Somoza's statist policies that assisted workers and peasants and expanded Nicaragua's industrial development. The Somocistas criticized the old political parties and their leaders in populist, almost pseudo-leftist terminology. A Somocista pamphlet that was circulated in Jinotega in January 1936 noted that "*the aristocracy had kept them (residents of Nicaragua) in ignorance and misery in order to dominate and exploit them more easily.*"[634]

Rhetorically, both Anastasio Somoza Garcia and his son Anastasio Somoza Debayle espoused corporative, populist, and even vaguely anti-capitalist sentiments. The ideological tempo against the business community was channeled when the wealthy classes backed political actions against Somoza or attempted to sabotage his social policies. President Somoza Garcia emphasized the corporative theme in 1937 that workers, landowners, and capitalists must work for the benefit of all.[635] Such rhetoric was to forestall any chance of communist or further pro-Sandino rebellion in Nicaragua and solidify the rule by the Somoza family. The son, Somoza Debayle, continued his father's tradition of espousing corporative and populist themes. Furthermore, Somoza Debayle also endorsed economic planning and even some state ownership of various sectors in Nicaragua. In December 1974, Somoza noted that "*I am completely sure that without the ordered distribution of wealth and the land political democracy is incomplete just as development and social justice for the less privileged is incomplete.*"[636]

Another facet of Somoza's assertions that would be especially shocking to American conservatives would be the Nicaraguan strongman's admissions that he was a leader in the progressive liberal mold. President Anastasio Somoza Debayle commented "*this has been a very liberal and nationalistic government where we mix socialism and free enterprise. What's happening today in the rest in the rest of Latin America and is shaking some people in the United*

---

[633] Cox, Jack and Somoza, Anastasio. Nicaragua Betrayed (Western Islands 1980)

[634] Knut, Walter. The Regime of Anastasio Somoza, 1936-1956 (University of North Carolina Press, 1993) pages 44-46.

[635] "Nicaragua Bans Communists" New York Times February 17, 1937 page 12.

[636] "President Somoza Gives Inaugural Address to Nation" Managua Domestic Service December 1, 1974

States happened in Nicaragua thirty or more years ago."[637] In February 1978, Somoza declared himself a capitalist and socialist noting that "*I am a devilish mixture that is called a liberal democrat by the Americans.*"[638]

Somoza also hit back severely at criticisms from Nicaraguan industrialists and landowners and their alleged sabotage of the economy and political structure. In January 1978, Somoza noted that "*the Liberal Party guarantees democracy, social justice, and the better distribution of the nation's wealth…(Somoza then) condemns the national lockout and strike called by the Conservative Party as a sign of Conservative capitalists attitude against the working masses.*"[639]

In May 1978, Somoza noted that "*It is under the shelter of these liberties that reactionary capitalists have tried to subject our country to chaos and the greatest upheaval that any nation has ever had to overcome…it is not fair that the weakest-the workers-should suffer because of the subversion by the rich and the communists.*"[640]

In August 1978, Somoza noted that "*…a small majority such as the capitalists who have tried to oppose the Liberal Party…Let us turn to the Right and Left and again see that we are part of a conglomerate which through good will and sacrifices has brought countless advantages to persons you do not know but who recognize that the Liberal conglomerate is the one which has brought the most happiness to the Nicaraguan people.*"[641]

Somoza noted in November 1978 that "*Twenty two years ago when I was chief director of the National Guard these men and I faced the same men and interests that today are trying to remove the Liberal Party from power. They are the same businessmen, industrialists, and builders whom the workers supported by the people did not allow to destroy Nicaragua's social security…*" Somoza noted that the PLN "*made it possible to have social justice for the worker in Nicaragua and for Nicaragua to be one of the most progressive countries in Latin America today.*" He also stated "*As you know very well gentlemen the conservatives, the businessmen, some industrialists and the construction sector in addition to some communist politicians allied to certain governments have chosen to bring bloodshed to the country.*"[642]

President Somoza noted in May 1979 that "*I have always stated and continue to reiterate that the social liberal revolution does not stop.*" He lambasted the "*subversion financed the reactionary capital which wants to change things in Nicaragua*" and "*the armed aggression launched by the capitalists together with the communists…*"[643]

Somoza stated that aggression against his government in the 1970s was "*launched by the capitalists in connivance with the communists*" and that "*Nicaraguan capitalists thought they could overthrow my government with the help of unscrupulous politicians in the United States*

---

[637] Diederich, Bernard. <u>Somoza and the legacy of U.S. involvement in Central America</u> (Markus Wiener Publishers, 2007) page 105.

[638] "Somoza Tells Brazilian Magazine He Will Not Resign" <u>Buenos Aires LATIN</u> February 8, 1978

[639] "Somoza Speech in Corinto" <u>Managua Domestic Service</u> January 28, 1978

[640] "Somoza Address to Workers on Labor Day" <u>Novedades</u> May 2, 1978

[641] "Somoza Announces Start of Electoral Campaign" <u>Novedades</u> August 14, 1978

[642] "Somoza Speaks at Hospital Dedication Ceremony" <u>Managua Domestic Service</u> November 19, 1978

[643] "President Somoza Delivers Labor Day Address" <u>Managua Domestic Service</u> May 1, 1979

and Venezuela...If Nicaraguan capitalists want to blackmail, I'll show them just who Anastasio Somoza is!"[644]

Even long after Somoza's overthrow, his family members refused to apologize for the actions that occurred under the dictatorship. They especially praised and highlighted the social and labor reforms enacted under the Somoza regime and compared them favorably to the Sandinistas. Alejandro Sevilla Somoza recalled to The Miami Herald in May 2000 that *"The people who hated our family were the rich business leaders who hated the things the Somozas did that cost them money...They didn't like social security, they didn't like women's suffrage, they didn't like having a labor code. Every single one of those things was started by my family. The labor code my grandfather wrote in 1938 was so liberal that when the Sandinistas got around to changing it, they actually took rights away from the workers."*[645]

The Somoza state intervened in the Nicaraguan economy after it took power in the mid-1930s. In August and September 1939, Nicaraguan merchants complained about the rise in import tariffs and price controls on basic goods. In December 1939, the Managua Chamber of Commerce communicated to the Minister of the Interior their opposition to the decree on maximum profits for private companies. Government employment increased from 5,321 in 1936-37 to 9,500 in 1944. In January 1938, the Somoza regime passed a law that limited profits for merchants. The Comision Ajustadora Nacional ensured that this law was followed. The Comision had the power to impose fines or even close down businesses that violated this law.[646] In September 1939, the Somoza-controlled Congress imposed an *"estado de emergencia economica"* which controlled Nicaraguan commerce until 1956.[647]

During and after World War II, this intervention continued to increase in leaps and bounds in Nicaragua. The book States, Ideologies, and Social Revolutions: A Comparative Analysis of Iran, Nicaragua, and the Philippines noted that *"The Nicaraguan government began active intervention in the economy to promote economic development following World War II. The state expanded the nation's infrastructure by building highways, roads, and rail systems...extending electric power; and, most importantly, allocating capital for economic investment."* In the 1960s, the National Economic Council compiled plans to reduce Nicaragua's vulnerability that would be felt by economic fluctuations of the world market. The Planning Office encouraged more self-sufficiency in agriculture and industry. The government also set up state enterprises such as Central Bank of Nicaragua, the National Bank of Nicaragua, the Mortgage Bank of Nicaragua, the Bank of Popular Credit, the National Development Institute (INFONAC), the National Assembly of Assistance and Social Foresight (JNAPS), the Irrigation Company of Rivas, the Agrarian Institute of Nicaragua (IAN), the National Company of Light and Power (ENALUF), the National Institute of Electrical Energy, and the Port Authority of Corinto.[648] However, there were occasions where the Somoza dictatorship disrespected private property outright and even nationalized the assets owned by American multinationals. Somoza

---

[644] Diederich, page 244.

[645] Garvin, Glenn. "Dynasty's heirs fight to regain seized Nicaragua property" Miami Herald May 7, 2000 Accessed From: http://www.latinamericanstudies.org/nicaragua/comeback.htm

[646] Knut, Walter. The Regime of Anastasio Somoza, 1936-1956 (University of North Carolina Press, 1993) pages 72-73.

[647] Ibid, page 201.

[648] Parsa, Misagh. States, Ideologies, and Social Revolutions: A Comparative Analysis of Iran, Nicaragua, and the Philippines (Cambridge University Press 2000) pages 59-61.

nationalized the port of Corinto, railroads, utilities, and properties of the United Fruit Company.[649]

As a result of the over-regulation of the economy, cronyism, and human rights violations, the business community continued to grouse about life under Somoza. Walter Knut commented that *"The regime's relations with the private sector were not entirely devoid of friction. By the early 1950s, the Somozas were a business empire on the same level as some of the much older families of Granada and León and had expanded into some very profitable ventures in addition to those acquired during the war years, which were mainly in agriculture and urban real estate. By 1950, Somoza was the principal shareholder of the internal airline, LANICA, and had set up his own liquor plant, Fabrica de Licores Bell. In 1953, he founded the sole national merchant marine company, MAMENIC Line, and also moved into the textile industry."*[650]

Walter Knut observed that *"The typical complaints now voiced by Nicaraguan business associations had to do with government controls on imports and foreign exchange and with increased taxation. The Banco Nacional was the main target of criticism, given both its administrative control of foreign exchange operations and its preponderance in the nation's credit transactions. In late 1947, the Managua Chamber of Commerce stated that the Banco Nacional's operations were deficient in all respects and that a better alternative would be a purely autonomous central bank not under the direct control of the executive branch of government..."*[651]

Knut also reported that *"...the exchange controls...received the most criticism. The Leon Chamber of Commerce stated flatly in July 1950 that eighteen years of state direction of the economy ('economia dirigida') had not yielded good results and that the exchange control mechanisms were largely to blame, in addition to the fact that foreign exchange always had been distributed to favor some and hurt others. Now was the time, the Leon Chamber said, to correct this policy, 'to free commerce from the heavy weight of the controls in order to enter into a new era of economic readjustments and individual liberties, which is the basic condition to achieve success in the development of the country's finances.'...In February 1951, the Managua Chamber of Commerce complained that procedures to request foreign exchange were excessively complicated and that the Banco Nacional bureaucrats dragged their feet in processing the forms."*[652]

In May 1953, the Managua Chamber complained that Somoza's economic system *"has created a situation that is untenable for nearly all branches of private enterprise."*[653] The Nicaraguan private sector also opposed Somoza's new taxes and social services that drained profits and resources from the business community. The Managua Chamber of Commerce and the Cooperativa Nacional de Agricultores publicly opposed to income tax proposals put forth by the Somoza regime. The Managua Chamber was very critical of the social security system in mid-1956 because of the large contributions that the private sector and the workers would have

---

[649] Diederich, Bernard. Somoza and the legacy of U.S. involvement in Central America (Markus Wiener Publishers, 2007) page 105.

[650] Knut, Walter. The Regime of Anastasio Somoza, 1936-1956 (University of North Carolina Press, 1993) page 198.

[651] Ibid, pages 200.

[652] Knut, Walter. The Regime of Anastasio Somoza, 1936-1956 (University of North Carolina Press, 1993) page 201.

[653] Ibid.

to make. The Social Security Institute retorted that Nicaraguan private industries made good profits and had no rights to support policies just so businessmen could keep their labor costs low.[654]

The complaints from the business community continued under the Somoza Debayle regime, especially by the end of the late 1970s. As of February 1979, Nicaraguan businessmen complained about Somoza's tax hikes, tight credit policies, and import restrictions. President Somoza responded to these gripes by asserting that *"I'm not interested in the profits of the private sector...I'm interested in the welfare of the Nicaraguan people. We can do without manufactures. As a mainly agricultural country, we can always eat rice and beans and sell our farm products on the world market."*[655]

To his credit, all of the Somozas who served as Presidents of Nicaragua were stalwart anti-communists who sincerely desired to stem communist influence in Central America. The Sandinistas and their international communist allies sought to force a withdrawal of American, Israeli, and other foreign support for the Somoza regime. Somoza's corruption and brutality were played up in the American liberal media, while Sandinista brutality was either ignored or under-reported. As the Sandinistas regrouped and reorganized after various defeats in the 1960s and early 1970s, they also sought to manipulate American liberal opinion and the Carter Administration into withdrawing assistance to and delegitimizing the authoritarian dictatorship of President Somoza. In 1977, Sandinista activist Miguel Bolanos and two other Nicaraguans formed a solidarity committee at Louisiana State University in Baton Rouge. Bolanos recalled that other solidarity committees were formed *"in other parts of the South. We sent all the money and other aid we collected to headquarters in Costa Rica. What we were creating became the National Network in Solidarity with the People of Nicaragua."* Bolanos noted that *"by 1978 the Sandinistas realized the value of the solidarity committees in the United States. So they placed a couple of key people from the Sandinista organization in charge of the solidarity network in this country. They were under orders from the Sandinistas Directorate."* Bolanos noted that the National Network in Solidarity with the People of Nicaragua was *"guided by the intelligence organs of Cuba."*[656]

Communist support for the Sandinistas was channeled primarily through Cuba. In the early 1960s, the Cubans provided the Sandinistas with training and weapons. However, such support waned and was reduced to safe haven and propaganda support until late 1977. In 1977 and early 1978, a high-ranking Cuban Communist Party Americas Department (DA) official, Armando Ulises Estrada met with the Sandinistas to unify the three major factions before conducting a general offensive against Somoza. In late 1978, Estrada developed smuggling networks to ship weapons to Sandinista troops. Arms were flown from Cuba to Panama under the leftwing dictatorship of Brig. Omar Torrijos. The weapons were then transshipped to Costa Rica, where the Sandinistas gladly took those arms. Cuban soldiers also appeared in northern Costa Rica to advise and support Sandinista troops. In early 1979, Cuba also organized, trained, and equipped an *"internationalist brigade"* that consisted of terrorists from South and Central America. They were tasked to fight alongside Sandinista soldiers. Cuban troops from the elite Directorate of Special Operations were also dispatched to assist the Sandinistas in the field by

---

[654] Ibid.

[655] "An ostracized regime runs out of money" Business Week February 5, 1979 page 38

[656] Whelan, James Robert and Jaeckle, Franklin A. The Soviet Assault on America's Southern Flank (Regnery Gateway, 1988) pages 344-345.

mid-1979. A number of these Cuban soldiers were wounded in combat with Somoza's troops and were flown back to Cuba via Panama. These Cuban forces maintained direct radio communication with Havana.[657] In March 1979, the National Guard of President Somoza captured a variety of weapons from Panama and Cuba. They included M-1 Garand rifles (from Cuba and Panama), Red Chinese-made RPG-2s, and Belgian FN FALs (from Cuba). Humberto Ortega admitted that *"Needless to say, the armament that was received played quite a decisive role in hastening the victory, and in some cases, in deciding a few battles which otherwise would have been lost."*[658]

The American abandonment of Somoza followed the same pattern of Cuba where anti-communist forces were marginalized and weapons shipments cut-off from the armed forces in engaged in battle against Red forces. The United States pressured Israel to halt weapons shipments to Somoza's forces in their battle against the Sandinista communists. Somoza believed that these weapons shipments, which included anti-tank and anti-personnel grenade rifles, could have saved the anti-communist forces. Another Israeli ship that was laden with weapons was diverted only miles away from the Nicaraguan coast.[659] Victory was assured to the Sandinistas, who have ruled Nicaragua directly and behind the scenes since July 1979.

Nationalist China Under General Chiang Kai-shek (1926-1949/1949-1975)

In 1912, revolutionaries overthrow the government of the Manchu Empire and replaced it with the Republic of China. By 1920, China fell into disorder and various warlord factions took over various regions of the country. However, the republicans (the Kuomintang or KMT) retook power by the late 1920s under the command of General Chiang Kai-shek. While the KMT were initially backed by the USSR and the Chinese Communist Party (CCP), an ideological split developed. The KMT and Communist forces clashed. Meanwhile, the KMT itself retained a highly nationalist and socialist platform which increasingly resembled fascism. This ideology originally developed from the notion of the Three Principles of the People-People's Livelihood. The Three Principles of the People represented the core of the KMT's philosophy as formed by Dr. Sun Yat-sen, the first President of the Republic of China. By 1931, the KMT fought both the communists and the Japanese militarist forces who invaded Manchuria in northern China.

From the beginning, the KMT under Chiang enacted policies which severely controlled private business, built up a large state-owned sector of the economy, and developed an ideological collectivism which looked upon Nazi Germany and Fascist Italy as models. In the late 1920s, he KMT forced industrialists and bankers to finance their army's Northern Expedition against the warlords and communists. It was noted during the late 1920s that *"Wealthy Chinese would be arrested in their homes or mysteriously disappear from the*

---

[657] United States Department of State. Bureau of Public Affairs "Cuba's Renewed Support of Violence in Latin America" December 14, 1981 Accessed From: http://www.latinamericanstudies.org/guerrilla/report-90.htm

[658] Kagan, Robert. A Twilight Struggle: American Power and Nicaragua, 1977-1990 (VNR AG 1996) pages 85-86.

[659] Jane Haapiseva-Hunter. Israeli Foreign Policy: South Africa and Central America (South End Press 1987) page 140.

streets…Millionaires were arrested as 'communists.'"[660] In 1935, the KMT broke the political power of the private banks. The government forced banks to buy government bonds, while the Bank of China and the Bank of Communications were forced to also accept these government bonds. By 1937, the government controlled over 70% of the banks in China. Eastman wrote *"These banking coups effectively ended the bankers' role as a political pressure group and demonstrated beyond doubt that it was the regime that controlled the capitalist rather than vice versa."*[661]

In the 1930s, the institutional framework of a collectivist economy was laid down by the KMT. By 1932, Chiang and the KMT supported the planned national defense economy or *kuo-fang ching-chi*. In November 1932, the KMT formed the National Defense Planning Commission to plan China's state-run industries in cooperation with Germany.[662] The KMT also mimicked the fascists and communists in their willingness to use their foreign capitalist enemies to modernize the Chinese state. The KMT Guideline on the Reconstruction of the People's Livelihood noted in November 1931 that *"As a nation which lags behind in production, China has to make use of her domestic and overseas Chinese capital in order to develop rapidly her national economy and the reconstruction of all production industries. In particular, she has to take full advantage of foreign capital and technology."*[663]

As World War II loomed in the horizon and the KMT retreated to the interior of China, the economy was placed in a straitjacket of government controls. By 1941, the Nationalist government created state monopolies for tobacco, matches, sugar, and salt. The regime also imposed *"compulsory borrowings"* of goods such as grain to feed the Nationalist armies. James Chieh Hsiung noted that *"In industry, the government moved far in the direction of state capitalism managed by an economic bureaucracy that grew much more quickly than the economy under its direction."* The Industrial and Mining Adjustment Administration relocated factories in Nationalist China. Economic management was shifted to the new Ministry of Economic Affairs (MOEA). MOEA was tasked with the *"economic administration of the whole nation."* The National Resources Commission (NRC) was given a mandate to *"develop, operate, and control"* major industries, mining companies, and *"other enterprises as designated by the government."* The Nationalists passed wartime economic regulations in 1938. The MOEA and NRC were provided powers to nationalize any industrial, mining, and electrical enterprises; to assume *"direct control of enterprises or products affecting daily necessities;"* to assume the management of firms that failed to *"effect measures of technical or administrative reform as ordered by the government;"* and to regulate the production, pricing, and export of specific products. Weng Wen-hao observed that the disconnection between the state (*kuo-yu*) and private (*min-yu*) enterprises was incorrect, since all *"nationally-owned industries in fact also belonged to the people."* In March 1942, the National General Mobilization Act subjected *"every person and every means of production"* to government control. Chi Ch'ao-ting approvingly noted that state-owned enterprises were the *"dominating feature"* of wartime economic policy in Nationalist China. In 1937, the NRC maintained 23 industrial and mining enterprises and fewer than 2,000

---

[660] Lloyd E. Eastman, Jerome Ch'en, Suzanne Pepper, Lyman P. Van Slyke. The Nationalist Era in China, 1927-1949 (Cambridge University Press, 1991) pages 16-19.

[661] Ibid.

[662] Kirby, William C. Germany and Republican China (Stanford University Press 1984) pages 78.

[663] Ibid, pages 78, 81.

staff members. By the end of 1938, the NRC possessed or controlled 63 enterprises. In 1942, the NRC controlled 40% of Nationalist China's industry. By 1944, the NRC owned 103 manufacturing, mining, and electrical enterprises in Nationalist China. Twenty eight of these NRC enterprises were private firms that were nationalized or publically-controlled companies owned by local governments. The NRC had, at its height, 12,000 staff members and 160,000 workers. By 1943, state-owned enterprises in Nationalist China rose from 15 to 35%. The Nationalist Chinese also leaned in the direction of an ideological attachment to the idea of a *"controlled economy."* NRC Vice-Chairman Ch'ien Ch'ang-chao noted that postwar Nationalist China should be *"following the socialist road."* Economics Minister Weng Wen-hao noted that postwar Chinese industrial planning should be *"close to socialism though not entirely identical."*[664]

Fred Simon confirmed that the intrusive and comprehensive state controls over the economy would be retained in postwar China: *"...the extension of government controls and the growth of the state industrial sector were not simply wartime 'emergency measures' but were to serve as the basis for an even greater state role in peacetime."* NRC planners such as Weng Wenhao, Qian Changzhao, and others believed that China would move along the path of *"socialization"* (*shehui-hua*) of the economy. Weng Wenhao called the Chinese policy *"close to socialism, though not entirely identical."*[665]

In October 1940, the Chinese Economic Reconstruction Society drew up the Outline of Economic Reconstruction in China. The Outline gave priority to defense related industries, which were to be developed *"as quickly as possible, as state enterprises"* according to a *"planned economy."* The Outline also noted that foreign economic investment would be necessary and welcome in Nationalist China. However, such investment would be regulated by the government in accordance to China's national development strategies. Industries located in the Japanese-occupied zones were to be nationalized by the Nationalist government through the NRC. The NRC and the American multinational corporation Westinghouse International entered into a joint venture to modernize and expand the Central Electrical Manufacturing Works. In the 1930s, the Nationalists noted that the *"national defense economy"* was to be entirely state-owned and state-managed as a first step forward to a *"controlled"* (*t'ung-chih*) economy. It was noted that *"...although technology transfer from advanced Western nations was essential to the creation of defense industries, the foreign role would take the form of technical assistance agreements, not equity ownership."*[666]

After the Japanese defeat in World War II, the communists resumed their war against the KMT. The extreme statist-socialist principles of the KMT along with the resultant corruption and inflation shattered the Chinese economy. Once again, the KMT decided to scapegoat and attack the business classes as the cause of the economic collapse in China during the late 1940s. In 1948, the Kuomintang attacked the merchants of Shanghai. Chiang Kai-shek sent his son Chiang Ching-kuo to restore economic control. Chiang Ching-kuo copied Soviet methods when he tried to jumpstart a social revolution by attacking middle class merchants. It also appeared that Chiang

[664] James Chieh Hsiung. China's Bitter Victory: The War With Japan, 1937-1945 (M.E. Sharpe 1992) pages 188-200.
[665] Denis Fred Simon. Science and Technology in Post-Mao China (Harvard University Asia Center, 1989) pages 31-33.
[666] James Chieh Hsiung. China's Bitter Victory: The War With Japan, 1937-1945 (M.E. Sharpe 1992) pages 188-200.

Ching-kuo was also at least partially sympathetic to aspects of Soviet Communism. In fact, he was observed reading the Collected Works of Lenin and other Marxist and communist literature.[667] He also enforced low prices on all goods to garner support from the proletariat. Chiang Ching-kuo also attacked the wealthy classes and seized assets and placed them under arrest.[668] By 1948, Chiang Ching-kuo arrested over 1,000 profiteers during price control enforcement. He addressed 5,000 Youth Army veterans in 1948 in Shanghai by exhorting them with slogans: *"Down with profiteers and speculators," "Make Revolution,"* and *"Root Out Corrupt Forces."* While Chiang Ching-kuo pledged to protect private property and enterprises, he also criticized *"so-called economists who claim that if we want to solve economic problems we should proceed from the economic point of view."* Instead, Chiang Ching-kuo felt that *"the economic structure is based on social and political forces."*[669] The American consul-general in Mukden reported that *"Puerile efforts have been made towards price control and to combat hoarding…the results…have been largely to enforce requisitioning of grain at bayonet-point for controlled prices and enable the resale of requisitioned grain at black market prices for the benefit of the pockets of rapacious military and civil officials."*[670]

After the conquest of mainland China by the Communist Party in October 1949, the Chiang Kai-shek regime fled to the island of Formosa (Taiwan). Taiwan was the remnant of the Republic of China and it was heavily backed by the United States. Chiang died in 1975 and his son Chiang Ching-kuo succeeded him as President of Taiwan (Republic of China or ROC). In the interim, Chiang continued his socialist policies of development on the island of Taiwan for various reasons. Chiang and the majority of the KMT officials clung to their socialist notions as defined in the People's Livelihood aspect of the Three Principles of the People. Secondly, Chiang and the KMT realized that in order to create a strong Republic of China on Taiwan, a crash program for industrialization and agricultural production was necessary from a practical point of view. After all, a strong economy would help preclude communist subversion. Contrary to the prevailing wisdom of most American anti-communists and conservatives, Taiwan retained a quasi-socialist, heavily regulated economy throughout the 1950s and 1960s. In May 1949, the Taiwan Production Board (TPB) was formed to stabilize the economy. The TPB was absorbed by the Economic Stabilization Board (ESB), which was established in 1951 with the advice of the United States. Thomas Gold noted that *"The state thus had bureaucratic agencies to guide all aspects of the economy in addition to its own unassailable position as the dominant capitalist…In the economy as well, the state dominated. It owned all large industrial concerns and banks. It stimulated agricultural production while ensuring its own control of the surplus…the state turned Taiwan's economy to import substitution in light industry to conserve funds, absorb labor, supply the domestic market, and accumulate capital rapidly. It selected cronies to become industrialists and made certain they depended on the state for capital, foreign exchange, equipment, raw materials, energy, and docile labor."*[671] He also wrote *"The state also*

---

[667] Taylor, Jay. The Generalissimo's Son (Harvard University Press 2009) page 42.

[668] Fenby, Jonathan. Generalissimo: Chiang Kai-Shek and the China He Lost (Da Capo Press 2009) pages 156-159 and 485.

[669] Taylor, Jay. The Generalissimo's Son (Harvard University Press 2009) page 42.

[670] Johnson, Paul. Modern Times (Harper Collins Publisher 1991) Accessed From: http://archive.org/stream/ModernTimes_305/42024947-19032115-Johnson-Paul-Modern-Times-the-World-From-the-Twenties-to-the-Nineties-Revised-Edition-Harper-Collins-1991_djvu.txt

[671] Gold, Thomas B. State and Society in the Taiwan Miracle (M.E. Sharpe 1986) pages 67-68.

controlled relations with the outside world. It allocated financial aid and commodities. It closely regulated trade. There was virtually no direct foreign investment. The state thus mediated external linkages--most of which were with other nations' officials--and did not permit an untrammeled private foreign presence or a segment of Taiwan's society to represent alien interests."[672]

As of 1953, government-owned enterprises in Taiwan accounted for 50-100% of the alcohol, tobacco, salt, transport, fertilizer, power, chemicals, sugar, timber, and cement production.[673] Specific industries covered in this statement were the sugar, oil, fertilizer, power, shipbuilding, and machinery, which were to remain under government ownership. According to Mendel, Nationalist red tape became the target of criticism by both Taiwanese and foreign businessmen.[674] An article in China News confirmed Mendel's point when it stated: "*Our bureaucracy has two faults. First regulations are too numerous and too cumbersome...Everything takes several times as long as it should...Second our whole bureaucratic system is based on mistrust and unwillingness to accept responsibility...Investors, workers, and their families are to be mistrusted...as sharpers and cheats awaiting the smallest opportunity to defraud the government.*"[675]

Even in the 1960s, the KMT was unwilling to loosen the government's hold on the economy in Taiwan. According to a Taiwanese Cabinet statement issued in 1965, the government "*has no intention to transfer to private capital those state enterprises vital to either national defense or economic development.*"[676] Even after Chiang Kai-shek's death in 1975, the Taiwanese KMT state owned many vital sectors of the economy. In 1980, the MOEA still owned fourteen business enterprises in petroleum, power, sugar, steel, shipbuilding, engineering, aluminum, fertilizer, petrochemicals, machinery, chemicals, mining, alkali, and phosphates, in addition to investments in other enterprises. The Ministry of Finance owned several insurance companies.[677]

One of the darker secrets of the KMT was its initial affinity for the German National Socialists during much of the 1930s. The KMT viewed the Nazis as a kindred ideological spirit, since both adhered to a collectivistic, socialist nationalism which sought an increase in the industrial and military power of their respective nations. Pro-Nazi Chinese KMT officials included Minister of War Ho Ying-chin, Secret Service Chief Tai Li, and the head of the Central Political Training Office Ho Chung-huan. For much of the 1930s, the Nazis even assisted the KMT with weapons, advisers, and industrial technology. In the 1930s, Nazi Germany built modern factories in China and equipped them with machinery. Germany also built up China's army with weapons and a modern arms industry. By 1937, China's army had over 80,000 German-trained officers and troops. Several hundred German troops and officers were stationed in China, which included General Alexander von Falkenhausen.[678] The journal of the Central Air

---

[672] Ibid, page 73.

[673] Mendel, Douglas. The Politics of Formosan Nationalism (University of California Press, 1970) pages 78-79.

[674] Ibid, pages 78-79.

[675] Ibid, pages 78-79.

[676] Ibid, pages 78-79.

[677] Gold, Thomas B. State and Society in the Taiwan Miracle (M.E. Sharpe 1986) page 143.

[678] James Chieh Hsiung. China's Bitter Victory: The War With Japan, 1937-1945 (M.E. Sharpe 1992) pages 5-6.

Academy analyzed the methods undertaken by the Nazis to *"overcome the class struggle"* and often provided the German version of international events such as the occupation of the Rhineland in 1936. In a cable to Berlin, the Nazi Consul and former adviser to Chiang Kai-shek, Hermann Kriebel reported positively on the *"proliferation of the fascist idea"* in China.[679] Tang Liang-li wrote pro-Nazi commentaries in the People's Tribune that praised the socialism of the Nazis. Shih Shao Pei praised Nazi social programs such as the KdF, improved class cooperation, better working conditions in the factories, and public service work camps. Another author for the People's Tribune praised *"the integration of the working masses…into the National Socialist state and the abolition of…the evil elements of modern capitalism."*[680]

Radical sections of the KMT also developed in the 1930s. They sought to promote radical KMT doctrines and promote a deepening of the nationalist and social revolution of Chiang Kai-shek. The Kuomintang-led New Life Movement of the 1930s opposed selfishness, individualism, and class warfare and instead advocated the cooperation of labor and capital for the common good of the nation.[681] Lloyd Eastman noted that *"The Blue Shirts were acutely conscious of the need for economic reforms. And, in view of their totalitarian concept of society, and considering the fact that economic laissez-faire-ism was everywhere under attack in the 1930s, it is not surprising that they advocated an economy that would be completely planned and controlled by the state. They called their projected economic system 'national socialism' (kuo-chia she-hui chu-i) - a term doubtless derived from Hitler's Germany. Under the system of national socialism, all productive activity would come under the purview of the government's planning apparatus, which would prepare production goals and detailed plans of development. The Blue Shirts did not attack the system of private enterprise per se. However, such critical areas of the economy as heavy industry, mining, large-scale transport and foreign trade would be managed directly by the state. There was to be no proscription on private profit, but it was stipulated that private capital had to be used for the benefit of society as a whole. It is worth noting that the economic controls proposed by the Blue Shirts would apply solely to productive enterprises; the distributive sector of the economy would be left to the free functioning of the market."*[682] The Blue Shirt Society attacked capitalism, individualism, communism, and supported what they called *"national socialism"* combined with Marxism, the nationalization of industry and education, and the collectivization of farming.[683]

Even after the German-Japanese Axis alliance terminated the feasibility of further KMT-Nazi relations, Chiang continued to cling to a fascistic nationalism during World War II. This was best illustrated in late 1943 when Chiang published China's Destiny. In this book, he condemned communism and liberalism as negative philosophies for China and held up

---

[679] Kirby, William C. Germany and Republican China (Stanford University Press 1984) page 162.

[680] Ibid, pages 165-167.

[681] Dirlik, Arif. "The Ideological Foundations of the New Life Movement: A Study in Counterrevolution" The Journal of Asian Studies August 1975 pages 970-971.

[682] Eastman, Lloyd. "Fascism in Kuomintang China: The Blue Shirts" The China Quarterly (January - March 1972) page 12.

[683] Kirby, William C. Germany and Republican China (Stanford University Press 1984) page 159.

Confucian principles as a model for China to follow. The English-language text was so hostile to the West that it was censored, lest the Americans and British would become displeased.[684] Madame Chiang feared that the *"prideful, socialist, anti-imperialist, and even anti-capitalist outlook"* of China's Destiny would alienate British and American support for the Nationalists. It was seldom published in English during the wartime period. It was published by the pro-communist editor of Amerasia Phillip Jaffe.[685] Even after 1943, the book China's Destiny was required reading for students in Nationalist-controlled territory and for all officials, military officers, and KMT members. It was noted that China's Destiny *"reflects Chiang's distinctly nationalist, highly anti-imperialist, and strictly authoritarian outlook, but on world affairs it struck a liberal, internationalist stance."* Chiang implored citizens that they *"must pay special attention to and not neglect for a moment, the duty of obeying the state's policy."* Chiang's second book Chinese Economic Theory (1943) was used in the KMT's Central Political Training Institute. This book called for a mixed, planned economy, a protectionist/nationalist trade policy, state-ownership of major industries, and *"control of private capital."* This book also urged Western economists to abandon materialism and selfish individualism and embrace a *"world of great harmony"* where *"human nature is developed to the highest point...no one will be able to earn a living by sitting idle...no one will be unable to find work."*[686] Chiang Kai-shek himself also noted in China's Destiny (1943) that *"A planned economy should be put into operation so that national defense and the people's livelihood may be fully co-ordinated and developed and China may become a strong national defense unit against aggression."*[687]

Chiang also wrote that *"The dispute between liberalism and communism was nothing more than a dispute concerning Anglo-American and Soviet ideologies. All these theories and political doctrines not only could not meet the needs of China's national life, but they were also inconsistent with the inherent spirit of China's culture: for any one of us to advocate these theories and doctrines indiscriminately is to forget completely that he is a Chinese and to miss completely the object of learning which is to make use of what is learned for the benefit of China. The result was only to make Chinese culture sink into a state of decay and disintegration. Under these circumstances Chinese scholars and politicians who misinterpreted liberalism and abused communism were disposed, openly or indirectly, intentionally or unintentionally, to take a foreign power's stand as their own and to take a foreign power's stand as their own and to identify a foreign power's interests with theirs. Nay, they even went to the length of putting a favorable color on imperialism and of becoming the tools of aggression."*[688] The KMT also continued their ideological molding programs from the 1930s in order to forge loyalty to the rule of Chiang Kai-shek and his interpretation of the Three Principles of the People. In 1944, Chiang Ching-kuo formed the school for the training of cadres of the Youth Corps of the Three People's

---

[684] Johnson, Paul. Modern Times (Harper Collins Publisher 1991) Accessed From: http://archive.org/stream/ModernTimes_305/42024947-19032115-Johnson-Paul-Modern-Times-the-World-From-the-Twenties-to-the-Nineties-Revised-Edition-Harper-Collins-1991_djvu.txt

[685] Taylor, Jay. The Generalissimo's Son (Harvard University Press 2009) page 261.

[686] "China's Destiny by Chiang Kai-shek" February 20, 2010 Accessed From: http://johnshaplin.blogspot.com/2010/02/chinas-destiny-by-chiang-kai-shek.html

[687] Chiang Kai Shek. China's Destiny (Dobson, 1947) page 125.

[688] Ibid, page 247.

Principles. It was to combine "*Leninist revolutionary method and neo-Confucian traditional ethics*" to the Youth Corps officials.[689]

From the 1930s to the 1970s, successive KMT platforms endorsed at least some level of state ownership of the economy, state regulation and subsidies for favored elements of the private sector, and corporative relations between labor and management. The November 1935 Manifesto of the Fifth National Congress of the Kuomintang stated "*In industrial development all major enterprises of immediate concern to national interests and people's welfare should be operated by the state in principle. Efforts should be made to revamp old state operated enterprises and develop new ones...labor management relations should be harmonized in the interest of general industrial development.*"[690]

The Manifesto of the Extraordinary National Congress of the KMT noted in April 1938 that "*...during the war, the Government must enforce the planned economy in accordance with the Principle of People's Livelihood, especially the part about economic reconstruction. Enterprises designated for state operation should be developed with state funds and operated under state regulation. Enterprises suitable for private ownership should be developed by private capital in accordance with the overall state plan and should be given government guidance and encouragement. Private enterprises shall be encouraged to grow with help from government banks. Heavy industry and transportation networks may not run contrary to the principle of the 'regulation of capital.'*"[691]

In September 1950, the Political Platform of the Kuomintang wanted to "*...endeavor in the framework of our national reconstruction plans, free the great masses of people from domination by monopolists and speculators and to make it possible for people in all walks of life to have a chance for fair and equitable development...We shall also urge the strict levying of the income tax, the inheritance tax, and the property tax in order to being about a fairer distribution of wealth in society...We shall, in the best interests of both labor and capital promote their mutual help and cooperation in order to step up social production.*"[692] In October 1952, the Platform of the KMT as approved by the 7th National Congress noted that "*enterprises as are related to the secrets of national defense or are of a monopolistic nature should be operated primarily by the state.*"[693] The Platform of the 9th National Congress of the KMT intended to "*Encourage private enterprise in all fields except those having to do with national defense or those of a monopolistic nature and safeguard the employment of those who protect the property and factories in the war areas and assist them in securing a share of ownership.*"[694] The KMT Political Platform as adopted by the 9th National Congress in April 1969 wanted to "*Formulate long range economic plans to develop basic and sophisticated industries, improve agricultural techniques, increase the exploitation and utilization of natural resources, and expand*

---

[689] Shao Chuan Leng. Chiang Ching-Kuo's Leadership in the Development of the Republic of China (University Press of America 1993) pages 7-9.

[690] Shieh, Milton J.T. The Kuomingtang Selected Historical Documents 1894-1969 (St. Johns University Press, 1970) page 161.

[691] Ibid, page 180.

[692] Ibid, page 231.

[693] Ibid, page 251.

[694] Ibid, page 285.

international trade and economic and technical cooperation…Encourage private ownership of industries except for those vital to national defense or of a monopolistic nature…"[695]

The KMT under Chiang Kai-shek and even Sun Yat-sen viewed aspects of Soviet Communism with a favorable eye. On the one hand, the KMT opposed undiluted Marxism, yet also appreciated Soviet strategies for industrial development and their fight against Western colonialism. The Soviet Union trained Kuomintang revolutionaries in the Moscow Sun Yat-sen University. In the West and in the Soviet Union, Chiang was known as the *"Red General."*[696] Movie theaters in the Soviet Union showed newsreels and clips of Chiang, at Moscow Sun Yat-sen University. Portraits of Chiang were hung on the walls. At the Soviet May Day Parade, Chiang's portrait was carried along with the portraits of Marx, Lenin, Stalin, and other communist leaders.[697] The full break with the Soviets occurred when Stalin sabotaged the KMT and Chiang from behind the scenes. In 1927, Stalin noted that the KMT was a *"sort of revolutionary parliament…Why drive away the Right when it is of use to us…When it is no more use we will drive it away."* Stalin stated that Chiang Kai-shek was to *"be squeezed out like a lemon and thrown away."*[698] From that point onward, Chiang became ideologically an uncompromising anti-communist. However, the Soviet culture within the KMT remained deeply embedded in that movement. This reality was reflected in the KMT's centralized political structure, collectivist ideology, and use of mass organizations to mobilize support for the Chiang dictatorship.

While the Chiang dictatorship fought communist subversion and officially banned trade with the communist mainland, goods leaked through the Bamboo Curtain. While it is unknown whether the KMT encouraged these low level trade relations, it did catch the attention of the United States. In 1956, Assistant Secretary of State Herbert Hoover Jr. noted that the Chinese Nationalists in Taiwan shipped to the communist People's Republic millions of dollars' worth of goods. It was believed that these goods were smuggled on junks and transshipped through Hong Kong. Exports from Taiwan to China totaled $7.3 million in 1953 and mostly consisted of sugar shipped through Hong Kong.[699] Trade between Taiwan and China totaled $1.1 million in 1962 and consisted of medicinal herbs, dates, lotus seeds, crabs, and other types of herbs. Taiwan exported raw sugar to China via intermediaries in Hong Kong.[700] After Chiang's death in 1975, the trade between Red China and Taiwan increased by leaps and bounds.

Occasionally, KMT sanctioned anti-Americanism reared its head in Taiwan during the 1950s and early 1970s. Previous KMT anti-Americanism was confined to the radical elements that surrounded Chiang Kai-shek. Some Kuomintang officials like secret service chief Dai Lai were very anti-American and desired the full expulsion of US influence from China.[701] Such sentiments arose from alleged misconduct by American personnel; President Nixon's betrayal of Taiwan to Red China; and the US-supported return of the Senkaku Islands from Taiwan to Japan.

---

[695] Ibid, pages 328-329.

[696] Pakula, Hannah. The Last Empress: Madame Chiang Kai-Shek and the Birth of Modern China (Simon and Schuster 2009) page 246.

[697] Taylor, Jay. The Generalissimo's Son (Harvard University Press 2009) page 42.

[698] Ibid, page 42.

[699] "Trade by Taiwan with Reds Bared" New York Times March 28, 1956 page 1.

[700] Gilbert, Lewis. "Peking and Taipei" The China Quarterly July-September 1963 page 59.

[701] Fenby, Jonathan. Chiang Kai-shek: China's Generalissimo and the Nation He Lost (Carroll & Graf Publishers) page 414.

The 1957 killing of a Chinese "*peeping Tom*" by a US military officer in Taiwan sparked the sacking of the US Embassy in Taipei. Anti-US signs which condemned "*foreign devils*" appeared on the embassy walls.[702] In 1971, government newspapers in Taiwan lambasted US "*betrayal*" and "*appeasement*" over the opening to Red China by the Nixon Administration. President Chiang ruefully noted "*Some countries today are myopic and lured by immediate advantage.*" Thirty Taiwanese students paraded in front of the US Embassy to protest Washington's moves. Taiwanese also demonstrated against the American return of the Senkaku Islands to Japan.[703] However, beneath these surface issues, the KMT always retained an anti-colonial, anti-Western bias leftover from the 1930s. An American official commented: "*You get the feeling that down deep they would like to tick us off.*" Government newspapers in Taiwan dubbed the United States the "*Ugly Americans*" and opined that our pro-China policy was "*ill conceived.*"[704]

Some of Taiwan's ill will toward the United States was justified by bipartisan betrayal of the KMT to the Communist Party. President Truman and some of his more philo-Maoist advisers viewed the Chinese Communist Party as a grouping committed to "*agrarian reforms.*" Consequently, American arms shipments to Chiang's forces were embargoed and even destroyed or re-routed to the Soviets! Colonel L. B. Moody was United States Army Ordinance Corps officer who served with the Donald Nelson mission to China. He remarked in April 1950 that "*the massive support of artillery, tanks, motor transport and aircraft to which western armies are accustomed is practically non-existent. The side which has the predominating infantry weapons, and especially the ammunition therefore, holds all the aces. You are asked to bear this in mind as this talk will endeavor to show that the foreseen and inevitable defeat of the Nationalist Armies was due to a Nationalist deficit in these items, and Communist superiority therein, resulting from persistent United States action.*" In 1946 and 1947, General George C. Marshall also embargoed arms to the Chiang Kai-shek government. In 1946, the communist agent Lauchlin Currie wrote an order on White House stationery which forbade any shipment of ex-Nazi firearms to the Nationalist forces. These arms were instead turned over to Soviet forces in their occupied zone in eastern Germany or just destroyed. After Japan surrendered in September 1945, stores of Lend Lease supplies intended for China were destroyed or thrown into the Indian Ocean. After July 1947, American weapons shipments to the Nationalists consisted of older weapons. Furthermore, the Chinese were also charged five to ten times the normal price for these firearms. The State Department also refused to allow American military personnel in China to provide advice in the battlefield. William C. Bullitt also remarked after a visit to China in 1948 that the American military mission also consisted of "*fellow travelers and Communist sympathizers.*"[705]

Ill-conceived American trade and foreign assistance policies were the two factors which aggravated the already existing leftist anti-colonialism present in the KMT. Chinese Nationalist leaders organized mass meetings in Shanghai to drum up anti-American feeling to pressure Congress to provide Lend Lease assistance. Extreme elements of the Nationalists also stirred up

[702] Trumbull, Robert. "Taiwan Is Seeking Repair of U. S. Tie; Chinese Still Angry" New York Times May 29, 1957 page 1.

[703] Kann, Peter. "Embattled Island" Wall Street Journal August 24, 1971 page 1.

[704] Durdin, Tillman. "Taipei Clings to Affiliate Ties" New York Times October 27, 1971 page 1.

[705] Utley, Freda. The China Story (H. Regnery 1951) Accessed From: http://www.fredautley.com/toolittle.htm

anti-American feeling in response to the dumping of US-made products into the Chinese market, thus bankrupting Chinese industries and hampering postwar recovery. These Nationalist extremists also hotly opposed General George C. Marshall's efforts to halt a complete victory over the Chinese Communist armies.[706]

South Korea Under Syngman Rhee, Generals Park Chung-hee, and Chun Doo-hwan (1945-1988)

After the defeat of the Japanese militarists in September 1945, Korea was divided into zones: a Soviet-occupied area in the North and a noncommunist, American-controlled one in the South. In the North, the Soviets established the superstructure of a hardline Stalinist communist totalitarian dictatorship under General Kim il-sung, while the United States provided lukewarm support for an increasingly authoritarian, anti-communist, and collectivist regime in the South led by Dr. Syngman Rhee. In 1948, both Korean zones became independent countries: the Republic of Korea in the South and the Democratic People's Republic of Korea in the North. Throughout the entire post-1945 history of the Korean Peninsula, the two nations fought a shooting war and the state of relations was relatively tense thereafter.

Although many of Dr. Rhee's American defenders cast him as an admirer of the American constitutional system, the evidence seems to contradict that observation. His earlier political platform was clearly socialist and assuredly not capitalist. Perhaps Rhee's radical platform was crafted to compete with the myriad of communist subversives who sought to recruit peasants and workers in order to stir unrest and invite a Soviet/North Korean invasion. In 1946, Dr. Rhee, who was the chairman of the South Korean Democratic Representative Council, called for the confiscation of Japanese property, the nationalization of heavy industry, mines, forests, utilities, banks, communications, and transportation. He also called for a planned economy, price controls, rationing, and state supervision of private enterprises. Compulsory education and progressive income taxation were also supported by Dr. Rhee.[707]

Dr. Rhee also developed a nationalist-collectivist ideology called *Il Min Chui*, which denounced individualism. Il Min Chu I noted that *"the nation's weakness was ascribed to individual attitudes asserting special interests. Our supreme objective is to carry on our affairs by sacrificing everything and uniting into one."* Dr. Rhee's opponents in the National Assembly were condemned people as individuals who *"have not learned the lesson of subordinating parts to the greater whole."*[708]

Dr. Rhee's *Il Min Chui* supported the termination of class cleavages and differences in wealth. *Il Min Chui* ideologist An Hosang stated *"Nation is more important than any individual or class and the state is bigger than any organization or party. It is natural for one people to regard nation and state as such...If we neglect the welfare of the whole nation and cling to one's own foreign thought and ideology our nation will not only be divided but also return to toadyism of the past."*[709] Dr. Rhee's theorist Ahn Ho-Sang noted that the workers and capitalists were

---

[706] United States Department of State The China White Paper, August 1949 Volumes 1-2 pages 170-171.

[707] Johnston, Richard. "Dr. Rhee Outlines Korean Program" New York Times March 3, 1946 page 34.

[708] Hee, Park Chung. To Build a Nation (Acropolis Books 1971) pages 107-108.

[709] Gi-Wook Shin. Ethnic Nationalism in Korea (Stanford University Press, 2006) page 102.

materialist in their outlook, who henceforth pursued their own class interests. Ahn supported the democracy according to the precepts of *Il Min Chui,* as opposed to communism and the British-American style of capitalist democracy. Dr. Rhee's ideologists opposed capitalism and communism and attempted to create a nationalism based on the principles of the *Il Min Chui.* Dr. Rhee's ideologists urged the people to move beyond the "*foreign ideological divide of left and right.*" In 1949, Ahn Jae-Hong supported the "*three equalities*" in wealth, education, and power. According to Ahn, real democracy should be pursued, while capitalist democracy (plutocracy) and communist democracy (class dictatorship) were to be rejected by South Koreans. The ideologues of *Il Min Chui* observed that capitalism and communism undermined the South Korean nation. In 1947, Dr. Rhee noted that "*Under the generous but confusing policy of American democracy, individualist egoism instead of resolute kukmin character grew, which would lead to the extinction of patriotic passion for the freedom of kukmin.*" Yang Woo-Jung noted in 1947 that workers could not escape exploitation under capitalism. According to Yang, the state and household were incompatible with capitalism, which based on exploitation, and communism, which denied the existence of the state.[710]

After 1948, President Rhee developed an authoritarian dictatorship which suppressed even the noncommunist opposition. The ruling party was President Rhee's badly misnamed Liberal Party. The South Korean economy was transformed into a corrupt, crony capitalist system where the government heavily participated in investments and regulations. Under President Rhee "*business more than ever became an adjunct of government and especially as the Liberal Party rose, enterprises became the fiefs of politicians.*"[711] Import and foreign exchange controls became a cash cow for the private sector and government elites during the period of President Rhee. The chief source of public funds for South Korean private businesses was the government-owned Reconstruction Bank.[712]

After President Rhee was overthrown in 1960, a democratic government took over in Seoul. However, in 1961, General Park Chung-hee dislodged the democratic republic and set up a highly authoritarian dictatorship. General Park dubbed his political ideology "*administrative democracy.*"[713] The concept of "*administrative democracy*" entailed authoritarian rule from the President. General Park also noted in January 1979 that "*There was a time where we copied and mimicked Western democracy just as it was…The result however was most unproductive, inefficient, confusing and disorderly as you are well aware.*"[714] General Park then became the President of South Korea until 1979, when he was assassinated. General Park represented a group of South Korean military officers who served under the Japanese militarists in 1930s. Consequently, they absorbed Japanese fascist-socialist ideas on economic administration and

---

[710] Ou-Byung Chae. <u>Non-Western Colonial Rule and Its Aftermath</u> (University of Michigan., 2006)

[711] Henderson, Gregory. <u>Korea the Politics of the Vortex</u> (Harvard University Press, 1968) page 198.

[712] Henderson, Gregory. <u>Korea the Politics of the Vortex</u> (Harvard University Press, 1968) pages 284-285.

[713] Khaled, Mortuza. "Park Chung-hee's Industrialization Policy and its Lessons for Developing Countries" 23-25, August 2007 Accessed From: http://www.geocities.ws/mortuzakhaled/park.pdf

[714] "President Pak Chong Hui Holds Press Conference January 19" <u>Korean Herald</u> January 20, 1979

labor-management relations. General Park sought to launch an export-driven industrial drive in the 1960s to convert South Korea from an economic backwater to a major world economic power. Clifford observed that *"Because of their training in the fascist-corporate state of the wartime Japanese empire, the military men of Park's generation had a clearer idea of how a state could organize capitalism than did either their seniors or their juniors."*[715]

South Korean scholar Jung-en Woo observed that the economic and political ideologies of General Park and his military colleagues were statist-nationalist with strong socialist/fascist tendencies: *"These were men of peasant origin and harbored, like ultranationalist Japanese officers in the 1930s, a peasants' suspicion of the wealthy. When they thought of capitalism, they thought of a conspiracy of the rich; when they entertained the notion of economic development, they thought of a rich nation and a strong army, and wartime Japan came to their minds; and when they awakened to the need for domestic resource mobilization, they badgered the rich and forced citizens, through campaigns and edicts, to salt away chunks of their salaries."*[716] Economist and former Prime Minister Nam Duck Woo observed that General Park *"was guided by several different thoughts. They were influenced by some academics who had a socialist approach."*[717] Given the leftist-sounding rhetoric which emanated from General Park and his colleagues, along with the mass arrests of big businessmen, the anti-communist press believed that the new South Korean leaders were crypto-Soviet agents or Reds. For example, General Park Chung-hee was dubbed *"Parkov"* in light of his revolutionary and alleged pro-Soviet sympathies.[718]

General Park sought to create a *dirigist*-state capitalist economy which absorbed many socialist features. A crucial part of General Park's economic program was economic nationalism and a drive to promote the export of manufactured goods. General Park noted in 1962 that *"Korean-style capitalism under Japanese colonial rule had guaranteed the pursuit of foreigner-colonialists' interests and, post-liberation, had degenerated into a hot-bed of corruption and dishonesty which assisted illicit profiteers who pursued profit-making with their government allies."*[719] He also noted *"The principle of free enterprise and respect for the creativity of private industry was adopted for in this way we believed that the private sector would be encouraged to act voluntarily. Under the plan however the economy was not entirely free since development of basic industries was directed by the government."*[720] In 1962, General Park noted that *"Where the appalling power of mammoth enterprise is concerned only with private profit under a self-assumed assertion of contribution to national development, there is no free competition...Therefore the state's coordination and supervisory guidance of mammoth economic strength, especially that of private enterprise becomes a key issue in a free economic policy."*[721] Park also noted that *"Guided capitalism was system of economic management*

---

[715] Clifford, Mark. Troubled Tiger: Businessmen, Bureaucrats, and Generals in South Korea (M.E. Sharpe, 1998) page 37.

[716] Ibid, page 42.

[717] Ibid, page 42.

[718] Ibid, page 37.

[719] Hyung-A Kim. Korea's Development under Park Chung Hee: Rapid Industrialization, 1961-1979 (Routledge 2004) pages 73-76.

[720] Hee, Park Chung. To Build a Nation (Acropolis Books 1971) pages 107-108.

[721] Park Chung Hee. Our nation's path: ideology of social reconstruction (Hollym Corporation, 1970) page 270.

designed to create an economic order that would guarantee the equalization of income and public benefit from the economy."[722] In January 1979, General Park also noted that *"...the economy cannot be developed by the government's or the people's efforts alone and that the government and people must cooperate with each other."*[723]

After General Park took over South Korean in a *coup* in 1961, his government formed the Supreme Council for National Reconstruction. The National Assembly was abolished and politicians, businessmen, and alleged *"profiteers"* were jailed and their wealth was confiscated. The military regime forced a group of speculators to parade through the streets of Seoul, bearing signs emblazoned with the accusation: *"I am a parasite."* General Park noted that *"freedom"* was misconstrued as the *"freedom to engage in smuggling, freedom to accept bribes and freedom to amass illegal fortunes."* Two dozen members of the South Korean big business community were arrested by the South Korean military. Other prisoners of General Park were paraded in Seoul's streets by South Korean paratroopers. They bore signs that read *"We will quit being hooligans and will become workers for the revolution."* Alleged *"hoodlums,"* dancers, and smugglers of imported goods were also arrested by the new regime. General Park banned fifteen political parties and 238 social organizations.[724] Clifford observed that *"This is the sort of rhetoric expected from a budding Communist state, not a country that would be heralded as a triumph of capitalist growth, but it is a revealing illustration of the mistrust--even hatred--that many Koreans had for businessmen."*[725] The confiscated wealth was to be conscripted for an ambitious program for industrialization. The Korea Annual reported that *"The Military Government carried out criminal punishment, through the revolutionary trial, of those involved in illegal amassment of wealth so as to meet and alleviate the people's (indignation) against such hated millionaires and former high-ranking government officials and generals... The confiscation (of illegally amassed wealth) shall be materialized through forced reinvestment in the specific plant projects that the 5-year Economic Development Plan envisaged. Thus, a number of plant projects including a cement plant, an oil refinery, an iron works, a fertilizer plant, etc. were designated as the target projects for the confiscatory investment."*[726]

After the initial pseudo-leftist revolutionary period, General Park reached a grand bargain with big business. He sought to construct an economically powerful South Korea and forced the South Korean business community to collaborate in the effort to foster rapid economic development.[727] Export-oriented industries received cheap loans and other subsidies from the Park regime. Clifford observed *"On one side he (General Park) controlled business through loans, periodic tax investigations and anticorruption campaigns. But he also presided over the*

---

[722] Khaled, Mortuza. "Park Chung-hee's Industrialization Policy and its Lessons for Developing Countries" 23-25, August 2007 Accessed From: http://www.geocities.ws/mortuzakhaled/park.pdf

[723] "President Pak Chong Hui Holds Press Conference January 19" Korean Herald January 20, 1979

[724] Clifford, Mark. Troubled Tiger: Businessmen, Bureaucrats, and Generals in South Korea (M.E. Sharpe, 1998) pages 37-38.

[725] Ibid, page 39.

[726] Ibid, page 41.

[727] Ibid, pages 37-38.

explosive growth of the chaebol, which were both fiercely competitive private companies--in the export sector-and privileged recipients of domestic oligopolies and monopolies."[728]

Under General Park, the government exercised sizable powers over the private economy. The director general of the South Korean National Physical Planning Bureau Cho Sung Il bragged that *"I could decide that a factory should go here...or there and I controlled the population of Seoul."*[729] In January 1976, the South Korean Economic Planning Board (EPB) was granted the discretionary power to grant tax advantages and subsidies to private industries. Any new private investment project was subjected to review by the special investment screening organ of the EPB.[730] In early 1973, General Park launched the Heavy and Chemical Industries Plan to increase the number strategic industrial plants, such as shipyards, heavy engineering plants, power generation equipment plants, steel mills, electronics firms, and chemical plants. Clifford noted that *"Korea had a large, cheap, well-educated work force; as Posco demonstrated, it could acquire state-of-the-art facilities, which would give it a leg up over its more established competitors; it could borrow money from abroad for investment; a protected domestic market provided a captive customer base; and its businessmen and government officials were used to international market pressures and could readily develop export markets."*[731]

In response, South Korean businessmen sometimes quietly complained about the oppressiveness of state controls over the economy. Daewoo Chairman Kim Woo Choong observed that *"The government tells you it's your duty and you have to do it, even if there's no profit. Maybe, after the year 2000, Korean businessmen will be able to put their companies' interests ahead of those of the government or of society."*[732] Kim Suk Won, chairman of the Ssangyong group, recalled that *"The government asked (the chaebol) to invest in key industries...Whether businesses liked it or not, they had to do it."*[733] Ssangyong chairman Kim Suk Won recalled that *"Foreign companies have a lot of complaints about laws and regulations, but remember, we are living with it."*[734]

The Korean Central Intelligence Agency (KCIA) harassed both the foreign and domestic business communities. One report told of a *"manager of a foreign bank branch in Seoul came into his office to find several garbled telexes. He asked his Korean secretary to notify the senders to resend the messages. She told her foreign boss that it would be easier simply to contact the KCIA, which kept copies of all incoming messages. She did, and a few hours later the bewildered manager received copies of his telexes, along with a card stating that these had been provided with the compliments of the KCIA."*[735] Former KCIA director Kim Hyung Wook stated to the US Congress that General Park *"imposed severe pressures and sanctions on businessmen who did not give him their undivided loyalty. In many cases, charges were fabricated and these individuals were sent to jail. In addition to imprisonment, the businesses of these individuals*

---

[728] Ibid, page 41.
[729] Ibid, page 165.
[730] "Law to Control Private Enterprises Cited" <u>Seoul Haptong</u> January 22, 1976
[731] Clifford, Mark. <u>Troubled Tiger: Businessmen, Bureaucrats, and Generals in South Korea</u> (M.E. Sharpe, 1998) pages 104-107.
[732] Ibid, page 113.
[733] Ibid, page 114.
[734] Ibid, page 123.
[735] Ibid, page 83.

were often confiscated." The government also possessed the power to destroy businesses by cutting off the flow of credits from state-owned banks.[736]

Perhaps in an effort to mirror the wartime Japanese militarist *Sanpo*[737] organization, General Park created the *Saemaul Undong* (New Village movement) in 1971 to mediate the differences between management and labor and to stimulate increased production in the farms and factories. *Saemaul Undong* was clearly a fascistic, corporative institution which sought to root out class struggle in South Korean society. The *Saemaul Undong* imposed discipline on the South Korean farmers and workers. Under *Saemaul Undong*, farm villages were electrified, while bridges, roads, irrigation canals, dikes, and small reservoirs were built. These infrastructure projects were built using virtually unpaid village labor. The three goals of *Saemaul Undong* were:

1) An increase in the living standards of the farmers.
2) Increased incomes for the farmers.
3) Promotion of *"spiritual enlightenment."*[738]

In 1972, General Park observed that *"The Saemaul movement is a training ground for Korean democracy to become acclimatized to our native soil. It is the breeding ground for genuine patriotism, and at the same time the workshop for putting into reality the spirit of the October Revitalizing (Yusin) Reforms."* General Park noted in 1979 that the purpose of the *Saemaul Undong* movement was to *"demonstrate the spirit of self-help, participation, cooperation, unity and the determination to work for themselves."* The *Saemaul Undong* movement fostered *"spiritual enlightenment"* and a sense of *"spiritual revolution"* within the rural South Korean population.[739]

However, the *Saemaul Undong* had a darker, more authoritarian side. General Park and other South Korean officials insisted on the villagers' obedience to *"community will"* and *"community decisions."* One Western observer reported that *"several recalcitrant families"* were *"evicted from the village—their belongings were taken from their homes and they were told to move elsewhere if they would not abide by community decisions."*[740]

The *Saemaul Undong* movement also extended into South Korea's industrial sector. In 1979, Park noted that *"The (Factory) Saemaul Movement as practiced in offices and factories is nothing different (from the Village Movement), since its basic spirit is one of diligence, self-help and cooperation...There should be close labor-management cooperation, with the company president making maximum efforts to improve pay and welfare for his employees and the latter fulfilling their duties with a sense of responsibility and sincerity, doing factory work as if they were doing their own personal work, and caring for the factory as if it were their own."* One of the slogans of the Factory Saemaul Movement clearly highlighted its corporatist mission:

---

[736] Ibid, page 83.

[737] The Sanpo organization sought to foster collaboration and harmony between the workers and management in wartime fascist-militarist Japan.

[738] Clifford, Mark. Troubled Tiger: Businessmen, Bureaucrats, and Generals in South Korea (M.E. Sharpe, 1998) pages 94-96.

[739] "President Pak Chong Hui 1975 New Year Press Conference" Seoul Domestic Service January 14, 1975

[740] Ibid.

"Employees like family; the company like my home."[741] General Park noted in January 1975 that *"Labor and management should maintain close mutual understanding and cooperation. Businessmen should make efforts to insure better treatment for workers within the limits permissible. The government will actively strive to achieve this goal."*[742] In January 1979 General Park noted that *"...the Saemaul Undong (New Community Movement) being positively promoted in urban communities and at all factories throughout the country is becoming the force to strengthen the spiritual drive of all citizens and discipline in society. Particularly notable is the factory Saemaul Undong which is creating a fresh atmosphere for labor management cooperation. By virtue of this movement labor management problems which are apt to arise in the process of industrialization are solved satisfactorily by purely Korean methods, a fact that is heartwarming to us all."*[743] General Park stated in 1979 that *"Employers...must treat their workers if they were their own family members, while the latter should regard the plant as 'our factory' or 'my factory.'"*[744]

Amazingly, some observers also compared the *Saemaul Undong* with communism. Hyung-A Kim noted that *"The political concepts, implementation, and methods of the Saemaul Movement are likewise reminiscent of Kim Il Sung's mass mobilization campaign of the 1960s, the Ch'ollima (Flying Horse) Movement."*[745] In 1990, the Polish Ambassador believed that the *Saemaul Undong* was a non-collectivist route to agricultural mobilization. Hence, he recommend usage of the *Saemaul Undong* for Polish agriculture. However, the Poles abandoned hope after they realized that the *Saemaul Undong* was too similar to communism.[746]

After General Park was assassinated in 1979, General Chun Doo-hwan took power and established yet another fascistic authoritarian dictatorship. He espoused the same corporative social system; a state regulated mixed economy, massive social welfare programs, and anti-communist Korean nationalism. President Chun noted in 1980 that *"The old era, characterized by colonial rule, uncritical emulation of the big powers, and easy going attitudes will be banished. It is inevitable."* He supported medical, old age, and unemployment benefits for all South Koreans.[747] In May 1981, President Chun remarked that close labor-management cooperation *"would contribute greatly to social and economic stability and national security."* He stated *"In order to survive the severe competition in the international market we have to enhance the per capita productivity of all the workers. Therefore effort should be made to reinforce labor-management cooperation as a means of attaining a better position in the international business arena."* Chun felt that the labor-management relationship should not be

---

[741] Hyung-A Kim. <u>Korea's Development under Park Chung Hee: Rapid Industrialization, 1961-1979</u> (Routledge 2004) pages 133-146.

[742] "President Pak Chong Hui 1975 New Year Press Conference" <u>Seoul Domestic Service</u> January 14, 1975

[743] "President Pak Chong Hui Holds Press Conference January 19" <u>Korean Herald</u> January 20, 1979

[744] Park Chung Hee. <u>Saemaul: Korea's New Community Movement</u> (Korea Textbook Company, 1979) page 251.

[745] Hyung-A Kim. <u>Korea's Development under Park Chung Hee: Rapid Industrialization, 1961-1979</u> (Routledge 2004) pages 133-146.

[746] Clifford, Mark. <u>Troubled Tiger: Businessmen, Bureaucrats, and Generals in South Korea</u> (M.E. Sharpe, 1998) pages 94-96.

[747] McDonald, Hamish. "Chun Set to Go" <u>The Age</u> August 25, 1980 page 13.

antagonistic but *"family-like."*[748] *Laissez faire* and free market economics were clearly discarded by General Chun's regime. A *Saemaul Undong* pamphlet from 1981 noted that *"Our social culture had been strongly tainted with the predilection of individualistic egoism and liberalism. In such a socio-cultural atmosphere and environment it was hard to come by the voluntary cooperation of some people for the sake of other people and for social and common interests."*[749] The same pamphlet also noted that *"Through the Saemaul Undong we have experienced a spirit of cooperation in the true sense of the word. In the process we have come to realize the importance of harmony between public and individual interests and also of integrated coordination between groups and individuals."*[750] The handbook also stated that *"...the nationalistic self is the characteristic of an individual who can extend his ideas beyond his individual self. As a member of a large community such as a nation, the self, in the sense of an inclusive idea, always has an opportunity to sublimate itself so as to contribute to the community."*[751] According to a 1982 government pamphlet, the *Saemaul Undong* was charged with creating a *"democratic welfare state."* It also noted *"Industrialists and workers should help each other and build a home like atmosphere and based thereon increase productivity and boost real incomes aware that industrial development serves as the base of national development."*[752]

Big business was urged to drop their opposition and obey the Chun government's planning targets. In August 1981, Chun urged that *"local businessmen should be more cooperative with the government in pushing ahead with the economic development plans based on the capitalist market economic principles."*[753] President Chun stressed that his government would maintain a market economy, while the state controlled 50% of the investment funds which were channeled through state-owned banks.[754]

The dictatorship of President Chun also sought to mould the social spirit of South Korea in a clearly fascist image where the private sectors of civil society was purged or corrupt, greedy, and anti-national attributes. General Chun Doo Hwan noted that *"Because of the phenomenal expansion of our society, traditional virtues, manners and moral dignity have faded away to be replaced by rampant materialism resulting in irregularities, injustice, corruption and mistrust. Unless these evils are erased, we cannot attain our true integrity as a nation...The current social reforms must be seen as ground leveling, the first step in the construction of a society of justice. A society of justice then would represent the revival of traditional values and the achievement of a moral ethic for a new age."* Under General Chun, the Special Committee engaged in a program to *"purge impure elements," "rectify amoral business activities,"* and *"purify the nation by rooting out various social vices."* Clifford compared the purges during the period of General Chun's rule with that of the communist experience: *"Students of Chinese purges, from both the pre-Communist and Communist periods, will find the tone of this extraordinary document familiar."* Former members of General Park's regime were arrested for corruption and their

---

[748] "Chon Tu-Hwan Urge Close labor-Management Ties" <u>Yonhap</u> May 23, 1981
[749] Institute of Saemaul Studies. <u>Saemaul Undong: Determination and Capability of the Koreans</u> (Institute of Saemaul Studies, Republic of Korea, 1981) pages 14-15.
[750] Ibid, page 32.
[751] Ibid, page 182.
[752] Republic of Korea. <u>Saemaul in New Age</u> (Republic of Korea, 1982) page 110.
[753] "Summary of Chon Tu Hwan's August 2 News Conference" <u>Korea Herald</u> August 4, 1981
[754] Stokes, Henry Scott. "Cracking Down in Korea" <u>New York Times</u> October 19, 1980 page SM28.

assets confiscated by the government. In July 1980, officials of the private sector and state-owned corporations were arrested *en masse.*[755]

The General Chun regime also severely cracked down on luxurious weddings, which were unsuccessfully banned under General Park's government. The purpose of the Special Measures to Eliminate Social Evils was *"to root out all social evils at their sources and reshape the consciousness of the people so as to help build up a bright and just society in the belief that such a just society cannot be built without eliminating the cancerous elements in our society."* In August 1980, publications deemed *"obscene, vulgar, (or) instigating social confusion and creating a mood of class consciousness"* were banned by the Special Committee. The wire services were merged into the nationalized Yonhap News Agency. Many private television stations were also nationalized. The state's monopoly on the media was thus assured.[756]

South Korean labor leaders, leftists, and other dissidents were interned in brutal, so-called *"re-education camps"* where at least 50 prisoners died.[757] In 1980, special camps were also set up by the Chun regime for the *"purification"* of businessmen, bankers, and their spouses and children in order to prepare them for the new era. Chun also told businessmen to forsake golf, expensive restaurants, parties, flashy cars, and other forms of luxury consumption. They were also told to wear worker's uniforms and to eat lunch with their employees.[758]

The Chun regime still controlled the commanding heights of the economy through outright state ownership. The state's influence was so pervasive that even communist rulers admired the South Korean system under General Chun. Clifford noted *"Still state-controlled, Posco has become one of the world's largest and most efficient producers, prompting admiration by its competitors in Japan, Germany, and the United States. Ironically, this admiration is perhaps even greater from the Chinese and Russians, who have been stunned that a state-owned steel company could be so successful. An oft-told story has Chinese leader Deng Xiaoping on a trip to Japan asking Japanese steelmakers how to develop his country's steel industry. The reply, from Nippon Steel's Inayama Yoshihiro, was to ask if China had a Park Tae Joon."*[759] Hyundai founder Chung Ju Yung observed that *"the only state-owned corporation to surpass a private enterprise in international competitiveness is Posco, not only in Korea but in the whole world."*[760]

By the late 1970s, South Korea engaged in indirect trade with a number of communist countries, including their Stalinist neighbor to the North. Such trade relations were largely apolitical commercial transactions that were not motivated by ideology. As of September 1979, it was reported that thirteen communist nations traded with South Korea. The top communist trade partners with South Korea included China, the USSR, and Vietnam. In 1978, two-way trade with the communist world totaled $40 million. The South Koreans imported agricultural and fishery products, raw materials such as logs and coal, and machinery and heavy and chemical goods

---

[755] Clifford, Mark. Troubled Tiger: Businessmen, Bureaucrats, and Generals in South Korea (M.E. Sharpe, 1998) pages 162-168.

[756] Ibid, pages 162-168.

[757] Ibid, pages 162-168.

[758] Thorpe, Norman. "South Korea Starts Campaign to 'Purify' Nation's Businesses" Wall Street Journal September 25, 1980 page 36.

[759] Park Tae Joon was the founder and first chairman of POSCO.

[760] Clifford, Mark. Troubled Tiger: Businessmen, Bureaucrats, and Generals in South Korea (M.E. Sharpe, 1998) page 74.

from the communist world. South Korea exported electronic products, color television sets, refrigerators, clocks, fertilizer, machinery, and textiles to their communist trade partners. In 1978, Romanian-South Korean trade totaled $7 million; Soviet-South Korean trade totaled $6.5 million; Yugoslav-South Korean trade totaled $4 million; Vietnamese-South Korean trade totaled $6.2 million; and Czechoslovak-South Korean trade totaled $3 million. Trade between China and South Korea totaled a paltry $40,000. Cuba's trade with South Korea was a minuscule $5,000.[761]

From 1979 to 1983, South Korea imported 1,262,000 tons of coal ($80 million) from North Korea. South Korea imported this coal from the North in order to solve a serious fuel shortage in the wake of the second oil crisis. This coal was imported by Sunkyong Ltd through trading companies in third countries.[762] This set the stage for the full opening of trade relations between South and North Korea in 1988.

As of January 1981, South Korean firms expanded trade with Red China. This trade in goods were channeled through intermediaries in Japan and Hong Kong. South Korean-Red Chinese commerce was believed to have been worth several million dollars. South Korea exported televisions, synthetic textiles, and machinery parts to Red China. China exported coal, silk fabrics, silk yarn, threads, and medicinal herbs to South Korea. Most of the South Korean firms involved in trade with China were small companies.[763] As of July 1981, the Chinese exported coal, oil, and raw materials to South Korea. The South Koreans exported bicycles, synthetic fabrics, and other goods to China. These goods were shipped via ports in third countries.[764]

The Philippines Under President Ferdinand Marcos (1965-1986)

In 1965, Ferdinand E. Marcos was elected as President of the Philippines on a populist and nationalist platform. He immediately implemented a program that theoretically fused a collectivist populism, nationalism, anti-communism, and clean government in a country that was plagued by corruption and inequalities. The communist Huks fought a long war of aggression against the government that was not concluded until the mid-1950s and concerns remained that the Red menace continued to threaten civil society. President Marcos formed the New Society Movement and later the New Republic Movement to drum up mass support for his dictatorship and to exercise control over the populace. With the onset of Islamic and communist terrorism by the early 1970s, President Marcos declared martial law for an unlimited period. During this period the government intervened heavily in the economy and regime allies profited handsomely from this economic system. Independent businessmen were tightly controlled and maligned as exploiters and oligarchs by the Marcos dictatorship.

President Marcos fused anti-Western nationalism with a corporative vision of the reconciliation of the social classes. This was to be accomplished through the New Society/New

---

[761] "Communist Countries-Trade" South Korean News Agency October 10, 1979

[762] "South Korean Energy Ministry Reportedly Imported Coal From North" Yonhap October 10, 1988

[763] Tetsuo Tamura and Nihon Keizai. "South Koreans seek China trade" The Japan Economic Journal January 13, 1981 page 4.

[764] "Trading between China and S Korea alleged" BBC Summary of World Broadcasts July 9, 1981

Republic Movements, regime propaganda, and government regulations. In June 1981, Marcos proclaimed that his "*New Republic*" would liberate the Philippines from the legacies of Spanish and American colonialism. Marcos noted further that "*It is unthinkable that we should approach this task as partisans to warring interests, creeds and ideologies…Our goal is to unite, not divide.*"[765] In May 1985, the comparably leftwing, corrupt Imelda Marcos remarked that "*most of the problems of the nation stems from our colonial mentality.*"[766]

The Marcos dictatorship also propounded self-sufficiency and a highly regulated private sector as its chief ideological pillars. Allegedly anti-social or exploitative businessmen were to be prosecuted or severely controlled by the state. In March 1985, President Marcos noted in a speech on Armed Forces Day that "*We believe that we must seek in our country today a transformation of our society, and that democracy has the capability to transform even a society burdened by a corrupt oligarchy. And we must bring about the authentic economic liberation of our people…The government shall set the atmosphere and perhaps the general guidelines, but it shall leave to free enterprise and the private sector the actual achievement of progress.*"[767]

In October 1983, Marcos announced a new economic policy that supported "*national productivity and restricted importations.*" It also would forbid "*hoarding or profiteering of goods at the expense of the public.*" Minister of Trade and Industry Roberto Ongpin warned that price controls would be extended "*if unscrupulous elements immediately jack up prices to an unreasonable level.*"[768] Marcos noted in September 1983 that "*Economic emancipation is one of the visible gains of the country during the martial law years…one of the objectives of the new society was economic emancipation and this was one of the immediate reforms he ordered carried out.*"[769]

In June 1985, Marcos noted that "*We set before ourselves even higher standards for social justice, providing among others the greater regulation of private income, on the one hand, and the broadening of social services in the forms of educational opportunities, health services, social welfare assistance…We have done all this without abandoning our basic belief in free enterprise. With the engine of growth in our society, without transforming our people into wards of society, we have made enterprise and self-reliance the watchword of our economic life. Everywhere self-reliance is the catchword…*"[770]

The reality of the Filipino economy was a highly corrupt statist crony capitalism backed up by a plethora of official state agencies and government-owned enterprises. The book States, Ideologies, and Social Revolutions: A Comparative Analysis of Iran, Nicaragua, and the Philippines noted that "*The imposition of martial law in 1972 enhanced state resources and*

---

[765] Suarez, Miguel C. "Marcos Inaugurated, Beginning New 6-Year Term" The Associated Press June 30, 1981

[766] "Mrs. Marcos on need for Filipino ideology Quezon City" Maharlika Broadcasting System May 21, 1985

[767] "Marcos Speech at Armed Forces Day Ceremonies" Quezon City Maharlika broadcasting system March 26, 1985

[768] "President Announces New Economic Policy" Far Eastern Broadcasting Company Manila October 8, 1983

[769] "Marcos explains economic gains under martial law" Quezon city RPN television September 15, 1983

[770] "Marcos Speaks at Independence Day Parade" Quezon City Maharlika Broadcasting System June 14, 1985

expanded state intervention in the economy. State intervention increased as the government stimulated its economic assets by borrowing and otherwise obtaining massive amounts of capital from international agencies and the United States government…With increased resources, the state redoubled its intervention in the economy and in capital formation and further restricted the operation of the market mechanism. State regulation, ownership, investment, finance, and expropriation expanded to an unprecedented extent. The state took ownership of Philippine Airlines and created the National Steel Corporation by taking offer several steel mills. Several multinational oil corporations sold all or part of their interests to the state-owned Philippine National Oil Company." The state also took over crony capitalist firms that failed as a result of mismanagement and theft. By 1986, the state-owned a large number of banks, finance corporations, hotels, mines, several mills for the production of paper, textiles, and sugar, as well as construction companies, shipping lines, and steel mills. By 1983, 208 state corporations existed, most of which were established after martial law. The government's National Food Authority took over wheat trading at the wholesale and at the retail levels. In 1972, the Marcos government redistributed land to more than 110,000 tenants, who ended up initially becoming some of the regime's most stalwart supporters.[771]

Jaime Ongpin, a prominent anti-Marcos businessman reported that $6 billion to $7 billion of the Philippines $26 billion foreign debt had been *"wasted because of misallocation to crony-type projects."* An independent economist Bernardo Villegas noted that *"The most damaging impact of crony capitalism emasculated the free- enterprise system and discouraged a lot of would-be investors."* Crony capitalism hampered competition in the economy and restricted access to credit. Ongpin noted that *"The government takes all the lemons and lets them keep the plums…But if you're not a crony, the government takes everything."* Prime Minister Virata noted that *"we have about 300 government corporations."* Former Philippine president Diosdado Macapagal noted that *"All in all, crony capitalism is most responsible for the dismal performance of the economy."* He characterized crony capitalism's attributes as consisting of *"overborrowing and wasting the proceeds of borrowing on nonproductive projects, extravagance and corruption."* Reuben Canoy, a former undersecretary of public information under Marcos, noted that *"The New Society was ushered in by a blare of slogans and promises that wafted like a breath of fresh air across a land made arid by influence peddlers, vested interests, political untouchables and sacred cows."* Vicente Gabriel, president of the Coconut Development Center of the Association of Southeast Asian Nations (ASEAN) remarked that *"While the monopolists are wallowing in wealth, owning mansions, palaces, jet planes, helicopters and Benzes, the coconut farmers cannot even send their children to school or provide medicines, clothing and shelter for their families."* Sugar planters complained vociferously about the lack of payment and mysterious losses of money concerning the Philippine Sugar Commission and the National Sugar Trading Corporation. Reportedly, the Corporation owed the planters at least $27 million.[772]

President Marcos and his political supporters in the government vigorously lambasted oppositionist businessmen and their political allies in an almost pseudo-leftist, Marxist fashion. This was an effort by the Marcos dictatorship to portray itself as the champion of the working

---

[771] Parsa, Misagh. States, Ideologies, and Social Revolutions: A Comparative Analysis of Iran, Nicaragua, and the Philippines (Cambridge University Press 2000) pages 63-66.

[772] Branigin, William. "'Crony Capitalism' Blamed for Economic Crisis" The Washington Post August 16, 1984 page A1

classes and an enemy of allegedly anti-national and greedy business elites. In September 1983, Marcos warned big business opposition engaged in public demonstrations that *"We have pictures of everything that happened; there are videotapes where the faces of men are very clear…We will look for these men…Whether they are members of big institutions like the Ayala Foundation, the Bank of the Philippine Islands…or the Development Bank of the Philippines, Security Bank and other banks, you can rest assured we will look for you."*[773] In October 1983, Marcos denounced the *"hydra-headed oligarchy"* who led political opposition to his rule.[774] In December 1983, the Far Eastern Broadcasting Company reported that President Marcos uncovered a *"clergy-bourgeois clique which aims to topple the government and seize power in the country."*[775] In January 1986, the pro-Marcos Maharlika Broadcasting System noted that *"It is now clear that Cory Aquino*[776] *is the candidate of the hacienderos, because she is one of them. In this way, we can expect her to work only for the landed gentry, the oligarchs and the rich. No wonder the workers and farmers of her own hacienda are now up in arms against her."*[777]

In February 1986, the Marcos government bused landless peasants to demonstrate outside the home of Corazon Aquino. This demonstration was publicized in the pro-government media, which portrayed Aquino and her business partners as heartless, exploitative oligarchs.[778]

Aside from some American anti-communists and multinational corporations, the Marcos regime had few sympathizers within the United States by 1986. The communist-turned fascist Lyndon LaRouche movement was one of the Filipino government's last bases of support within the United States. In the fall of 1985, Fusion Energy Foundation (FEF)[779] spokesman Uwe Parpart and LaRouche's security chief, Paul Goldstein traveled to Manila to advise Marcos. They led a delegation of the LaRouche front Schiller Institute to meet with Marcos. This meeting with the LaRouchians was widely reported in the Philippine press. LaRouche noted that his aides warned Marcos: *"They're going to coup you."* LaRouche noted that if Marcos *"had taken the kinds of actions we'd recommended…he would not have been couped."* Paul Goldstein reported that Marcos was opposed by the Israeli Mossad and Jewish businessmen.[780]

---

[773] Chapman, William. "Marcos Says He Will Crack Down on Foes" The Washington Post September 26, 1983 page A15.

[774] "Philippine President Denounces Opposition Forces" Xinhua General News Service October 17, 1983

[775] "Marcos exposes 'clergy-bourgeois clique'" Far Eastern Broadcasting Company December 20, 1983

[776] Corizon Aquino was the daughter of key anti-Marcos opposition leader Benigno Aquino. She eventually became President in 1986, after Marcos was deposed and fled the country.

[777] "Government Radio Calls Cory Aquino 'Oligarchs' Candidate'" Quezon City, Maharlika Broadcasting System January 29, 1986

[778] White, Michael. "Marcos uses reform to attack Aquino estates" The Guardian (London) February 5, 1986

[779] The Fusion Energy Foundation (FEF) was one of the myriad of LaRouchian fronts that promoted, among other policies, an expansion of the number of government-subsidized nuclear power plants in the United States.

[780] King, Dennis. Lyndon LaRouche and the New American Fascism (Doubleday, 1989) Accessed From:

http://archive.org/stream/LyndonLaroucheAndTheNewAmericanFascism/LLNAF_djvu.txt

Even two decades after Marcos' overthrow, the LaRouchians continued to serve as apologists for that corrupt regime. In 2004, the LaRouche publication Executive Intelligence Review (EIR) noted that *"The popular memory of Ferdinand Marcos today, in the U.S. and in the Philippines, is largely shaped by the massive disinformation campaign created in the early 1980s by the circles around then-Secretary of State Shultz, and his deputy Paul Wolfowitz. Marcos was accused of corruption, human rights violations, plunder, and even the murder of a political opponent, Benigno Aquino—and this caricature is repeated ad nauseam still today. While Marcos was not without faults, he was by far the last Filipino head of state to have understood the challenge of true leadership in a world slipping towards chaos. His overthrow by the Shultz cabal had nothing to do with the charges issued publicly, but were intended to stop his national development policies, and his international collaboration with LaRouche and others in countering the genocidal policies of the IMF, and bringing into being a new world economic system based on development and justice."*[781]

The Marcos dictatorship also engaged in rhetorical attacks against Western values and the United States in particular for Washington's criticisms of human rights violations, corruption, and crony capitalism. Some of these attacks were lodged directly against the United States, while many verbal assaults were targeted at the vaguer term of *"imperialism."* In August 1978, President Marcos noted at the 58th International Law Association Conference that *"Human rights cannot be utilized as a vehicle for a new moral imperialism and especially when developed countries continue to ignore the demand for more equitable distribution of resources world-wide and for increasing development assistance to the Third World…The developed countries can continue to ignore the call for international economic order only at the risk of major dislocation in the world community."*[782] In June 1981, the Marcos election campaign was characterized by anti-American rhetoric. Marcos and the nationalists accused US Ambassador to Manila Richard W. Murphy of interference in the internal politics of the Philippines.[783] In December 1982, Information Minister Gregorio Cendana noted that *"To this day, the Western media seek to impose on us and on other Third World peoples the most insidious form of intellectual imperialism… By presuming to interpret for us events not only in the world but here in our own country, Western media are conditioning us to think not for ourselves, but as the imperialist powers want us to think."*[784] In May 1983, Marcos noted that *"We have no intention of allowing such misconceived neo-colonialist tendencies to, in any way, influence any of our policies."*[785] In April 1984, an editorial in a pro-Marcos Manila daily said that the Congressional

[781] Billington, Mike. "Shultz and the 'Hit Men' Destroyed the Philippines" Executive Intelligence Review December 24, 2004 Accessed From: http://www.larouchepub.com/other/2004/site_packages/econ_hitmen/3150philipp_coup.html

[782] "Critics of human rights policies assailed at Manila law meeting" The Globe and Mail (Canada) August 29, 1978

[783] Sheilah Ocampo. "Filipino election has anti-US flavor" Christian Science Monitor June 15, 1981 page 6.

[784] Redmond, Ron. "Newspaper shut for questioning Marcos war record" United Press International December 17, 1982

[785] Del Mundo, Fernando. "Marcos accuses Asian Wall Street Journal of sowing intrigues" United Press International May 29, 1983

decisions regarding aid to the Philippines smacked of *"born-again imperialism."*[786] In January 1986, Labor Minister Blas Ople noted that America's *"mindless policy toward a close ally"* represented *"real meddling"* in Filipino affairs and *"imperialist retribution."* Ople noted at a forum that *"I can see a whole arsenal of destabilizing weapons being trained against the Philippine government...President Marcos is being destabilized because he refuses to bow down to this new American imperialism."*[787] In February 1986, Marcos noted that *"Sadly, there are those in foreign lands who for their own reasons have willingly picked up the theme, impugned the integrity of our recent presidential election and have even called for foreign intervention in our national affairs...We deplore these actions as the acts of ungracious electoral losers and of modern-day imperialists who evidently think that a nation like the Philippines would willingly submit to their dictates and wishes."*[788]

Sometimes, the militant anti-American rhetoric from Marcos and his political allies translated into demonstrations in front of the US Embassy in Manila. In February 1986, a group of 50 pro-Marcos Filipino demonstrators shouted *"Down with U.S. Imperialism!"* and *"Sen. Lugar, CIA Terrorist"* and then burned a U.S. flag and chanted slogans against imperialism. This group was organized by a wing of President Ferdinand Marcos' ruling New Society Movement (KBL). These demonstrators protested US Senator Richard Lugar (R-Indiana) when he visited the Philippines. Marcos' political affairs minister, Leonardo Perez called U.S. Ambassador Stephen Bosworth a *"self-anointed American praetorian guard of democracy in the Philippines."* KBL spokesman J.V. Cruz remarked that US support for the pro-Aquino forces was the *"umbilical cord that has always tied Namfrel to colonialist elements in the United States."*[789] In April 1986, over 4,000 pro-Marcos demonstrators marched on the US Embassy in Manila. The pro-Marcos demonstrators burned US flags in front of the Embassy and shouted slogans such as *"Oust the U.S.-Cory Dictatorship."*[790] One demonstrator Juan Castello Jr noted *"We want the imperialist Americans to bring President Marcos back to Manila...We will not leave the American Embassy until President Marcos is brought back."*[791]

It also appeared that the Marcos dictatorship sought to align itself with the Soviets and other radical states in an effort to prove its credentials of a Non-Aligned Third World state, to derive economic benefits, and to spite Washington for its attacks. It appeared that the comparatively more leftwing Imelda Marcos was the go-between in negotiations and visits to the USSR and other radical leftist dictatorships. In October 1985, Imelda Marcos herself remarked that the world's problems *"have their roots in injustice, intolerance, greed and dominance by the*

---

[786] Gee, Marcus. "U.S. pressure builds on President Marcos" United Press International April 11, 1984

[787] Branigin, William. "Marcos Supporter Charges U.S. Plot; Campaign Manager Accuses 'Elements' of 'Transpacific Conspiracy'" The Washington Post January 28, 1986 page A10.

[788] Briscoe, David. "Marcos Tells World Election Is None Of Its Business" The Associated Press February 21, 1986

[789] Burgess, John. "Manila Turns Anti-U.S. on Cue; Government Suspected of Bringing in Demonstrators" The Washington Post February 11, 1986 page A10.

[790] Yabes, Criselda. "4,000 Marcos Loyalists March On U.S. Embassy" The Associated Press April 15, 1986

[791] Wren, Christopher S. "Supporters of Marcos March on US Embassy in Manila" The New York Times April 16, 1986 page A12.

strong....The solutions to these problems rest not in man's acquisitive nature, but in his sense of justice and sense of community."[792]

In October 1981, Iraqi Oil Minister Tayih Abd Al-Karim pledged to Imelda Marcos that Baghdad would sell the Philippines oil at *"friendship prices."* She also signed a trade agreement with Iraq. Saddam Hussein also promised Marcos that Iraq would import more Filipino guest workers.[793]

In July 1982 Zinaida Kruglova, Chairman of the Presidium of the Union of Soviet Societies for Friendship and Cultural Relations with Foreign Countries noted that *"The Soviet public attaches great significance to consolidating peace and stability in Asia, and it is determined to promote further relaxation of tension on the continent."* Kruglova spoke at the 10th Anniversary Meeting of the Philippines-USSR Friendship Society in Moscow. This meeting was attended by prominent Filipinos such as the Governor of Metropolitan Manila Imelda R. Marcos. Marcos remarked that *"I visited the Soviet Union ten years ago at the time when our countries had not yet established diplomatic relations. Today, we note with gratification that Soviet-Philippine relations have changed for the better. The two states have established friendly ties which are constantly growing stronger, thanks to the efforts of both sides. We Filipinos support the Soviet Union's peace initiatives, expressing the interests of detente and disarmament."*[794] In July 1983, Marcos warned that *"We would have to enter some kind of modus vivendi with the Soviet power which would mean that all of Southeast Asia, perhaps all of Asia, would be under the control of the Soviet Union."*[795]

Marcos allowed members of the Philippine Communist Party to visit the Soviet Union for consultations. The Soviet Union congratulated Marcos on his victory in the rigged February 1986 elections. Philippine Ambassador Romeo Fernandez noted that *"When the new Soviet ambassador presented his credentials he must have known that not a single Western country of even our closest ASEAN (Association of Southeast Asian Nations) associates had congratulated Mr. Marcos for his victory...But the Soviet ambassador conveyed his best wishes and congratulated him on his re-election."* Imelda Marcos was a regular visitor to the USSR and was flattered by the communists. Manila became a sister city of Moscow and Imelda was president of the Soviet-Philippine Friendship Society. An American diplomat noted that *"The Soviets maybe thought that through winning President Marcos the Philippines would distance itself from the Americans... It will never happen."*[796] Even the Soviet press started to defend Marcos, who they viewed as a belated victim of American imperialism. Pravda noted in 1986 in reference to the US-led anti-Marcos effort: *"Prattling about 'defense of democracy,' the fight against corruption and concern for 'justice' is merely camouflage, propaganda cover for Washington's major*

---

[792] Fein, Esther B. "Marcos Offers View of Sad World" The New York Times October 19, 1985 page 5.

[793] "Other Reports; Iraq's pledge to Philippines on Oil" Far Eastern Broadcasting Company Manila October 10, 1981

[794] "Visit to Moscow by Mrs. Marcos; Philippine-USSR Society anniversary meeting" TASS July 9, 1982

[795] Redmond, Ron. "Praise, ridicule for Marcos ultimatum on U.S. bases" United Press International July 10, 1983

[796] Redden, Jack. "Collapse of Marcos regime ends Soviet courtship" United Press International March 2, 1986

political objective."[797] One American diplomat concluded that *"The Russians seem to be playing a complex game, encouraging Marcos, although they detest him, while also trying to aid the guerrillas…What they really seek is to keep the pot boiling. They know that's to their advantage and Washington's disadvantage."*[798]

An example of a communist *"people's war"* aggression against a non-communist regime occurred in The Philippines from the 1940s until well into the 1990s and 2000s. The first initial communist attack via *"people's war"* was through the Communist Party guerrillas known as the Huks. As of July 1950, it was reported by a former US Army Private First Class Ronald Dorsey that the Soviet Union was in communication with the Huks communist guerrillas in The Philippines. Dorsey deserted from the US Army and fought with the Huks. The Soviets issued advice to the Huk leadership on tactics and issued propaganda and directives. The Red Chinese also maintained links via radio communication and other means. Chinese Communist army forces infiltrated The Philippines in the guise of Nationalist Chinese refugees and aided Filipino leftist dissidents.[799] Another source indicated that *"The Huks remained almost exclusively an organization of Filipinos. Some foreigners, however, joined them, including quite a few Chinese Communists and a handful of Americans. Ronald Dorsey left the U. S. Navy to become a Huk officer. Another was the American Communist, William J. Pomeroy of Rochester, N.Y., who served in the Philippines in the U. S- Army during the war. On his discharge he returned to the Islands, married a Filipino girl, and joined the Communist high command. Pomeroy was the intelligentsia in the Communist cause. He was a thoroughgoing Marxist, trained in dialectical materialism."*[800] Another report noted that *"Communist China strongly influenced the PKP partly because of the proximity of the Philippines to China. Chinese Communists were smuggled into the Philippines from Mainland China to advise the PKP on the military and non-military aspects of fomenting a people's revolution. One of these Chinese Communist advisers, a colonel in the People's Liberation Army (PLA), was the Huk's first instructor in guerrilla warfare. Chinese military advisers brought with them the guerilla tactics tested in their wars against the Japanese and Nationalist Chinese."*[801] The Huks clearly would have implemented a totalitarian-Stalinist state if they took power in The Philippines. One author noted that *"The Huks carried out a campaign of raids, holdups, robbery, ambushes, murder, rape, massacre of small villages, kidnapping and intimidation. The Huks confiscated funds and property to sustain their movement and relied on small village organizers for political and material support."*[802]

The Communist Party of the Philippines (CPP) and their military arm New People's Army (NPA) sought to conquer the country from pro-US governments. At first, the Red Chinese backed the New People's Army with weapons and training. In 1976, China withdrew this

---

[797] "Soviets Say United States Interfering in Philippine Affairs" The Associated Press February 22, 1986

[798] "In Soviet, A Shift to Increasing Support for Marcos" The New York Times February 23, 1986 page 17.

[799] "Soviet-Huk Tie Alleged" New York Times June 9, 1950 page 14.

[800] Douglas, William O. North From Malaya (Doubleday & Company Garden City NY 1953) Accessed From:
http://archive.org/stream/northfrommalayaa011715mbp/northfrommalayaa011715mbp_djvu.txt

[801] "PEFTOK: The Philippine Expeditionary Force to Korea (1950-1955)" Accessed From:
http://www.reocities.com/peftok/Peftokpoor.html

[802] Senauth, Frank. The Making of the Philippines (AuthorHouse 2012) pages 59-60.

assistance and slowly other communist powers and revolutionary movements replaced Beijing as the dominant patron of the NPA.[803] The CPP/NPA sought to implant a brutal dictatorship once they seized the whole country. In January 1985, the CPP called for the establishment of a "*People's Democratic Republic,*" termination of all treaties with the U.S., cancel all foreign loans, and create "*people's tribunals*" that will "*try and punish the enemies of the revolution.*" Other goals included nationalize the assets of the "*big foreign capitalists;*" cancel all foreign loans; collectivize agriculture; nationalize industry and institute central planning; and seek support from "*revolutionary movements and organizations abroad.*"[804] The actions in the NPA-occupied zones of The Philippines lent credence that they would implement totalitarian rule if they conquered Manila and dislodged the current government. In late 1985, an internal CPP purge in Northern Mindanao was characterized by brutal mass executions of villagers suspected of being spies. The body count totaled at least 690 victims.[805] Four defecting NPA commanders reported that "*the people at the top lived as bourgeoisie and they gave privileges to their friends.*" They even charged certain high level NPA and CPP members of financial corruption.[806]

There were splits in the CPP leadership on whether to continue its alliance with Red China or to switch to supporting the USSR. Captured NPA soldiers reported that Soviet made weapons were sent to the communists. The Christian Anti-Communist Crusade reported that "*There are many prongs to the Soviet attack on the Philippines. One prong operates through the front organizations, the World Peace Council and the World Federation of Trade Unions, which promote opposition to the U.S. bases in the Philippines and to so-called U.S. Imperialism. A second prong is the remnants of the PKP. A third is the courting of President Marcos and his administration. As the American press and Congress have become increasingly hostile to President Marcos, the Russians have become increasingly friendly. Art and trade exhibits are being held and economic aid is being offered to the harassed Marcos Government.*"[807]

A Filipino labor unionist reported to the Christian Anti-Communist Crusade that his labor group made tactical alliances with the Communists to "*cripple the economy of the country*" by mass strikes. This form of economic pressure would force the current Filipino government to collapse.[808]

---

[803]"New People's Army" Mapping Militant Organizations Stanford University Accessed From: http://www.stanford.edu/group/mappingmilitants/cgi-bin/groups/view/149

[804] Fisher, Richard D. "The Communist Threat to Reviving Democracy in the Philippines" Heritage Foundation Reports April 23, 1986 Accessed From: http://www.heritage.org/research/reports/1986/04/the-communist-threat-to-reviving-democracy-in-the-philippines

[805] Fisher, Richard D. "Confronting the Mounting Threat to Philippine Democracy" Heritage Foundation Report September 3, 1987 Accessed From: http://www.heritage.org/research/reports/1987/09/confronting-the-mounting-threat-to-philippine-democracy

[806]Schwarz Report October 1, 1984 Accessed From: http://www.schwarzreport.org/Newsletters/1984/october1,84.htm

[807]Schwarz Report October 1, 1984 Accessed From: http://www.schwarzreport.org/Newsletters/1984/october1,84.htm

[808]Schwarz Report April 1, 1986 Accessed From: http://www.schwarzreport.org/Newsletters/1986/april1,86.htm

There were occasional reports of Soviet and bloc intervention in the Philippines on behalf of the CPP/NPA rebels. In 1978, Cuban advisers were reported to have trained NPA terrorists in central Luzon. In 1979, arms were said to have been off-loaded from a Soviet ship in Davao del Sur. In 1981, Philippine officials reportedly intercepted "*Soviet hydrographic ships*" with "*sensor equipment*" docking at southern ports.[809] Soviet KGB agents entered the Philippines posing as East Germans and provided training, arms, money, and propaganda. They also sought to establish ties with Islamic terrorists of the Moro National Liberation Front (MILF). Some of the KGB agents also posed as businessmen, tourist, cultural workers, and German gold prospectors.[810] A surrendered NPA rebel named Welijado Basanez reported that three Soviet agents posing as ship crew members distributed weapons and documents to NPA troops in Surigao del Sur.[811] The Aquino government reported in 1987 that Soviet planes and submarines were sighted six times in the past month off eastern Mindanao, southeastern Luzon and Palawan Islands, in the South China Sea. Former NPA rebel and Mayor Ernesto Camino of Gagwait stated that Soviet advisers were training rebels in southern Mindanao.[812]

The Christian Anti-Communist Crusade documented that "*An observer at the last plenary session of the CPP[813] held in the jungles of Mindinao reports that he heard that the Soviet Union was offering: 1) Money; 2) Material, including weapons; 3) Books and books and books, which are reported to already be in the warehouse at the embassy.*" The Crusade also reported "*that a team of Filipinos is undergoing training in Vietnam.*"[814]

Richard Fisher of the Heritage Foundation noted that "*Since at least the late 1970s, the CPP has received indirect funding from the Soviets. Moscow has tried to conceal this relationship by making connections with CPP members in third countries and pursuing highly visible relations with the former Marcos government. Former KGB agent Stanislav Levchenko told the House Intelligence Committee that, while he was based in Tokyo from 1975 to 1979 for the KGB he witnessed Soviet money being passed to CPP messengers. Negotiations between Soviet and CPP representatives are alleged to have been conducted in Australia.*"[815]

Levchenko himself testified about the method of delivering payments to the Communist Party of the Philippines (PKP): "*I had to go to the Communist party headquarters in Moscow. And there was an accountant who brought a sack with money and this money went into a special*

---

[809] Kessler, Richard J. "Are the Soviets Sneaking Up on the Philippines?" Washington Post July 26, 1987 page B1.

[810] Driberg, D. "KGB Arms Claim as Rebels Ambush Aquino's Forces" Courier Mail March 9, 1987

[811] Costello, D. "Soviets Handed Out Arms in Philippines, Rebel Says" Courier MailMarch 7, 1987

[812] "Aquino Aide Says Soviet Ships And Planes Violate Philippine Territory" Associated Press August 23, 1987

[813] Acronym for the Communist Party of the Phillipines.

[814] Schwarz Report April 1, 1986 Accessed From: http://www.schwarzreport.org/Newsletters/1986/april1,86.htm

[815] Fisher, Richard D. "The Communist Threat to Reviving Democracy in the Philippines" Heritage Foundation Reports April 23, 1986 Accessed From: http://www.heritage.org/research/reports/1986/04/the-communist-threat-to-reviving-democracy-in-the-philippines

suitcase and I had to give him a receipt and then this money was special couriered. And in Japan a KGB officer who knows spy tradecraft technique delivered that money."[816]

In September/October 1986, the CPP/NPA established party to party relations with North Korea and the Korean Workers Party (KWP). The CPP/NPA sent Sixto Carlos while the North Korean side was represented by Ho Tam, who was an alternate member of the KWP Politburo. A second meeting between the CPP, NPA, and KWP discussed *"important issues including the US military bases in the Philippines, the CPP-NPA alliance with the Moro National Liberation Front, and the purchase of arms for the communist movement. They also tackled the question of how the KWP could send arms to the CCP in the Philippines."*[817]

By the 1980s, the NPA reportedly restored ties with the Red Chinese. The Chinese and North Koreans were also reported to have attempted to ship firearms in 1987 to the communist New People's Army fighting against the governments of Marcos and Aquino.[818] In 1988, reports indicated that special NPA assassins were trained by Red China. Reportedly, such Chinese-trained assassins killed US military officers stationed in The Philippines.[819] The Islamic Moro guerrillas were also aided by communist countries. In January 2005, it was reported that the Moro Liberation Front (MILF) bought 10,000 M-16 armalite rifles, hand grenades and other firearms from North Korea. The MILF allegedly paid $2.2 million to North Korea for the weapons.[820]

In January 1987, officials of the Maoist Communist Party of the Philippines noted that the Soviets offered *"unlimited arms and funds"* to the New People's Army (NPA). In May 1987, the American Naval Pacific Fleet Commander Admiral James Lyons noted that the Soviets supplied aid to the NPA. Czechoslovakia and other East European countries also sent weapons via Malaysia to the Filipino Communists. KGB agents reportedly conducted training of Filipino Communists right on the soil of their native country.[821]

Indonesia Under General Suharto (1965-1998)

In 1965, the leftwing dictator of Indonesia President Sukarno was overthrown in a military *coup d'état* led by General Suharto. By 1968, all of Sukarno's powers were stripped and General Suharto solidified his authority. In order to comprehend the dynamics of the Suharto takeover in 1965, one must also explore the dictatorship of President Sukarno. Defecting Czechoslovak General and to Warsaw Pact planner Jan Sejna noted that *"Sukarno was a total Soviet puppet"* and the Czechs used Indonesia for narcotics distribution in 1960. The Soviets

---

[816] "Moscow's Gold: Soviet Financing of Global Subversion" National Observer Number 40 Autumn 1999 Accessed From:
http://www.nationalobserver.net/1999_autumn_campbell.htm

[817] "Philippines President Responds to Allegations of NPA-DPRK Ties" Manila Broadcasting Company January 29, 1990

[818] Del Mundo, Fernando. "Government Thwarts Rebels Arms Deal with China, North Korea" United Press International November 12, 1987

[819] Mickolus, Edward F. and Simmons, Susan L. The Terrorist List (ABC-CLIO 2011) page 188.

[820] "Philippine MP Demands Probe Into Moro Group's Links to North Korea" Pilipino Star Ngayon Web Site January 9, 2005

[821] Golan, Galia. The Soviet Union and National Liberation Movements in the Third World (Unwin Hyman 1988) pages 80-81.

directed the Czechs to create this network in Indonesia, Burma, and India as a means of demoralizing the non-communist world through drug addiction, winning agents of influence through corruption, and gaining more hard currencies.[822]

Sukarno aligned Indonesia closely with communist nations such as Red China, the Soviet Union, North Vietnam and assorted leftwing dictatorships such as Nasser in Egypt and Sihanouk in Cambodia. China provided Indonesia army troops in 1964 with weapons, while supplying arms to the Indonesian Communist Party (PKI) in 1965. The Indonesians received a total of 25,000 arms to Sukarno loyalists and PKI militants. In early 1965, a high level Indonesian political and military delegation returned from Peking with a pledge to *"strengthen their contacts in the military field."*[823]

The Indonesians also sought to forge a new order in Asia in concert with the communist and other anti-Western powers. In January 1965, Sukarno called for the creation of a new United Nations based on the Nefos or New Emerging Forces against the Oldfos or Old Established Forces.[824] Fic noted that Sukarno and his Foreign Minister Dr. Subandrio noted that the Soviets and Chinese and the *"New Emerging Forces of the Afro-Asian national liberation movements, would create a New World Order of peace, prosperity, social justice, and cooperation."* Sukarno noted in August 1964 speech that *"No evil spirit, no genie, no devil can prevent Korea, Vietnam, Cambodia and Indonesia...from uniting themselves in the march towards a New World."* During a high level meeting of Indonesian diplomats at the UN Mission for Indonesia in New York, Foreign Minister Dr. Subandrio noted that a secret military agreement was signed with China. This agreement was to commit Chinese troops, which would assist Indonesia in attacks against Malaysia. China would permit Sukarno to absorb Borneo and Singapore. This meeting included the Indonesian Ambassadors to Canada, the United Nations (UN), the United States, Mexico, Belgium, and other countries. Indonesia agreed that China could occupy territory of Malaysia north of Singapore. Ten thousand Indonesian and Chinese troops stationed near the Thai border would be used in these conquest plans. The Soviets and Chinese pledged to support the removal of American bases in Southeast Asia. The Indonesians also planned to split the alliance between the United States and Britain over America's policies in Indochina. In April 1965, Sukarno held the 10th Anniversary of the First Afro-Asian Conference held in Bandung. Jakarta was decorated with flags and banners, erected arches, and imported luxury limousines transport guests. The Chinese, North Korea, North Vietnam, the Vietcong, the Pathet Lao, and leftist revolutionaries from North Kalimantan all dispatched delegations to this conference.[825]

The Indonesians also seriously pursued the development of a nuclear weapons program to assert its ascension as a rising, anti-Western Third World power. Both the communist powers and the Western powers were approached by the Sukarno regime and even provided some limited assistance to the Indonesian nuclear program. In 1961, Indonesia purchased an American-made General Dynamics nuclear reactor, which produced its first nuclear reaction in 1964. The Indonesians also welcomed China's explosion of an atomic bomb in 1964. Indonesian Minister of Public Relations Roeslan Abdulgani noted that China's atomic bomb *"would open*

---

[822] Douglass, Joseph D. Betrayed (AuthorHouse, 2002) page 430.

823 Gill, R. Gates. Chinese Arms Transfers (Praeger, 1992) page 56.

[824] "Sukarno's Motive Is Seen As Plan for Rival to U.N." New York Times January 4, 1965 page 1.

[825] Fic, Victor M. Anatomy of the Jakarta Coup: October 1, 1965 (Abhinav Publications, 2004) page 112.

the eyes of the West to the fact that from now on their encirclement of the peoples of Asia and Africa would be of no avail." Minister of Revenues, Expenditures, and Supervision Hassan praised China's atomic bomb as "*a matter worthy to be hailed not only by the Chinese people but by the Indonesian people as well.*" Many other Indonesian government ministers expressed their congratulations through the Chinese Ambassador in Djakarta. In a presidential law on atomic energy in November 1964, Sukarno noted that nuclear power is "*important for the people and the nation in finishing the national revolution and because of that should be possessed and mustered by the nation.*" In November 1964, Indonesian Army Brig. Gen. Hartono of the Army Ordinance Department noted to the state news agency Antara that by 1965, Indonesia would possess the atomic bomb. Between 1958 and 1965, less than 300 Indonesians went abroad for nuclear training. Hartono noted that Indonesia "*could immediately mobilize nuclear physicists to start working on the fabrication of a nuclear bomb.*" By 1965, there were reports that the Chinese were training Indonesian engineers at its nuclear plants. In February 1965, Hartono alleged that 200 Indonesian scientists were working on tests for a nuclear bomb. The Rector of University Indonesia Sumantri toured China's atomic plants and set up collaboration with the Indonesian military and the Institute of Technology in Bandung. In 1965, Sukarno upgraded the atomic energy program to the National Atomic Energy Agency. In July 1965, Sukarno announced "*God willing Indonesia will shortly produce its own atomic bomb.*" Sukarno noted that the bomb would be used to "*guard our sovereignty, guard our homeland.*" Brigadier General Sabur traveled to France in August 1965 to purchase an atomic bomb or equipment for its production in exchange for $800,000. In August 1965, Sukarno noted to a group of Japanese journalists that "*Indonesia's preparations to explode its first atom bomb are progressing smoothly without being affected by international events.*"[826]

The Indonesians also utilized its intelligence service to subvert its neighbors and to aggressively collect information. Subandrio sent Indonesian Intelligence (BPI) agents to Kalimantan to recruit communist elements and train them in West Java at a police school. In 1963, this training was completed and was at first called the Special Force, which then became the Sarawak People's Guerrilla Force (PGRS). The BPI also took over a dormitory in East Jakarta and filled it with leftist Malayan and Singaporean exiles that were flown to Indonesia aboard commercial flights and then given paramilitary training at the National Police School. In July 1963, Operation A was launched which attacked Malaysia with Indonesia Marines, police, and Air Force troops, who were loyal Sukarno supporters. In 1964, the BPI sought to incite Singapore to separate from the Malaysian union. In 1963, the BPI stationed agents in Singapore, Rangoon, and Bangkok. In 1964, the BPI stationed agents in Hong Kong, Kuala Lumpur, Phnom Penh, Tokyo, Vientiane, Morocco (to monitor the Arab world), and Portuguese Timor. In 1963, BPI agents sifted through British Embassy documents that were left behind by PKI mobs.[827]

Foreign Minister Subandrio admitted to the UN that Indonesian troops infiltrated into Malaysia to "*resist neo-colonialism.*" In March 1965, Subandrio worked with the NKKU to form the United National Revolutionary Front of North Borneo, which unified the guerrilla forces from Brunei, Sabah, and Sarawak. In September 1965, the North Kalimantan Communist Party was formed with Indonesian assistance with the guerrilla force North Kalimantan People's

---

[826] Cornejo, Robert M. "When Sukarno Sought the Bomb" <u>The Non-Proliferation Review</u> Summer 2000 Accessed From: <u>http://cns.miis.edu/npr/pdfs/72corn.pdf</u>
[827] Conboy, Kenneth J. <u>Intel: Inside Indonesia's Intelligence Service</u> (Equinox Publishing, 2004) pages 36-40.

Force (PARAKU). By October 1965, PARAKU started its operations with support from the PKI. After the PKI attempted coup in October 1965, the Indonesian Army and Sarawak Communist Organizations continued joint operations. In December 1965 the Sarawak police observed that there was *"no indication of any change in the attitude of the Indonesian Army to Sarawak Communist elements."* In March 1966, there was a heavy battle between Sarawak Communist/Indonesian troops and Sarawak government forces supported by the British. In August 1966, the Crush Malaysia campaign was ended.[828]

The Indonesian government under President Sukarno also borrowed the communist strategy of opening luxury hotels to Western businessmen with an eye to influencing them to increase trade with Djakarta and to collect any useful intelligence about their intentions. An American architect Abel Sorenson built the Hotel Indonesia, which was completed in the early 1960s.[829] Australian author C.J. Koch noted that the Hotel Indonesia resembled *"a luxury ship in mid-ocean"* and was *"majestically expensive."* The hotel had its own power supply and purified water, which made it an oasis of Western luxury in the sea of poverty stricken Indonesian socialism. Koch reported that *"No Indonesians were allowed inside the hotel except the generals and the very influential top brass of the government...It was very much a Western island in the middle of Jakarta."* He recalled that the air conditioning units at the Hotel Indonesia were bugged and that Indonesian agents would listen to guests' conversations from their office in the basement. The Hotel was financed by Japanese reparations from their occupation during World War II and was owned by the Sukarno government.[830] The Hotel Indonesia was managed for the government by Intercontinental Hotels Corporation.[831] The Hotel featured 586 rooms, a swimming pool, and two tennis courts.[832] Room charges were payable in hard currency and the hotel displayed an American-style coffee shop, luxurious restaurant, and a well-stocked bar. As of July 1963, guests lodged at the Hotel Indonesia included Soviet technical advisers, Japanese businessmen, and American oil company workers.[833] As of 1965, Indonesia imported Japanese, European, and American-made automobiles which then used by government officials and prosperous citizens.[834]

Western business interests and governments also continued to provide direct assistance as well as tradable goods to Indonesia under Sukarno. Despite Indonesia's Soviet alignment, the United States even shipped arms for Sukarno's armed forces. In 1964, it was reported that Dutch businessmen visited Indonesia and stayed at the Hotel Indonesia. Their visits were trade missions to the Sukarno government. One American company used Dutch experts to buy Sumatran rubber for direct shipment to the United States. The Netherlands Bank and Bank of Indonesia signed an agreement in 1964 regarding the exchange of credits.[835] In 1964, Japan issued

---

[828] Lau, Albert. <u>Southeast Asia and the Cold War</u> (Routledge, 2012) pages 121-123.

[829] Kalb, Bernard. "American Architect Introduces the Skyscraper to Indonesia" <u>New York Times</u> March 26, 1961 page R1.

[830] Torchia, Christopher. ""Hotel Indonesia: Still a Place to Stay" <u>Manila Bulletin</u> August 30, 1999 Accessed From: http://www.travelsmart.net/article/100852/

[831] King, Seth. "Austerity in Jakarta" <u>New York Times</u> July 20, 1963 page 7.

[832] Torchia, Christopher. ""Hotel Indonesia: Still a Place to Stay" <u>Manila Bulletin</u> August 30, 1999 Accessed From: http://www.travelsmart.net/article/100852/

[833] King, Seth. "Austerity in Jakarta" <u>New York Times</u> July 20, 1963 page 7.

[834] Sheehan, Neil. "Mud and High Hopes" <u>New York Times</u> February 20, 1965 page 3.

[835] "Dutch Resuming Indonesian Role" <u>New York Times</u> March 29, 1964 page 8.

Indonesia a $12 million credit. As of 1964, Indonesia had contracts with the following oil companies: Caltex Pacific, Standard Oil, Texaco Inc., and Shell Indonesia. These investments earned $250 million per year, with Sukarno collecting 60% of this revenue.[836] Between 1949 and 1965, the United States provided over $800 million in loans, grants, and surplus commodities to Indonesia. Since 1959, the US provided Indonesia with $20 million per year of military arms. The US was a customer of 16% of Indonesia's exports, while Sukarno received from Uncle Sam cotton, foodstuffs, and machinery.[837] In 1963 the United States provided spare parts for Indonesia's fleet of C-130 transport planes. These planes were sold to the Indonesian Air Force in 1959. The United States also had a military training program with the Indonesian armed forces. The C-130s were used to ferry Indonesian troops to attack Malaysia.[838] Not unsurprising was the criticism of American aid to Sukarno by politically informed citizens within our own country. For example, an American technician who worked in Indonesia for 3 years wrote Congressman William Broomfield (R-MI) complaining *"I am getting very tired of working three months of the year paying taxes so that the US government can support corrupt governments and communist nations…we the United States government have supported more corrupt dictators than any other nation in history. When we support such corrupt dictators we only force the masses into communism."*[839]

Even after Suharto took *de facto* control of the government in late 1965, Sukarno retained the presidency of the Republic until 1968. He and his cronies in the government continued to issue pronounced anti-Western statements and even blamed the PKI coup attempt on imperialism. A conference directed against the presence of Western military bases (KIAPMA) was also convened in this period. In November 1965, the Indonesian Press Agency reported that intellectuals and scientists pledged their *"determination to continue the struggle against neo-colonialism, imperialism, and counter-revolutionary subversive elements."*[840] In December 1965, Sukarno urged an alliance of China, Cambodia, Indonesia, North Korea, and North Vietnam to confront the United States and the West.[841] In December 1965, General Nasution stated *"in Southeast Asia the man in the street has become conversant with the tactics and the pains taken by the imperialist British and the USA."* Nasution noted that the *"Neokolim are practically taking their guns on Indonesia's doorstep."*[842] In late 1965, the KIAPMA hosted delegations in Indonesia from 27 countries and terrorist movements, such as China, North Vietnam, North Korea, North Borneo National Liberation Front, Malayan National Liberation League, and the Vietcong.[843] In August 1966, Sukarno urged Indonesia to host a Conference of New Emerging Forces as an effort in *"the struggle against imperialism."* He defended *"guided democracy"*

---

[836] "Indonesia Grasps For a Firm Straw; Inflation Spiraling" New York Times January 13, 1964 page 37.
[837] Trager, Frank. "The U.S. And Indonesia: A Tragedy In Diplomacy" New York Times August 29, 1965 page SM26.
[838] Handler, M.S. "U.S. Scales Down Help to Indonesia" New York Times November 22, 1963 page 1.
[839] "Thefts Alleged in Indonesia Aid" New York Times November 2, 1963 page 5.
[840] "Demand for Red Ban Pressed in Jakarta" New York Times November 5, 1965 page 4.
[841] "Sukarno Seeking to End China Rift" New York Times December 19, 1965 page 13.
[842] "Nasution Scores US and Britain" New York Times December 21, 1965 page 14.
[843] Brackman, Arnold C. The Communist collapse in Indonesia (WW Norton and Company 1969) page 107.

against *"liberal or parliamentary democracy."*[844] In September 1966, Sukarno urged that Red China should attack American forces in Vietnam from the north, while Indonesia would attack from the south.[845] In January 1967, Sukarno charged that the PKI uprising was the result of *"the cunning of neokolim subversion."*[846]

The period under Suharto's rule was officially known in Indonesia as the New Order. He extended and redefined aspects of Sukarno's philosophy called *Pancasila*, which was originally a socialist, anti-Western nationalist ideology. Under Suharto, *Pancasila* rejected communism, liberal capitalism (known as *"free fight"* liberalism to the Indonesians), and all other atomizing doctrines. The rhetoric employed by General Suharto and his supporters had a pseudo-leftist, almost Marxist veneer. Suharto clearly sought to develop an authoritarian collectivism which rejected capitalism, communism, and other ideologies which atomized the Indonesia state and its peoples. Hill noted that *"Great emphasis has been put on the centrality of Pancasila as the ideological basis of Indonesian nationhood, with any 'deviation' to the left or the right, either towards communism, 'laissez faire capitalism,' or Islamic extremism being deemed a potential threat to national unity."*[847] In 1983, the Suharto government ordered all political parties to adopt *Pancasila* as their guiding philosophy.[848] The ruling party coalition became known as *Golkar*.

In 1975, Suharto noted that *"Pancasila society is a socialist-religious society based on a rejection of capitalism, feudalism, colonialism, and imperialism."*[849] In February 1977, Minister of Defense and Security and Commander of the Indonesian Armed Forces General Maraden Panggabean noted that *"capitalism is as dangerous as communism and the only way to overcome both these threats is to strengthen our confidence in implementing and serving pancasila."*[850] President Suharto noted in October 1978 that *"Indonesia could also not tolerate ideas based on liberalism, individualism, capitalism, and totalitarianism...such as ideas arose from the philosophy of individualism and liberalism of the West which is not in line with our spirit of togetherness which we are developing."*[851] In February 1982, Jakarta OANA reported that Home Affairs Minister Amir Makhmud stated *"It will be empty talk if we speak of legacy if what we are leaving behind would be merely political time bombs whose indications would plunge towards social democracy, communism, or a la Kartosuwiryo Islam, capitalism or feudalist compartments of the country. We must continue strengthening pancasila democracy."*[852] In October 1988, Suharto noted that *"History taught us that both liberalism with its free competition system and oppressive Nasakom concept were unable to allow our nation to implement national development. In fact, development in all sectors is the only way for us to*

---

[844] "Sukarno Repeats Call for Parley" <u>New York Times</u> August 17, 1966 page 6.

[845] "Sukarno Says US Tries to Kill Him" <u>New York Times</u> September 7, 1966 page 5.

[846] "Sukarno Denies Role in Uprising" <u>New York Times</u> January 11, 1967 page 7.

[847] Hill, Hal. <u>Indonesia's New Order: The Dynamics of Socio-Economic Transformation</u> (Allen & Unwin, 1994) page 26.

[848] Ariel Heryanto and Sumit K. Mandal. <u>Challenging Authoritarianism in Southeast Asia: Comparing Indonesia and Malaysia</u> (Routledge, 2003) pages 102-104

[849] Bourchier, David. <u>Dynamics of Dissent in Indonesia: Sawito and the Phantom Coup</u> (Equinox Publishing 2010) page 6.

[850] "Panggabean Briefs Parliament on Security, Defense" <u>Jakarta Suara Karya</u> February 7, 1977

[851] "Suharto Marks Failed Coup: Communism Remains Latent Danger" <u>Hong Kong AFP</u> October 1, 1978

[852] "Minister Warns Against Undermining Elections" <u>Jakarta OANA</u> February 24, 1982

realize the ideals of the proclamation of independence, namely proper public welfare and an increasing national level of intelligence. While liberalism and communism are compatible for other nations, it is certain that liberalism, communism and other ideas influenced by liberalism and communism will not be compatible with our identity and our basic ideas on common life based on an Indonesian identity."[853] In December 1993, Suharto noted that *"those who were seeking to establish a Western-style democracy, rather than a democracy based on consensus…were obstructing further development."*[854] The Indonesian Times also noted that *"Our parliament has banned communism and Marxism in our country and will not permit liberalism, capitalism, and otherism's other than Pancasila to operate in Indonesia. This is our internal affair. We choose the ideology best suited to our country and people."* [855]

Suharto's dictatorship undertook an intense indoctrination campaign to promote and brainwash Indonesians into his version of the collectivist *Pancasila* philosophy. In the 1970s, state leaders introduced *Pancasila* Moral Education (PMP) and Guidelines for the Comprehension and Implementation of *Pancasila* (P4) indoctrination courses. The PMP and P4 courses stressed *"the whole idea of the collectivity of the nation"* that were *"expressed through functional groups"* of the *"Big Golkar Family."* Workers' strikes were regarded as being in *"contradiction with the principles"* that comprised the ideology of *Pancasila.*[856]

While private enterprise and foreign investment was promoted by Suharto's dictatorship, major economic players remained under the control of the state. Furthermore, the Suharto regime subsidized domestic Indonesian producers in an effort to develop an indigenous economy. Suharto formed the *Golkar* to mobilize support for his dictatorship from all classes of the Indonesian populace. It should be pointed out that Suharto heartily rejected capitalism and free market economics. President Suharto placed great emphasis *"on the notion that Indonesia is not and should not be a 'capitalist' society…"*[857] Emmerson wrote that General Suharto *"was uncomfortable with the extreme pursuit of self-interest in unfettered markets, which he disparaged as 'free-fight capitalism.'"*[858] Schwarz observed that *"More broadly, the notion that the government exists to protect the poor against 'greedy capitalists' is one which both Sukarno and Soeharto have supported."* Suharto himself outlined *"Our goal, (is) the greatest possible prosperity for the most number of people, not like what is the case in liberal countries."*[859] Sadli noted in 1988 that *"One of the economic doctrines of the New Order is that it is against 'free fight competition,' because the latter is too much identified with 'capitalism,' which even the*

---

[853] "Suharto Warns Golkar Congress of Dangers of Communism and Liberalism" Jakarta home service October 25, 1988

[854] Ariel Heryanto and Sumit K. Mandal. Challenging Authoritarianism in Southeast Asia: Comparing Indonesia and Malaysia (Routledge, 2003) pages 102-104

[855] "Trade Urged With Eastern Bloc Jakarta" Indonesia Times November 19, 1982

[856] Porter, Donald J. Managing Politics and Islam in Indonesia (Routledge 2013) pages 30-31.

[857] Hill, Hal. Indonesia's New Order: The Dynamics of Socio-Economic Transformation (Allen & Unwin, 1994) page 27.

[858] Emmerson, Donald K. Indonesia beyond Suharto: Polity, Economy, Society, Transition (M.E. Sharpe, 1999) pages 162-163.

[859] Schwarz, Adam. A Nation in Waiting: Indonesia's Search for Stability (Westview Press 2008) pages 82-83

New Order cannot embrace."[860] Hill wrote that "*It is a mistake to view the change in regime in 1966 as a switch from a 'socialist' to a 'capitalist' or 'free market' regime. There remains a deep-seated mistrust of market forces, economic liberalism, and private (especially Chinese) ownership in many influential quarters in Indonesia.*"[861]

In February 1974, President Suharto asserted that the stimulation of native Indonesian private enterprise was not the equivalent of support for liberal capitalism: "*This does not mean that we have allowed Indonesia's economic progress to turn and head toward capitalism. Not in the least.*"[862] Suharto also believed that the long term economic policy of his dictatorship was to convert a large part of Indonesia's economic sectors into government-subsidized cooperatives. President Suharto noted in August 1981 that "*...in the long run it is co-operatives that must be the backbone of the Indonesian national economy...The government had not allowed the propagation of a liberal climate, continued to hold the reins, giving orientation to the development of the private sector, so that it is the prosperity of the people, common prosperity, that is given priority...*"[863] In fact, in 1990, Suharto shocked Indonesia's wealthiest ethnic-Chinese businessmen when he requested them to redistribute their wealth by selling up to a quarter of their companies' shares to cooperatives. Suharto also desired to have the ten "*strategic industries*" under continued state ownership.[864]

Even during the 1990s and the intense onset of globalization, the Suharto dictatorship sought to distinguish its economic model from the liberal capitalist model. An editorial in the Indonesian newspaper <u>Kompas</u> noted in December 1994 that the economy was "*a blend between the market economy (or capitalist or liberal economy) and one with centralized planning. We exercise a market economy with the government playing a dominant interventionist role in policy and planning. We have always believed that capitalist or liberal economy is not suitable for Indonesia as only the strong will survive in that system where competition knows no humanity and where the common people will live in misery and ruin. It seems to us that in the market economy mechanism in the capitalist economy there is bare and murderous competition in which the government cannot intervene nor stop.*" The editorial also noted that "*There has been a kind of evolution in that system and an improvement in what was considered bad in the capitalist or liberal economy*" in countries such as the United States. It also observed that "*...in the capitalist or liberal economy of developed countries there is strong and effective government intervention.*"[865]

Indonesian officials also remarked that the government's encouragement of foreign investments did not mean surrender to capitalism and the free market. The Suharto regime employed the same justifications as the communist bloc in the effort to attract foreign multinationals to invest in Indonesia. In August 1982, <u>The Indonesia Times</u> noted "*In analyzing the impact of foreign investments on our economy we may say that our economic development*

---

[860] Hill, Hal. <u>Indonesia's New Order: The Dynamics of Socio-Economic Transformation</u> (Allen & Unwin, 1994) page 116.

[861] Ibid, page 66.

[862] "President Suharto's February 6th Address to Governor's Conference" February 6, 1974

[863] "The President on the Economy; President Suharto in his Independence Day speech" <u>Indonesian News Agency</u> August 26, 1981

[864] Emmerson, Donald K. <u>Indonesia beyond Suharto: Polity, Economy, Society, Transition</u> (M.E. Sharpe, 1999) pages 162-163.

[865] "Liberalized Trade is not Liberalism" <u>Jakarta Kompas</u> December 8, 1994

has been stimulated and helped by Western capitalists. It does not mean that we are going capitalistic. Of course we must always guard ourselves against any pull towards capitalism which is against the spirit and letter of our Constitution."[866] In April 1992, Radius Prawiro, Coordinating Minister for Economic Affairs noted that *"foreign investors should be reminded that the Indonesian government will not allow the economic system to develop along the lines of free-fight liberalism."*[867]

The Suharto dictatorship also sought to launch an export drive to dump products into foreign markets as a means of gaining hard currency and economic clout. This mirrored the efforts of other Asian dictatorships such as South Korea and the communist bloc (China, Romania, the Soviet Union, *et al*). Cooney wrote that *"The New Order government found itself forced to reorient its investment and industrial policies to adopt an export-oriented industrialization strategy. It saw Indonesia as competing with other low-cost Asian states for foreign capital in labour-intensive industries such as textiles."*[868]

Even Suharto's program for domestic economic liberalization did not correlate with the abolition of the state's control of the economy. In March 1988, Suharto noted that *"I must inform the assembly that the deregulation and debureaucratisation policy does not at all mean we have ushered in liberalism. We have implemented this policy to stimulate creativity and to encourage all available forces in our society to share and expand common responsibility for development…"*[869]

Economists in Indonesia during the Suharto years were steeped with collectivist and even socialist viewpoints. In 1989, economist Bruce Glassburner requested 36 members of Indonesia's political elite to describe their economic ideology. He found that most Indonesian politicians held statist economic beliefs and were hostile toward free enterprise. In March 1993, the Islamic leader Imaduddin observed that the technocrats that were dropped from the Suharto economy *"were directing a capitalist economy which is not in line with the 1945 Constitution, thus it is only natural if they were replaced."*[870]

Despite the anti-communism of the Suharto dictatorship, the state still played a large role in guiding, controlling, and even owning sizable segments of the Indonesian economy. The roots of this economic structure lay chiefly with:

1) The ideological roots of contemporary, mainstream collectivist Indonesian political economy (*Pancasila*).
2) The nationalistic desire of Suharto to develop a native entrepreneurial class to compete with the ethnic Chinese and foreign-owned companies.

Sri Majangwoelan commented that *"Despite privatization, the state still plays a big role in the economy as clearly indicated by the existence of Pertamina, Bulog, the state electricity*

---

[866] "Indonesia Times Views Role of Foreign Investment" <u>Jakarta Indonesia Times</u> August 6, 1982

[867] "Indonesia Plans Full Foreign Ownership of Firms" <u>Central News Agency–Taiwan</u> April 15, 1992

[868] Sean Cooney, Tim Lindsey, Richard Mitchell and Zhu Ying. <u>Law and Labour Market Regulation in East Asia</u> (Routledge, 2003) pages 39-40.

[869] "President Suharto's Speech to the People's Consultative Assembly" <u>Jakarta television</u> March 7, 1988

[870] Schwarz, Adam. <u>A Nation in Waiting: Indonesia's Search for Stability</u> (Westview Press 2008) pages 82-83

company, PLN, the telephone company, the national flag carrier, the state road agency and other leading companies controlled by some of the ministries Yet, the state's dominance of the super layer of the economy cannot be merely perceived as an attempt to neutralize the negative impact of economic liberalization on society. In fact, state capitalism has continuously provided patronage funds within the new economic environment. It has been also used massively to promote business interests of the families of power holders. More importantly, it has been an important means to remove the idea of political succession by the fact that the President now places his children in the vanguard of the resurgence of an indigenous Indonesian entrepreneurship to redress imbalances created by Chinese economic dominance." Suharto regime officials were involved in the *"allocation of oil drilling, leases, mining leases, forestry concessions, import and export licenses, government contracts for construction and supply, and state bank credit."*[871] Various state owned enterprises under Suharto included the state electricity company (PLN), the state shipping company Pelai, the state oil company Pertamina, and the state aircraft company IPTN.[872] State-owned enterprises such as Pertamina, Bulog, IPTN, and other large, strategic industries became economic fiefdoms of the New Order, *Golkar*, and armed forces.[873] The Suharto government also maintained a National Planning Agency and regional planning boards which developed Five Year Plans and Twenty Five Year Long Term Plans.[874]

Both the Sukarno and Suharto regimes strictly controlled the labor unions in Indonesia. In fact, the Indonesia labor movement was an arm of the state and an instrument in the development of a fascist-style corporative labor-management arrangement. In 1973, the government-controlled All-Indonesia Workers Federation (FBSI) was formed. Activities conducted by the SPSI included social events such as volleyball, *karate*, table tennis, and badminton games.[875] In 1974, *Pancasila* Industrial Relations (HIP or *Hubungan Industrial Pancasila*) was created by the Suharto government. He noted that under HIP, *"there is no place for confrontation."* Other HIP ideologists contrasted the *"partnership"* of Indonesian labor-management relations with the *"confrontational"* type of relations that existed in *"liberal"* North America, Western Europe and Australia.[876]

By the 1980s, the FBSI was transformed into the All-Indonesia Workers' Union (SPSI). The Suharto government controlled the SPSI. In 1985, Manpower Minister Sudomo ordered that all unions needed to join the SPSI. The leadership of the SPSI were dominated by the ruling *Golkar* party and officers of the armed forces. Companies with more than 25 employees were

---

[871] Sri Majangwoelan. "The Political Economy of the Marginalization Process in Indonesia's 'New Order'" Accessed From: http://www.collectionscanada.gc.ca/obj/s4/f2/dsk2/ftp04/mq22802.pdf

[872] Hill, Hal. Indonesia's New Order: The Dynamics of Socio-Economic Transformation (Allen & Unwin, 1994) page 37.

[873] Sri Majangwoelan. "The Political Economy of the Marginalization Process in Indonesia's 'New Order'" Accessed From: http://www.collectionscanada.gc.ca/obj/s4/f2/dsk2/ftp04/mq22802.pdf

[874] Hill, Hal. Indonesia's New Order: The Dynamics of Socio-Economic Transformation (Allen & Unwin, 1994) page 67.

[875] Hadiwinata, Bob S. The Politics of NGOs in Indonesia: Developing Democracy and Managing a Movement (Routledge 2003) pages 65 and 182.

[876] Berger, Mark and Borer, Douglas. The Rise of East Asia: Critical Visions of the Pacific Century (Routledge, 2002) pages 183-184.

required by the Suharto government to establish a unit of the SPSI in their plant or business. The government's policy of *Pancasila* Industrial Relations, workers and employers were to solve their problems and disputes through state intervention. Workers needed permission from the arbitration tribunals and the Manpower Ministry to engage in a strike. In 1991, the Indonesian Observer admitted that *"Indonesian labourers have virtually been delivered to their employers' arbitrariness and greed."* Since the SPSI was controlled by the state, it was not recognized by the International Confederation of Free Trade Unions.[877]

In 1966, the New Order elaborated an *"independent"* and *"active"* foreign policy in the pronouncements of the Provisional People's Consultative Congress (MPRS). While General Suharto dropped the Sukarno-era ideological alliances with the communist world, he did retain an *"anti-imperialist"* stance. Furthermore, relations with the Soviet Union, Red China, North Korea, Vietnam, and other communist countries were never fully severed. State-owned and private Indonesian companies also professed to garner profits from sales to the communist world. Weinstein noted that *"Sometimes using language not markedly different from that of the Sukarno years, the MPRS strongly reaffirmed its vigorous opposition to imperialism and colonialism and pressed for continued efforts to foster Asian-African solidarity."* Such principles were outlined in the document titled Indonesia's Foreign Policy as Based on the Pantja Sila Principles (1966). Weinstein noted that *"Soeharto's definition of imperialism has perhaps been closer to Sukarno's than one might have expected."* In 1967, General Suharto defined imperialism as *"teachings or practices or intentions in any form on the part of one state...to dominate or exploit another state...merely for its own interests."* Ali Sastroamidjojo noted in June 1973 that anti-imperialism and the efforts to raise living standards were part of the same national struggle of the New Order.[878]

In 1967, Admiral Muljadi visited Moscow. The Soviets agreed to provide spare parts for Indonesian Navy vessels. In 1967, the Soviets transferred submarine charging equipment to the Indonesians at Surabaya Naval base. By 1969, the flow of Soviet spare parts to the Indonesian armed forces was reduced to a trickle.[879] With US encouragement, improvements in Soviet-Indonesian relations became a reality by 1969. By 1974, the Soviets resumed aid to the Indonesian mining and electric power industries. Loans were sought from Warsaw Pact countries and Yugoslavia. By 1975, Indonesia purchased rice from North Korea. The Suharto regime also signed trade agreements with Poland and the USSR. Foreign Minister Malik supported the concept of expanded trade with communist countries.[880]

It also appeared that the Suharto regime sought to undermine pockets of stalwart opposition to economic relations with the communist world. The motivations behind this campaign appeared to be commercial. Vice President Adam Malik noted in November 1982 that *"Therefore at the present stage of economic crisis we should approach the communist countries which need Indonesian commodities. For example the Soviet Union needs Indonesian coffee."*

---

[877] Schwarz, Adam. A Nation in Waiting: Indonesia's Search for Stability (Westview Press 2008) pages 258-259.

[878] Weinstein, Franklin B. Indonesian Foreign Policy and the Dilemma of Dependence (Equinox Publishing 2007) pages 170-171.

[879] Brackman, Arnold C. The Communist Collapse in Indonesia (W. W. Norton & Company, 1969) page 241.

[880] Weinstein, Franklin B. Indonesian Foreign Policy and the Dilemma of Dependence (Equinox Publishing 2007) pages 170-171.

The Indonesia Times complained "...*because of our bitter experiences with communism in our recent history there is a tendency to give more emphasis to the danger from communism than from liberalism and capitalism. In its turn this tends to create communist phobia in our country. On the other hand it leads us to be oblivious of the latent danger of liberalism and capitalism. There is a trend now in our country among young people to automatically like people from Western countries and avoid people from Eastern countries.*" The Indonesia Times also noted "*on the contrary the government wants the traders to exploit all the possibilities to augment trade with the Eastern European countries so that we can overcome export stagnation we are experiencing due to the world recession...**We must learn from the Western countries themselves how they fight to maintain their profitable trade relations with the countries of Eastern Europe**.* "[881] The Soviets also maintained a support network within the ruling circle of Suharto's government and network of supporters who read the nationalist newspapers Merdeka and Sinar Harapan. Merdeka had a wide readership among elements of the Indonesian military elite and was reportedly funded by a Soviet bank. General Suharto visited Moscow in September 1989 after he attended the NAM Conference in Yugoslavia. Suharto thanked the Soviets for their aid in territorial disputes with Malaysia. He also noted that Indonesia maintained no hostility against communist countries.[882]

South Vietnam Under Diem

After the conclusion of the First Indochina War between the French and the communist-led Viet Minh in 1954, Vietnam was divided into two countries: the communist-ruled North led by President Ho Chi Minh and the South led by its President Ngo Dinh Diem. Ho was an ardent Stalinist communist who established a totalitarian state in the North under the thumb of the Workers' Party of Vietnam. Diem evicted the pro-French monarchy of Emperor Bao Dai and became a highly authoritarian President who implemented a collectivist nationalist program based on the imported philosophy of Personalism. The philosophy of Personalism had its origins in France and maintained its share of Vietnamese adherents. Ngo Dinh Diem, Ngo Dinh Nhu, and other high level officials of the South Vietnamese regime espoused Personalism and attempted to remold society according to its precepts. Diem, a staunch anti-communist, also aligned himself closely with the United States, who in turn provided military and civilian advisers, arms, and economic aid. However, by the early 1960s, the United States under the Kennedy Administration grew weary of Diem's police state tactics and tried to push various political reforms. The South Vietnamese regime responded with communist-style propaganda assaults against the United States, which displeased Washington even more. Eventually, Diem was overthrown by a group of South Vietnamese Army generals in 1963.

Diem sought to create a nationalist dictatorship that espoused anti-communism and anti-colonialism in general. While the economy would remain in private hands, the Diem regime reserved the right to intervene or even create government-owned enterprises. The goals of Diem and Nhu as stated by Bernard Fall was to make "*the South Vietnamese regime as a sort of anti-communist people's democracy whose major difference with its Communist North Vietnamese*

---

[881] "Trade Urged With Eastern Bloc Jakarta" Indonesia Times November 19, 1982
[882] Gennadii Illarionovich Chufrin and Mark Hong, Kah Beng Teo. ASEAN-Russia Relations (Institute of Southeast Asian Studies, 2006) page 31.

twin is its attitude toward the practice of Catholicism and the ownership of rubber plantations. "[883]

The regime also had a sort of an official political party. Diem's brother Ngo Dinh Nhu established the Personalist Revolutionary Labor Party (Can Lao) in the mid-1950s and it played a role in mobilizing support for the government.[884] The National Revolutionary Movement (NRM) of President Diem also was involved in the propagation of Personalism. Personalism itself was supposed to be a collectivist philosophy that rejected liberal capitalism and communism and endorsed nationalism. President Diem described Personalism as the *"reconciling of the demands of collective discipline and social justice with those of individual liberty."*[885]

In 1955, Ngo Dinh Thuc set up a Personalist School in Vinh Long to train civil servants. In 1954, the Revolutionary National Movement (NRM) was formed under the Diem regime as consisting of *"revolutionary forces from all classes of the population."* Civil servants and peasants were forced to join the NRM. Ngo Dinh Nhu admired the performance of the official Vichy organizations in Indochina during World War II and the communist organizations. Thus, Nhu desired the creation of an organization and philosophy that would imitate and compete with the Viet Cong and Worker's Party of Vietnam. Nhu was so passionate about his beliefs that he enjoyed lecturing to CIA officials on the evils of capitalism and communism, the true nature of Vietnamese society, and the advantages of the spiritual East over the materialist West.[886]

The official ideological positions and Constitution of the South Vietnam also reflected the heavy influence of Personalism. In the 1956 <u>History of the Constitution of the Republic of Vietnam</u> the South Vietnamese government of Diem allegedly displayed *"the thirst for social justice all."* The <u>History</u> noted that the *"needs of humanity in the whole which were injured these last centuries by capitalist and communist imperialisms, the concrete emanations of extremist individualism and collectivism."* It also noted that *"...the heritage of French imperialism-of democratic individualism, pushed to the contradiction of true democracy...has never been regarded as a blessing by Vietnamese, who suffered for nearly a century under the double standard of colonial 'justice.'"*[887]

In April 1956, President Diem noted to the National Assembly that *"Numerous constitutions have been drawn up and promulgated in the past with the intention of setting up Democracy. During the 18th and 19th centuries, constitutions were drawn up which established political regimes, later known as political democracies, in which individualism and economic liberalism were advocated as proper formulas to emancipate man and lead mankind toward happiness. While this system in its appreciation brought relative freedom to a minority of its citizens, at the same time it lessened the effectiveness of the state, which became impotent to*

---

[883] Fall, Bernard. <u>The Two Vietnams</u> (Praeger, 1966) page 250.

[884] Donnell, John C. "National Renovation Campaigns in Vietnam" <u>Pacific Affairs</u> March 1959 pages 79-80.

[885] President Ngo Dinh Diem on Democracy (Addresses relative to the Constitution) Press Office, Saigon: 1958 Accessed From:
http://ngothelinh.tripod.com/President_Diem_April_17_1956.html

[886] Fitzgerald, Francis. <u>Fire in the Lake</u> (Little, Brown, 1972) page 120.

[887] The Constitution of the Republic of Vietnam Saigon-Vietnam The Secretariat of State for Information Accessed From: http://www.virtual.vietnam.ttu.edu/cgi-bin/starfetch.exe?IknObAeTfUuJL0OlB12lAqge@cK3kMQ.OXDkLEvfMJzWsODO3loNZ0frl YlkQuM0FETARIxp2WErDTlkO7Q18Hv6lWWLGFvN5PrHlt.ejp0/2390309002.pdf

defend collective interests and to solve social problems...The risks of relapsing into anarchy and servitude brought about by the internal feudalism or foreign imperialism that lies in wait for all newly emancipated peoples weigh more heavily on our country than on others, because of our geographic position..." The South Vietnamese constitution under Diem noted that "*Economic forces should associate in the exercise of power in the form of a National Economic Council composed of representatives of union and professional groups and which will present suggestions and opinions on bills of economic interest.*"[888]

In July 1957, President Diem noted in a speech that "*First of all, national sovereignty has been wrest from the establishment of a republican regime based on the philosophy of Personalism...Our success is due to the choice of a correct policy based on the social conditions of Vietnam, in accord with the people's aspirations and with human progress...In fact, to liberate the people in order to liberate the individual, it was necessary to know who oppressed, exploited, and trampled on the human dignity of the Vietnamese people; They are the colonialists, the feudalists, and the Communists...In the past three years, we have stabilized the market, regularized prices and assured economic rights for the Vietnamese.*"[889]

In an April 1963 speech to Personalist militants, Ngo Dinh Nhu stated: "*This preoccupation, this approach does not aim at satisfying a few intellectual bourgeois whims. It is not either destined to justify any regime, for the concept and the process of development of the policy of strategic hamlets have already given the impetus to a total re-examination of the doctrine, of the organization as well as of the technique of all regimes, in particular of the present regime of the Republic of Vietnam.*"[890]

Nguyen Ngoc Tho, the Vice President of South Vietnam, noted that "*The Personalist economic system aims at developing personal freedom, insuring human dignity and realizing social justice. On the one hand, we must avoid the liberalism of the Capitalistic system with its cyclical evils of unemployment and economic crisis; on the other hand, we must keep away from the Communistic system which calls itself socialism with its false and inhuman class struggle. The golden mean which brings about harmony between the human person and the organized society is the economic cooperation practiced under the organizational form of cooperatives which insure the public rights of the group as well as the private right of the individual while, at the same time, developing the community of life.*"[891]

---

[888] President Ngo Dinh Diem on Democracy (Addresses relative to the Constitution) Press Office, Saigon: 1958 Accessed From:
http://ngothelinh.tripod.com/President_Diem_April_17_1956.html

[889] President Ngo Dinh Diem's Speech on Third Anniversary of Accession to Office July 7, 1957 Accessed From: http://www.virtual.vietnam.ttu.edu/cgi-bin/starfetch.exe?5SDbolBjEAiBzEERe.0KTn2vRPz8@0B5lJM2K4jfRNftTKiszLo2QxotRCsJ9wDUggCIIrO85eLAEyg.lfQqSkdMJ8f2I68jH6XIieUJoxA/2321507007.pdf

[890] Friendly Talk to the Militants by Political Counsellor Ngo Dinh Nhu April 17, 1960 Accessed From: http://www.virtual.vietnam.ttu.edu/cgi-bin/starfetch.exe?OyYzGngxsZ201YWkY4mY7spTP5O2iVPaDZRAvHhbA9BlcVs9jQXa4dVP2p@OnFOzhsgL2MSHyafDBTFNC@PMW6w5a5ks3kEUNaZ3GYrH3rE/0440728001.pdf

[891] Trued, M.N. "South Viet-Nam's Industrial Development Center" Pacific Affairs Volume XXXIII Number 3 September 1960 Accessed From: http://www.virtual.vietnam.ttu.edu/cgi-bin/starfetch.exe?5FSSyVWHx6UQn8s39F1BzZPu8XgVGB7QD@CDMLEFsBpdnCQZCBquTwdxoapFVfm2cDd4bAY0Q5mFwqqWdlWfwisb4fwJuloOR2k.B9kUVEU/2321907001.pdf

South Vietnamese Personalist ideologists believed that *"individualism gives birth to 2 twins: one is called colonialism and other is communism."* They noted that *"we must naturally endorse a new conception about private ownership; basic private ownership is respected and if the right to private ownership is too broad it must be coordinated with the interest of those people who have contributed to the reconciling individual and collective demands."* They noted that *"...the man conceived as an individual like in free capitalism is an abstract man...conception of man as an individual is abstract..."* Nhan Vi noted that capitalists *"say we are prone to a theory close to communism."*[892]

In October 1962 President Diem noted to the National Assembly that *"....The State has played an important role in industrial development, by helping and encouraging investments, by associating itself with private national and foreign capital, and by itself creating industrial enterprises the stocks of which will later be sold to individuals."*[893]

The Personalist philosophy was also apparent in the development of the economic structure in South Vietnam, which neither free market nor communist. In September 1955, Prime Minister Diem declared an economic program to encourage Vietnamese farmers and business people and halt the influence of French owned colonial monopolies in an effort to *"perfecting the independence of the country in the economic field."* Diem noted that Vietnamese companies and state-owned corporations would manage industries vital to national security and public utilities.[894]

In September 1955, President Diem brushed aside whether the South Vietnamese economy would be *"capitalist or socialist"* and supported unified national efforts to achieve reconstruction. While Diem sharply castigated foreign investors during the French colonial period, he invited foreign businessmen into South Vietnam and assured them they would not *"have to fear either a sudden nationalization of their enterprises...or a regime of exorbitant taxes, or difficulties in the transfer of their annual profits."* In March 1957, a Presidential Declaration on economic policy supported *"free enterprise in the framework of a Plan in which the role of the Government will be essentially to orient, coordinate and assist private enterprise."* The Declaration also supported the policy of the government reserving *"the right to participate in the ratio of over 51% in certain enterprises of vital importance to the nation's economy or affecting national security- e.g., transportation, power, etc."*[895]

Diem's Personalism sought a balance between capitalism and socialism. Personalist literature and Diem's early policy pronouncements outlined a program for some state-owned

---

[892] "Personalism-Vietnamese Specialists; Also Others Somewhat Relevant" Accessed From: http://www.virtual.vietnam.ttu.edu/cgi-bin/starfetch.exe?ZpiN626oJTWQ6EiXIiiSeAtYL1R2.5kxhxjBNF6WXLZaISSDpE4Q9KSKoh EGU25yGXKmPpRf4NUmHhOmUcZVvpYsMn8zJsiRsZ.h4KCAtWY/0720314001.pdf

[893] Message of the President of the Republic to the National Assembly October 1, 1962 Accessed From: http://www.virtual.vietnam.ttu.edu/cgi-bin/starfetch.exe?UDo1jWwY3UpOdt28vLRbvoU2JYuQ44IcOM4WYlbfCpn3Vv8CZLB8lNM 9bbdBZe1G9G5NmCRmF7fGY3U5IraSwoUAyNiX124@mzleMNR05Ds/2390802003A.pdf

[894] "Declares War on Monopolies" <u>Saint Joseph Gazette</u> September 19, 1955 page 13.

[895] Musolf, Lloyd M. "Public Enterprise and Development Perspectives in South Vietnam" <u>Asian Survey</u> Volume 3 Number 8 August 1963 pages 357-371.

enterprises. Personalist literature in South Vietnam supported the nationalization of big businesses if they engaged in abusive practices.[896]

The Diem regime formed the Industrial Development Center (IDC) and the National Investment Fund in 1957 to promote industrial development in South Vietnam. In 1956, the Diem government enacted anti-Chinese ordinances which impaired businesses owned by ethnic Chinese. In 1956, the South Vietnamese government created the National Agricultural Credit Office. In the end of 1957 and 1958, the Sugar Company of Vietnam was formed to take over the French-owned Hiep Hoa sugar mill and the Bien Hoa saw mill. The Diem regime created the state-run Tan-Mai Saw Mill Administration. In 1959, Diem increased the South Vietnamese government's share of ownership in Air Vietnam to 75%. The South Vietnamese regime created the National Office for Electrification, Nong-Son National Coal Mine Administration, the Railroad Administration of Vietnam, and other railway systems and hydroelectric dams. General Director Thai noted that agrarian reform bonds in South Vietnam could be exchanged as shares in mixed companies which was to serve as *"a particularly suitable method of mobilizing capital in agriculture for the building of industry"* and thus achieving *"the stage of social capitalism without passing through the process of concentrated capitalism."* A US adviser to the IDC noted that *"The (Vietnamese) Government envisaged what would be, in many respects, a giant holding company with a substantial role in government-owned industries, whereas the U. S. officials conceived the IDC primarily as a catalyst for private initiative, especially for small and medium-sized industries."*[897]

Diem's adviser Law Professor at Saigon University and Vu Quae Thuc at the National Conference of Vietnamese Engineers and Technicians noted in June 1959 that *"The present 'semi-liberal' economy must be ended. The only way…is to follow our government in its planning."*[898]

Diem noted in October 1962 that *"Cooperation between the management and their employees is becoming more and more active and fruitful. The collective agreement of the rubber plantations has been followed by that of the banks and many others. On the national level, the participation of workers' representatives in the elaboration of economic plans for the country has been consecrated by the appointment of numerous trade union leaders to the National Economic Council."*[899]

Lastly, the Diem dictatorship reacted in a hostile manner towards the negative reporting of much of the American mainstream press and the Kennedy Administration's appeals for political reforms. In November 1960, a South Vietnamese government-supported committee charged that a coup against Diem was aided by *"colonialists and imperialists, American, French,*

---

[896] Ibid.

[897] Ibid.

[898] Trued, M.N. "South Viet-Nam's Industrial Development Center" <u>Pacific Affairs</u> Volume XXXIII Number 3 September 1960 Accessed From: <u>http://www.virtual.vietnam.ttu.edu/cgi-bin/starfetch.exe?5FSSyVWHx6UQn8s39F1BzZPu8XgVGB7QD@CDMLEFsBpdnCQZCBqu TwdxoapFVfm2cDd4bAY0Q5mFwqqWdIWfwisb4fwJuloOR2k.B9kUVEU/2321907001.pdf</u>

[899] Message of the President of the Republic to the National Assembly October 1, 1962 Accessed From: <u>http://www.virtual.vietnam.ttu.edu/cgi-bin/starfetch.exe?Ms6sSxBCKjBdEiHCWZgvtY6rvQZAqTb9IusYj9faHPnv.aMPGtZPb9O2AO 9y37X7yEMWMjN@pHPsVUeiai1mtykut0i8oYQiKMLItxSwQNY/2390802003B.pdf</u>

and British."[900] The Saigon newspapers <u>Thoi Bao</u> and <u>Tu Do</u> stated in 1961: *"Republic of Vietnam Is Not A Guinea Pig for Capitalist Imperialism-Is It Not Time to Revise Vietnam American Collaboration?"* It was alleged that US *"interference"* in South Vietnam was to gain *"profits"* under the *"exploitation policy of the capitalist imperialists."*[901] In 1961, the South Vietnamese government-controlled press accused the US of pursuing the *"capitalist imperialist policy of exploiting and seeking gains."* Red China immediately picked up and disseminated this story throughout Asia.[902] Diem denied suppression of the Buddhists in 1963 alleging that *"any allegation to the contrary is nothing but an imperialist invention."*[903] In 1963, the South Vietnamese referred to the Voice of America as not *"the voice of the Government of America at all, but the voice of a group of capitalists who control it."* American journalists and diplomats were also closely watched and followed by the South Vietnamese police and intelligence services.[904]

Singapore Under Prime Minister Lee Kwan Yew

In 1965, the anti-communist socialist politician Lee Kwan Yew became prime minister of the city-state of Singapore after the British ceded independence to that nation. The People's Action Party (PAP) became the only ruling party in the authoritarian state of Singapore. The PAP at first hewed to a democratic socialist ideology and by the 1970s, shifted to a guided, authoritarian capitalism with strong collectivist overtones. The PAP's opposition on the Left was lambasted in sometimes Marxist terms. For example, a propagandist for the PAP regime noted that *"...the discerning Singaporean is not impressed when petit-bourgeois amateur European revolutionaries call, from the comfort of their universities, for the violent overthrow of the government in Singapore."*[905] On other occasions, the PAP viewed themselves as the vanguard of progressive socialism in Singapore and the enemy of laissez-faire free markets. The same propagandist noted that *"Taking an overall view of Singapore's economic policy we can see how radically it differed from the laissez faire policies of the colonial era. These had led Singapore to a dead end, with little economic growth, massive unemployment, wretched housing, and inadequate education. We had to try a more activist and interventionist approach. Democratic socialist economic policies ranged from direct participation in industry to the supply of infrastructure facilities by statutory authorities and of laying down clear guidelines to the private sector as to what they could and should do."*[906] The former head of the NTUC noted *"One of the major policy achievements of democratic socialists in Singapore has been to*

---

[900] "Saigon Drops Charge" <u>New York Times</u> November 19, 1960 page 2.

[901] Trumbull, Robert. "Saigon Resisting US Reform Plan" <u>New York Times</u> November 27, 1961 page 1.

[902] Frankel, Max. "U.S. May Call Home Envoy If Saigon Refuses Reforms" <u>New York Times</u> December 1, 1961 page 1.

[903] "Diem Tells Thant Asia Is Imperiled" <u>New York Times</u> September 25, 1963 page 3.

[904] Halberstam, David. "Saigon Reported to Post a Watch on Persons Who See Americans" <u>New York Times</u> September 13, 1963 page 1.

[905] Nair, C.V. Devan. <u>Socialism That Works...The Singapore Way</u> (Federal Publications, 1976) page 77.

[906] Nair, C.V. Devan. <u>Socialism That Works...The Singapore Way</u> (Federal Publications, 1976) page 77.

eliminate acute class divisions and dissensions within the Republic."[907] In 1977, Guenther Scholz of the Bonn office of Deutsche Welle interviewed Lee Kuan Yew of Singapore and asked: *"Would you name the system in Singapore as socialistic or capitalistic? Answer: We have a mixed economy. There are certain sectors of the economy which are run by the State like the public utilities, transport, shipping, the airlines, and so on. To that extent, the factors of production are in the hands of the state but we do not believe that we have either the management capacity or the technical know-how or the marketing to be able to run the many industries which we have brought into Singapore. So they are in the private enterprise sector. So it is a mixed economy but the bias of our social policies is towards equal opportunities in health and education for everyone."*[908]

The political and economic realities in Singapore were that of an authoritarian collectivism that combined private enterprise and state socialism. Christopher Lingle noted that *"In terms of its domestic policies Singapore's policies share as many notable similarities with state socialism than with free market capitalism...Clearly the regime is regime is driven more by political opportunism than by a commitment to free markets or any free market ideology."* The PAP government was heavily involved in savings and investment, monopolies in the telecommunications companies, public housing/real estate, and industries such as newspapers, shipping, ship building transportation, and others. A National Wages Council was created in 1972 and a Monetary Authority (MAS) manipulated exchange rates to sustain the export industrialization drive. All banks were to be licensed by the MAS. Foreign banks are not allowed to compete with domestic banks inside Singapore. The government-owned companies Temasek, MND, Singapore Technology Holdings, and Singapore Health Corporation controlled 74.7% of the profits. The National Trade Union Congress (NTUC) was controlled by the government. This state of affairs prompted Lingle to comment that *"Singapore joined the ranks of socialist states where top leaders of the ruling party also served as officials in the trade union movement."* Massive North Korean-style demonstrations were also held to support PAP rule. In 1994, the National Day rally celebrated the *"cohesive community,"* concept of *"Total Defense,"* where thousands of *"Spiritual Warriors"* marched. *"A Better Tomorrow"* was hoped for. In 1991, a government document published by the Ministry of Community Development created the *"Singapore Shared Values."* They were *"nation before community and society above self,"* *"family as the basic unit of society,"* *"consensus instead of contention,"* and *"racial and religious harmony."*[909]

Despite its stated anti-communist policy and adherence to the ASEAN alliance, Singapore also broke the embargoes on trade with the Indochinese communist nations in the pursuit of economic self-interest. In 1982, the Japanese News Agency commented that *"Singapore is carrying on active commerce with Vietnam behind a facade of scathing criticism leveled on the political and diplomatic fronts against the communist country's invasion of Kampuchea in December 1978. This island country is a major centre of trade and trans-*

---

[907] Ibid, page 99.

[908] "Lee: We have to be practical for that's the only way we can survive" The Straits Times April 26, 1977 Accessed From:
http://newspapers.nl.sg/Digitised/Article.aspx?articleid=straitstimes19770426-1.2.57&sessionid=b1b9cc6981c248769ca0be2f6b303982&keyword=%22democratic+socialism%22+and+%22Lee+Kuan%22&token=kuan%2clee%2cand%2csocialism%2cdemocratic

[909] Lingle, Christopher. Singapore's Authoritarian Capitalism (Sirocco, 1996) pages 62-66.

shipment, and Vietnam apparently has found Singapore's services to its advantage."[910] As of February 1982, Singapore's trade with Vietnam was paid through barter transactions. Vietnam imported from Singapore goods such as cement and other construction materials, edible oil, certain foods, and general merchandise. Vietnam exported to Singapore items such as rice, beans, and peas. Singapore exported to Vietnam 30,000 tons of wheat with the assistance of the Moscow (Soviet) state-owned Narodny Bank.[911]

Singapore also engaged in commercial transactions with the hard-line Maoist/Stalinist Khmer Rouge communist and later the Vietnamese puppet communist (PRK) regimes in Kampuchea. In May 1978, it was reported that Singapore and communist (Khmer Rouge-ruled) Democratic Kampuchea intended to resume trade relations after a visit to Phnom Penh by a Singaporean trade delegation. Goods were to be shipped back and forth between Singapore and Kompong Som. The Singaporean International Trade Company (INTRACO) and the Democratic Kampuchean Committee on Foreign Trade were to coordinate the trade.[912]

Kampuchean official Pen Sovan was informed by National Bank officials that *"goods in Singapore are cheaper than in neighboring countries such as Thailand. Also we can export our goods to sell in Singapore."*[913] PRK puppet Prime Minister Hun Sen reportedly commented *"If the government can't carry out this trade and the people can, we allow them to do it."*[914] Prime Minister Hun Sen noted to a foreign journalist that "*You have seen our markets are filled with goods from Japan, Thailand and Singapore…Therefore the so-called economic blockade is not effective at all. That is why they cannot strangle us to death…If the government cannot conduct this kind of trade, the people can do it and we will allow them to do it.*"[915]

In early 1989, the PRK puppet trading company KAMPEXIM exported 10 tons of crepe to Singapore. This company also exported tires for cars, motorcycles and bicycles, slippers, sandalwood and jute bags to the Singapore.[916] This trade was carried through "*private*" merchants and was tolerated by the PRK communists. Singapore ships called at the port of Phnom Penh and delivered $2 million worth of goods in 1985. Destinations for these goods included state-controlled "*private*" enterprises and international relief agencies.[917]

Singapore's financial institutions were also used by the PRK and North Korea for various banking transactions. The Kampuchean (PRK) Central Bank officials noted that they desired to establish relations with the Narodny Bank branch in Singapore which "*would allow access to the international market in the area.*"[918] The office of the Workers Party Room Number 39 was the central clearinghouse of virtually all hard currency operations of North Korea. The North Korean

---

[910] "Japanese View of Singapore-Vietnam Trade" Japanese News Agency February 6, 1982

[911] Ibid.

[912] "Bilateral Trade with Cambodia to be Resumed" Singapore Domestic Service May 17, 1978

[913] Gottesman, Evan. Cambodia After the Khmer Rouge (Yale University Press, 2004) pages 121-122.

[914] "Cambodia: A Country Study" Accessed From: http://lcweb2.loc.gov/frd/cs/khtoc.html

[915] Richburg, Keith B. "Cambodians Fight Poverty Through Free Enterprise; Vietnam Takes First Steps Toward Change" Washington Post April 9, 1987 page A1.

[916] "International Relations; Export and import goods" SPK July 6, 1989

[917] "Cambodia: A Country Study" Accessed From: http://lcweb2.loc.gov/frd/cs/khtoc.html

[918] Gottesman, Evan. Cambodia After the Khmer Rouge (Yale University Press, 2004) pages 121-122.

Trade Representative in Singapore was a major player in these financial operations for Room 39.[919]

Pakistan Under General Mohammed Zia ul-Haq (1977-1987)

In 1977, General Mohammed Zia ul-Haq seized power from the Islamic Socialist dictator President Zulkifar al-Bhutto. He established an equally and highly authoritarian dictatorship that imposed martial law and extreme Islamic Sharia. Zia's title was President and Chief Martial Law Administrator (CMLA) and ruled Pakistan with an iron fist until his death in an airplane crash in 1987. In summary, General Zia imposed a form of Islamic totalitarianism which was never fully compatible with American interests. Furthermore, while ideologically anti-communist, General Zia continued to pursue relations with nations such as Red China and North Korea.

In order to comprehend the dynamics of the Zia dictatorship, one must briefly explore the Bhutto regime of the 1970s. Both General Zia and President Bhutto were clearly authoritarian rulers who rejected various facets of the West in favor of Islamic collectivism. The ruling party under President Bhutto was known as the Pakistan People's Party (PPP). It combined socialism and Islamic fundamentalism into the political culture of Pakistan. President Bhutto was described as *"undemocratic, more oppressive and more intolerable than the two martial law regimes, which preceded his government."* Bhutto developed a Pakistan People's Party (PPP) paramilitary force and a special police force called the Federal Security Force (FSF). The FSF attacked rival Islamists and rightist opponents. In November 1975, the FSF physically assaulted and expelled dissenting members of the Pakistani national legislature.[920] Perhaps in an effort to deceive the West into providing more aid, Bhutto instructed his PPP to drop references to the scary term *"Islamic Socialism"* and instead use *"Islamic Egalitarianism"* during the spring 1977 election.[921]

Bhutto also strengthened Pakistan's relationship with the Soviet Union, Red China, North Korea, and radical Arab states. Pakistan shared the deep Islamic antipathy to Israel and sought to use its resources to aid the Arab effort to conquer the Middle East's only true free nation. During the Yom Kippur War of 1973, President Bhutto provided diplomatic, material, and political support to the Arab aggressors. President Bhutto instructed the Pakistani Mission to the United Nations (UN) to assist the Arab delegations in building a united diplomatic front against Israel. Pakistani doctors and nurses were dispatched to the Arab Socialist and pro-Soviet despotisms of Egypt and Syria. Pakistani pilots fought with the Syrians against Israel, while some Pakistani Army battalions were stationed near Damascus. President Bhutto also developed what he termed the *"Islamic Bomb."* He noted that *"We know that Israel and South Africa have full nuclear capability. The Christian, Jewish and Hindu civilizations have the capability. The communist powers also possess it. Only the Islamic civilization was without it, but that position was about to change."*[922] Pakistani support for anti-Israel, anti-Zionist causes continued into the Zia

---

[919] "Kim Jong-il controls $2-billion slush fund, sources say" The Korea Herald February 21, 2000

[920] Abdus Sattar Ghazali "Islamic Pakistan: Illusions and Reality" Accessed From: http://ghazali.net/book1/chapter_7.htm

[921] Saha, Santosh C. Religious Fundementalism in Developing Countries (Greenwood Press 2001) page 20.

[922] Ibid, page 18.

dictatorship. Also, General Zia continued to modernize and expand the "*Islamic Bomb*" project of Pakistan as a means of Islamabad's stature on the world stage and to possess the military means to attack India and Israel.

Aside from the USSR and especially China, Bhutto's Pakistan increased the scope of the relationship with the virulently anti-American communist regime in North Korea. In 1971, Bhutto visited North Korea to procure weapons. An agreement was signed between North Korea and Pakistan in September 1971. The North Koreans agreed to export ammunition and conventional weapons to Pakistan. The Pakistanis paid the North Koreans in American dollars. In November 1972, diplomatic relations were fully opened between North Korea and Pakistan.[923] The North Korean-Pakistani relationship was expanded during the Zia regime. General Zia also aligned himself with the communist North Korean position on unification with the South (Republic of Korea). A document dated from March 1978 was drawn up by the Hungarian Embassy in Pakistan. This document confirmed that Islamic Pakistan sought to continue political and military relations with North Korea: "*In confidential conversations, the Pakistani side confirmed that despite the removal of Bhutto from power, they do not intend to make changes in the bilateral relations between Pakistan and the DPRK, and they will maintain the friendly relationship...In the question of Korean reunification, they support the North Korean efforts 'to create a unified Korea under the leadership of Kim Il Sung,' which are based on the resolutions of the UN...The Pakistani government asked North Korea to intensify its efforts to rearm the Pakistani armed forces, and increase its arms shipments—small arms and anti-armor weapons. According to journalists, they were given such a promise (by the DPRK).*"[924]

During the Iran-Iraq War, North Korean weapons shipments to Tehran were shipped in Pakistani trucks from Karachi and through Baluchistan. Pakistani army officers trained Libyan officers on the usage of North Korean-made weapons. The Pakistani Inter-Services Intelligence (ISI) and the North Koreans cooperated in endeavors to procure technology from West Germany and other capitalist countries. North Korea provided the ISI with lists of technologies needed by the communists.[925]

Well into the 1980s, economic relations were also forged between Islamic Pakistan and North Korea. In October 1982, North Korea and Pakistan signed a technology, economic, scientific, and cultural agreement.[926] In November 1986, the North Koreans and Pakistanis signed their first joint venture agreement for the manufacture of pipe fittings. The North Koreans provided the equipment and the technical experts, while Pakistan provided land and buildings.[927] In March 1987, the North Korean Minister for Foreign Trade Choe Chong-kun noted that "*there were bright prospects for the further promotion of co-operation between the two countries.*"[928]

---

[923] Raman, B. The Rediff Special April 8, 2003 Accessed From: http://www.rediff.com/news/2003/apr/08spec.htm

[924] Hungarian Embassy in Pakistan, Telegram, 16 March 1978. Subject: DPRK-Pakistani Relations March 16, 1978 Accessed From: http://digitalarchive.org/document/116009

[925] Raman, B. The Rediff Special April 8, 2003 Accessed From: http://www.rediff.com/news/2003/apr/08spec.htm

[926] "Economic Co-operation Agreement between Pakistan and N Korea" North Korean Central News Agency October 28, 1982

[927] "International Relations; North Korea First Joint Venture" Xinhua November 12, 1986

[928] "DPRK Foreign Trade Minister optimistic over co-operation with Pakistan" Karachi home service March 14, 1987

The Zia dictatorship also sought to maintain the military relationship with Red China, since Pakistan possessed large quantities of arms previously procured from Beijing. In 1980, Pakistan received F-6 jet fighters and modified SA-2 ground to air missiles from China. Chinese technicians worked with the Pakistanis in modifying their F-6 fighters to carry US-built Sidewinder AAMs. A batch of Sidewinder missiles were diverted to China by the Pakistanis. The Sidewinder AAMs were then copied by the Chinese for use in their Air Force's fleet of F-6 fighters.[929]

Despite Washington's stated opposition to anti-Western Islamic totalitarianism, Presidents Carter and Reagan continued to provide assistance and trade privileges to the Zia dictatorship. Pakistan was a fascistic dictatorship which fused collectivism and Islamic fundamentalism together. Independent political parties and groups which represented civil society were banned or severely controlled. In October 1979, a diplomat called the Zia regime "*a naked dictatorship. There's no sunshine in it.*"[930] In October 1979, Zia closed Pakistani newspapers considered engaging in the "*poisoning the minds of the people.*" Zia noted over radio and television that the Army overthrew the Bhutto regime because politicians "*preferred party interests to national interests.*"[931]

The Pakistani regime of President Zia and his Islamic fundamentalist supporters were very outspoken in their denunciation of Western political and cultural values. In January 1980, General Zia lectured American correspondents to "*Forget about your Western ideals and Western standards of freedom and democracy...We are in a Moslem developing country. And Islam says if somebody says anything against your integrity, against your religion, against your everything, chop him -- teach him a lesson.*"[932] In August 1982, the government-backed party, the *Jamaat-e-Islami*, dubbed women's rights movements as "*agents of Western imperialism.*"[933]

General Zia openly admitted his intention of creating a non-Western dictatorship based on total adherence to radical Islamic doctrines. In November 1982, Zia noted that "*I and my colleagues will surely fulfill our mission of Islamizing our national polity...The day is not far off when the spirit of Islam will be visible in every sector of society.*"[934] In March 1984, President Zia stated that he wanted "*to purge the society*" of "*professional political monopolies*" and create a "*true*" Islamic government. He predicted that "*We will bring about democracy which reflect our Islamic values and traditions.*"[935] In December 1984, General Zia concluded that "*There is*

[929] "Pakistan Purchases, Upgrades PRC Fighter Aircraft" Indian Express November 9, 1980

[930] Auerbach, Stuart. "Pakistan Moves Toward Islamic Authoritarianism; Pakistan Adopting Strict Islamic Code" The Washington Post October 21, 1979 page A1.

[931] Auerbach, Stuart. "Pakistani Chief Puts Off Election, Tightens Martial Law Controls, Zia Postpones Elections, Broadens Army Powers" The Washington Post October 17, 1979 page A1.

[932] Auerbach, Stuart. "Pakistanis Are Restless Under Zia's Fragile Rule; Regional Divisions, Resistance To Military Rule Put in Question Support for Zia in Pakistan; News Analysis" The Washington Post January 21, 1980 page A1.

[933] Stokes, John. "Pakistani regime taking aim at hard-won women's rights" The Globe and Mail (Canada) August 27, 1982

[934] Evans, Richard. "Pakistan's interest-free-banking law is still adjusting to the profit motive" Christian Science Monitor March 13, 1986 page 21.

[935] "Zia vows to return government to Allah" United Press International March 12, 1984

no room for Western democracy in Pakistan."[936] In March 1984, General Zia noted that *"Islamic unity in its true sense will be established in Pakistan…The entire administration including the head of state and all elected persons will be the functionaries of Allah and the holy prophet…All ideological contradictions in the constitution will be eliminated."* General Zia noted that the *"gates of the (representative) assemblies will not be opened for bad characters and the people who do not observe Islamic values… We will bring about democracy which reflect our Islamic values and traditions."*[937]

Despite pronouncements directed at Western investors and anti-communists, General Zia did not fully implement a program to denationalize the economy. While General Zia sought to undo the socialist legacy of the Bhutto regime, he did not wish to destroy the concept of state involvement in the economy of Pakistan. He adhered to the notion of an Islamic economy that rejected liberal capitalism and communism. In the eyes of General Zia, an Islamic economy stipulated a still powerful role for governmental intervention. General Zia maintained state ownership of major industries and banks, while privatizing some firms. General Zia dubbed this economic state of affairs a *"mixed economy."*[938] Furthermore, Pakistani officers maintained plum positions as directors of state-owned enterprises and government economic agencies. They jealously guarded their positions from any hint of de-regulation and privatization. In December 1983, the Karachi Domestic Service reported that General Zia discussed the economic ideology of the Islamic dictatorship in Pakistan: *"Turning to the economic aspect of the Islamic system, Zia notes the uniqueness of the system, saying it does not favor capitalism or socialism."*[939]

Zia also recommended an Islamist corporatist system which reconciled the class struggle between management and labor. In July 1977, General Zia noted that *"Therefore not only will the interim government preserve all the facilities granted to workers but will protect them from every exploitation. It is true that some factory owners have taken undue advantage of the ban on trade union activity imposed by martial law. But corrective action was taken in time…It is the duty of the industrialists to insure the prosperity and welfare of labor. They should give them the maximum of just facilities and should abjure undue profiteering."*[940]

Another tenet of the economy of Pakistan under General Zia was Islamic banking, which outlawed interest. General Zia himself pledged to rid Pakistan of *"the curse of interest."* The Committee on Islamization stated in 1980 that *"the Islamic rejection of interest is in effect a rejection of the entire capitalistic system: an interest free economy is in fact an exploitation free economy."*[941] Dr. Khurshid Ahmad, a Deputy Minister for Planning in the Zia government,

---

[936] Abel, Allen. "One paper, 39 pictures of President Pakistan's Zia only rider on trail" The Globe and Mail (Canada) December 14, 1984

[937] "Zia vows to return government to Allah" United Press International March 12, 1984

[938] Auerbach, Stuart. "Pakistani Chief Puts Off Election, Tightens Martial Law Controls, Zia Postpones Elections, Broadens Army Powers" The Washington Post October 17, 1979 page A1.

[939] "Zia Ul Haq Addresses Religious Conference 18 December" Karachi Domestic Service December 18, 1983

[940] "General Zia Ul Haq Addresses Nation 27 July" Karachi Domestic Service July 27, 1977

[941] Esposito, John. Islam and Politics (Syracuse University Press, 1998) pages 181-182.

predicted that *"If we implemented fully Islamic principles in banking and economics in this country, I am convinced we could change the face of Pakistan within 10 years."*[942]

Shafqat observed that *"Although Zia-ul-Haq was totally opposed to Bhutto's policies and programs, he did not take any major steps to reverse the status of institutions that had been nationalized by his predecessor, and most of these enterprises remained government-owned-and-operated throughout the relatively lengthy Zia regime (1977-1988). The Zia government's attempts at privatization were extremely limited and half-hearted at best...One explanation for the Zia regime's lack of interest in denationalization lies in the nature of a military government. Contrary to popular belief, a military government (whose main objective is to remain in power) is, to a great extent, a status quo government...There were certain other reasons too, for not moving toward privatization. The power elite -- ministers, civil and military bureaucrats -- were able to obtain immense benefits from these institutions. A conspicuous example is the huge loans advanced by nationalized banks to those in power; loans that were, in many cases, never repaid and were simply 'written off.' The ruling elites continued to have their friends and relatives appointed in state-owned banks and industries. Bureaucracy, which had extended its domain, also continued to be a beneficiary, and many bureaucrats were able to find lucrative positions, with numerous perquisites, in public enterprises. As noted earlier, another major group in the society, labor, had been able to obtain security in the nationalized industries. The military government did not wish to earn the displeasure of these powerful sections of society through denationalization and the handing over of banks and industries to private individuals whose management style would be different and who would be guided in personnel matters by market factors. The Zia government, therefore, was not interested in presiding over the dissolution of the economic empire it had inherited from the Bhutto regime."* In 1980, as many as one fourth of the 35 to 40 top bureaucratic-governmental positions were held by the military officers. Many military officers controlled state-owned enterprises such as Pakistan International Airlines (PIA), Pakistan Water and Power Development Authority (WAPDA), Pakistan Agricultural Storage & Services Corporation (PASSCO), National Logistics Cell (NLC), and the National Transport Research Center (NTRC). The Fauji Foundation was also a large employer of retired army officers. During the Zia regime, it expanded into a monolithic economic powerhouse which covered the industrial, medical, services, and real estate sectors.[943] As of February 1981, Pakistani Army officers acquired much wealth and had enough assets to build lavish houses and import new cars. They also received prime positions in state-owned enterprises and ministries. One such state agency, the Water and Power Development Authority (WAPDA) was massively monopolized by military officers that it was nicknamed *"Wanted Army Personnel -- Dead or Alive."*[944]

Various Pakistani and Western observers confirmed that the *"privatization"* program of the Zia regime was not implemented in a comprehensive fashion. In August 1986, a Karachi banker noted that *"The deregulation so far is just window dressing. The general attitude of the government is that it doesn't want to lose control."* A Western diplomat noted that *"The*

---

[942] Hollick, Julian Crandall. "Islamic banking aims to close poverty gap" <u>Christian Science Monitor</u> December 6, 1982 page B4.

[943] Shafqat, Saeed. <u>Civil-Military Relations in Pakistan: From Zulfikar Ali Bhutto to Benazir Bhutto</u> (Westview Press, 1997) page 201.

[944] Shlachter, Barry. "Political Unrest in Pakistan Challenges Military" <u>The Associated Press</u> February 27, 1981

government has said the private sector will be the engine for the growth, but it remains more of a statement than a national policy."[945] In November 1981, a Western diplomat noted that "*It's the generals and the senior officers who are raking it in…Take a look at how many retired officers head business companies. It's a patronage system to reward service and head off complaints.*" In Peshawar, generals lived in luxurious British cantonments. Army trucks transported their children to school. Officers shopped for duty-free goods in the Persian Gulf states. They also drove in late model imported cars. One businessman reported that "*I was asked for 20,000 rupees (about $2,000) as a bribe to have my telephone and telex shifted to a new building…Fortunately, I knew some influential people and I didn't have to pay in the end. If you don't have contacts, you pay…We say that corruption has been nationalized now…*"[946]

One of the strictest forms of economic control during the Zia dictatorship was price controls and anti-hoarding operations directed at the shopkeepers and businessmen in Pakistan. As of October 1979, the Zia regime attempted to keep prices low and increase industrial productivity. Hoarders were given a week to bring their goods on the open market, while shop owners were ordered to prominently displayed their price lists. Special paramilitary squads of the Zia regime combed villages, towns, and cities to arrest merchants who violated government economic mandates. Mobile military courts followed these squads, who possessed steady supplies of canes to beat up offending businessmen. In Hyderabad, two businessmen were whipped in the stadium for hoarding and black market activities. They bled profusely and were carried off to a 1 year prison sentence.[947] Pakistani newspapers ran stories of "*vigilance squads*" which caught merchants hoarding sugar and other food products to drive prices up. These merchants who violated price control laws were beaten by the "*vigilance squads.*" In the Raja Bazaar near Rawalpindi, Army troops fined every merchant between $10 and $30 for a variety of minor offenses. Kale Khan was described by the Zia government as "*a notorious smuggler*" and was beaten by the "*vigilance squads.*"[948]

General Zia also banned strikes and lockouts.[949] Labor strikes were crushed and unions were strictly controlled by the state. As of June 1981, Zia decreed punishment by flogging, fines, and five years of slave labor for participants and leaders of "*go slow movements*" and labor strikes in government departments and state-owned enterprises.[950]

New taxes for social welfare and on bank deposits were levied by the Zia regime. In 1980, the Zia regime imposed a compulsory *zakat* tax for social welfare measures.[951] By September 1980, Zia imposed a 2.5% tax on all fixed bank deposits, which hit the Pakistani middle class hard. A group of middle class men called General Zia "*the biggest beggar of them*

[945] Tefft, Sheila. "Economic Surge Wanes in Pakistan" Journal of Commerce August 21, 1986 page 5A.

[946] Willis, David K. "Paradoxical Pakistan; Camels and Color TV, Nuclear Power and 'Nationalized Corruption'" Christian Science Monitor November 25, 1981 page B12.

[947] "Pakistan; Spendthrift with a cane" The Economist October 27, 1979 page 63.

[948] Auerbach, Stuart. "Pakistan Moves Toward Islamic Authoritarianism; Pakistan Adopting Strict Islamic Code" The Washington Post October 21, 1979 page A1.

[949] "Pakistan; Spendthrift with a cane" The Economist October 27, 1979 page 63.

[950] "International News" The Associated Press June 15, 1981

[951] Hollick, Julian Crandall. "Islamic banking aims to close poverty gap" Christian Science Monitor December 6, 1982 page B4.

all" for taking all of the *zakat* money. This tax netted the government $90 million.[952] A prominent Pakistani banker in Islamabad noted that *"Nobody is in business to help cover somebody else's losses...All they care about is making a profit. It doesn't matter what a holy book said 1,400 years ago."*[953]

General Zia called upon the nationalized Pakistani banks and the 17 foreign-owned banks in Pakistan to search for ways to make their operations more *"moral"* and *"godly."* Kurshid Ahmad, an economist for the fundamentalist *Jamaat-e-Islami* party, felt that the bankers' markup (or service charges to replace interest) was *"a disguised form of interest payment."* Some of the foreign-owned banks in Pakistan cooperated with the government in molding their operations according to the strictures of Islamic financial practices. Grindlays signed special agreements with the Zia regime that adhered to Islamic banking principles.[954]

While the Islamist dictatorship of General Zia cooperated with the United States in ventures against the Soviet occupation of Afghanistan, other events pointed to a less than friendly relationship. After Iran fell to the Soviet-supported Islamists in February 1979, Pakistan decided to withdraw from the fractured CENTO alliance. In March 1979, the Zia regime formally withdrew Pakistan from the Central Treaty Organization (CENTO). Agha Shahi, foreign affairs adviser to President Zia, noted that this decision was made *"in light of new realities"* as a result of which *"the alliance had lost its relevance to Pakistan's security concerns."*[955] The Pakistanis also excoriated the American attempt to rescue the hostages at the American Embassy in Tehran. There were two probable motivations for the Pakistani reaction. One was the close geographical proximity of Iran and Pakistan. If Pakistan took a pro-US position on Iran, then the Ayatollahs could potentially launch a subversive campaign to subvert and overthrow the Zia regime. Furthermore, both the dictatorships of General Zia and Ayatollah Khomeini were of an anti-Western persuasion and retained common political cultures and ideological orientations. In April 1980, a Pakistani Foreign Ministry spokesmen condemned the attempted US rescue of hostages held in anti-US, Islamist Iran. The Pakistani Foreign Ministry pledged support for the Ayatollah's Iran in its *"struggle to defend its sovereignty and national honor."* The Pakistani spokesman noted that the US rescue mission was an *"adventurous act undertaken by (a) U.S. military task force in flagrant violation of international norms and law ostensibly to rescue the American hostages...This aborted attempt to rescue the (U.S. Embassy) hostages (in Tehran) by the use of force could also have far-reaching consequences for the peace and security of the region."*[956]

Other anti-American protests and actions were the result of an Islamist hatred of the United States. Such anti-US riots and demonstrations had at least the tacit approval of the Zia dictatorship. In November 1979, government-sanctioned Pakistani mobs burned down the US Embassy. Even more disturbing was the fact that it took 5 hours for Pakistani troops to finally quell the Islamist militants and rioters. Islamic students were joined by *"workers and layabouts"* who were taken to the Embassy by the state-owned Punjab Transport Corporation buses. These

---

[952] Auerbach, Stuart. "Pakistan's Official Turn to Islam Collides with Tradition" The Washington Post September 8, 1980 page A24.

[953] Evans, Richard. "Pakistan's interest-free-banking law is still adjusting to the profit motive" Christian Science Monitor March 13, 1986 page 21.

[954] Ibid.

[955] "International News" The Associated Press March 12, 1979

[956] "Pakistan Condemns U.S. Raid" The Associated Press April 25, 1980

Islamist mobs shouted *"Kill the American Dogs."* They also taunted US diplomats by calling them *"imperialist pigs."*[957] In November 1979, Thomas Gene Putscher, a US Embassy staff member noted that while the Embassy was sacked by Islamic militants, Pakistani soldiers *"didn't do a damn thing"* to help. Putscher noted that *"No Pakistani soldiers tried to help me when I was taken by the students…They were there, including at least one officer. I called for them, but there was just no response they didn't do a thing, a damn thing."*[958]

Lastly, the Zia dictatorship strongly resented American support for the State of Israel. Pakistan had long counted itself as a part of the anti-Zionist alliance and this was not abated under the Zia regime. Furthermore, the Zia regime also believed that America was controlled by the Jews, who they felt encouraged a less friendly policy towards Pakistan. As of October 1982, it was noted that *"Anti-American sentiment in this Moslem country (Pakistan) has risen perceptibly since the massacre of Palestinian refugees in Beirut…The resentment has manifested itself mostly in the state-controlled press, which has dwelled on U.S. backing of Israel in its presentation of graphic and grisly accounts of the killings of refugee women and children by Israeli-supported Christian troops. Typical of the coverage was a bannered front-page account in Jang, an Urdu-language daily published here, which carried just beneath its massacre headline a photograph of President Reagan and an accompanying headline declaring, 'Reagan Justifies Massacre.' A story underneath appeared to distort earlier statements by the U.S. president that attempted to explain Israel's motivation for moving its troops into West Beirut before the massacre. The English-language daily, The Moslem, published in Islamabad, carried on its front page the day after news of the massacre broke a photograph of piles of corpses, accompanied by detailed accounts of past U.S. support of Israeli military actions."* In September 1982, the Zia government sponsored a series of meetings and demonstrations where Israel, the United States, and its supporters were condemned. The government ordered factories, offices, and schools to close in order to enhance participation in the anti-American, anti-Israel demonstrations and meetings.[959]

In September 1981, President Zia remarked that there was a *"very effective"* lobby that campaigned in the United States against a $3.2 billion aid package to Pakistan. Foreign Minister Agha Shahi accused the *"Zionist Lobby"* of opposing aid to Zia's Pakistan.[960] In August 1981, General Zia noted that *"Zionist aggression and expansionism as well as foreign armed intervention in the internal affairs of Muslim states, can be faced successfully only through promotion of Islamic solidarity and cooperation at all levels."*[961] In October 1982, the Pakistani *Majlis-i-Shoora* (Federal Advisory Council) adopted a resolution which called for the *"collective*

---

[957] Shalchter, Barry. "Report Pakistani Troops Took Five Hours to Aid Embattled Embassy" The Associated Press November 22, 1979

[958] Schlachter, Barry. "American Says Pakistani Soldiers Watched Him Beaten" The Associated Press November 22, 1979

[959] Claiborne, William. "Beirut Massacre Triggers Increase in Anti-American Sentiment in Pakistan" The Washington Post October 3, 1982 page A24.

[960] "Zia Says Anti-Pakistan Lobby Active In Washington" The Associated Press September 23, 1981

[961] "Pakistan President Calls Upon Muslim Community to Support Liberation of Occupied Arab Territories" Xinhua General News Service August 22, 1981

defence of the Islamic Ummah (community) to frustrate the Zionist entity designs."[962] In September 1982, General Zia condemned the massacres of Palestinians in Lebanon by Israeli-backed right wing Christian militias. He expressed *"our deep anguish and indignation over the premeditated massacre of hundreds of innocent Muslim men, women and children will doubtlessly be reflected."* Various rallies were held in Pakistan that condemned the *"Israeli Zionists for the massacre of Lebanese civilians in west Beirut and expressing sympathy for the Afghan refugees who have been driven from their homeland."*[963] In September 1983, the Pakistani Minister of Information Raja Zafarul Haq remarked that *"The international media are surely and securely in the hands of the Jews."*[964]

The Bhutto and Zia dictatorships also contributed men and material to the Arab war efforts against Israel. Thousands of Pakistani military advisers served in the armies of Saudi Arabia and the Persian Gulf states. Pakistani pilots flew Jordanian and Syrian fighter planes during the 1967 Six Day and 1973 Yom Kippur Wars. The Pakistanis shot down Israeli Air Force planes. At least 50 Pakistani volunteers fought with the PLO against Israel in 1982. After 1973, Pakistan and the PLO signed an agreement for the training of PLO officers at Pakistani military academies. During the First Intifada of 1987, pro-PLO rallies were held in Pakistan and the Zia regime sent the PLO food and medical supplies.[965] In September 1980, the Beirut newspaper <u>Al-Liwa</u> reported that the PLO signed military agreements with Red China, North Korea, and Zia's Pakistan. The PLO was trained in weapons, technology, and battle techniques.[966]

The Zia dictatorship also aligned itself with anti-Western causes that masqueraded as anti-colonialism. This arose from Pakistan's continued desire to remain a credible member of the Non-Aligned Movement. Hence, Pakistan issued diplomatic and political support to Soviet-supported communist terrorist forces in southern Africa. In an October 1982 visit to North Korea, General Zia called for the *"elimination of the colonial system, in whatever form, from every part of the world, for liquidation of racism, for discouragement of arms race and for the establishment of a just and peaceful order throughout the world."*[967] In an October 1982 visit to North Korea, General Zia noted that Pakistan wished to *"discourage anti-peace forces, and to encourage peace-forces everywhere."*[968]

In May 1979, President Zia al-Haq noted that *"Pakistan will fully support all efforts to hasten the process of Namibia's march to independence...Pakistan, a founding member of the United Nations Council for Namibia, is proud of its close association with the Namibian*

[962] "Other Reports; Pakistan calls on Moslem world to unite against Israel" <u>Karachi home service</u> October 14, 1982

[963] "Pakistan President Urges Remembrance of Massacred Refugees" <u>Xinhua General News Service</u> September 28, 1982

[964] "Pakistan; Another world Zionist plot?" <u>The Economist</u> September 10, 1983 page 42.

[965] Yegar, Dr. Moshe. "Pakistan and Israel: An Ongoing Hostility" <u>Jewish Political Studies Review</u> 19:3-4 (Fall 2007) Accessed From: http://www.jcpa.org/JCPA/Templates/ShowPage.asp?DRIT=5&DBID=1&LNGID=1&TMID=111&FID=625&PID=0&IID=1899&TTL=Pakistan_and_Israel

[966] "In Brief: General Outcome of Abu Jihad's Far East visit" <u>Israel home service</u> September 9, 1980

[967] "Pakistan President's Visit to North Korea" <u>KCNA</u> October 25, 1982

[968] "End of Pakistan President's Visit to N Korea" <u>KCNA</u> October 27, 1982

people's just struggle for self-determination and independence...the decisive factor in the liberation struggle of the valiant people of Namibia is their perseverance in the face of adversity and the dedication of the national liberation movement SWAPO. I am confident that their heroic efforts will soon be crowned with success."[969]

In October 1984, General Zia called for South Africa to release all PAC and ANC prisoners. A Xinhua report noted that General Zia condemned *"the repressive policies of the Pretoria regime and its continued denial of human, political and socio-economic rights to the majority of the people of South Africa...Pakistan...has always extended full support to the just struggle of the people all over the world, particularly in South Africa, against colonialism, imperialism and racism in all their manifestations. Pakistan regards the racial segregation followed by the racist minority regime of Pretoria as a crime against humanity and a threat to international peace."*[970]

In September 1986, General Zia asserted at the Non-Aligned Movement summit in Zimbabwe that Pakistan should support the *"inevitable strife of liberty in southern Africa and to concentrate on the issue of apartheid...Pakistan will co-operate with SWAPO, the ANC and the Pan-Africanist Congress in their crusade for self-determination and human dignity."*[971]

Saudi Arabia

Saudi Arabia was another questionable Islamist ally of the United States in the Middle East during the Cold War and the post-1991 period. The relationship between the Saudis and the United States stemmed primarily from oil imports and proximity to the vital Persian Gulf region. Saudi Arabia was ruled by a royal family (the al-Saud dynasty) since the 1930s. They exercised an iron grip over that country through strict adherence to the Wahhabist variant of Islam. The economic structure was a blend of state controlled and subsidized private enterprise with government-owned businesses. Politically, the al-Saud's maintained a near totalitarian grip over their subjects replete with secret police and special morality squads which exacted great brutality against dissenters and other nonconformists.

Perhaps the most comprehensive examination of the Saudi royal dictatorship and its operations against American and Western interests came from Mohammed Abdalla Al Khilewi. Khilewi was the First Secretary at the Saudi Arabian Mission to the United Nations in New York who defected in August 1994. The Saudis clearly had a pervasive espionage operation in the United States that harassed Jewish rightwing organizations and sought to manipulate American foreign policy through influence operations. Khilewi revealed that the Saudi UN Mission in New York gathered intelligence on the Jewish Defense League (JDL) and also installed wiretaps at their headquarters. Khilewi remarked that the Saudi intelligence *"has a big budget that allows it to plant agents almost everywhere. You will find them in human rights organizations, in the United Nations, and in Washington, D.C."* Khilewi remarked that the Saudis engaged in influence and disinformation operations to manipulate American public opinion and to discredit oppositionists abroad: *"If politicians and the media are their old target, scholars are the new*

---

[969] "Pakistan Reaffirms Support for Namibian People's Struggle for Independence" <u>Xinhua General News Service</u> May 5, 1979

[970] "Pakistan Supports Just Struggle of Azanian People" <u>Xinhua General News Service</u> October 11, 1984

[971] "Ziaul Haq's Address on 4th September" <u>Karachi home service</u> September 9, 1986

one. This explains why the government is so active on the Internet, where you find them listed under various committees and organizations. In an effort to know and to control everybody who researches the country at universities and research centers, it sets up seemingly anti-Saudi websites. These serve two purposes: First, as a gatekeeper they make known who's doing what. Second, they spread misinformation, which is made the more plausible by also giving out correct information. I recommend you don't believe what you read on the Internet about Saudi Arabia unless you know who is sponsoring the site and you examine every piece of information." [972]

In an interview with Barbara Walters, Khilewi noted that Saudi diplomats carried firearms, including machine guns. He also revealed that the Saudis spied against Americans in the United States and on American military installations in Saudi Arabia. Khilewi was also instructed at a Saudi diplomatic school on how to smuggle bombs and weapons inside men's suits. [973]

The Saudis also supported violently anti-US terrorists such as Hamas and the pro-Soviet PLO. Khilewi also revealed that *"The Saudi support for Hamas consists of money and logistic support. I am not revealing a secret here, by the way. The Saudi government in Riyadh announced its unconditional support for Hamas. And in an interview with Qatari television April 26, 1998, Sheikh Ahmad Yasin, the founder of Hamas, confirmed this by thanking the Saudis for their support…It gave money to Ramzi Yusuf, the mastermind behind the World Trade Center bombing, right after he traveled to the Philippines from his base in Pakistan…I know that during his time in the Philippines, Ramzi Yusuf received a large amount of money from a Saudi citizen carrying a Saudi diplomatic passport."* Khilewi also reported that *"…in Saudi Arabia three groups can carry a diplomatic passport—royal family members, diplomats, and intelligence."* [974]

From 1968 onwards, public fundraising for the PLO Fatah was freely permitted within Saudi Arabia and the state-controlled press was instructed to support it. In 1968, Saudi contributions to the PLO totaled $100,000 per month. Beginning in 1969, the Saudi government and *"private"* individuals also provided substantial aid to the PLO terrorists. By 1973, Saudi Arabia disbursed $1.2 million per year to the Fatah PLO. Between 1973 and 1981, the Saudis provided the PLO with over $1 billion. In 1980, the Saudis remitted a gift of $40 million to the PLO. In 1982, a PLO delegation visited Saudi Arabia and collected $250 million from the King. [975]

After 1974, the Saudis became the main financier of Palestinian terrorism. In 1989, the PLO received $85 million, while Hamas received $72 million from Saudi Arabia. From 1977 to August 2001, the funding of PLO and Hamas terrorists was overseen by the former Saudi intelligence chief Prince Turki. [976] The Saudis donated hundreds of millions of dollars, US-made explosives, ammunition, and small arms to the PLO. [977] In 1987, the Saudis donated $9.5 million

---

[972] "Mohammed Al Khilewi: 'Saudi Arabia Is Trying to Kill Me'" Middle East Quarterly September 1998 Accessed From: http://www.meforum.org/article/409

[973] "'The Secrets of the Kingdom'-Saudi Terrorist Support" ABC NEWS-20/20 June 24, 1994

[974] "Mohammed Al Khilewi: 'Saudi Arabia Is Trying to Kill Me'" Middle East Quarterly September 1998 Accessed From: http://www.meforum.org/article/409

[975] McForan, Desmond. The World Held Hostage (Oak-Tree Books, 1986) pages 51-53.

[976] Leitzinger, Antero. "Roots of Islamic Terrorism" Global Politician September 11, 2007 Accessed From: http://www.globalpolitician.com/23436-terror-russia

[977] Davis, Leonard J. and Decter, Moshe. Myths and facts 1982 (Near East Report, 1982) pages 184-186.

to the PLO in order for that terror group to expand its influence in Gaza Strip and West Bank. In 1986, the Saudis provided the PLO with $86 million and paid the salary of Mohammed Abu Abbas who was the mastermind behind the hijacking of the *Achille Lauro*.[978] Starting in the 1970s, the Saudis developed an alliance with the Muslim Brotherhood. In the 1980s, the French scholar Olivier Roy noted "*In the 1980s a kind of joint venture was established between the Saudis and the Arab Muslim Brothers.*"[979]

In the name of anti-Semitism, the Saudis even supported neo-Nazi groups in the United States to spread the anti-Israel message. This was part and parcel with the overt anti-Jewish ideology of the Saudi royal family itself. The prejudices against the Jews reached to the level of xenophobia within Saudi Arabia. King Faisal saw to it that all Saudi hotels rooms had copies of the Protocols of the Elders of Zion and the Quran. No Jews were allowed to enter Saudi Arabia unless the visa was personally approved by King Faisal.[980] One well-known example of Saudi support to the American neo-Nazi community occurred in the 1970s. In the late 1970s, the Saudi government retained the services of American neo-Nazi William Grimstead as a lobbyist in the United States. The Saudis also funded international Islamist organizations, such as the World Muslim Congress (WMC). The WMC secretary-general Dr. Inamullah Khan was a trusted advisor to the Saudi royal family. Dr. Khan wrote a letter to the crypto-Nazi Liberty Lobby's newspaper The Spotlight, praising its "*superb in-depth analysis*" and stating that the newspaper deserved "*the thanks of all right-minded people.*" The Saudi-supported WMC was both anti-Soviet and anti-American. For example, a headline from the WMC newspaper Muslim World read "*U.S. and USSR — Both Serve Zionist Interests.*"[981]

The Saudis also maintained strategic military cooperation with various adversaries of the United States, such as Baathist Socialist Iraq and Red China. Khilewi revealed Saudi secret documents which indicated that the royal regime supported Iraq's nuclear program to the tune of $5 billion between 1975 and 1990. The Saudis also attempted to obtain nuclear weapons from the USSR and Pakistan. Khilewi remarked that Saudi Arabia "*will pay anything to acquire a nuclear capability as long as the cost is just money…I'd say the Saudi government has since 1975 spent at least $7 billion on nuclear armaments. It paid millions of dollars to buy nuclear reactors for what it likes to call 'scientific' and 'peaceful' uses. It also spent millions of dollars for nuclear research and data collection. But most of the money went to support nuclear programs in other countries—Iraq and Pakistan.*"[982] Khilewi reportedly attended a meeting in 1989 between teams of Saudi and Iraqi nuclear specialists regarding the status of Baghdad's nuclear weapons program. Khilewi also reported that teams of Saudi scientists received nuclear training in Iraq during the 1980s. The Saudis also developed a nuclear research center at the

---

[978] Packwood, Bob and Cranston, Alan. "No More Arms for the Saudis Until They Show Friendship" The New York Times August 23, 1987 page 23.

[979] Gold, Dore. Hatred's Kingdom: How Saudi Arabia Supports the New Global Terrorism (Regnery Publishing 2012) page 101.

[980] Weston, Mark. Prophets and Princes: Saudi Arabia from Muhammad to the Present (John Wiley & Sons 2011) page 201.

[981] Lee, Martin A. "Holocaust Deniers Unite" Intelligence Report Spring 2002 Accessed From: http://www.splcenter.org/get-informed/intelligence-report/browse-all-issues/2002/spring/the-swastika-and-the-crescent/deniers

[982] "Mohammed Al Khilewi: 'Saudi Arabia Is Trying to Kill Me'" Middle East Quarterly September 1998 Accessed From: http://www.meforum.org/article/409

military base in Al Suleiyel. It was staffed by 100 Islamic technicians and three Westerners.[983] Khilewi also revealed that the Saudis attempted to purchase a nuclear reactor from Red China in 1989 via an American firm. A letter from the Chinese Nuclear Energy Industry Corporation to Prince Abdel Rahman was dated from January 1989. It noted that Red China would sell research reactors to Riyadh. The Prince was to receive a 5% commission on this deal. A February 1989 letter to a senior official at Riyadh University described a visit to Red Chinese nuclear industries. Prince Abdel Rahman indicated that Saudi Arabia needed a *"nuclear reactor and training program."* In May 1986, an official Saudi letter to the American firm Marine Services Limited confirmed receipt of documents for a *"Miniature Neutron Source Reactor."* In 1985, Khilewi reported that the Saudis purchased CSS-2 medium range ballistic missiles from Red China.[984]

Saudi Arabia also funded various Soviet clients in the Middle East on the pretext of halting Islamist Iranian expansion (by aiding Iraq) and smashing the State of Israel in a series of conventional invasions. During the 1973 Yom Kippur War, Saudi Arabia sent a squadron of US-made Bell 205 Iroquois helicopters to Egypt, which ignored the American conditions of sale. Saudi Arabia also provided Egypt with 38 Mirage 3 jets, British-made Lightning jets, and dozens of light British-made tanks. In mid-1975, Senator Clifford Case (R-NJ) noted that Saudi F-5E jets participated in a military exercise in Syria.[985] The Saudis also pledged assistance to Qaddafi in Libya in the event of sanctions by the United States.[986] As of December 1986, the Saudis provided the Baathist Socialist dictatorship of Syria with $540 million per year. This aid kept Syria afloat economically.[987]

Various American corporations arguably enabled Saudi anti-Israeli policies. For example, the American firm Vinnell Corporation was paid by the Saudis to recruit 1,000 US soldiers to train the Saudi National Guard. It should be noted that the Guard's commander, Amir Abdullah ibn 'Abd Aziz al Saud expressed his hatred of the *"Zionist enemy in Palestine."* On Riyadh Radio he stated *"How can an Arab or Moslem accept the continuation of this bitter state of affairs particularly since Zionist ambitions know no limits? These ambitions are a danger threatening the Arab and Islamic worlds and indeed the whole world."* He told the radio that he hoped to acquire *"the latest weapons."* The Guard also ordered large numbers of Cadillac Gage armored cars with 90mm cannons. Hence, the Guard's new American weapons and training could have been conscripted in the fight against Israel.[988]

Former USAF General Joseph Churba expressed concern about the increasingly pro-Saudi and Arabist shift in American Mideast foreign policy under President Reagan. General Churba observed that after Reagan won the 1980 election, his Administration increasingly became a *"spokesman for sub rosa factions in his administration: Arabists in the State*

---

[983] Coll, Steve and Mintz, John. "Saudi Aid to Iraqi A-Bomb Effort Alleged; Asylum-Seeking Diplomat Says Riyadh Secretly Gave Baghdad Money and Technology" The Washington Post July 25, 1994 page A12.

[984] Lewis, Paul. "Defector Says Saudis Sought Nuclear Arms" The New York Times August 7, 1994 page 20.

[985] Rosenfeld, Alvin. The Plot to Destroy Israel (Putnam 1977) page 202.

[986] Packwood, Bob and Cranston, Alan. "No More Arms for the Saudis Until They Show Friendship" The New York Times August 23, 1987 page 23.

[987] Walker, Tony. "State of war burden for Syria's economy" The Globe and Mail (Canada) December 15, 1986 page B12.

[988] Rosenfeld, Alvin. The Plot to Destroy Israel (Putnam 1977) pages 210-211.

Department, those under the direct influence of the oil interests, and outright ignoramuses vulnerable ipso facto to both Arabists and oil people."[989] Churba was also opposed by elements within the "*Republican Party, circles sympathetic to the PLO opposed me and my positions.*" The pro-Arab shift was felt in the Reagan Administration. Naturally, this was a continuation of President Carter's appeasement of Israel's Arab enemies. The Reagan Administration:

1) Provided the Saudis with F-15 technology, which was allegedly passed to pro-Soviet Syria.
2) Provided the Saudis with satellite intelligence on Israel.
3) Supplied intelligence on the IDF to the Saudis which was then passed to Moscow's satellites of Iraq and Syria.[990]

The Saudis themselves engaged in policies and actions that were clearly hostile towards American interests. Deep down, America was viewed by the Saudis as an infidel nation that was nevertheless needed by the al-Saud monarchy to counter Soviet and later Iranian influences in the Persian Gulf region. Otherwise, Saudi leaders displayed a not-so-thinly disguised hatred of the United States. Such feelings were held by a long succession of Saudi royals. In early 1949, Saudi Foreign Minister Prince Faisal noted in the official Saudi gazette <u>Umm al-Qura</u> that "*The Arab world appeared to be under the misapprehension that they were fighting the Jews…**We are not fighting the Jews but the tyrannical imperialist states whose greedy aims are to captivate the nations of the world in order to enslave and exploit the weak…The true enemies of the Arabs in Palestine are not the Jews…but the imperialist states of Great Britain, the United States of America, and the Soviet Union*.*"*[991] Anti-Western and anti-American feelings also reached a fever pitch under King Faisal (1964-1975). King Faisal hoped to form a united front of Islamic nations against communism, Zionism, and imperialism.[992] In June 1967, in response to the Israeli strikes against the Arab countries, King Faisal exhorted "*To jihad citizens! To jihad!*" at a giant rally in Riyadh. Oil workers employed by Aramco went on strike for a week. Students who attended the University of Petroleum threw rocks and damaged several American military residences.[993] King Faisal noted that "*…imperialism aims to oppress other people and rule them in wholly different ways. As to the forces of Zionism, they know that cooperation among Muslims would put an end to the evil expansionist idea of international Zionism in Islamic and Arab countries.*"[994] King Faisal also promised Egyptian President Sadat that he would reduce oil exports to the West if events required it. One week later, on television, King Faisal told an NBC News correspondent that "*America's complete support for Zionism against the Arabs makes it extremely difficult for us to supply its petroleum needs.*"[995]

---

[989] Churba, Joseph. <u>The American Retreat</u> (Regnery Gateway, 1984) pages 27-29.

[990] Churba, Joseph. <u>The Washington Compromise</u> (University Press of America 1995) pages 76-85.

[991] Gold, Dore. <u>Hatred's Kingdom: How Saudi Arabia Supports the New Global Terrorism</u> (Regnery Publishing 2012) page 69.

[992] Weston, Mark. <u>Prophets and Princes: Saudi Arabia from Muhammad to the Present</u> (John Wiley & Sons 2011) page 202.

[993] Ibid, page 201.

[994] King Faisal. <u>Faisal speaks</u> (Kingdom of Saudi Arabia, Ministry of Information 1966) page 48.

[995] Weston, Mark. <u>Prophets and Princes: Saudi Arabia from Muhammad to the Present</u> (John Wiley & Sons 2011) page 213.

One Saudi general noted to American reporters that Riyadh would look to the Arab bloc to assist them first *"and to you last."* An official of Defense Minister Sultan's office noted that the United States was the primary threat to the Saudi oil fields. Another Saudi official admitted that there was only one positive outcome of the Camp David Accords: *"Yes, the death of Sadat."*[996] In 1981, Secretary of Defense Caspar Weinberger was told during a visit to Saudi Arabia: *"We don't want your Rapid Deployment Force."* One Saudi general remarked *"You are just arms salesmen and we pay cash."*[997] The Saudis threatened the United States for attempting to fill the US Strategic Petroleum Reserve; pressured Oman for permitting a American base in that country; attempted to sabotage the US-brokered Camp David Accords; and expelled the CIA Station Chief in Saudi Arabia. The Saudis also refused the US to build bases in that country in the 1970s and 1980s.[998]

Unfortunately, the United States sealed its slow death of energy independence under President Reagan in his first term. This measure was undertaken clearly in the name of short-sighted geopolitics and commercial profits. In 1983, the United States provided Saudi Arabia a unilateral no-embargo pledge as an inducement to the Saudis to increase their purchases of US food products. Agriculture Secretary John Block noted *"there is a great deal of interdependence"* in the economic relationship between the Saudis and the US. Block argued that the doctrine of *"comparative advantage"* should determine trade policy between the Saudis and the US. He noted *"They have a comparative advantage in the production of oil, and we have a comparative advantage in food."*[999] The short-sighted free traders also sought to cripple American energy independence, thus ensuring continued dependence on imported oil from politically unstable regions and authoritarian regimes. This is discussed in my book Red Dawn In Retrospect: Soviet-Chinese Intentions for Conquest of the United States.

Despite being cast by pro-Arab and corporate globalists within the State Department as *"moderates,"* Saudi Arabia sought to destroy Israel. The Saudis also fought in the wars of 1948 and 1973 against Israel with conventional armies.[1000] Even in the 1980s, the Saudis threatened Jordanian King Hussein with economic sanctions if he entered into direct negotiations with Israel.[1001] Saudi King Khalid noted on January 28, 1981 that *"The Moslem nation has asserted anew that the liberation of holy Jerusalem from the claws of Zionism is a must."* Crown Prince Fahd noted on May 18, 1979 that *"We would spare no effort to force Egypt's President Anwar Sadat to renounce his newly signed peace treaty with Israel."* Fahd also stated in 1977 to Al Hawadess that *"We will never recognize Israel. We don't have to recognize anyone we don't want to recognize."* Foreign Minister Saud ibn Faisal noted in a 1977 interview that *"Not only will Saudi Arabia sacrifice its oil and financial resources, but also the blood of its sons."* Saudi

---

[996] Churba, Joseph. The American Retreat (Regnery Gateway, 1984) pages 50-53.

[997] Packwood, Bob and Cranston, Alan. "No More Arms for the Saudis Until They Show Friendship" The New York Times August 23, 1987 page 23.

[998] Davis, Leonard J. and Decter, Moshe. Myths and facts 1982 (Near East Report, 1982) pages 184-186.

[999] Lippman, Thomas W. "U. S. Gives Saudis No-Embargo Pledge; Inducement to Buy More Food Products" The Washington Post May 10, 1983 page D7.

[1000] Davis, Leonard J. and Decter, Moshe. Myths and facts 1982 (Near East Report, 1982) pages 184-186.

[1001] Packwood, Bob and Cranston, Alan. "No More Arms for the Saudis Until They Show Friendship" The New York Times August 23, 1987 page 23.

Oil Minister Sheik Yamani noted in February 1981 that *"We are prepared to use all that we have, even to fight and shed our blood, in order to liberate Jerusalem and Palestine."*[1002]

By the 1980s, the Saudis also expanded trade relations with the Soviet Union and Red China. The Saudis and the communists were motivated to engage in such mutual trade for reasons of commercial profit and to diversify its international relationships. While the Saudis were intensely anti-communist, ideology did not prevent Riyadh from underwriting the the purchase of Soviet weapons by radical Arab Socialist dictatorships.

Initially, the early Saudi monarchs and princes were sympathetic to the anti-colonial and anti-Western positions of the Soviet Union, especially under Stalin. Prince Faisal traveled to the USSR in 1932 and visited factories, military academies, and an oil field on the Caspian Sea. He met with Stalin and persuaded Stalin to increase the number of pilgrimages made by Soviet Muslims to Mecca.[1003] In fact, the Soviet diplomat Karim Hakimov assisted King Saud in creating the modern Saudi state. In reality, Hakimov was a communist revolutionary who deceptively posed as a devout Islamist. He conducted a pilgrimage to Mecca to strengthen his *bona fides* with the Saudi ruling elites. On the initiative of Hakimov, the World Muslim Congress (WMC) was formed in 1926 in Mecca. The WMC, which is anti-American to this day, strategized various methods that the Islamic world could utilize to throw off Western colonialism. Hakimov was purged by Stalin by 1937 and King Saud promptly broke diplomatic relations with the USSR. Saudi trust towards the Soviet Union was damaged for decades to come.[1004]

Occasionally, Soviet sympathizers made their way to the court of the al-Saud family. Muhammad Maruf ad-Dawalibi was the former Prime Minister of Syria and founder of the Islamic Socialist Front in the fall of 1949. He noted in April 1950, that Arabs would prefer *"thousands time more to become a Soviet Republic than to be spoils of Jews."* After September 1951, Ad-Dawalibi requested that Arab leaders push harder for Soviet support. He was exiled from Syria and became a councilor of Saudi King Khalid.[1005]

By the 1960s, the USSR sought an improvement in its relations with the Saudis under the rubric of a common anti-Zionism. The Soviets also scoped for more progressive-minded Saudi royals who might display some commonalties with socialism. The Soviets sought to improve relations with Saudi Arabia when Faisal became King in 1964. An Izvestia correspondent reported that King Faisal wanted to develop good relations with the USSR. The correspondent also spoke of the *"positive measures"* of social and economic reforms undertaken by King Faisal.[1006] While King Faisal was very anti-communist, he did support the USSR indirectly through Saudi payment for Soviet weapons shipped to Egypt. These Saudi-subsidized Soviet-made weapons were used by Egypt to attack Israel. In 1973, the Saudis paid for Sadat's Soviet-

---

[1002] Davis, Leonard J. and Decter, Moshe. Myths and facts 1982 (Near East Report, 1982) pages 184-186.

[1003] Weston, Mark. Prophets and Princes: Saudi Arabia from Muhammad to the Present (John Wiley & Sons 2011) page 168.

[1004] Preobrazhensky, Konstantin. "Communists and Muslims: The Hidden Hand of the KGB" Accessed From: http://leninandsharia.com/docs/preobrazhensky.pdf

[1005] Leitzinger, Antero. "Roots of Islamic Terrorism" Global Politician September 11, 2007 Accessed From: http://www.globalpolitician.com/23436-terror-russia

[1006] Yodfat, Aryeh Y. and Abir, M. In the Direction of the Persian Gulf (Psychology Press, 1977) pages 53-54.

made weapons. Egyptian President Sadat flew to Riyadh to inform King Faisal that the Soviet weapons were delivered to Cairo and that war with Israel was imminent.[1007]

By the 1980s, the Soviets stepped up their campaign to woo the Saudis based on a common anti-Zionism, mutual aid for the PLO, and even their joint opposition for American support for Israel. In 1974, the Syrians reportedly attempted to forge a rapprochement between Saudi Arabia and the Soviet Union based on issues of common agreement.[1008] In 1982, the PLO mediated discussions with the Soviets and Saudis on re-opening relations between the two countries.[1009] In 1979, the Soviets were seeking to split Saudi Arabia and the United States over Iran and the Camp David Accords.[1010]

The Saudis also made statements to the effect that they would align or purchase weapons from the Soviets, especially if arms from the Americans were not forthcoming. Saudi King Khalid noted at the Islamic Conference of January 1981: *"Our loyalty should not be to either the Eastern bloc or the Western bloc but to Allah, His Prophet and the Islamic masses everywhere in the world."* In 1980, Crown Prince Fahd told Al-Hawadess *"We are not compelled to be friends with the Americans. There are many doors wide open to us, be it on the military, technological, or economic level...We can easily replace the Americans."* In September 1981, Prince Khaled ibn Sultan, the director of planning for the Saudi Air Defense Command, informed the Los Angeles World Affairs Council that the Saudis would consider buying Soviet made arms: *"To protect ourselves, our land, and our heritage, we are willing to deal with the devil himself if it is in our best national interests."*[1011] In February 1981, Crown Prince Fahd noted to a Swedish reporter that *"There are no restrictions of our arms purchases...If Sweden agrees to sell us weapons, we will buy. If we find the doors to American and Western arms markets closed, we might turn to the Soviet Union for buying the weapons we need."*[1012]

Meanwhile, the Saudis even provided credits to communist countries. Clearly, business and profits trumped ideologies. As of January 1981, Gulf Riyadh Bank managed the syndication of three to four loans to the Soviet bloc. Gulf Riyadh managed or led the syndication of the following loans: $150 million for Hungary and $117 million for Yugoslavia.[1013] By the mid-1980s, Soviet-Saudi trade also experienced an uptick. In 1985, Soviet-Saudi trade totaled over 405 rubles. During the same year, Soviet imports from Saudi Arabia totaled over 378 million rubles.[1014] As of October 1985, Soviet exports to Saudi Arabia included machinery, equipment and transport facilities, metal-cutting machine tools, forging presses, drilling rigs, cars, and pipes. In 1984, Soviet exports to Saudi Arabia included goods such as building materials and cement. Saudi exports to the USSR consisted mainly of fuel and raw materials.[1015] As of January

---

[1007] Weston, Mark. Prophets and Princes: Saudi Arabia from Muhammad to the Present (John Wiley & Sons 2011) page 213.

[1008] "Syrians in Favor of Saudi Soviet Dialog" Le Monde December 31, 1974

[1009] "PLO Official on Saudi Soviet Relations Mediation" Foreign Broadcast Information Service Review February 3, 1982

[1010] "Soviets Attempt Rapprochement with Saudis" Cairo Akhbar Al-Yawm February 10, 1979

[1011] Davis, Leonard J. and Decter, Moshe. Myths and facts 1982 (Near East Report, 1982) pages 184-186.

[1012] "Fahd Threatens to Turn to Moscow for Arms" The Associated Press February 23, 1981

[1013] "Arab oil money helps bail out the East bloc" Business Week March 23, 1981 page 39.

[1014] "International Relations; Trade With Arab Countries" TASS March 28, 1986

[1015] "International Relations; Saudi Arabia: Trade" TASS October 4, 1985

1988, Saudi Arabia sold wheat to the Soviet Union and Red China. These trade relations were seen by Western diplomats as a *"gentle thawing of the Arab country's anti-Communist stance."*[1016]

Saudi funds to the USSR under Gorbachev were even diverted into the activities of international communist subversion. In a secret February 1991 memo, CPSU International Department head Valentin Falin recommended that Soviet Communist Party debts to friendly companies in Japan, France, Italy, Britain, Austria, and Greece should be paid from untied hard currency credits provided to Moscow by Saudi Arabia and South Korea.[1017]

Saudi ports and funds were also harnessed for Soviet and Eastern Bloc weapons shipments to Baathist Socialist Iraq during the war with Iran (1980-1988). As of November 1980, Saudi Arabia allowed three of its ports to be used for the transshipment of weapons to Iraq. Ships from Yugoslavia, France, and East Germany unloaded their weapons cargos at the Saudi ports of Jidda, Yenbo, and Qadhima.[1018] In March 1981, Saudi Arabia reportedly bought Soviet-made tanks, field artillery, and ammunition which were then shipped to Iraq.[1019] As of February 1981, diplomatic sources indicated that 100 Soviet-made T-54 and T-55 tanks were shipped from East European nations and unloaded at Saudi ports on the Red Sea. They were trucked to Iraq.[1020] As of November 1981, Israeli military intelligence chief Major General Yehoshua Saguy reported that Saudi Arabia transferred Soviet-made weapons to Iraq. These Soviet weapons were shipped from unidentified European sources, unloaded at Saudi ports, and transported by truck to Iraq.[1021] As of May 1987, it was reported that *"Soviet trade with Saudi Arabia almost certainly represents an extension of its trade with Iraq. Saudi sales to the USSR are used to assist the Iraqi balance of payments."*[1022]

The Saudis also paid for Soviet weapons destined to Baathist Socialist Syria, which was ruled by the tyrant President Hafez- al-Assad. In November 1981, the Saudis paid for the Soviet weapons imported by Syria, which included MIG-27 fighters, tanks, and APCs.[1023] In 1986, the Saudis provided Syria with $700 million in order for the Baathist Assad regime to purchase Soviet-made weapons such as SS-21 ballistic missiles.[1024]

Contrary to the blatant displays of material wealth and commercialism in the Saudi economy, the government played a strong role in guiding, nurturing, and even owning large sections of the national economy. The Saudi economic ideology adhered to an Islamist ideology that rejected free market capitalism, socialism, and communism. It also supported a planned

---

[1016] "Saudi Arabia selling wheat to Soviet Union and China" The Globe and Mail (Canada) January 18, 1988

[1017] "Ivashko, Falin, and Hard Currency" Russian Press Digest October 27, 1991 page 3.

[1018] "Saudi Ports Handle Iraqi War Supplies" The New York Times November 21, 1980 page A14.

[1019] "Saudi Arabia Reported Buying Soviet Tanks, Arms" Cairo MENA March 2, 1981

[1020] "Iraqis Reported to Get About 100 Soviet Made Tanks" The New York Times February 4, 1981 page A4.

[1021] "Israeli Says Saudis Send Iraq Soviet Arms" The Associated Press November 12, 1981

[1022] "Paying for Soviet weapons" MidEast Markets May 11, 1987

[1023] "Saudis Financing Soviet Syrian Deal" Ma'ariv November 20, 1981

[1024] Packwood, Bob and Cranston, Alan. "No More Arms for the Saudis Until They Show Friendship" The New York Times August 23, 1987 page 23.

economy with a plethora of subsidies to encourage Saudi economic independence from the major world powers, especially during periods of reduced oil exports.

The Saudis hewed to a collectivist economic worldview which stemmed from their Islamic and anti-Western bias. Such sentiments gained steam under the iron-fisted, but reformist King Faisal. In a speech in communist Guinea in 1966, King Faisal noted "*So if Islamic principles were properly applied, there would not be capitalism and there would not be poverty and there would be no oppression or illness, because Islam is the solid basis for every virtue and every benefit.*"[1025] King Faisal also stated in 1966 that "*What is called progressiveness in the world today and what reformers are calling for, be it social, human or economic progress is all embodied in the Islamic religion and laws. We are going ahead with extensive planning, guided by our Islamic laws and belief, for the progress of the nation...We have chosen an economic system based on free enterprise because it is our conviction that it fits perfectly with our Islamic laws and suits our country...*"[1026] King Faisal implicitly noted in 1973 that he was a revolutionary: "*Revolutions can come from thrones as well as from conspirators' cellars.*" Mark Weston noted that King Faisal "*built highways, ports, and power stations and gave his people cradle to grave security: free schools and medical care, easy loans for homes and farm equipment, and heavily subsidized food and utilities.*"[1027]

During the 1980s, the Saudi Muslim clergy and government-controlled press continued to reject capitalism. In 1983 Saudi Television noted "*Islam then turned toward recovering its control over its capabilities and economic resources only to be surprised that many of the sons of the Islamic world believe that there is no way to usefully exploit these economic resources except by following an Eastern or Western system, that is capitalism or Marxist socialism.*"[1028] One Saudi Islamic writer noted in the mid-1980s that the "*Zionists*" were supported by "*Western imperialist capitalism.*" Two Saudi lecturers at the Islamic University of Medina for Islamic law and *da'wa* wrote deep criticisms of the West and capitalism in their book The Methods of Ideological Invasion of the Islamic World: "*In the economic field that means the flag of capitalism, in the political field that means the principles of democracy, and in the social field it waves the principles of freedom.*"[1029]

Even during the 1990s and 2000s, the Saudis continued their denunciations of Western liberal free market economics. In 1994, the well-spoken and urbane Saudi Prince Bandar noted that "*The state opens doors to its citizens and enables them to contribute to the process of the economic development, they succeed in performing their mission that will be a good thing, but if they fail to attain success the state assists them and enables them to try again...So the Kingdom, like the capitalist countries, open its doors to the citizens for contribution to economic*

[1025] King Faisal. Faisal speaks (Kingdom of Saudi Arabia, Ministry of Information 1966) page 87.

[1026] Champion, Daryl. The Paradoxical Kingdom: Saudi Arabia And the Momentum of Reform (Columbia University Press 2005) page 128.

[1027] Weston, Mark. Prophets and Princes: Saudi Arabia from Muhammad to the Present (John Wiley & Sons 2011) page 229.

[1028] "Television Discussion of Islamic Ijtihad" Jiddah Ukaz June 17, 1983

[1029] Gold, Dore. Hatred's Kingdom: How Saudi Arabia Supports the New Global Terrorism (Regnery Publishing 2012) page 96.

development, but at the same time through its social insurance system, it appear to be like a socialist country. We have successfully taken the best things from capitalism and socialism."[1030]

In May 2002, Crown Prince Al-Rashid supported labor unions in the West as a tool in fighting unrestrained capitalism and praised Saudi worker-employer relations in a typically corporative, collectivist fashion: "*Labour unions were established when independent capitalism held sway to protect the workers' rights at a time when they did not have guarantees from the law. Their history went through much violence and strikes and some of these caused the destruction of the whole economy in several countries. We in the kingdom, and through the clear concepts of Islamic sharia, are eager to give the worker his full rights according to the best labour legislation in the most advanced countries. Through its regulations that are derived from God's sharia, the state has set itself as the workers' protector and the defender of their rights. Hence there is nothing at present to warrant the establishment of labour unions. There are several acceptable alternatives, including the professional and scientific associations of which there is a growing number in the kingdom, such as the labour and the various trade committees. We hope that these establishments will be active and play their role in full alongside the state in a cordial and peaceful way that avoids the violence and chaos that labour organizations in several countries had fallen into.*"[1031]

The economic crisis in the United States during the years 2008 and 2009 only heightened Saudi criticism of economic liberalism. In October 2008, the Saudi writer Husayn Shubakshi noted that "*In the 1960s, US economist Milton Friedman won the Nobel prize for economics because of his theories about liberal economy which always demanded to leave the markets operate alone without any government intervention at all because the markets 'have a secret hand' and the ability to correct themselves...But events of the current stage prove without any doubt that Friedman's theories are the biggest loser and that capitalism 'becomes a beast' if it is left without control and supervision. The French and Swedish examples probably appear like a beacon in the present darkness...The world is watching the rebirth of the economic system and the end of the barbaric capitalist and stupid management era.*"[1032]

Various writers and scholars also confirmed the strong role that the Kingdom played in the Saudi economy, thus proving false the image that the rulers in Riyadh were strict adherents to Western-style capitalism. The anthropologists Soraya Altorki and Donald Cole noted that in Saudi Arabia: "*...Landownership involves registration and must conform to the guidelines set by the state as do commercial establishments. The importation of a laborer requires approval by an agency of the state and rules and regulations concerning that laborer must be followed once he is employed...The state also provides a major source of entertainment and the news through its radio and television networks. It has also become the major source of loans and subsidies to build houses or development agricultural enterprises...The state has become the single most employer in the community.*"[1033]

[1030] "Islam is a way of life: Prince Bandar; 'Extremism is against Islamic spirit'" <u>Moneyclips</u> August 3, 1994

[1031] "Saudi crown prince on US visit, peace initiative, Iraq, other issues" <u>Al-Sharq al-Awsat web site</u> May 12, 2002

[1032] Husayn Shubakshi. "Saudi writer urges 'bold' steps to protect immature markets from crisis" <u>Al-Sharq al-Awsat website</u> October 13, 2008

[1033] F. Gregory Gause. <u>Oil Monarchies: Domestic and Security Challenges in the Arab Gulf States</u> (Council on Foreign Relations, 1994) pages 50-59.

One source noted that "*The Saudi elites and religious establishment do not believe in capitalism, or democracy or gender equality. What we call freedom they think of as chaos.*"[1034] In October 2001, conservative historian and Reagan Administration economic adviser Bruce Bartlett noted that "*The discovery of oil in the 20th century encouraged further state centralization in Saudi Arabia. As the State Department's latest report on economic policy and trade practices notes, 'Parastatal enterprises, such as Saudi ARAMCO (oil) and Saudi Basic Industries Corp. (SABIC - petrochemicals), and utilities, among others, dominate the economy.' Consequently, there is little entrepreneurship in the Saudi economy. Oil wealth provides a good education for any Saudi male who wants one. But lacking opportunities for careers outside government, few study business, economics or engineering. Many pursue degrees in Islamic studies and are unemployed more or less permanently after graduation. Generous government benefits provide for their needs and foreigners do most of the manual labor, leaving large numbers of Saudis with nothing to do except bemoan their condition and look for scapegoats to blame for it.*"[1035]

The book Saudi Arabia: A Country Study noted that "*The stated goal of Saudi rulers has been to improve the economic conditions of the country's citizens while retaining the society's Islamic values.*" Since the 1950s, the modern, centralized state in Saudi Arabia intervened in the economy to promote development. The size and scope of the state grew in relation to the Saudi economic structure. In 1952, the government of King Saud formed the Saudi Arabian Monetary Agency (SAMA). In 1962, the General Petroleum and Mineral Organization (Petromin) was formed. In 1958, the IMF also successfully recommended to the King of Saudi Arabia the creation of a government planning organization. In 1965, the Central Planning Organization was formed. In 1975, the Organization was reorganized and upgraded to the Ministry of Planning. It closely planned the performance and development of various Saudi economic sectors. The First Development Plan of 1970-75 focused on the development of capital projects in the defense, education, transportation, and utility sectors. The Second Development Plan of 1975-80 implemented social welfare goals such as free medical service, free education and vocational training, interest-free loans and subsidies for the purchase of homes, subsidized prices for essential commodities, interest-free credit for people with limited incomes, and extended social security benefits and support for the indigent.[1036]

In 1981, Saudi economic plans outlined the government's concern that "*alien values and the spirit of materialism*" would threaten Islam through development and modernization programs. Deputy Planning Minister Faisal Bashir remarked that "*I am an optimist...I think we came out of the 1970s very well. But we must not compromise our basic principles. I would call those Islam and our belief in the family.*" The 1980-85 economic plan envisioned investments totaling $300 billion for social improvements, defense, agriculture, and gas-based petrochemical plants. Minister of Planning, Hisham Nazer remarked to the visiting Prime Minister Thatcher that all Saudis were entitled to free education and health care, unemployment and injury benefits,

---

[1034] United States Senate. Committee on the Judiciary. Testimony of Steve Emerson "Saudi Arabia: friend or foe in the war on terror?" November 8, 2005 Accessed From: http://www.investigativeproject.org/documents/testimony/324.pdf

[1035] Bartlett, Bruce. "Misreading the scorecard" The Washington Times October 31, 2001 page A20.

[1036] "Saudi Arabia: A Country Study" Accessed From: http://lcweb2.loc.gov/cgi-bin/query/r?frd/cstdy:@field(DOCID+sa0136)

and essential goods having their prices subsidized by the state. He noted "*It may sound as if the Saudi Government is following a policy of handouts…But the policy is to insure a minimum standard of living and beyond that the good life will have to be earned.*"[1037]

The Saudis also sought to promote an independent industrial and oil extraction sector to contribute to the nation's economic independence and increase its hard currency reserves. In the 1970s, the Saudi government built the industrial cities of Yanbu and Jubayl and formed the Saudi Basic Industries Corporation (SABIC), which was 70% owned by the government. Other government-owned enterprises in Saudi Arabia included the national oil and gas marketing company (Petromin), the regional electric companies, some of the major hotels, a steel mill, the maritime facilities company working for the oil industry, and the national cement company. In Saudi Arabia, government-owned cooperatives provided food products at subsidized prices.[1038]

In 1972, the Saudi government purchased 25% ownership of the Arab-American Oil Company (Aramco). By 1988, Aramco was converted to a completely Saudi-owned company called the Saudi Arabian Oil Company (Saudi Aramco). Petromin held part ownership in Saudi enterprises that specialized in products such as fertilizers, steel, and petrochemicals. The Saudi private sector received financial aid from the Saudi Industrial Development Fund (SIDF). It was noted that "*The government owned all subsoil resources and permitted joint ventures with Petromin for exploration and mining activities…The government has played an instrumental role in developing the manufacturing sector by directly establishing industrial plants, mainly in the basic industries sector, such as petrochemical, steel, and other large manufacturing enterprises. Also, it has developed manufacturing through direct loans, mainly by the SIDF and through industrial subsidies, offset programs, set-asides, preferential buying programs, and tariffs.*" As of 1992, SABIC owned at least fifteen major industrial enterprises.[1039]

The Saudis also sought to develop self-sufficiency in food production through state involvement and subsidies. Saudi Arabia utilized price supports and subsidies to fund farming made possible by oil profits.[1040] Saudi agriculture was assisted by the Ministry of Agriculture and Water, the Saudi Arabian Agricultural Bank (SAAB) and the Grain Silos and Flour Mills Organization (GSFMO). SAAB provided interest-free loans to farmers.[1041]

The Saudis also developed a banking system which adhered to the policy framework of Islamic and semi-nationalist ideology. SAMA's charter stipulated that it would conform to Islamic banking law. Hence, it was officially forbidden to generate a profit or tender interest payments. In 1975, the government embarked on a program of Saudi participation in ownership

---

[1037] "Saudis Shield Islam From 'Alien Values'" New York Times April 26, 1981 Accessed From: http://www.nytimes.com/1981/04/26/world/saudis-shieldi-islam-from-alien-values.html
[1038] F. Gregory Gause. Oil Monarchies: Domestic and Security Challenges in the Arab Gulf States (Council on Foreign Relations, 1994) pages 50-59.
[1039] "Saudi Arabia: A Country Study" Accessed From: http://lcweb2.loc.gov/cgi-bin/query/r?frd/cstdy:@field(DOCID+sa0136)
[1040] F. Gregory Gause. Oil Monarchies: Domestic and Security Challenges in the Arab Gulf States (Council on Foreign Relations, 1994) pages 50-59.
[1041] "Saudi Arabia: A Country Study" Accessed From: http://lcweb2.loc.gov/cgi-bin/query/r?frd/cstdy:@field(DOCID+sa0136)

of foreign banks that operated in the Kingdom. In order to curb fraud and speculation, SAMA tightly regulated the activities of the money changers since the 1980s.[1042]

Organizations that were part of the fabric of civil society in Saudi Arabia were tightly controlled as a means of maintaining the Islamic, collectivist authoritarian society that the al-Saud royal family was committed to upholding. The Ministry of Information and the 1964 Press Law regulated the Saudi media, thus precluding the development of truly private and independent investigative reporting institutions.[1043] Independent labor unions were illegal while chambers of commerce were supervised by the government.[1044] Saudi Arabia's labor code forbade strikes and collective bargaining and also called for arbitration of labor disputes and rules on proper treatment of workers.[1045] The unspeakably brutal religious police (*mutawwiin* or the Committees for the Propagation of Virtue and Prevention of Vice) enforced the Islamic *sharia* law in the Kingdom. In 1990, the *mutawwiin* conducted raids on wealthy and influential Saudis. This force totaled 20,000 in 1990 and were one of the pillars of the severe social controls exerted by the ruling Islamist monarchs in Riyadh.[1046]

Iran Under Shah Mohammed Reza Pahlavi (1941-1979)

In 1941, the pro-Nazi regime of Reza Shah Pahlavi was overthrown and his son Mohammed Reza took over as Shah (Emperor) of Persia (which later became Iran). Mohammed Reza Pahlavi proved to be more amenable to the Western allies, especially the United States and Great Britain. By the beginning of the Cold War, the Shah was firmly in the anti-communist camp and fended off Soviet subversion attempts through the Tudeh (Communist) Party and various other leftwing parties. The Soviets also sought to gain influence through the leftist-nationalist authoritarian Prime Minister Dr. Mohammed Mossadeq, who was overthrown by the Shah and the CIA. Moscow also established puppet dictatorships in Azerbaijan and Kurdistan in northern Iran in 1945. After Soviet troops were withdrawn from these northern puppet states in 1946, these leftwing dictatorships collapsed upon advances by Iranian Army troops. During the 1950s, 1960s, and most of the 1970s, the Shah established a highly authoritarian dictatorship that espoused a Great Persian nationalism. Furthermore, the Shah rejected capitalism, communism, and European-style socialism and supported his own variant of a collectivist economy. On that point, Mohammed Reza Pahlavi was in full ideological agreement with his father, who was also an ardent statist and interventionist in the economy of Iran.

In respect to the economy, the Shah rejected free market capitalism and communism in favor of a system that was a hybrid of private enterprise, socialism, and the institutions of a modern welfare state. Such statist and interventionist policies were started by Mohammed Reza

---

[1042] "Saudi Arabia: A Country Study" Accessed From: http://lcweb2.loc.gov/cgi-bin/query/r?frd/cstdy:@field(DOCID+sa0136)

[1043] "Saudi Arabia: A Country Study" Accessed From: http://lcweb2.loc.gov/cgi-bin/query/r?frd/cstdy:@field(DOCID+sa0136)

[1044] F. Gregory Gause. Oil Monarchies: Domestic and Security Challenges in the Arab Gulf States (Council on Foreign Relations, 1994) pages 50-59.

[1045] Ibid, pages 50-59.

[1046] "Saudi Arabia: A Country Study" Accessed From: http://lcweb2.loc.gov/cgi-bin/query/r?frd/cstdy:@field(DOCID+sa0136)

Pahlavi's father, Reza Shah Pahlavi. He was an ardent admirer of aspects of Hitler and Stalin's rule and economic management. Reza Shah Pahlavi's admiration for communist and Nazi economic administrative policies was made apparent during his rule in the 1930s and the beginning of the early 1940s. Jahangir noted: "*While the country's basic legal recognition of private ownership, free enterprise, and a free labor movement remained in effect the government's economic policies showed notable departures from the capitalist norm. Reza Shah's programs seemed to have much in common with those of the nonmarket economies although he himself was a rabid anti-communist, staunch fiscal conservative, and personally a shrewd entrepreneur…he was always an economic interventionist if not a economic determinist. His strict exchange control policy, restrictions on foreign travel, bilateral clearing agreements, and anti-union posture were the type of policy instruments used at the time by Moscow and Berlin.*"[1047] In order to extend government control and promote Westernization, Reza Shah Pahlavi overhauled the administrative machinery and vastly expanded the bureaucracy. He created an extensive system of secular primary and secondary schools. In 1935, Reza Shah Pahlavi established the country's first European-style university in Tehran. These schools and institutions of higher education became training grounds for the new bureaucracy and helped create a new middle class. Reza Shah Pahlavi also expanded the road network; successfully completed the Trans-Iranian railroad; and established a string of state-owned factories to produce such basic consumer goods as textiles, matches, canned goods, sugar, and cigarettes.[1048] By the end of the late 1930s, Reza Shah Pahlavi allocated 20% of the state budget for industrialization projects. These subsidies resulted in the establishment of 64 factories. He raised import tariffs and supported state-owned industries, which numbered 346 in 1941.[1049]

Shah Mohammed Reza Pahlavi's economic ideology categorically rejected *laissez faire* doctrines and called for the imposition of a planned economy within a framework of a mixed socialist and privately-owned system. Shah Mohammed Reza Pahlavi dubbed his economy *"a free enterprise economy assisted by the state."* The Shah noted that *"pure capitalism is not a secret of productivity and economic democracy; a mixed capitalist/socialist economy is."* The Shah felt that the state should regulate and assist private enterprise in *"the public interest."* He also believed that the government should own enterprises and industries *"when that will benefit the people as a whole."*[1050] Other Iranian ministers such as Minister of the Economy (1962-1970) Alinaqi Alikhani commented that the Shah was a superior form of a socialist.[1051]

The Shah uttered assertions and speeches which contained more than mere tinges of Marxist-sounding rhetoric. The Shah's regime in the 1960s and 1970s opposed Iran's *"feudal and capitalist ruling clique"* and *"social conflict and injustices."* The Shah's government also endorsed the *"necessity of reducing class differences by the just distribution of national*

[1047] Amuzegar, Jahangir. The Dynamics of the Iranian Revolution (SUNY Press, 1991) page 145-147.

[1048] "Iran: A Country Study" Accessed From: http://lcweb2.loc.gov/cgi-bin/query/D?cstdy:2:./temp/~frd_7E27::

[1049] Chaichian, Mohammed. Town and Country in the Middle East (Lexington Books, 2009) page 98.

[1050] Amuzegar, Jahangir. The Dynamics of the Iranian Revolution (SUNY Press, 1991) page 145-147.

[1051] Cronin, Stephanie. Iranian Russian Encounters (Routledge, 2013) pages 45-46.

wealth. "[1052] The Shah described the Iranian parliament (*Majlis*) as belonging "*to the ruling class of landowners and profiteers.*" He noted that Iran's natural food and fuel resources and heavy industries should not "*fall into the hands of greedy individuals or monopolistic corporations.*" The Shah was concerned that these corporations would "*become the successors of the former feudal minorities by whom the country was ruled in the past. If this happened the new society in Iran would be afflicted with another exploitative ruling class.* "[1053] In his description of "*economic democracy,*" the Shah stated that "*none of the ideologies based on enmity and antagonism and on crushing a class or classes for the gain of other classes, or on the exploitation of individuals or classes by other classes or individuals can be acceptable to us because these ideologies are essentially contrary to our national spirit, culture, and way of thinking.* "[1054] The Shah informed the Italian leftwing journalist Oriana Fallaci that "*my White Revolution is an incentive to work. It is a new original kind of socialism and…believe me in Iran we're far more advanced than you and really have nothing to learn from you.*"[1055] The Shah even asserted in 1974 that "*We are more socialistic than the Labor Party because we have started the whole thing. You think that Iran with an emperor with all that money is a capitalist country. Steel is nationalized; copper is nationalized; posts and telegraph telephones, railways, and even water.*"[1056]

The Shah in Iran carried out a program of massive economic planning in the 1960s and 1970s, which developed the infrastructure and industries of the country. Historian Paul Johnson noted that these US-educated Iranian economic planners "*had the arrogance of party apparatchiks and a Stalinist faith in centralized planning, the virtues of growth, and bigness.*" The Shah noted that his White Revolution combined "*the principles of capitalism…with socialism, even communism.*"[1057]

Parsa wrote that "*the Iranian government was the…nation's single largest banker, industrialist, employer, and landlord by the end of the Pahlavi regime. Increased state resources, including support from the United States, along with weaknesses in industrial capital and the private sector, combined with reduced social support to produce favorable conditions for the expansion of state intervention in the Iranian economy.*" By 1975, it was reported that 60% of the industrial development in Iran was funded with government resources. In 1976, the Shah's government owned 130 large factories and workshops. The Iranian state also entered into an additional 55 joint venture agreements with domestic and foreign corporations. The Shah's government owned all Iranian petroleum plants, four large petrochemical plants, all oil refineries, machine-tool plants, steel, aluminum, copper, cement, textile, sugar mills, tobacco, and cigarettes, and the Iranian Carpet Company. Almost 69% of the financial capital was held by

---

[1052] Ibid, page 36.

[1053] Mohammed Reza Pahlavi. Iran, Philosophy Behind the Revolution (Orient Commerce Establishment, 1971) page 55.

[1054] Ibid, pages 60-61.

[1055] "The Shah of Iran: An Interview with Mohammad Reza Pahlevi" The New Republic December 1, 1973 Accessed From: http://www.newrepublic.com/article/world/92745/shah-iran-mohammad-reza-pahlevi-oriana-fallaci

[1056] Nayar, Kuldip. "Shah Remembers the Days of Moussadek" Times (London) June 27, 1974

[1057] Johnson, Paul. Modern Times (Harper Collins Publisher 1991) Accessed From: http://archive.org/stream/ModernTimes_305/42024947-19032115-Johnson-Paul-Modern-Times-the-World-From-the-Twenties-to-the-Nineties-Revised-Edition-Harper-Collins-1991_djvu.txt

the Shah's government. The state owned the railroads, airlines, National Arya shipping, communications facilities, many utilities, all major dams, and a sizable number of insurance companies and agro-businesses.[1058] The Government Factories Corporation was tasked with the sale of selected state corporations. These facilities were reconstituted as joint stock companies. In a 1971 interview, the Shah stated that heavy industries such as oil, gas, steel, water, power, and petrochemical sectors would remain nationalized.[1059]

During the mid-1970s, the Shah sought to combat "*industrial feudalism*" through a variety of measures. They included the suppression of land speculation, increased housing construction, the sale of shares in private and government owned industries to workers, "*fair pricing*" of goods, and anti-profiteering campaigns.[1060] The peasants were collectivized in the 1970s into "*consolidated agricultural management.*"[1061]

When inflation drove up prices in the 1970s, the Shah sent youthful thugs to arrest "*profiteering*" shopkeepers and small businessmen.[1062] As of November 1975, <u>Business Week</u> reported that "*…businessmen are upset over some of the turns that Iran's domestic policy has taken. Alarmed by inflation…the Shah imposed price controls on virtually everything this summer. Squads of government inspectors, aided by eager students, were urged to report prices that they considered excessive. Though judgments were often arbitrary, many businessmen were fined for infractions. Among them was the French manager of a lubricating oil company jointly owned by Exxon Corp. and an Iranian group. Some price violators were even jailed, and in at least two cases, Iranians were exiled to the provinces.*" <u>Business Week</u> also reported that "*Another difficulty, far worse, is the new law requiring that the biggest companies in Iran offer 49% of their shares to their workers or the Iranian public. A further concern is yet another law that limits the amount of equity that foreigners can hold in Iranian companies from 15% in the food and textile industries to up to 35% in high-technology concerns. These domestic moves have already scared off some multinationals or led to changes in their investment plans.*" Prime Minister Amir Abbas Hoveyda noted that foreign multinationals had many opportunities to make heavy profits, though not to "*profiteer.*"[1063]

The Shah also strictly controlled the labor unions, which rapidly became corporative arms of the dictatorship. The 1959 Labor Law ordered that labor unions be approved by the Ministry of Labor. The unions were also run by SAVAK officers. It was reported that "*In some factories SAVAK officials have their own officers, and some foreign businessmen who have worked in Iran have been heard to complain about these powerful and interfering agents of the Iranian state to whom they have to pay salaries and from whom they must, on occasion, accept instructions. Precisely because their job is not only to repress but also to induce cooperation*

[1058] Parsa, Misagh. <u>States, Ideologies, and Social Revolutions: A Comparative Analysis of Iran, Nicaragua, and the Philippines</u> (Cambridge University Press 2000) pages 56-59.
[1059] Mohammed Reza Pahlavi. <u>Iran, Philosophy Behind the Revolution</u> (Orient Commerce Establishment, 1971) page 95.
[1060] Amuzegar, Jahangir. <u>The Dynamics of the Iranian Revolution</u> (SUNY Press, 1991) page 145-147.
[1061] Johnson, Paul. <u>Modern Times</u> (Harper Collins Publisher 1991) Accessed From: http://archive.org/stream/ModernTimes_305/42024947-19032115-Johnson-Paul-Modern-Times-the-World-From-the-Twenties-to-the-Nineties-Revised-Edition-Harper-Collins-1991_djvu.txt
[1062] Ibid.
[1063] "Iran Rethinks Its Grandiose Goals" <u>Business Week</u> November 17, 1975 page 58.

these SAVAK agents can, and sometimes do, create difficulties for management." Production was organized along military lines at the factories of the Military Industrial Organization (MIO). Union officials and factory managers were armed, while workers wore military uniforms at plants run by the Military Industries Organization (MIO).[1064]

On May Day 1974, the Shah addressed four thousand *"syndicate representatives"* who were bused to Sacadabad Palace. He promised housing, factory shares, workers' holiday, and *"justice against exploiting employers."*[1065] The SAVAK also arranged for workers to conduct pro-Shah demonstrations. Labor Minister Moini noted at the Third Iranian Labor Congress of May 1976 that *"workers should strive to work harder, improve their skills and raise productivity in an effort to repay their debts to the Shahanshah."*[1066]

The Shah's propaganda machine noted that the state-run labor unions rejected class conflict and supported what it called *"class compromise"* under the rubric of *"national unity."* Prime Minister Hovieda noted that *"Fortunately in Iran we neither have a class struggle nor do we believe in it. We are all united as one nation, attempting to achieve the goals of the great Iranian Revolution."*[1067]

State ideologists at the National Labor Congress of 1977 refused to term workers the proletariat and that it was only the Western working class that thought in terms of *"class war."* The conference noted that the boss was no longer a *"karfarma (employer or capitalist) which is reminiscent of class privileges"* but a *"karama which is appropriate to the hearty cooperation of all groups in the new system of production...in the era of Revolution."* In 1976, the Shah unified all of unions into the Organization of Iranian Workers which then joined the Rastakhiz Party.[1068]

By the 1970s, the Shah also seemed to adopt leftwing propaganda in his denunciations of Western capitalism, imperialism, and exploitation by foreign firms. In January 1974, the Shah noted that *"I believe that in the past we were exploited by colonialist power and by the capitalist world."*[1069] In December 1976, the newspaper Rastakhiz noted that *"The Third World and all the anti-colonialist elements of the world express their hatred towards Yamani for selling the interests of his nation to the imperialists."* An editorial of Kayhan denounced Saudi Oil Minister Ahmed Yamani as a *"stooge of capitalist circles, and a traitor not only to his own king and country, but also the Arab world and the Third World as a whole."* Rastakhiz noted that the anti-Shah opposition was *"a group of misguided agents of alien policies and puppets of international imperialism."*[1070]

[1064] Halliday, Fred. "Trade Unions and the Working Class Opposition" MERIP Reports October 1978 pages 11-12.

[1065] Abrahamian,Ervand. Khomeinism Essays on the Islamic Republic (Berkeley, Los Angeles, Oxford 1993) Accessed From:
http://publishing.cdlib.org/ucpressebooks/view?docId=ft6c6006wp;brand=ucpress

[1066] Halliday, Fred. "Trade Unions and the Working Class Opposition" MERIP Reports October 1978 pages 11-12.

[1067] Moaddel, Mansoor. Class, Politics, and Ideology in the Iranian Revolution (Columbia University Press, 1993) pages 126-127.

[1068] Bayat, Assef. Workers and Revolution in Iran (Zed Books, 1987) page 60.

[1069] "Shah Gives Views on Oil in Der Spiegel Interview" Tehran Domestic Service January 6, 1974

[1070] Legum, Colin and Shaked, Haim. Middle East Contemporary Survey Volume 1 1976-1977 (The Moshe Dayan Center, 1999) pages 33 and 270.

The Shah also rejected Western-style political systems in favor of his authoritarian, nationalist, and corporative monarchy. In March 1977, the Shah noted that *"The difficulties of the West are due to lack of discipline and the way work is managed; whereas in Iran, there is not one minute of workers' strikes."*[1071] The Shah stated *"Western attitudes but with essential differences without the West's permissiveness, carelessness, and lack of patriotism."* He also criticized the West for being *"voracious,"* *"exploitative,"* and *"unfair in your trade dealings"* with Iran.[1072] The Shah noted in July 1978 that *"We cannot copy the West because of its weak points. And we cannot follow Communism because it is not human, and (Communists) have many weak points too: they are behind in technology and other things. So we will try to find something in between."* The Shah also remarked that *"The greatest external threat is the weakness of the West. It is paralyzed. Traumatic. Divided…I am doing what is necessary for my country, and we see to our defense. Whenever this country stands, it will decide about the fate of East Asia and the Middle East. The only thing the West can do is put its own house in order."*[1073]

The Shah and his propaganda apparatus also expressed great displeasure at the alleged subversion of Iran by British institutions. Often, the Iranians would express such opposition to Britain in typical leftwing, anti-colonialist terms. As of December 1978, the running joke in Iran was *"What do you see when you pull the beard off a mullah?" The answer: "A stamp saying made in Britain."* The Shah's government engaged in anti-US and anti-British propaganda. The BBC Tehran correspondent was regularly reprimanded by the Shah's government. The Iranians also threatened the British Embassy with a loss of business and trade contracts. A pro-Shah newspaper displayed the letters *"BBC"* with the *"C"* wrought into a hammer and sickle.[1074]

By the early 1970s, the Shah developed a mass political party that was supposed to serve as a tool to mobilize support for the monarchy. It was known as the National Resurgence Party or Rastakhiz. The Shah's Rastakhiz Party supported what it termed *"social discipline"* which encouraged *"constructive criticism"* that opposed *"destructive violence and pessimism."*[1075] Rastakhiz adhered to the concept of *"democratic centralism"* and sought to absorb the best of capitalism and socialism, thus proclaiming the elimination of class and social conflicts in Iran. A Central Committee and Political Bureau led Rastakhiz, while all classes of Iranians were organized into subgroups of this organization.[1076]

The Rastakhiz Party of the 1970s consisted of ex-*Tudeh* (communist) Party members who felt that this new party was based on Leninism capable of leading Iran into a modern society, mobilize the masses, and break down class barriers.[1077] Ex-communists who became officials in the Rastakhiz Party included Dr. Mohammed Baheri and Parviz Rassouli.[1078]

[1071] Parsa, Misagh. Social Origins of the Iranian Revolution (Rutgers University Press 1989) page 143.

[1072] Lewis, Flora. "Iran: Future Shock" New York Times November 12, 1978 page SM17.

[1073] "'Things Will Be Different'" Newsweek July 24, 1978 page 56.

[1074] Randal, Jonathan C. "Iranians Mix Fact with Fiction in Long Crisis Over Shah" The Washington Post December 15, 1978 page A33.

[1075] Housego, David. "More shoulders than one" The Economist August 28, 1976 page 10.

[1076] Abrahamian, Ervand. Iran between two revolutions (Princeton University Press, 1982) pages 439-442.

[1077] Ibid, pages 439-442.

[1078] Ladjevardi, Habib. Labor Unions and Autocracy in Iran (Syracuse University Press, 1985) page 208.

The Rastakhiz Party also consisted of an assortment of intellectuals such as SAVAK officers, renegade and unrepentant Marxists, and *"gurus of cultural authenticity."* The Shah and the Rastakhiz also opposed colonialism and imperialism, especially of the international oil cartel. During the 1970s, ex-communists served in the Shah's government. Ex-communists who served in the Shah's regime included Riza Qutbi, head of the National Iranian Radio and Television; and Ihsan Naraqi was the head of Tehran University's Institute of Social Research. Leftists wrote for the regime newspapers Kayhan, Ittila'at, and Ayandigan. Leftists also headed official agencies such as the Center for Intellectual Development of Children and Young Adults, Franklin Publishers, and the Center for Translation and Publication of Books.[1079] By June 1975, squads of Rastakhiz Party toughs denounced shopkeepers as *"profiteers"* and *"hoarders"* who raised their prices above the *"official"* limits. Over 8,000 Iranian businessmen were arrested in these sweeps, including the Habib Sabet, the head of Pepsi-Cola in Iran, and Mohammed Vahabzadeh, the representative of BMW.[1080] Perhaps not unsurprisingly, the Rastakhiz Party squads of students and workers were nicknamed the *"little Red Guard"* for their militant and often anti-capitalist physical attacks on Iranian businessmen and shopkeepers who violated government regulations and price controls. They also insisted on massive wage increases for Iranian workers. The Party was under the control of the Ministers of Interior and Economy.[1081]

The Rastakhiz Party also spewed forth anti-colonialist and anti-imperialist rhetoric worthy of the USSR and China. In January 1978, the Extraordinary Congress of the National Resurgence Party in Iran condemned *"the colonialists' machinations and deceptions against the independent nations struggling to expunge the vestiges of colonialist policies…"* The principles of the Party were the *"manifestation of our national cohesion against avaricious colonialist designs."* The Party noted that *"The Iranian nation knows that the colonialists have mobilized their forces against the nations of the Third World have covertly begun extensive cooperation and have striven toward setting up new colonialist bases."* The Party supported the *"obliteration and destruction of colonialism in all its shapes and hues."*[1082] The Rastakhiz leadership also blamed colonialism for the Shah's repression of demonstrations in the late 1970s. Mr. Ameli, Deputy Secretary General of the Rastakhiz Party, noted in April 1978 that colonial agents created riots and demonstrations which in turn forced the Shah's government to repress these demonstrators.[1083] In fact, the Rastakhiz Party and the *komitehs* and Islamic Republican Party of the mullahs shared a common theme of collectivism and hostility to the West in their respective programs. In fact, some of the main features of Rastakhiz *"resurfaced as official ideology under the Islamic Republic."*[1084]

While the Shah was deeply suspicious of the Soviets and allowed American intelligence monitoring bases to be established in northern Iran, relations with Moscow became progressively warmer by the late 1960s. The Shah sought to convey the outward image that he was a truly non-aligned power that was not a mere puppet of the United States. The Soviets and the Shah also desired mutually beneficial economic relations between the two nations. In May 1978, a secret

---

[1079] Cronin, Stephanie. Iranian Russian Encounters (Routledge, 2013) pages 36-37.

[1080] Housego, David. "More haste, less speed" The Economist August 28, 1976 page 21.

[1081] "Iran; Watch out, if you're rich" The Economist December 13, 1975 page 54.

[1082] "National Resurgence Party Congress Issues Resolution" January 4, 1978

[1083] "Rastakhiz Official Scores Acts of Colonial Agents" Tehran Domestic Service April 12, 1978

[1084] Cronin, Stephanie. Iranian Russian Encounters (Routledge, 2013) pages 36-37.

telegram from the Romanian Embassy in Tehran to the Foreign Ministry's Fourth Directorate noted that *"Amir Afshar Aslan, Chief of Protocol at the Imperial Court told me that the North Korean Vice-President, on the occasion of his recent official visit to Iran gave the Shah an invitation from comrade Kim Il Sung to visit the DPRK…**Afshar said that the visits the Iranian monarch is undertaking in several countries, including in socialist countries, have as purpose the strengthening of Iran's cooperation with all states, irrespective of their social regime, and (thus), to demonstrate the universality of Iran's foreign policy**…We think that Iran's wide opening to socialist countries, manifested in visits to Czechoslovakia and Poland in 1977, Bulgaria and Hungary in May 1978, Romania and the GDR in September 1978, and Democratic People's Republic of Korea and PRC in 1979, have the following purposes: **Given the evolution of the region in which Iran is located, strengthening relations with the USSR and other socialist countries (with which Iran has considerable mutually advantageous economic and commercial ties) is imperative. Through these actions, Iran wants to prove the independence of its foreign policy from the US and Western states in general**. At the same time, (Iran) is (sending them) a warning (especially the US against the opposition to deliver the advanced weapons systems Iran had requested) that the Iranian government can adopt a rapprochement policy with socialist states and (a policy of) relative distancing from the West, if Iran is not granted the appropriate attention and importance. In essence, however, Iran's foreign policy will continue to be based on its close alliance with the US, on whose support (Iran) is counting in case a conflict breaks out."*[1085]

Despite the Shah's ideological anti-communism, military relations were also developed with the USSR in the late 1960s and early 1970s. Under the Shah's regime, the Soviets trained 500 Imperial Iranian Army officers in the 1960s and 1970s and sent military advisers to assist the Shah. The Soviets also built a military hardware production complex outside Tehran and also sold armored vehicles to Iran during the Shah's tenure in power.[1086]

Since 1967, the USSR was Iran's third largest arms supplier. Since January 1967, the Soviets provided the Shah $370 million in weapons and military-related goods. It was observed that *"The Shah's acceptance of Soviet arms reflected his declining fear of Soviet intentions toward Iran and the general rapprochement between the two countries that began early in the 1960s."* The Iranian-Soviet arms agreements of 1967 covered the Shah's purchase of 700 armored personnel carriers, 8,500 miscellaneous vehicles, 600 23mm and 80 57mm anti-aircraft guns, and spare parts and ammunition. In 1970, the Iranians purchased from the USSR 136 130-mm (M-46) field guns and 1,500 RPG-7s. In August 1971, the Shah also acquired 30 ZSU-23-4 anti-aircraft guns. From 1967 to 1971, the Shah received from the Soviets BTR-50 and BTR-60 armored vehicles, artillery guns, anti-aircraft guns, and BM-21 multiple rocket launchers.[1087]

The Shah's Iran also maintained economic relations with the Soviet satellite regime in Afghanistan under the thumb of the People's Democratic Party (PDPA). In July 1978, the Afghan communist regime sought increased aid from the Shah's Iran. President Nur Mohammed

---

[1085] Telegram 075.359 From the Romanian Embassy in Tehran to the Romanian Ministry of Foreign Affairs May 30, 1978 Accessed From: http://digitalarchive.org/document/116430
[1086] Ashton, Nigel and Gibson, Bryan. The Iran-Iraq War: New International Perspectives (Routledge 2013) pages 233-236.
[1087] Central Intelligence Agency, Directorate of Intelligence May 1972 Intelligence Memorandum Recent Trends in Iranian Arms Procurement Accessed From: http://2001-2009.state.gov/documents/organization/70713.pdf

Taraki noted on Iranian State Radio that the Shah's government should *"not only continue its aid but to increase it."* President Taraki spoke of Afghanistan's *"great feelings of friendship towards Iran"* and noted that Iranian aid would greatly contribute to the success of the Afghan Five Year Plan.[1088]

American multinational corporations also provided the Shah's regime with the technology and hardware to develop Iran into a regional economic and military power. Sometimes these firms were also complicit in the repressions carried out by the SAVAK. For example, in 1974, Rockwell signed a deal with the Shah's Iran to supply the SAVAK with a highly-automated computer network. A former National Security Agency official admitted that the Rockwell equipment could be used *"by the Iranian secret police, the SAVAK, to help locate dissidents inside the country and for other internal security functions."*[1089]

By the late 1970s, the Shah retained only American anti-communists and the stalwart socialists of the National Caucus of Labor Committees (NCLC) as his only supporters within American public opinion. American anti-communists such as the John Birch Society expressed concern that the Soviets and their allies were behind the unrest in Iran in the late 1970s and viewed the Shah as a modernizing and pro-Western leader that would check Moscow's machinations in the region. The NCLC probably admired the Shah's statist and interventionist economic programs and were possibly bribed by the Iranian government to collect information on opposition forces. In 1978, the LaRouchian NCLC passed information to the Iranian intelligence and secret police service (SAVAK). They also passed a secret memo to the Shah as to how to save his regime from the Islamists.[1090]

Despite the outward professions of friendship, economic and military relations, the Soviets and their allies also engaged in a very ambitious and successful disinformation program to discredit the Shah. Former Czechoslovak intelligence officer Ladislav Bittman wrote that *"Moscow pursued a two-track policy toward the Shah: respectable non-involved relations on the one hand, and covert operations to undermine his government on the other. The Soviets praised the anti-U.S. movement against the Shah and tolerated Khomeini's religious fanaticism, while attempting to push the Iranian revolution toward communist ends under the vanguard of a well-financed and well-organized Tudeh communist party."*[1091]

Sometimes this disinformation altered Western perceptions of the Shah and enhanced his reputation as a brutal dictator. The ultimate motivation for the Soviet disinformation campaign was to push for a social explosion and the eventual termination of all American assistance to the Shah. Manouchehr Ganji wrote *"A voice cassette surfaced in media circles outside of Iran on which it was claimed that one could hear the voice of the Shah himself addressing his generals before his departure: 'After my departure, do all that you deem necessary for me to return, even if rivers of blood should flow!' The cassette was widely played on radio and television broadcasts all through Europe, the United States, and the rest of the world. A few days later,*

[1088] Housego, David. "Afghanistan Seeks Aid" The Financial Times July 28, 1978 page 6.
[1089] Cavanagh, John. "Business in the Shah's Iran" Multinational Monitor December 1980 Accessed From: http://www.multinationalmonitor.org/hyper/issues/1980/12/cavanagh.html
[1090] King, Dennis. Lyndon LaRouche and the New American Fascism (Doubleday, 1989) Accessed From: http://www.lyndonlarouche.org/fascism19.htm
[1091] Waller, J. Michael. "International terrorism: The Communist connection revisited" August 20, 2003 Accessed From: http://acmeofskill.com/2003/08/international-terrorism-the-communist-connection-revisited/

voice experts reported that the cassette was a fake and that the voice heard on it was not the voice of the Shah but an imitation. By that time, the intended damage had already been done. No degree of denial could have changed the situation. In 1981, Michael Ledeen and William Lewis revealed how the KGB had fabricated the cassette and through a so-called 'SAVAK defector' placed it in the hands of 'Iranian students' in Texas."[1092]

The Soviets and their Middle Eastern allies supported the various leftwing guerrillas that battled the Shah's army and police forces. In September 1978, the Majlis revealed that a SAVAK report outlined the fact that the *"communists have a nineteen point plan for violent unrest in Iran."* In 1976, Iranian Prime Minister Amin Abbas Hoveyda held a press conference where he alleged that anti-Shah rebels maintained ties to the KGB, the Popular Front for the Liberation of Palestine (PFLP), and Qaddafi's Libya. The PFLP trained these guerrilla soldiers, while Libya provided funds.[1093] The anti-Shah opponents and Islamists in Iran were also aided in varying degrees by the PLO, Cuba, East Germany, Syria, and Algeria.[1094]

The *Mujahideen e-Khalq* and *Fedayeen e-Kalq* guerrillas were funded with KGB money.[1095] Former US Ambassador to Iran William Sullivan reported that the *Fedayeen e-Kalq*, the *Mujahideen e-Khalq*, and the *Tudeh* were trained in PLO camps, Libya, and East Germany. Sullivan also reported that these rebels possessed AK-47 rifles.[1096] Anti-Shah terrorist groups such as the Organization of Iranian People's Fedayeen Guerrillas (OIPFG) and Organization of Mujahedin of the People of Iran (OMPI) reportedly trained in South Yemen, Iraq, PLO camps in Lebanon, Libya, and Cuba. These anti-Shah terrorist groups maintained troop levels of at least 4,000.[1097] Soviet arms destined to Iranian leftists were channeled through PLO affiliates in Iraq.[1098]

The Soviets and their Middle Eastern clients also sabotaged the Shah's regime through labor strikes and mass demonstrations. In mid-December 1978, the Soviets encouraged mass demonstrations in Iran against the Shah.[1099] Iraq and Syria also sent agitators to participate in the anti-Shah demonstrations.[1100] South Yemeni agents were dispatched to foment strikes at the refineries and oilfields in Abadan.[1101]

Meanwhile, the Iranian Communist (*Tudeh*) Party actively played a role in helping to spearhead the political subversion of Iran under the Shah. The *Tudeh* (Communist) publication

---

[1092] Manouchehr Ganji. Defying the Iranian Revolution (Greenwood Publishing Group, 2002) page 100.

[1093] O'Ballance, Edgar. Tracks of the Bear (Presidio, 1982) pages 142-146.

[1094] Manouchehr Ganji. Defying the Iranian Revolution (Greenwood Publishing Group, 2002) page xxviii.

[1095] O'Ballance, Edgar. Tracks of the Bear (Presidio, 1982) pages 142-146.

[1096] Manouchehr Ganji. Defying the Iranian Revolution (Greenwood Publishing Group, 2002) page 40.

[1097] McDonald, Congressman Larry P. "Moscow's Hand in the Iranian Civil Strife" Congressional Record January 31, 1979 pages 1630-1633.

[1098] Phillips, James. "Afghanistan: The Soviet Quagmire" Heritage Foundation October 25, 1979 Accessed From: http://www.heritage.org/research/reports/1979/10/afghanistan-the-soviet-quagmire

[1099] Ibid

[1100] Ibid.

[1101] Ibid.

Navid was published in the printing presses of the Soviet Embassy in Tehran.[1102] The oppositionist *Tudeh* Party received support from the KGB and broadcasted propaganda from East Germany via Radio Iran Courier.[1103]

Despite the exchange of goods and proclamations of friendship, the communist Afghan regime also cooperated with Moscow to undermine and overthrow the Shah's dictatorship. Once the communist PDPA leader Nur Mohammed Taraki took over Afghanistan, Soviet-trained agents moved into Iran and infiltrated mosques, schools, Shiite monasteries, bazaars, and oil fields.[1104] The KGB took over the Afghan intelligence service and set up training camps for Iranian terrorists.[1105] The Soviet-controlled Afghan Secret Service (*Estekbarat*) also coordinated activities among the 500,000 Afghans that resided in Iran.[1106] Soviet weapons destined to Iranian Baluchistan were transshipped through communist Afghanistan.[1107] Two Soviet-controlled camps in Afghanistan provided communist indoctrination and terrorist training to Pakistani and Iranian radical leftists. During the demonstrations of 1978, the Iranian authorities arrested Afghans. According to former Prime Minister Shahpour Bakhtiar, 200 armed men crossed the border from Afghanistan in January 1979. There was a *"historically close working relationship which has existed between Afghanistan's Khalq Party and the pro-Soviet Iranian Tudeh Party…"*[1108]

The Soviets and their *Tudeh* allies also developed close relations with Khomeini's Islamists. Starting in the late 1960s, the KGB funneled hundreds of thousands of dollars to Khomeini while he was in exile in Najaf in Baathist Iraq.[1109] A Soviet radio station in the USSR beamed anti-Shah propaganda and coded messages to Islamic activists fighting the Shah.[1110]

Khomeinist Sadegh Ghothzadeh was reported by European intelligence services to have ties to Libyan intelligence and the Communist Parties of Italy and France. The *Tudeh* formed the Democratic Union of the People of Iran, which was a united front of the communists and Islamists committed to overthrowing the Shah. It sold 300,000 copies of the Communist Manifesto and thousands of Lenin's works in Tehran. Slogans such as *"Death to the Shah,"* *"Long Live the Islamic Democratic Republic," "Power to the People,"* and *"Long Live the Revolution."*[1111] The Tehran correspondent for Le Figaro Thierry Desjardins reported the Islamist identity of interests with the *Tudeh* in an interview with National Front (Islamist) leaders Karim

---

[1102] Rees, John. "How Jimmy Carter Betrayed the Shah" Review of the News February 21, 1979 pages 31-48.

[1103] McDonald, Congressman Larry P. "Moscow's Hand in the Iranian Civil Strife" Congressional Record January 31, 1979 pages 1630-1633.

[1104] Rees, John. "How Jimmy Carter Betrayed the Shah" Review of the News February 21, 1979 pages 31-48.

[1105] McDonald, Congressman Larry P. "Moscow's Hand in the Iranian Civil Strife" Congressional Record January 31, 1979 pages 1630-1633.

[1106] Phillips, James. "Afghanistan: The Soviet Quagmire" Heritage Foundation October 25, 1979 Accessed From: http://www.heritage.org/research/reports/1979/10/afghanistan-the-soviet-quagmire

[1107] Ibid.

[1108] Ibid.

[1109] Adams, Nathan M. "Iran: Ayatollahs of Terror" Readers Digest January 1985 page 41.

[1110] Ibid.

[1111] Rees, John. "How Jimmy Carter Betrayed the Shah" Review of the News February 21, 1979 pages 31-48.

Sanjabi and Ayatollah Talebani (Shiite Leader in Tehran): *"On the philosophical level no agreement is possible between us and the atheist Marxists but on the political and social level we agree with them."*[1112] In June 1978, the *Tudeh* Party publication <u>Navid</u> published an article titled "*The Tudeh Party and the Muslim Movement*" called for an "*anti-dictatorial broad front*" which tasked the mullahs to play a "*vanguard role*" in the overthrow of the Shah.[1113] In December 1978, *Tudeh* head Iraj Eskandari wrote an article for <u>World Marxist Review</u> which stated "*When Muslim leaders like Ayatollah Khomeini oppose imperialism, declare that the Shah's regime is anti-popular and anti-Islamic and say that it must be overthrown then we consider this a positive occurrence."*[1114] In 1978, Khomeini also noted that under the Islamic Republic, the *Tudeh* would be allowed to function as long as it does not serve "*foreign interests."* In January 1979, <u>Pravda</u> noted that Khomeini would be backed by the USSR because he and his Islamists had "*a long established reputation as opponents of tyranny."*[1115]

Early on, Khomeini was committed to the implementation of an Islamic theocracy in Iran and not a democracy as some of his Western supporters would have liked to believe. In December 1968, the magazine called <u>The Middle East</u> quoted Khomeini indicating that Iran was to become an "*Islamic Republic*" where all Western influence would be eliminated. In an interview in the Lebanese newspaper <u>as-Safir</u>, Khomeini confirmed in January 1979 that the new Islamic Republic would not "*leave room for pro-American leaders."*[1116] Khomeini proposed to impose on the Iranian people 80 lashes for drinking alcohol, public stoning of adulterers, and cutting off a thief's hand. One of Khomeini's close aides noted to <u>Newsweek</u> that "*you don't cut off the whole hand-just the fingertips*" which the aide felt was more respectful of human rights as opposed to Saudi Arabia and Libya, who severed the entire hand off.[1117]

In a November 19, 1978 interview in <u>Pravda,</u> Brezhnev noted that any foreign (read: American) intervention in Iran would be considered by the USSR a "*security matter."*[1118] Perhaps Brezhnev was hinting at a Soviet invasion of Iran in the event the United States directly intervened to protect the Shah and his dictatorship. Meanwhile, the Soviets maintained many nests of subversion in Iran under the cover of diplomatic, trade, and cultural missions. The KGB and GRU operated in the Shah's Iran at the following locations:

1) The Soviet Embassy in Tehran.
2) Consulates in Isfahan, Tabriz, and Mashad.
3) The Soviet trade mission.
4) Technicians and engineers in the Aryamehr steel mill.
5) Deep cover illegals who were Farsi-speaking Soviets from Azerbaijan.

Other Soviet fronts in Iran included the:

[1112] McDonald, Congressman Larry P. "Khomeini Lines up with the PLO Terrorists" <u>Congressional Record</u> February 21, 1979 pages 2967-2968.

[1113] McDonald, Congressman Larry P. "Moscow's Hand in the Iranian Civil Strife" <u>Congressional Record</u> January 31, 1979 pages 1630-1633.

[1114] Ibid.

[1115] Ibid.

[1116] Ibid.

[1117] Rees, John. "How Jimmy Carter Betrayed the Shah" <u>Review of the News</u> February 21, 1979 pages 31-48.

[1118] McDonald, Congressman Larry P. "Moscow's Hand in the Iranian Civil Strife" <u>Congressional Record</u> January 31, 1979 pages 1630-1633.

1) Novosti offices.
2) A Soviet-owned transport company.
3) A Soviet hospital in Tehran.
4) The Iranian-Soviet Cultural Society.[1119]

As a result of the very real brutality of the Shah and the vast amount of Soviet-inspired propaganda, the Carter Administration decided to grease the skids for the overthrow of the Shah and his eventual replacement with the anti-American Islamic Republic. In 1979, President Carter dispatched General Robert Huyser, the deputy commander of NATO in Europe, to beg the Iranian military not to launch a *coup* and to permit Khomeini to seize power.[1120] A former Iranian diplomat in the United States reflected that "*President Carter betrayed the Shah and helped create the vacuum that will soon be filled by Soviet trained agents and religious fanatics who hate America.*" Khomeini supporters within the Iranian Embassy such as Djafar Faghih boasted of their ties with officials of the National Security Council (Gary Sick and William B. Quandt) and the State Department. Former Attorney General and roving leftwing activist Ramsey Clark secretly arranged for Khomeini supporters to meet with the State Department's Iran Task Force, Senators, Congressman, and the US Mission to the UN (Andrew Young). Ambassador Young himself believed that Khomeini would "*eventually be hailed as a saint.*"[1121] By March 1979, Khomeini and his Islamist seized total power in Iran. The negative repercussions of President Carter's actions against the Shah remain to this day. Despite the Shah's intense authoritarianism, the United States undertook a strategic blunder in allowing the overthrow of the Shah's monarchy.

South Africa Under the Afrikaner Nationalist Party

The period of the iron-handed rule of the racial collectivists of the Afrikaner Nationalist Party was perhaps one of the many misunderstood periods of African history. On the one hand, Marxists of various stripes viewed the rule of the Nationalists in South Africa as merely the extension of the domestic and even foreign capitalist classes, while a number of sincere and committed anti-communists viewed the regime as an ally of the West during the Cold War and a bastion of free enterprise. This chapter will dispel some of these myths and will prove that the government of the Nationalist Party organized the South Africa economy on a statist-socialist model with some corporative labor policies for white workers. Furthermore, the system of apartheid (state-mandated racial segregation/oppression) was really a huge exercise in social engineering and collectivism which placed the needs of one racial group over almost all others. The Afrikaner Nationalists won the parliamentary elections in the Union of South Africa in 1948 and quickly became the dominant party. Immediately after the electoral victory, the Nationalist implemented an authoritarian system where the state had massive police powers. Furthermore, the Nationalists never shed their belief that the state should be heavily involved in developing a modern South African economy. State-owned enterprises, agencies, and subsidies proliferated during the period of Nationalist rule from the 1940s until the 1980s.

[1119] Ibid.

[1120] O'Ballance, Edgar. Tracks of the Bear (Presidio, 1982) pages 142-146.

[1121] Rees, John. "How Jimmy Carter Betrayed the Shah" The Review of the News February 21, 1979 pages 31-48.

The Afrikaner nationalist movement maintained a long-held anti-capitalism that arose in its opposition to British colonialism. While Dutch émigrés settled in South Africa (Boers or Afrikaners), the British became the top colonial power by the 1800s. Afrikaner commandos fought the British in the Boer War of the late 1800s and early 1900s. While the Afrikaners lost the war, they concentrated their energies on developing economic assets, labor unions, and politically nationalist movements that clung to racially collectivistic ideas. The Afrikaner Nationalists spewed anti-capitalist rhetoric which exhibited an almost Marxist flavor. In 1900, Jan Smuts remarked that *"It is ordained that we, insignificant as we are, should be amongst the first people to begin the struggle against the new world tyranny of capitalism."*[1122]

By the 1930s, prominent Afrikaner Nationalists such as Dr. D.F. Malan fused a socialistic anti-capitalism with anti-Jewish prejudices. Furlong wrote that *"Malan had identified one at the very founding of his new movement: Hoggenheimer…No Jew could feel safe, given the understandable identification of the Hoggenheimer stereotype in the popular South African imagination with Jewish businessmen. The Hoggenheimer cartoon character appeared with increasing frequency in Die Burger."*[1123] Furlong also pointed out that Malan and the Nationalists did not represent capitalism in South Africa: *"**Despite the widespread belief of many Marxian historians that the apartheid state is essentially a creature of capitalism, its creators, the Malanite Nationalists, had nothing but scorn for large-scale capitalism. An anti-capitalist message was at the heart of the Malanite program, on a par with the protection of Afrikaner identity, not least because capitalism was seen as synonymous with British and Jewish oligarchy.**"* Malan condemned the pro-British Smuts government at the 1934 Cape Nationalist Party Congress because it was not formed *"…to the advantage of the farmer and the poor man, but to the advantage of (tot voordeel van) the money power (geldmag) and the imperialist, his ally, who behind the scenes was exceptionally active in obtaining this policy."* Malan supporters on the Federal Council of the old National Party asserted in June 1934 that *"We feel that the basis as it stands of the new Party (the United Party) is going to make a stronghold for imperialism and capitalism, and that it is impossible for the farmer, the worker and the poor man in the long run to find safety in it and must necessarily find a new home."*[1124] Some Nationalists even blatantly admitted their preference for the creation of a socialist economy in South Africa. In 1934, Dr. Hendrik Verwoerd presented a paper to the People's Conference on the Poor White which called for *"a socialist state."*[1125]

Clearly, the Nationalist Party program of the 1930s and early 1940s stipulated the creation of an authoritarian, socialistic, and racist state for a fully independent South Africa. The Draft Constitution of the Nationalist Party was influenced by German National Socialism and neo-Calvinism. It upheld the philosophy of Christian Nationalism and supported a republic for South Africa. The President of the Republic would be *"responsible to God and the volk alone."* The mass media would be forbidden to undermine the security of the republic, good morals, and the independence and dignity of the nation. The president could dismiss a cabinet minister and

---

[1122] Peron, Jim. "Apartheid's Dirty Little Secret" Accessed From: http://www.freerepublic.com/forum/a3b8531ad4d8d.htm

[1123] Die Burger was the main Nationalist Party newspaper.

[1124] Furlong, Patrick Jonathan. Between Crown and Swastika (Witwatersrand University Press, 1991) pages 53-54.

[1125] Louw, P. Eric. The Rise, Fall, And Legacy Of Apartheid (Greenwood Publishing Group, 2004) pages 37-38.

provide the prime minister with wide powers to rule in national emergency periods. The parliament in the projected republic was to consist of the *Volksraad* (People's Assembly) and a Communal Council. The Council was organized along corporative lines according to occupations. The Council could also contain presidential appointees on issues such as "*Indian Infiltration*" (*Indierindringing*) and "*Jewish overpopulation*" (*Joodse oorbevolking*).[1126] Another Afrikaner extremist Piet Meyer praised the notion of the *volk* as "*the real employer, and not the capitalist*" in a fascist state.[1127] Malan noted that "*...it (the republic) shall be protected effectively against the capitalistic and parasitical exploitation of its people as well as against the undermining influences of hostile and unnational elements.*"[1128]

A senior member of the Nationalist Party and head of the board of the Nasionale Pers (National Press), referred to "*our archenemies*" as forming an unholy alliance between "*Imperialists,*" "*Capitalists,*" and "*Communist Jews.*" A.L. Geyer of the Purified Nationalist Party and the editor of <u>Die Burger</u> launched a massive intellectual attack on "*Hoggenheimer*" in November 1934 under the titled "*The Chief Enemy in the National Struggle.*" Hoggenheimer was a portly, cigar-smoking cartoon character who portrayed the typical, greedy Jewish capitalist. Geyer also opposed the "*imperialist, who was obsessed with love of another country, Britain... But Hoggenheimer has no patriotism and no National feeling at all. Not the interests of the volk nor even of humanity, but self-seeking and own interests pure and simple control his actions. The Dark Money Power is a tumor in the body of the capitalist system.*"[1129]

By the early 1930s, a number of prominent Afrikaners formed a secret society called the *Broederbond*. Its mission was the creation of an independent, nationalist, and authoritarian power structure. The *Broederbond* called for in its program of 1933: "*Abolition of the exploitation by foreigners of (South Africa's) national resources...the nationalization of finance and the planned coordination of economic policy*"[1130]

During the late 1930s and during World War II, a pro-Nazi Fifth Column of extreme nationalist Afrikaners developed in the form of the *Ossabrandwag* (OB). The OB was sympathetic to Nazi Germany and hostile to Britain. The OB opposed South African participation on the Allied side during World War II, even when the Union government declared war on the Axis. In January 1944, a secret German source indicated that the OB was "*based on the Fuhrer-principle, fighting against the Empire, the capitalists, the communists, the Jews, the party and the system of parliamentarism...on the base of national-socialism.*" OB members refused to enlist in the Union armed forces and even assaulted service members. In February 1941, OB members launched an assault on Union armed forces members that resulted in 140 injuries. The OB developed the *Stormjaers* paramilitary force which engaged in sabotage against the Union government. They dynamited electrical power lines and railroads and disconnected telegraph and telephone lines.[1131] The OB youth wing, the *Boerejeug* (Boer youth), managed

---

[1126] Furlong, Patrick Jonathan. <u>Between Crown and Swastika</u> (Witwatersrand University Press, 1991) pages 194-195.

[1127] Ibid, page 96.

[1128] Ibid, page 192.

[1129] Ibid, pages 36-37.

[1130] Hazlett, Thomas W. "Apartheid: The Concise Encyclopedia of Economics" Library of Economics and Liberty Accessed From: http://www.econlib.org/library/Enc/Apartheid.html

[1131] "Ossewabrandwag" Accessed From:
http://en.wikipedia.org/wiki/Ossewabrandwag#cite_note-5

"*officers' training camps*" with a curriculum of topics such as "*Healthy National Socialism*" and "*National Socialism versus Capitalism and Communism.*"[1132]

The OB supported the abolition of political parties as a part of the "*Revolution of the 20th Century.*" The OB supported the creation of a racist Afrikaner republic with National Socialism. The OB's ideology stressed the socialism of Nazism and opposed "*imperialism.*" Such leftist views were viewed by other nationalists as an attack on the concept of private property. Even the hard-line Nationalists criticized the OB's radicalism as being "*communistic.*"[1133] The second commandant-general of the OB J.F.J Van Rensburg dubbed himself the "*Leader of Disciplined Afrikanerdom.*" Van Rensburg noted in an address to the Afrikaanse Nasionale Studentebond in Stellenbosch in February, 1941 that "*...And with it (democracy) will be buried capitalist imperialism and its disasters...They do not need to accuse us of being opposed to capitalistic democracy (kapitalistiese demokrasie). It is not an accusation but rather an honor.*"[1134] One Regional OB officer W.R. Laubscher noted that "*The Arbeidsfront of the OB will not only fight against communism's forerunner, namely capitalist exploitation, but replace it once and for all by the saving grace of socialism tailored to the volk. For the urbanized Afrikaner worker who is exploited under the democratic system of capitalism, there is only one choice: the OB or communism.*"[1135]

Aside from the OB, other pro-Nazi personalities and groups existed in wartime South Africa. Hertzog was another admirer of Nazi Germany. In October 1941, he sharply opposed "*liberal capitalism*" and the multiparty system of government.[1136] Another radical Nationalist Johannes Du Plessis wrote in Die Nuwe Orde (The New Order) that there was a need for a local version of the worldwide revolution for a new political and social-economic system. Du Plessis praised a variety of communist and fascist dictators as positive examples of revolutionaries. They included Premier Salazar of Portugal, General Secretary of the Communist Party of the Soviet Union/Premier Joseph Stalin, Italian Fascist dictator Prime Minister Mussolini, and Nazi German Chancellor Adolf Hitler. Du Plessis believed that an Axis victory was possible, but despite the outcome of World War II, an anti-capitalist and anti-liberal revolution would occur on a worldwide basis.[1137] Oswald Pirow's New Order Study Circle supported the end of "*liberal capitalist democracy*" and the creation of White Christian National Socialist Republic where political parties, elections, and parliament would be abolished.[1138] Malan tried to draw pro-Nazis into the Nationalist camp by noting that 80 to 85% of the New Order's program was already in the Nationalist Party's program. Malan noted that the New Order's program would be carried out "*in letter and in spirit*" when the Nationalist Party took over South Africa.[1139] Many of the former pro-Nazi South Africans in the Greyshirts, *Stormjaers*, OB, and the New Order

---

[1132] O'Meara, Dan. <u>Volkskapitalisme</u> (Cambridge 1983) pages 206-207.

[1133] Ibid, pages 130-131.

[1134] Furlong, Patrick Jonathan. <u>Between Crown and Swastika</u> (Witwatersrand University Press, 1991) pages 139-140.

[1135] Marx, Christoph. <u>Oxwagon Sentinel</u> (LIT Verlag Munster, 2009) pages 474-475.

[1136] Furlong, Patrick Jonathan. <u>Between Crown and Swastika</u> (Witwatersrand University Press, 1991) pages 154-155.

[1137] O'Meara, Dan. <u>Volkskapitalisme</u> (Cambridge 1983) pages 164-165.

[1138] Ibid, page 125.

[1139] Ibid, pages 182-183.

Movement held some of the senior positions in the police, armed forces, and civil service in post-1948 South Africa.[1140]

Even the Malanite Nationalists retained their anti-capitalist, anti-Jewish, and anti-British sentiments during World War II. For example, J.F. Strijdom and Malan expressed their joint opposition to "*Jewish-British*" capitalism and the Union's connection to the British Empire.[1141] During a 1941 speech at Stellenbosch University, Malan noted that British-style democracy and capitalism were due to collapse.[1142] In September 1941, the Afrikaner business publication Volkshandel stated: "*Every sober-minded, thinking Afrikaner is fed up to the top of his throat with so-called laissez-faire—let-it-be—capitalism, with its soul-destroying materialism and the spirit of "every man for himself...We are sick of it because of...the condition which makes the Afrikaner a spectator in the business of his own country.*"[1143]

During the first two decades of Nationalist rule, various anti-capitalist policies and socialist rhetoric continued to emanate from Pretoria. P. Eric Louw noted that "*Under Malan, Strijdom, and Verwoerd, this variant of anti-capitalism was a powerful subtext of Afrikaner nationalism. It began to weaken during Vorster's premiership and was finally abandoned by P.W. Botha's NP.*" From the 1930s to the 1950s, this Afrikaner nationalism intensely disliked liberal and English capitalism, which was termed "*Engelse geldmag*" or English money power.[1144]

During the late 1940s, the Nationalists also displayed a simultaneous hostility towards foreign capital and a grudging pragmatic admission that such economic resources needed to be harnessed for industrial and technological development. In March 1947, the Volkshandel expressed concern about the penetration of British and American capital into the South African economy.[1145] The Afrikaner business association (AHI) was concerned that the economy was "*increasingly being controlled from abroad*" and urged the state to limit foreign holdings in any new undertaking to 49%.[1146] According to a March 1948 edition of Volkshandel, foreign investment was necessary to stimulate the development of natural resources. However, the same article in Volkshandel also asserted that the state should ensure that national companies owned banking and strategic industries.[1147] Dr. Albert Hertzog stated in April 1949 that "*I am satisfied that for all those who look to the future of South Africa there is only one solution and that is that, irrespective of any other key industries, the gold mining industry should be nationalized by the state.*"[1148]

Throughout the 1950s, the various Afrikaner Nationalist leaders continued their spouting of anti-capitalist and even anti-Western rhetoric in terms that were almost at times

---

[1140] Laurence, John. The Seeds of Disaster (Gollancz, 1968) pages 33-34.

[1141] Furlong, Patrick Jonathan. Between Crown and Swastika (Witwatersrand University Press, 1991) pages 206-207.

[1142] O'Meara, Dan. Volkskapitalisme (Cambridge 1983) pages 182-183.

[1143] Ibid, page 152.

[1144] Louw, P. Eric. The Rise, Fall, And Legacy Of Apartheid (Greenwood Publishing Group, 2004) pages 37-38.

[1145] O'Meara, Dan. Volkskapitalisme (Cambridge 1983) page 146.

[1146] Ibid, pages 146-147.

[1147] Ibid, pages 146-147.

[1148] Bunting, Brian. Rise of the South African Reich (Penguin Books, 1969) Accessed From: http://www.american-buddha.com/rise.reich13.htm

indistinguishable from the Soviets and Chinese. In August 1951, South African Minister of Defense Erasmus noted that "*The financial dictators must not be surprised if their action acts as a boomerang and that for the sake of existence an urge is created particularly among poor people and workers, to place our gold riches where it is still practicable under the control of the people...*"[1149] In May 1958, South African Minister of Lands Paul Sauer criticized "*American dollar imperialism in Africa.*"[1150]

The Afrikaner leaders also courted the industrial workers during the 1950s. B.J. Vorster noted to the House of Assembly in February 1956 that "*We know one person only to whom we owe an explanation, and that is the White worker in South Africa who has brought the National Party to the position it occupies today and who will keep it in that position in the future.*"[1151] Hertzog noted in 1953 that "*we are largely a party of workers.*"[1152]

During the 1950s and 1960s, the Nationalist government continued to oppose free market capitalism and enthusiastically supported state intervention in the economy. In February 1955, Minister of Native Affairs Hendrik Verwoerd accused industrialist Harry Oppenheimer of "*pretending to work in the public interest while in reality serving only the interests of capitalism.*"[1153] South African businessman A.D. Wassenaar noted that the South African government was hostile to the concept of the undiluted profit motive. He quoted one cabinet minister's speech to the Senate. The cabinet minister stated: "*...that the government is of the opinion that certain essential services should in the general interest, be provided to the society on a non-profit basis.*"[1154] A Nationalist government minister noted that "*The task of government is to protect those who make agriculture their life task against capitalists who would ruin them and create monopolistic conditions.*"[1155] In October 1958, Die Transvaler noted that "*There are people who (argue that)...simply everything...must be made subordinate to their so-called economic laws...It is fortunate that under a Nationalist government these worshippers of economic laws have never had their way but that a nobler and higher goal has been striven after—the maintenance of white civilization.*"[1156]

In 1960, an official commission condemned the erosion of the traditional Afrikaner rural class, which created a "*tendency towards unsound class distinction on the platteland.*" It criticized the "*morgenheimer*" who was "*cheque book farmer*" who conducted his business from an urban office.[1157] In 1965, conservative NP members criticized the merger of Federale Mynbou

---

[1149] "'Monopolies' Attacked" The Financial Times August 14, 1951 page 1.

[1150] "Foreign Investment Doubts in South Africa" The Financial Times May 28, 1958 page 5.

[1151] Bunting, Brian. Rise of the South African Reich (Penguin Books, 1969) Accessed From: http://www.american-buddha.com/rise.reich13.htm

[1152] "The Great Evasion; The golden harvest" The Economist June 21, 1980 page 6.

[1153] Ingalls, Leonard. "Apartheid Seen As 2-Sided Policy" New York Times February 19, 1955 page 3.

[1154] Wassenaar, A.D. Assault on Private Enterprise (Tafelberg, 1977) pages 145-146.

[1155] Peron, Jim. "Apartheid's Dirty Little Secret" Accessed From: http://www.freerepublic.com/forum/a3b8531ad4d8d.htm

[1156] Williams, Walter E. South Africa's War Against Capitalism (Praeger, 1989) Accessed From: http://www.cato.org/pubs/wtpapers/south_africa/

[1157] Leftwich, Adrian. South Africa: Economic Growth and Political Change (Allison & Busby, 1974) page 264.

and General Mining as a plot to strangle Afrikaner companies in the face of the giant Anglo-American Corporation.[1158]

While in power, the official Nationalist press also called for the development of a corporative state that would mediate all class and industrial conflicts for the greater interest of the *Volk*. In February 1949, Inspan noted that *"How different would the world be if capital and labor everywhere became allies? If each helped and served the other: if the capitalist strove to provide as many as possible of the good things in life for the worker; and if the worker strove to give the capitalist the best and most abundant labor."*[1159] In January 1949, Inspan noted that *"We must combat the devouring cancer of class divisions and incorporate every Afrikaner worker as an inseparable part of the body of the volk."*[1160] A representative of the Afrikaner labor movement *Reddingsdaadbond* (RDB) stated to Die Transvaler in 1952 that workers *"form the kernel of the nation. That is why we must see the incorporation of the Afrikaner worker as one of the main objects of the Reddingsdaadbond. The incorporation of Afrikaner workers into the organic unity of the volk meant they were to be rescued from the claws of the un-national power of the trade unions."*[1161] In February 1949, Inspan stated *"the relationship between worker and capitalist is interdependent. As they shared the same national interests, strikes should not be allowed."*[1162] In November 1950, Inspan supported the notion that *"Were Afrikaners in charge, exploitation would wither away in the cooperative organic unity of the volk. Afrikaners would never exploit fellow Afrikaners who did their duty and worked."*[1163]

The extreme statist and even socialist tendencies in the South African economy were the subject of commentaries by historians and observers of various political persuasions. The conservative, pro-Thatcher, ex-Laborite historian Paul Johnson noted in Modern Times that South Africa enlarged *"its state sector"* and adopted *"a 'command economy' attitude…"* Johnson also described the *"flagging"* of the once vibrant South African economy the result of *"apartheid-style Big Government."* Johnson observed that *"social engineering was raised into the central principle (indeed philosophy) of government in the form of apartheid."*[1164]

Ann Seidman commented that *"…the South African government has long intervened directly in the economy through a series of parastatals, state corporations which co-operate closely with the private sector. These are closely inter-linked through capital and members of their boards of directors to the government, on the one hand, and to the mining finance houses that dominate the private sector, on the other hand. There is, in other words, no such thing as the 'free play of market forces' in the South African economy."*[1165]

[1158] Ibid, page 269.

[1159] O'Meara, Dan. Volkskapitalisme (Cambridge 1983) page 161.

[1160] Ibid, page 158.

[1161] Ibid, page 87.

[1162] Ibid, pages 88-89.

[1163] Ibid, page 89.

[1164] Johnson, Paul. Modern Times (Harper Collins Publisher 1991) Accessed From: http://archive.org/stream/ModernTimes_305/42024947-19032115-Johnson-Paul-Modern-Times-the-World-From-the-Twenties-to-the-Nineties-Revised-Edition-Harper-Collins-1991_djvu.txt

[1165] Seidman, Ann. "Why U.S. Corporations Should Get out of South Africa" A Journal of Opinion Volume 9 Number 1/2 Spring-Summer 1979 pages 37-41.

Leftwing historian Joseph Hanlon noted that *"The role of the government in the economy is closer to that in socialist countries than capitalist ones. Many of the largest corporations are parastatals…The private sector is tightly regulated."*[1166]

Adam wrote that *"state intervention in the private sectors of the economy as well as through state controlled corporations is not merely balancing an unstable boom, as in other capitalist countries, but is the very prerequisite of the settlers' survival. While state economic activity initially aimed primarily at the protection and promotion of the Afrikaner proletariat, it has now assumed the role of guaranteeing rapid, though differential material advancement for all groups including the non-white proletariat. Severe legislative restrictions on private profit which would not be tolerated by big business in Western countries are accepted more easily in South Africa because of the potentially extreme instability of laissez faire racialism."*[1167]

The high level South African Communist Brian Bunting even admitted that the apartheid regime implemented a quasi-socialist economy: *"State control over a certain sector of the economy is common to a number of capitalist countries, but in few has it progressed as far as in South Africa, where the State owns or controls, land and forests, post, telegraphs and telephones, railways and airlines, broadcasting and a host of other public services. The State has entered the field of private industry in electric power generation (Escom), printing, the manufacture of arms and ammunition, the production of iron and steel (Iscor), heavy engineering (Vecor), insecticides, oil, gas and chemicals from coal (Sasol), and fertilisers (Foskor). Through the Industrial Development Corporation, the state has become, together with private capital, a permanent shareholder in a host of industries, mining and finance, aircraft manufacture, oil, textiles, shipping etc. Nevertheless, the idea of nationalization or some form of direct State control has remained in the background of Nationalist economic thinking, to be put on view from time to time as a threat whenever non-Afrikaans big business shows signs of proving recalcitrant."*[1168]

Murphy noted that *"In 1948 the Nationalists (Afrikaner party) won the election and became the governing party and although they vehemently denied, it had very socialistic policies."*[1169]

The pro-free trade, free market <u>The Economist</u> noted in 1980 that the older Nationalist Party economists adhered to ideological positions that were almost indistinguishable from the far Left of the British Labor Party: *"Talking to the older generation of Nationalist economists is uncannily like talking to the postwar generation of English Labour party planners. They remind you that originally Nationalism was anti-capitalist, protectionist, centralist and, above all, planned."*[1170]

The South African business magnate A.D. Wassenaar noted that Afrikaners possessed an innate political culture of a simultaneous preference for capitalism and socialism: *"Thus Afrikanerdom has maneuvered itself into a frame of mind such that it is intensely capitalist and*

[1166] Hanlon, Joseph. <u>Beggar Your Neighbours: Apartheid Power in Southern Africa</u> (Indiana University Press, 1986) page 14.

[1167] Adam, Heribert. <u>Modernizing Racial Domination: South Africa's Political Dynamics</u> (University of California Press 1971) page 173.

[1168] <u>The African Communist,</u> Issues 40-43 (South African Communist Party, 1970) page 90.

[1169] Murphy, John J. <u>The Regime-Looking In: South African Short Stories</u> (AuthorHouse 2012) page 9.

[1170] "The Great Evasion; The golden harvest" <u>The Economist</u> June 21, 1980 page 6.

jealous of the freedoms which it enjoys under the system of free enterprise. Everyone is a capitalist as far as his personal interests are concerned and also a lover of land as property; but otherwise and at the same time he is inclined to be a socialist, enlisting state assistance as far as possible; demanding state intervention to curb Hoggenheimers; advocating state control of certain industries; ready to welcome price control; sometimes even advocating a dictatorship because he thinks that after 28 years of Nationalist government this dictatorship which he has in mind would be a dictatorship of his own government. Almost every Afrikaner regards communism as a foul system against which we should continue to fight and he gives his government full credit for doing so. But to many, socialism is something not quite as objectionable which can be accepted. When asked to define socialism and communism so as clearly to bring out any difference most get tangled up with words in a quite pathetic way. "[1171]
Wassenaar also wrote that many Afrikaners also supported the concept of government ownership of major services and companies: *"Everybody in the RSA[1172] appears to accept as quite natural the idea that all these services should be state conducted. This unquestioning acceptance is probably due to brainwashing through custom."*[1173]

Perhaps the most detailed analysis of the nature of the South African economy was provided by the historian Patrick Furlong. Furlong outlined the statist-collectivist and even fascist-corporative policies that the Nationalists implemented after 1948 in the realm of economic controls, government ownership of various sectors, and labor-management arbitration. He noted that the Nationalists attempted to *"crush African trade unionism, barring Africans from membership in state-recognized unions in 1953, removing their right to strike, and offering an alternative system of 'plant-level committees' and state-appointed labor officers. When some employers continued to recognize African trade unions, the government prohibited the deduction of dues. Although 'coloreds' and Indians could still belong to mixed state-recognized unions, no new mixed unions received government recognition, and trade union leaders were often 'named' under the Suppression of Communism Act and banned or detained..."*[1174]

Furthermore, Furlong also discussed the development of a plethora of state-owned corporations under the regime of apartheid: *"Just as Hitler and Mussolini forged an alliance of state and capital to promote 'national' economic interests, so the Nationalist government used the massive expansion of state involvement in the economy to further the interests of an indigenous Afrikaner entrepreneurial class, and to reduce the threat of a widening gap between rich and poor Afrikaners. State corporations multiplied in number, including not only the long-established ISCOR (Iron and Steel Corporation) and ESCOM (Electricity Supply Commission) as well as South African Railways, but also SASOL, the state oil company, the Atomic Energy Board, and ARMSCOR, the state armaments and munitions monopoly. Furthermore, the state-run Industrial Development Corporation, the instrument which the Nationalists hoped to use to encourage expansion in manufacturing, developed a close relationship with private Afrikaner companies like Federale Kunsmis (Federal Fertilizer), and by 1960 the Development Corporation had invested 171 million pounds in industrial projects, partly through loans, but primarily in the form of holdings in new enterprises. Such developments strengthened the role of*

[1171] Wassenaar, A.D. <u>Assault on Private Enterprise</u> (Tafelberg, 1977) page 124.

[1172] The RSA was the acronym for the Republic of South Africa.

[1173] Wassenaar, A.D. <u>Assault on Private Enterprise</u> (Tafelberg, 1977) page 139.

[1174] Furlong, Patrick Jonathan. <u>Between Crown and Swastika</u> (Witwatersrand University Press, 1991) pages 255-256.

the Afrikaner-controlled state in the economy and helped to create and train Afrikaner capitalists who would otherwise have been unable to compete with established English-speaking and often British-owned economic interests…"[1175] The development of these state corporations even predated the 1948 electoral victory of the Nationalists. Although the British-oriented parties were dominant in the pre-1948 era, the Afrikaner Nationalists possessed enough political clout to impose aspects of their economic agenda. For example, the South African Iron and Steel Company (ISCOR) was formed in 1927 by the government of General Hertzog as a state-owned iron and steel company.[1176]

By the 1960s, the role of the government in the South African economy reached an all-time high. The Marketing Act guaranteed South African farmer high prices for their products.[1177] Economist Walter Williams noted that government-owned industries in South Africa included ARMSCOR, ESCOM, ISCOR, SASOL, SABC, SATS, and SAA. The National Marketing Council administered South African agriculture. It controlled prices through the Price Control Act of 1964. The Group Areas Act of 1950 controlled housing transactions, while the Industrial Conciliation Act of 1956 supervised the labor market.[1178] The Nationalist Party created or expanded 22 state-owned enterprises such as ISCOR, ESCOM, ARMSCOR, and SASOL. The annual expenditure of the public sector rose from 36.5% in 1946 to 53% in 1966. Professor J. L. Sadie of Stellenbosch University noted that 35% of all working Afrikaners were employed in the public sector.[1179] In South Africa, the sale of coal was subject to price controls. The government's Petrick Commission recommended that an Energy Planning and Coordinating Board be established. Wassenaar termed that step *"a worse evil than nationalization"* of the coal industry.[1180]

The Afrikaners also implemented harsh and racist labor market controls to assure privileges for its workers: *"At the same time, white workers, predominantly Afrikaners, were protected by statutory measures that allowed the minister of labor, in terms of the 1956 Industrial Conciliation Act, to reserve jobs for particular racial groups 'in any industry, trade or occupation.' Three years later this law was amended to permit the minister to reserve jobs even where the autonomous white-controlled industrial council of a particular industry opposed such steps…A planned economy could not accommodate resistance from whites who failed to see the advantages of such a system; such a degree of state regulation of labor went far beyond longstanding reservation of better-paying mining jobs for whites, and Hertzog's encouragement in the twenties of a 'civilized labor' policy that favored the employment of whites or, to a lesser extent, of 'coloreds' rather than Africans in both the public and the private sector. The post-1948 Nationalists wanted a more exclusivist, comprehensive, and statutorily enforced policy more in keeping with government by blueprint."*[1181] Bunting even admitted that apartheid labor controls bore no resemblance to free market capitalism: *"South Africa began to experience ever-*

[1175] Ibid, pages 255-256.

[1176] Wassenaar, A.D. Assault on Private Enterprise (Tafelberg, 1977) page 123.

[1177] O'Meara, Dan. Volkskapitalisme (Cambridge 1983) page 100.

[1178] Williams, Walter E. South Africa's War Against Capitalism (Praeger, 1989) Accessed From: http://www.cato.org/pubs/wtpapers/south_africa/

[1179] "The Great Evasion; The golden harvest" The Economist June 21, 1980 page 6.

[1180] Wassenaar, A.D. Assault on Private Enterprise (Tafelberg, 1977) pages 45 and 48.

[1181] Furlong, Patrick Jonathan. Between Crown and Swastika (Witwatersrand University Press, 1991) pages 255-256.

increasing government intervention to ensure White supremacy and put an end to laissez faire policies."[1182] Clearly, the most radical racialist Nationalists viewed big, centralized government as a tool to enhance the economic privileges of Afrikaner enterprises and laborers. Prime Minister Hendrik Verwoerd noted that the problem of Afrikaner poverty could be solved "*by temporary discrimination in their (Afrikaner) favour…even if it should superficially resemble favouritism…The only organisation in the country which has the power to deal really effectively with the problem is undoubtedly the Government.*"[1183] Some observers argued that the collectivist labor policies of apartheid even resembled socialism. Reason Magazine author Frances Kendall wrote that "*…blacks and to a lesser extent coloreds live under conditions of almost pure socialism. Virtually every aspect of black life has been provided and controlled by the state-from houses, hospitals, and nurseries, to schools and transport. Until very recently, genuine private ownership of land and free exchange of land rights were prohibited in black areas. The government has controlled the trade unions and not allowed blacks to move freely from job to job.*"[1184]

The United States and elements of the South African business community criticized the collectivist and socialist nature and programs that took root during the period of Nationalist Party rule. The US Commerce Department issued a report criticizing South Africa in 1953 for racial tensions, discrimination of non-white skilled laborers, and the creation of state owned enterprises such as SASOL, ISCOR, ESCOM, state railways, and the posts and telegraphs agency all had the effect of discouraging American investment in that country.[1185]

Jan Marais of the Trust Bank criticized massive amounts of state-owned and semi-state companies for competing with the private sector. Marias also denounced the Nationalist Party for enacting too many laws and promoting the excessive regimentation of the economy. In punishment, the Nationalist Party withdrew 3 million rands from the Trust Bank for these remarks. Another entrepreneur Jan Hupkes criticized some government economic policies and in response, the headlines of the hard-line Afrikaner Nationalist newspapers screeched "*Afrikaans business tycoon slams government policy.*" Furthermore, Nationalist Party activists whispered "*I always knew he was a SAP.*"[1186] Hupkes estimated that 70% of businessmen would welcome a new government, since the Nationalists greatly increased corporate taxation.[1187]

On the other hand, the Afrikaner Nationalists were sensitive to domestic and international criticisms of its collectivist and regimented economy. Government spokesmen and propaganda booklets sought to dispel the notion that Nationalist economic policy was socialistic or as A.D. Wassenaar stated: "*a freeway to communism.*" The Afrikaners needed Western investment to acquire the technology which would allow South Africa to build a modern industrial state, to repress the African natives, and to maintain a strong military force. The last thing the Nationalists wanted was more negative international publicity, especially criticisms from Western and American anti-communists. The South African Department of Information

---

[1182] Peron, Jim. "Apartheid's Dirty Little Secret" Accessed From: http://www.freerepublic.com/forum/a3b8531ad4d8d.htm

[1183] Ibid.

[1184] Kendall, Frances. "South Africa's Only Hope?" Reason Magazine January 1987 page 39.

[1185] "South Africa Hurt Over US Report" New York Times November 26, 1953 page 11.

[1186] The SAP was the acronym of the pro-British South Africa Party.

[1187] Leftwich, Adrian. South Africa: Economic Growth and Political Change (Allison & Busby, 1974) pages 270-272

publication <u>Pillars of the South African Economy</u> noted in 1964 that "*Doubts have been expressed concerning these enterprises on the score of their pointing to socialism. South Africa aligns itself openly and unequivocally with the Western democracies and the system of private industrial enterprise. There is no danger of the country becoming socialized in the prevailing ideological sense of the term. Like all Western democracies, South Africa does offer a measure of social security to its people and the State Industrial Corporations must be seen as a contribution thereto. They have been established with the express purpose of promoting private enterprise. The term State Industrial Corporation may be misleading, for all such enterprises in the Republic are a form of partnership between the State and private capital. They are, in truth, only sponsored enterprises.*"[1188]

By the 1960s, the Soviet-funded South African Communist Party also sought to distance Nationalist economic policy from socialism. The South African Communists did not want the "*good name*" of socialism to be ruined by any association with apartheid. The SACP publication <u>The African Communist</u> noted in 1963 that "*Nationalisation of certain industries and services by a capitalist state must not be confused with socialism. In South Africa the state controls certain vital industrial undertakings as steel (ISCOR) and coal-derived oil and petrol (SASOL). The railways, airways and harbours are state-owned and operated. But no sane African could claim that control or even ownership by the criminal apartheid state has anything at all in common with socialism.*"[1189]

By the late 1970s and early 1980s, the more enlightened elements of the Nationalist Party (the so-called *verligtes*) took over the government. P.W. Botha became the State President and sought to enact policies to privatize certain state-owned enterprises and introduce free market-oriented reforms in the South African economy. The hard-line factions of the Afrikaner Nationalists and other splinter groups vociferously opposed these policy recommendations. The more prominent of these splinter groups included the neo-Nazi Afrikaner Resistance Movement (AWB), the Conservative Party, and the *Herstigte Nasionale Party* (HNP). These splinter extremists professed a statist-populist and outright socialist agenda combined with undiluted doctrines of Afrikaner racial supremacy. The AWB supported the nationalization of natural resources from "*volks alien companies.*" All foreign control of basic industries were be halted and that some of these industries be nationalized. Land owned by foreigners was to be confiscated for communal uses and speculation in land was to be outlawed. Medical services were to be provided free of charge to mothers and children, which Kemp noted was a similar policy introduced by the ANC communists in the post-1994 government.[1190] Professor F.A. van Jaarsveld of South Africa noted in the late 1970s that the AWB desired an Afrikaner dictatorship, the nationalization of the gold mines and industries, and a corporative state modeled on Fascist Italy. Professor van Jaarsveld was very critical of the AWB and was tarred and feathered by members of the group for his public views.[1191] Elements of the Botha government also tied the socialist ideologies of the ANC and the AWB together as representing the collectivist, extremist threat to the political and economic reforms. The Minister of Manpower Pietie du Plessis noted in May 1986 that "*One has to think very seriously about what we are dealing with in the*

[1188] Department of Information. <u>Pillars of the South African economy South Africa</u>. (The Department 1964) page 5.

[1189] <u>The African communist</u> Issues 12-19 (South African Communist Party 1963) page 63.

[1190] Kemp, Arthur. <u>Victory or Violence</u> (Forma Publishers, 1990) pages 19-21.

[1191] "Afrikaner Militants" <u>Patterns of Prejudice</u> Volume 13 Issue 4 1979 page 23.

AWB...The AWB rejects the political system, just like the ANC. It stands for the nationalization of property, just like the ANC. And it rejects democracy in South Africa, in the same way as the ANC and its people's democracy. The ANC's tactics of violence also remind one of the AWB. The CP has fully associated itself with the AWB. Just like Umkhonto we Sizwe is the military wing of the ANC, I am not sure whether the CP is not the political wing and the Stormtroopers (Stormvalke) the military wing of the AWB. [1192]

The *Herstigte Nasionale Party* (HNP) adhered to a socialist ideology which endorsed the government-directed creation of jobs and businesses for Afrikaners. It favored the white working class and maintained ties to the Mineworkers' Union and White Building Workers' Union. [1193] The HNP characterized Botha's privatization program as *"the already over-concentration of economic power in the hands of a small number of persons...The population as a whole gain nothing by privatization and is increasingly exposed to monopolistic practices. A nation must through state enterprise be protected against exploitation by financial interests intent on more and more profits, irrespective of the effects on the country and society."* [1194]

The Conservative Party (CP) broke away from the Nationalists over the reforms to liberalize the apartheid system. The CP also vocally opposed Botha's privatization program and other free market-oriented reforms. The CP also opposed privatization of state owned enterprises and characterized such a process as *"handing over the state's assets to big business"* thus resulting *"in a monopoly capitalist situation only equaled in the communist world where the state owns everything."* The CP also noted that *"There should be a healthy balance between private enterprise and state control, the latter being important for the strategic legs of the economy such as oil supplies, transport, hospitals, etc."* [1195] As of November 1988, privatization of South African state-owned enterprises was opposed by the Conservative Party and white trade unions as being a *"sale of the (Afrikaner) family silver."* [1196] Rooyen concluded that the South African Conservative Party *"indicated a preference for a strong state presence in the economy."* The CP supported influx control, closing of central business districts to non-white businessmen, and for strict state controls and outright curbs on private monopolies and multinational corporations. The CP opposed privatization and cutbacks in spending for government-owned weapons plants, such as ARMSCOR and ATLAS. The CP was also anti-US, calling it an *"imperialistic"* nation. Furthermore, the CP opposed America's *"self-serving interference"* in South Africa in respect to its apartheid policies. It took an anti-American, pro-Saddam position during the Gulf War of 1990-1991 and lambasted the Nationalist government of President F.W. De Klerk for siding with the US and UN. [1197] The Conservative Party in South Africa asserted in 1987 *"The CP will reassess its whole attitude towards for example the US and Sweden, and if necessary will even expel foreign diplomats whose countries declare economic war against us as we do not wish to have spies from those countries reporting on our activities and exposing the identity of our friends."* [1198]

[1192] "S African Minister on AWB Links with Conservative Party" <u>SAPA</u> May 30, 1986

[1193] Rooyen, Johann Van. <u>Hard Right</u> (I.B. Tauris 1994) page 70.

[1194] "HNP on Economic Policy Questions" <u>Johannesburg Star</u> April 23 1987

[1195] "CP on Economic Policy Questions" <u>The Johannesburg Star</u> April 23, 1987

[1196] Robinson, Anthony. "Rolling Along Private Lines" <u>Financial Times</u> November 30, 1988 page 23.

[1197] Rooyen, Johann Van. <u>Hard Right</u> (I.B. Tauris 1994) pages 68-69.

[1198] "CP on Economic Policy Questions" <u>The Johannesburg Star</u> April 23, 1987

To be fair, the economic reforms proposed or cautiously enacted by President Botha did not fully roll back the influence and power of the state over the economy. In addition, with the looming military and political threat from the constellation of communist states and occupation armies in the north, the Botha regime decided to implement the policy of Total Strategy. The Total Strategy plan stipulated the regimentation of the economy to serve the needs of the military-oriented state for the possible, future communist invasion of South Africa and internal terrorism wrought by the ANC. Hard-line statist collectivist Nationalists also resisted the implementation of any far-reaching liberal economic reforms. Janine Aron, Brian Kahn, Geeta Kingdon noted that *"While some privatization and deregulation occurred in the 1980s, the intensification of trade and financial sanctions against South Africa curtailed any remaining appetite for liberalization...Despite the privatization of ISCOR and SASOL, other state enterprises such as ESKOM and ARMSCOR remained firmly under the control of the state."*[1199]

Hanlon noted that under Botha *"...the new relationship (between the private sector and government) never really got off the ground. Tensions between business and government increased in 1982 and 1983."* The National Key Points Act of 1980 authorized the Minister of Defense to designate a military *"key point"* at any private company and establish a militia and establish security precautions. Over 600 key points were established and the SADF ordered more military goods to be locally produced and foreign imports were subjected to high tariffs.[1200]

Under President P.W. Botha ARMSCOR, SASOL, and ISCOR developed strong ties with the private sector and the SADF through sales to the army and security forces, along with ties to state agencies and planning bodies. For example, CSIR was completely tied to defense research. The Atomic Energy Act as amended in 1979, the National Petroleum Supplies Procurement Act of 1970 as amended in 1979, the National Key Points Act of 1980, and the Petroleum Products Amendment Act of 1979 ordered private companies not to disclose information about their operations.[1201]

Even the Soviets admitted that South Africa, even under Botha, retained perhaps one of the most government-controlled economies outside the communist world. The resource South Africa: A Country Study reported that *"South African economists in the 1980s described the national economy as a free-enterprise system in which the market, not the government, set most wages and prices. The reality was that the government played a major role in almost every facet of the economy, including production, consumption, and regulation. In fact, Soviet economists in the late 1980s noted that the state-owned portion of South Africa's industrial sector was greater than that in any country outside the communist bloc. The South African government owned and managed almost 40 percent of all wealth-producing assets, including iron and steel works, weapons manufacturing facilities, and energy-producing resources. Government-owned corporations and parastatals were also vital to the services sector. Marketing boards and tariff*

[1199] Janine Aron, Brian Kahn, Geeta Kingdon. South African Economic Policy under Democracy (Oxford University Press 2009) page 5.

[1200] Hanlon, Joseph. Beggar your neighbours: apartheid power in Southern Africa (Indiana University Press, 1986) page 14.

[1201] Grundy, Kenneth W. The Militarization of South African Politics (I.B.Tauris, 1986) pages 45-47.

regulations intervened to influence consumer prices. Finally, a wide variety of laws governed economic activities at all levels based on race."[1202]

The Nationalists also mirrored the Communists in their utilization of domestic and international business to bolster and modernize the economy without verbally sacrificing their core ideological principles. While the Soviets and other communist powers sought global conquest, South Africa desired regional hegemony and the retention of the political monopoly of the Nationalist Party. Laurence noted that "*Without the despised Rooinek[1203] with his skills, money, and sophistication the Afrikaner volk are completely vulnerable.*"[1204] Eben Donges stated at the RDB congress in 1941: "*The aim of a struggle against the capitalist system does not mean that you are opposed to capital as such. The movement (RDB) is against the system which concentrates capital in a few hands.*"[1205] Sanlam managing director Dr M.S. Louw noted that "*If we want to achieve success we must make use of the technique of capitalism as it is employed in the most important industry of our country, the gold industry. We must establish a financial company which will function in commerce and industry like the so called 'finance houses' in Johannesburg.*"[1206] Nico Diederichs noted before the annual assembly or Bondsraad of the Broederbond in 1944 that "*in order to fight capital, capital was necessary.*"[1207] Prime Minister Verwoerd remarked in the late 1950s that "*There is a natural desire on the part of every country to retain control over its economic destiny…The encouragement of local capital formation was one of the guiding principles of our financial policies during the past decade…But…foreign capital can still be of great assistance in the development of our resources…Moreover, in many cases desirable development will not take place without the technical knowledge and business skill which accompany foreign capital…We will continue to welcome the participation of foreign investors…provided this did not conflict with the general principle of a country retaining control over its economic destiny.*"[1208]

Despite their distrust towards foreign capitalists, the South African Nationalists lured American and Western multinational corporations with subsidies and cheap labor. For example, American and British companies sited factories in the Bantustan border areas.[1209] Laurence also reported that a campaign was "*mounted and sustained by industrialists with large investments in South Africa and who wish to keep international pressure away from their exceptionally profitable undertakings there…*"[1210] The South Africa Foundation provided guided tours for foreign businessmen that became known as "*The Treatment.*" These controlled tours were encouraged by the South Africans and international business ostensibly for "*fact finding*" purposes. Foreign business visitors were not familiar with South Africa, rarely asked the wrong

---

[1202] "South Africa: A Country Study" Accessed From: http://countrystudies.us/south-africa/63.htm

[1203] Rooinek was an Afrikaner pejorative slang term for foreigner.

[1204] Laurence, John. The Seeds of Disaster (Gollancz, 1968) page 56.

[1205] O'Meara, Dan. Volkskapitalisme (Cambridge 1983) page 151.

[1206] Harsch, Ernest. South Africa: white rule, black revolt (Monad Press: distributed by Pathfinder Press, 1980) page 51.

[1207] O'Meara, Dan. Volkskapitalisme (Cambridge 1983) page 221.

[1208] Seidman, Gay W. Manufacturing Militance: Workers' Movements in Brazil and South Africa (University of California 1994) pages 75-76.

[1209] Laurence, John. The Seeds of Disaster (Gollancz, 1968) page 125.

[1210] Ibid, page 131.

questions, wined, dined, and entertained luxuriously, and never permitted to speak in private with carefully picked educated black South Africans.[1211]

According to Laurence, the phrase "*don't harden the hearts of the Nationalists*" was used by British and American businessmen when the Nationalists were elected in 1948. American and British industrialists believed that if the Nationalists were treated with kid gloves, then their odious policies would soften and the situation would improve in South Africa. This theory was also propounded by the same multinational corporations and the adherents of the policy of engagement in respect to trade and economic cooperation with communist countries. The South African government hit back at American companies whenever an unfriendly policy was enacted against the Nationalists. When the American government halted arms shipments to South Africa, the South African government temporarily boycotted the purchase of Ford trucks and cars for the South African police, army, and government agencies.[1212] It was also clear that part of South Africa's commerce with the West modernized the agencies of repression. By 1982, South Africa purchased 2,500 shock batons from an unnamed United States manufacturer. This sale was licensed by the Commerce Department. Jean Sindab, executive director of the Washington Office on Africa, noted that "*We are appalled and outraged that the Reagan administration would approve this sale. Sending shock batons to South Africa clearly places the Reagan administration on the side of the apartheid regime's growing repression against the majority Black population.*" These batons were used to torture political prisoners and were sold to a "*private*" South African company.[1213]

By 1980, American firms accounted for 33% of South Africa's motor vehicle market; 44% of the oil market; and 75% of its computer market. General Motors and Ford plants in South Africa made cars and trucks destined for the South African market (including some to the military and police) and for export to Europe. Firestone and Goodyear sold tires to private South African companies and government agencies. A General Electric affiliate, SAGE, supplied geothermal turbines to South Africa's nuclear program. ITT also held shares in a South African firm that produced communications equipment. Some of this equipment was sold to the police and the South African naval base at Simonstown. Shell BP, Texaco, Mobil, and Caltex refined oil at South African refineries. Shell BP also helped the state-owned company Petrochem build a petrochemical industry in South Africa. Another American firm Flour provided engineering and construction services to SASOL. IBM supplied computers to South African government-owned enterprises and state agencies such as the Atomic Energy Board, the Industrial Development Corporation (IDC), and the Council for Scientific and Industrial Research. IBM computers also were used in the Johannesburg Stock Exchange and for military communications in Namibia. Control Data, Honeywell, and Sperry supplied computers for the military and police along with private South African companies. Citicorp and Chase Manhattan Banks provided loans to private and government owned South African companies.[1214]

[1211] Ibid, pages 147-148.
[1212] Ibid, page 274.
[1213] "South Africa gets shock batons from U.S." Multinational Monitor October 1982 Accessed From: http://www.multinationalmonitor.org/hyper/issues/1982/10/southafrica.html
[1214] Seidman, Ann Wilcox. Apartheid, Militarism, and the US Southeast (Africa World Press 1990) pages 66-67.

Polaroid sold film to the South African government for the development of passbooks. In the face of international outcry, Polaroid pledged to stop direct sales as of 1974.[1215] However, after 1974, the South African affiliate of Polaroid continued to sell South Africa film without informing its parent in the United States. The ITT affiliate in South Africa, Standard Telephone and Cables (STC) produced communications equipment for the Simonstown Naval Base and the police. It was reported that 70% of STC's sales was with the South African government. South African General Electric (SAGE) produced militarily applicable equipment such as industrial controls, capacitors, and locomotives. SAGE also produced equipment for the state-owned electrical company ESCOM. AEG-Telefunken provided components for Project Advocaat, which was an advanced military communications system for the SADF. Motorola sold 15% of its goods to agencies of the South African government. Motorola sold two-way radios to the South African police. IBM supplied computers to the SADF, police, and nuclear program. South Africa purchased a US-made nuclear reactor under the guise of the Eisenhower Administration's program of Atoms for Peace. Allis-Chalmers helped install the reactor in South Africa. South African nuclear scientists were trained at the US Atomic Energy Commission (AEC) laboratory in Oak Ridge. As of 1976, the United States provided enriched uranium to South Africa. The Foxboro Corporation sold two computers to South Africa's Pelindaba nuclear complex. The state-owned enterprise SASOL had its plants built with the assistance of US and West German multinationals. From 1972 to 1976, the US Export-Import Bank insured $691 million in trade with South Africa. In 1977, the Export-Import Bank funded shipments of turbo-commander aircraft destined for the South African military-industrial complex.[1216]

As of 1977, the South African army used weapons systems imported from Britain, France, and the United States. These weapons included Centurion Mk 10, Patton, M-41 Walker Bulldog, M-47 Patton, and AMX-13 tanks; Staghound and Shorland MK 3 armored cars; M-113AI, V-130 Commando, Piranha, Short SB 301, and M3A1 armored personnel carriers; and Sexton 88mm, M-7 Priest 105mm, and M-109 155mm self-propelled guns. The United States and France supplied aircraft and helicopters such as Impala II jets, F-104G Starfighter jets, F-51D Cavalier counter-insurgency planes, Mirage F-1 and Mirage 3 fighters, and Iroquois, Alouette, Puma, and Gazelle helicopters.[1217]

A spokesman for General Motors noted in 1977 that "*We've been there over 50 years and we plan to be there for a long time to come.*" Over 350 American companies invested in South Africa as of December 1977. American banks in South Africa provided loans and credits to mostly government entities and state-owned companies worth $2.2 billion. The Chase Manhattan Bank senior official in South Africa Stephen Pryke noted that "*We're just carrying on as before and we'll shortly be moving to bigger premises.*" In November 1977, a new American Chamber of Commerce was opened in Johannesburg. Amongst its members were the executives of Esso Standard Oil and Colgate Palmolive. Caltex also spent $134 million to enhance refining capacity in South Africa. A Caltex representative in New York noted that "*We're doing it because of an expanding market.*" As of December 1977, Britain was South Africa's largest trading partner

---

[1215] "Major Firms May Have to Justify Their South African Investments" Bangor Daily News January 22, 1974 page 26.

[1216] Seidman, Ann. "Why U.S. Corporations Should Get out of South Africa" A Journal of Opinion Volume 9 Number 1/2 Spring-Summer 1979 pages 37-41.

[1217] Gervasi, Sean. "Arms for Apartheid" Southern Africa August 1977 Accessed From: http://kora.matrix.msu.edu/files/50/304/32-130-E82-84-al.sff.document.af000018.pdf

followed by the United States. Citibank, Manufacturers Hanover, Morgan Guaranty Trust, and Chase Manhattan directly loaned money to the South Africa government and state-owned companies such as ESCOM and ISCOR. Once again, the South African government justified this trade on the grounds of procuring the best possible foreign technology and not any love for Western investors. Theo Vorster of the South African Consulate General noted that *"We aren't as concerned with the capital situation as we are with attracting technology."*[1218]

The policy of setting aside labor privileges to white Afrikaner workers was endorsed by racialist, pro-Nationalist, and even some leftist unions and stridently opposed by big business. South African big business desired a labor market system where they could hire the best workers unconstrained by various restrictive laws and regulations. The Afrikaners imposed the Colour Bar Act and the Civilized Labor Policy to push African natives out of privileged jobs within South Africa, thus reserving these positions for whites. Lord Oliver, a socialist and supporter of the unions, wrote in his 1927 book The Anatomy of African Misery that capitalists would not go along with racist economic-labor laws: *"The mine manager, however, does not see white men and black men, he sees only grades of labour—and it is the technique of his training, from which he could not depart, to try to reduce his labour costs by the most economic blending of dear grades with cheap. He had the impiety to attempt to take the Kaffir out of his traditional South African place and to use him to blackleg the white men. Why not? He is not a sociologist or a politician (as an aside let me clue you in advance that the main architect of apartheid later turned out to be both a sociologist and a politician). He is not a sociologist or a politician, he is a capitalist organizer of industry. South African racial tradition and trade union principles, therefore, invariably coalesce in demanding that the Kaffir shall not be given such opportunity to improve his status. A conventional colour bar is established by collective bargaining in the mines, and it is demanded that it shall be made stable by the sanction of the law."*[1219]

Bunting observed that *"...it seemed that the Natives had fallen out of the frying pan into the fire. The white workers who had gone on strike and taken up arms for a 'white South Africa' were defeated on the industrial field in 1922; but they won a political victory in 1924. The Pact Government was soon to entrench the white workers as an aristocracy of labour by writing into the constitution of South Africa a law which made it illegal for black persons to be employed in skilled work. The 'Colour Bar Act' did not come until 1925, but already in August 1924, the new Government began to put into practice its 'civilized labour policy' which consisted in sacking Native in Government employ and replacing them by white men."*[1220]

Africans and Indians were also pushed out of the business community, thus giving government enterprises and subsidized Afrikaner firms a distinct competitive edge. It was reported at the 1964 Nationalist Party Congress at Johannesburg that *"Delegate after delegate arose and demanded a total trade boycott of South Africa's Indian traders."*[1221]

Native Africans were relegated by the Nationalists to near slave labor status both in speech, policy, and action. Private farmers paid the government 750 pounds for a *"loan"* of a

---

[1218] Jensen, Michael C. "The American Corporate Presence in South Africa" New York Times December 4, 1977 page 145.

[1219] Peron, Jim. "Apartheid's Dirty Little Secret" Accessed From: http://www.freerepublic.com/forum/a3b8531ad4d8d.htm

[1220] Ibid.

[1221] Laurence, John. The Seeds of Disaster (Gollancz, 1968) page 46.

black South African prisoner for several years of virtual slave labor.[1222] In a visit to the United States, an Afrikaner minister of the Dutch Reformed Church noted to a South Africa Bureau of Race Affairs conference that *"Notwithstanding that the American Negro is treated on a different level he is lazy, as unreliable, as immoral, as enslaved to liquor and as black as the Bantu in South Africa."* Prime Minister Verwoerd compared black South African workers with oxen, stating that they were not integrated into the agricultural economic community. Another Nationalist Party speaker stated that there was no difference between the use of black South African labor and machinery as far as human rights was concerned.[1223]

The South African Nationalists also mirrored the Communists and Nazis in constructing a propaganda and disinformation apparatus which portrayed that country as a land of social reforms, racial harmony, and political stability. When the Nationalist Party took over South Africa in 1948, they reorganized the State Information Office and concentrated on the propaganda campaign abroad. Overseas information officers were transferred to the supervision of the State Information Office of the Department of the Interior. The Office cooperated with government organizations such as the South African Tourist Corporation. The Information Office's budget was 50,000 pounds per year in 1948 and grew to 2 million pounds by 1968. The 1951 Annual Report of the Information Office noted that *"the South African Information Office in the USA is in fact serving two states, the USA and the vast organization of the United Nations with its exceptional potentialities for spreading news influencing world opinion."* In 1951, an Information Office was opened in Washington DC (one already existed in New York) and 1963 and an Office was opened in San Francisco. The New York Office *"concentrates on lobbying"* the foreign press in the United Nations (UN).[1224] South African tourist promotion efforts were carried out by the state-owned South African Tourist Corporation (SATOUR) and South African Airways.[1225] SATOUR maintained offices in New York, Los Angeles, West Germany, Australia, and New Zealand.[1226] Examples of South African propaganda measures included information distributed *"overseas in pamphlets, films, television items, statements by ambassadors, by friendly industrialists with their eye on a rich country with a cheap controlled labor force, and in advertisements and in news items written by the South African Department of Information."*[1227] South Africa House and Pretoria's Embassy in London distributed The Transkei and the Case for Separate Development to prospective immigrants and investors in South Africa.[1228] South African embassies and tourist offices distributed massive amounts of propaganda books, booklets, brochures, pamphlets, and leaflets. Advertisements on foreign television, radio, and newspapers enticed businessmen and governments for *"profitable investment opportunities."*[1229]

A senior member of the South African Embassy noted in 1965 that *"apartheid is being implemented with great care and benevolence in order to provide the richest possible future for all...White South Africans will labor sincerely and conscientiously and with Christian humility to do our best to reconcile any facts of history with the needs of the future."* The Department of

[1222] Ibid, pages 47-48.

[1223] Ibid, page 98.

[1224] Ibid, pages 142-143.

[1225] Ibid, page 163.

[1226] Ibid, page 325.

[1227] Ibid, page 78.

[1228] Ibid, page 109.

[1229] Ibid, page 130.

Information pamphlet <u>This Is South Africa</u> noted *"South African social security measures are all embracing and include: Pensions and grants for the aged, the blind, the physically and mentally disabled, and the veterans of four wars."* The same pamphlet noted that *"all the country's peoples benefit"* from these social security measures.[1230] Another annual South African propaganda book dated from 1966 praised the *"far-sighted labor legislation"* as resulting in virtually no strikes and consequential labor peace.[1231]

In 1987 and 1988, $28 million was allocated to the South African Department of Foreign Affairs for *"communications and image-building"* programs overseas. During the 1980s, the South African government retained more than 15 lobbying and public relations firms in the United States to promote Pretoria's image. In 1978 and 1979, the so-called Muldergate scandal revealed that the South Africans maintained a propaganda budget of $50 million per year. The South Africans engaged in at least 160 propaganda operations, many of which were in the United States. The South Africans funneled money to the rightist publisher John McGoff in an effort to purchase <u>The Washington Star</u> and <u>The Sacramento Union</u>. In 1976 and 1978, the South African propaganda official Eschel Rhoodie revealed that the South Africans covertly funded campaigns to unseat leftist Senators John Tunney (D-CA) and Dick Clark (D-IA). Rhoodie also claimed that the South Africans bribed American labor union officials to prevent a refusal to unload South African ships. The South Africans retained an embassy in Washington DC and consulates in New York, Chicago, Beverly Hills, and Houston, and honorary consuls in Mobile, Salt Lake City, Seattle, and Phoenix. Officials at these embassies and consulates sought to propagandize the Pretoria line and promote imports of minerals into the American market.[1232]

South African diplomats resident in the United States fought criticisms of their country with both charm and jabs that displayed a heavy helping of moral equivalence. In the mid-1970s, James Sanders observed that there was an *"invasion"* of South Africans in Washington DC during that time period. He noted that the general tone at South African Embassy parties were *"Hey look-we're nice people-have some more champagne."*[1233]

However, Sanford Ungar also reported that South African diplomats resident in the United States were specifically trained to disarm critics of apartheid through the use of moral equivalence. It was a tactic that Communist and Nazi-ruled nations used to neutralize international political opposition to their regimes. Ungar wrote that *"South Africa's isolation— its almost universal condemnation by the outside world — often causes its spokesmen to defend themselves by accusing others. The skill of mocking those who try to occupy a higher moral ground is actually taught. One incident that occurred in 1978 was especially telling. At a training session for South African diplomats in the inner sanctum of the magnificent Union buildings in Pretoria, tempers are high. The diplomats, self- consciously sharpening their debating skills for overseas encounters, demand that a visiting American justify the 'selective application' of Jimmy Carter's human rights policy to South Africa and a few other vulnerable states. South African diplomats have made themselves experts on the mistreatment of American*

[1230] Ibid, page 88.

[1231] Ibid, page 151.

[1232] Leonard, Richard. "Apartheid Whitewash: South Africa Propaganda in the United States" Africa Fund December 1988 Accessed From: http://kora.matrix.msu.edu/files/50/304/32-130-F6B-84-32-130-F6B-84-al.sff.document.af000257.pdf

[1233] Sanders, James. <u>South Africa and the International Media 1972-1979</u> (Psychology Press, 2000) page 79.

Indians, a subject they feel provides effective ammunition for returning the fire of Americans who are critical of the South African political system. It gives them an opportunity to say, in effect, 'Clean up your own backyard first, before you complain about us.'"[1234]

In order to propound the myth that South Africa was a compassionate, harmonious country, state-owned radio was quickly utilized by the Nationalists. Prime Minister Verwoerd noted in October 1965: *"The Voice of South Africa will beam truth and goodwill to all parts of the globe…it will counter that which is so harmful to the welfare of this continent and to civilization as a whole."*[1235] Government radio was also used by the Nationalists to brainwash the native Africans, thus encouraging them to work for the welfare of the white minority. The Minister of Posts and Telegraphs Hertzog noted in respect to the state-owned Radio Bantu in April 1964 that *"The radio is the only way to get through to the Bantu and to reach his soul. It has an important role to play in the creation of good relations and goodwill between white and black…The establishment of Radio Bantu is an even greater security measure for the country than the police force, and for that reason the whole population must help put it on a sound footing."*[1236]

The South Africans also stationed intelligence officers abroad to monitor and even battle their communist and leftwing opponents. In 1969, the Bureau of State Security (BOSS) was formed by the Nationalists as the premier intelligence service. Previous to BOSS's formation in 1969, South African intelligence was named Republican Intelligence. In 1971, there were reportedly 10 trained intelligence officers at the South African Embassy in London and 12 others operated elsewhere in London. In 1966, Gordon Winter underwent a staged imprisonment for anti-government activities and was deported to Britain where he penetrated anti-apartheid organizations. Other intelligence officers such as Hans Lombard and Jean Legrange also undertook such work.[1237] In December 1982, a South African BOSS warrant officer Joseph Klue was expelled from Britain for spying. It was noted that Klue *"is known to have run a network of agents spreading fear in Britain and in Europe from the London embassy in Trafalgar Square."*[1238] As of 1977, it was reported that South African BOSS agents were trained by West Germany (BND) and the United States (CIA) as a part of the common battle against communism.[1239]

In order to retain Western and American investment and trade, the Nationalists carefully hid their Nazi-like proclivities from the public's view. A pro-Verwoerd British citizen admitted in 1962: *"The Nationalists have the right idea; they are much shrewder than you think. They are following the same path as Hitler did, but they will not be as hasty as he was. They are going very slowly now, but they will smash their enemies in the end."*[1240] The South Africans also implemented Soviet-style Potemkin village tours for sympathetic foreigners. These foreign

---

[1234] Ungar, Sanford. Africa (Simon & Schuster, 1989) pages 228-229.

[1235] Laurence, John. The Seeds of Disaster (Gollancz, 1968) page 78.

[1236] Apartheid Propaganda Offensive Accessed From: http://www.historicalpapers.wits.ac.za/inventories/inv_pdfo/AK2145/AK2145-C3-5-011-jpeg.pdf

[1237] Barber, James and Barratt, John. South Africa's Foreign Policy (CUP Archive, 1990) page 116.

[1238] "South African Accused of Being Spy in Britain" Toledo Blade December 16, 1982 page 2.

[1239] "Were South African Spies Trained In America?" Observer-Reporter July 25, 1977 page 31.

[1240] Laurence, John. The Seeds of Disaster (Gollancz, 1968) page 318.

guests would then transmit the message that South Africa was a civilized nation that the West could conduct business with. A religious minister from New Zealand commented in 1965, that *"It is one thing to visit South Africa as an official guest and to move through the country on a carefully prepared itinerary seeing only what the government wants you to see. It is quite another thing to live in the situation and share in the suffering brought about by the apartheid policy."*[1241]

Even during the 1960s, various extreme nationalists and even neo-Nazis made their pilgrimages to Nationalist-ruled South Africa and met with high level officials. They were also given exposure in the state-owned South African media. For example, the SABC introduced a minor British right winger as a *"well-known statesman."* The SABC also played the Nazi Horst Wessel song on Afrikaner national days.[1242] Segregationist elements in the Deep South also maintained supportive ties with official and private South African organizations. The student body at an Afrikaner university located in Pretoria transmitted a cable to white racist groups in the South who supported white supremacy. An American segregationist was welcomed into South Africa and spoke in favor of racial separation on the SABC. He also gave *"scientific"* racist lectures at Pretoria University. Laurence noted that *"more and more American industrialists, ministers of religion, teachers, and journalists from segregationist societies in the USA are visiting South Africa every year and once there are being furnished with extensive and carefully prepared propaganda material stressing the desirability and divine origins of race segregation and the wickedness and dangers of integration."* One group of fourteen right wing and segregationist American journalists visited South Africa in early 1966 and pledged to write articles praising apartheid and opposing integration. South Africans who visited the United States disseminated anti-Black stereotypes and praised the peace, prosperity, and alleged Christian values of apartheid.[1243]

The British fascist Oswald Mosley visited South Africa during the apartheid years and met with the Prime Minister and top government officials. Mosleyite official William Webster also visited South Africa in order to drum up financial assistance for his movement in Britain. The Candour League was another British racialist group that maintained ties with the South African government. In 1963, Adolf von Thadden of the West German National Democratic Party (NPD) visited South Africa and met with prominent Nationalist Party politicians.[1244]

While much of the international Left excoriated the South Africans, at least one communist-oriented group appeared to have cooperated with the apartheid regime. This group was the National Caucus of Labor Committees (NCLC) of Lyndon LaRouche. It appeared that the NCLC admired aspects of the statist-developmentalist economic approach that the Afrikaners utilized in their industrialization and modernization programs. Starting in 1978, NCLC officials met with South African diplomats in New York and Washington. In the late 1970s, David Cherry authored a report for the NCLC Africa File, which described a sympathetic group of South African *"humanists"* such as the pro-Nazi Nicolaas Diederichs and the industrialist Anton Rupert. The NCLC noted in internal reports that the apartheid regime intended to export *"humanism"* to the rest of Africa. The NCLC called for the expansion of the contract labor

---

[1241] Ibid, page 148.
[1242] Ibid, page 182.
[1243] Ibid, pages 144-145.
[1244] Bunting, Brian. Rise of the South African Reich (Penguin Books, 1969) Accessed From: http://www.american-buddha.com/rise.reich4.htm

system in Mozambique as a means of pressuring that communist nation to abandon its support for the ANC.

Furthermore, the NCLC's intelligence gatherers passed reports on anti-apartheid, leftist, and communist activists to the South African Bureau of State Security (BOSS). South Africa's embassy information officer in Washington DC Karl Noffke stated that "*They (the NCLC) wanted to alert us about certain forces they think are bad for South Africa--the British, the Wall Street bankers, and so forth.*" The LaRouchians continued its intelligence gathering for BOSS as late as the mid-1980s. At that time, the LaRouchians shed much of their communist rhetoric and assumed a position that combined nationalism, socialism, populism, and totalitarianism all wrapped up as "*Mom, God, and Apple Pie.*"

The NCLC also convened conferences in the United States that promoted foreign investment in South Africa. In May 1978, the NCLC held a Conference on Industrial Development of Southern Africa in Washington DC under the auspices of the Fusion Energy Foundation (FEF).[1245] This Conference was attended by diplomats from the USSR, France, various African nations, and two observers from the South African Embassy. The NCLC also supported the efforts of American banks in disbursing low-interest loans to the apartheid government.[1246]

To be fair, the South Africans viewed the LaRouchians with some concerns. A South African professor and former government official Dr. van Rensberg remarked that the NCLC were "*a bunch of dangerous crackpots.*"[1247] Karl Noffke, information counselor of the South African Embassy in Washington, noted that the "*main purpose*" of the NCLC in their meetings with the South Africans was to "*reveal their philosophy…They wanted to alert us about certain forces they think are bad for South Africa: the British, the Wall Street bankers, and so forth. They presented themselves as a conservative right-wing group, but seemed to have socialistic tendencies as well.*" Les de Villiers, a former South African information official at their Embassy in Washington DC, noted that NCLC officials from its Africa Sector "*gave me this spiel about the U.S. and Israel conspiring against South Africa. (They) left me two tabloids which dealt with South Africa's problems in a singularly naive fashion--I threw them out.*"[1248]

In the nascent days of Afrikaner nationalism, admiration for Soviet Communism was not unusual. Both opposed liberal capitalism and British imperialism and adhered to a socialistic form of collectivism. The Soviets sought to undermine the British in South Africa via political action, attempted revolution, and strikes. The early Afrikaner nationalists displayed an attitude towards Russian Bolshevism (Communism) that was strikingly different to their stances after the 1920s. The American ex-communist Nathaniel Weyl observed that "*The leaders of the Nationalist Party…viewed Bolshevism at first with pronounced sympathy, regarding it as a nationalist, anti-capitalist movement similar to the struggle they waged and lost against British*

[1245] King, Dennis. Lyndon LaRouche and the New American Fascism (Doubleday, 1989) Accessed From: http://lyndonlarouche.org/fascism19.htm

[1246] King, Dennis. Lyndon LaRouche and the New American Fascism (Doubleday, 1989) Accessed From: http://lyndonlarouche.org/ourtown3.htm

[1247] King, Dennis. Lyndon LaRouche and the New American Fascism (Doubleday, 1989) Accessed From: http://lyndonlarouche.org/fascism19.htm

[1248] King, Dennis. Lyndon LaRouche and the New American Fascism (Doubleday, 1989) Accessed From: http://lyndonlarouche.org/ourtown3.htm

imperial rule."[1249] When Malan served in the Union parliament, he asserted that *"Communism in Russia stands for the same things as Nationalism in South Africa."*[1250] General Hertzog noted at a Nationalist Party Congress in November 1919 that *"I say that Bolshevism is the will of the people to be free…Why do people want to oppress and kill Bolshevism? Because national freedom means death to capitalism and imperialism. Do not let us be afraid of Bolshevism. The idea in itself is excellent."* Malan noted in January 1920 that *"The aim of the Bolshevists was that Russians should manage their own affairs without interference from outside. That was the same policy that Nationalists would follow in South Africa. The Bolshevists stand for freedom, just like the Nationalist Party."*[1251]

However, these sentiments quickly translated into a short-lived cooperation between the Nationalists and Communists in South Africa. Both forces were faced with the common enemies of British capitalism and colonialism and were determined to cripple those adversaries through industrial strikes and demonstrations. Edward Roux noted in his book <u>Time Longer Than Rope</u> that *"the communists did what they could to help the Nationalists into power…"*[1252] Jan Smuts noted that his moderate nationalist, pro-British Union government was defeated by an *"unholy alliance between Christian Afrikaner and Bolsheviks."*[1253] During a 1922 mine-workers strike, Nationalists and South African Communists shouted slogans such as *"Workers of the world unite and fight for a White South Africa."*[1254] Roux reported that *"The Afrikaner strikers sang the 'Red Flag' in English to the tune of the old republican 'Volkslied,' and the Marxist socialists, not to be outdone, refurbished an old May Day banner so that its slogan read, ironically enough, 'Workers of the World fight and unite for a White South Africa.'"*[1255]

The Afrikaners also endorsed Left-Right cooperation in the South African political realm under rubric of a united front against capitalism. Malan noted at the Cape Congress of the Nationalist Party in 1923 that his Party and the Labor Party were both *"squarely opposed to capitalistic and monopolistic domination and exploitation of the people. In the existing circumstances…co-operation between the Nationalist Party and the Labour Party is not only completely justified but is also a clear and urgent patriotic duty."*[1256]

Even elements of the early South African Communist movement uttered guarded praise of the Nationalists' racist job reservation policies. As early as 1911, the South African Communist W.H. Andrews spoke out *"against the encroachment of coloured labour in the skilled trade unions of South Africa…The Government was guilty of a crime not only against the white people, but against the nigger himself in forcing him to go to the mines and work for the*

[1249] Peron, Jim. "Apartheid's Dirty Little Secret" Accessed From: http://www.freerepublic.com/forum/a3b8531ad4d8d.htm
[1250] Ibid.
[1251] Bunting, Brian. <u>Rise of the South African Reich</u> (Penguin Books, 1969) Accessed From: http://www.american-buddha.com/rise.reich2.htm
[1252] Peron, Jim. "Apartheid's Dirty Little Secret" Accessed From: http://www.freerepublic.com/forum/a3b8531ad4d8d.htm
[1253] Ibid.
[1254] Bunting, Brian. <u>Rise of the South African Reich</u> (Penguin Books, 1969) Accessed From: http://www.american-buddha.com/rise.reich2.htm
[1255] Peron, Jim. "Apartheid's Dirty Little Secret" Accessed From: http://www.freerepublic.com/forum/a3b8531ad4d8d.htm
[1256] Ibid.

benefit of the capitalist class." Another South African Communist Sydney Bunting noted to the left-wing unionist F.H.P. Cresswell: "*There may be something in this white labour policy of yours.*"[1257]

By the 1930s, much of the pro-Soviet sentiments that emanated from Afrikaner Nationalists disappeared. Henceforth, anti-communism became one of the ideological orthodoxies of the Afrikaner Nationalist Party. During the late 1940s, 1950s, and 1960s, the South African government suppressed all hints of communist activities and Soviet espionage. In February 1956, the South African government ordered the Soviet Consulates in Pretoria and Cape Town to be ejected from the country. The South African government maintained that the Soviet consulates "*cultivated and maintained contact with subversive elements in the Union, particularly among the Bantu and Indian population*" and that the Soviet Consulate in Pretoria served as a "*channel of communication between such elements and the authorities of Soviet Russia. Furthermore the same channel has been used for the diffusion of communist propaganda directed particularly at the Bantu population in transgression of the law of the land which proscribes communist propaganda in any form.*" Meanwhile, the Afrikaners allowed the Czechoslovaks to maintain a "*listening post*" and "*base of operations*" at their consulate in Pretoria as of 1956.

In the same breath, the South Africans also asserted that "*the termination of Soviet consular representation in the Union does not involve the discontinuance of diplomatic, trade, and other relations with which can in future be conducted by the Soviet Ambassador to London through the medium of the Union's commissioner there.*" Ultimately, South Africa was still interested in maintaining profitable commercial relations even with its ideological enemies. As of 1956, the South Africans still sold wool and meat to the USSR.[1258]

South Africa's trade with the communist world actually increased by the 1960s and soon became a source of international embarrassment for Pretoria, Moscow, and Beijing. Both sides desired the products and profits derived from this sort of international trade. At the same time, both the Soviets and South African Nationalists also wanted to project the image of ideological purity to their allies and other international supporters. According to an Eastern World report of November 1964, Red Chinese representatives reassured the owners of Hong Kong firms that handled Peking's trade for South Africa that business with Pretoria would continue uninterrupted. The South Africans also held a trade exhibition on the grounds of a Chinese Communist-owned business. In an article dated from an October 1965 issue of the East African Standard, the Kenyan Minister of Commerce and Industry J. G. Kiano estimated that Chinese-South African trade totaled $21 million. Chinese Communist official Chen Yi claimed that these stories purposely vilified China because the capitalist nations "*could not cover up their own ugly features.*" In August 1963, the Afrikaner Nationalist newspaper Die Burger and the Johannesburg Sunday Times bragged in August 1963 that their trade with Red China was flourishing due to the activities of private traders, third parties, and an unnamed international trade organization. The South Africans imported a large number of products from Red China and even paid hard currency for these goods. By the 1960s, the Chinese even incurred a trade deficit

---

[1257] Ibid.

[1258] Ingalls, Leonard. "South Africans Order Soviet Out" New York Times February 2, 1956 page 1.

with the South Africans. In May 1963, 163,000 tons of South African corn was sold to Red China.[1259]

The Times of Zambia reported that Chinese trade with South Africa totaled 20 million rand per year. Furthermore, The Times of Zambia also noted that *"The Peking leaders skillfully used the trade fair of the Republic of South Africa in Hong Kong in the autumn of 1964 to sign a secret ten year trade agreement with the republic!"* In January 1964, the Times of India reported that the China National Cereals, Oils, and Fats Import-Export Corporation maintained trade links with South Africa through the French firm Louis Dreyfus. In 1962, China exported pharmaceuticals, textiles, and light machinery to South Africa in exchange for 1 million pounds worth of food grains. In 1963, the South Africa Foundation reported that South African exports to China increased and consisted of mainly maize worth 2.25 million pounds in the first two months of that year. In March 1963, South Africa ceased to publish figures on its trade with China as a result of the international embarrassment of both Beijing and Pretoria. In 1963, a South African trade commissioner visited Peking. In November of the same year, Prime Minister Verwoerd office sent a booklet to China's state buying agencies that explained the benefits of trade with South Africa.[1260] Trade by 1971 totaled over 10 million pounds. As of 1971, China supplied South Africa with oil in exchange for copper, diamonds, lead, and zinc.[1261]

Well into the 1980s, the South Africans also conducted trade with the USSR and a number of its Eastern European satellites. As of 1963, Soviet and Polish ships stopped at South African ports such as Cape Town. Polish ship cargoes carried goods such as asbestos and chemicals destined to South Africa. As of 1963, Ghana supplied cocoa to South Africa through third parties. As of 1963, South Africa shipped maize to Red China.[1262] Johannesburg radio reported in May 1981 that South African imports from the communist world totaled 25 million rand. These imports included chemicals and electrical and heavy machinery from the Soviet Union, East Germany, Hungary, Bulgaria, Czechoslovakia, Poland, Romania, Cuba, Mongolia, and Albania.[1263] As of February 1982, it was reported that the Romanians bartered ammonia for South African maize. Reportedly, Hennie Nel, general manager of the Maize Board, visited communist Romania.[1264] The East Germans exported Wartburg cars to the South African market starting in 1957. These trade transactions were conducted through the South African-based corporations Kolipex and the Kimberley Export Company Ltd.[1265]

By the late 1980s, elements of the internationalist-minded business and Nationalist Party elites viewed Gorbachev as a *"new,"* less threatening type of Soviet ruler worthy of conducting economic relations with. These sentiments were aired by South African officials in respect to trade relations. Other South African businessmen were deeply resentful of American sanctions

---

[1259] Prybyla, Jan S. "Pragmatic Marxism-Peking Style" Challenge Volume 15, Number 2 November/December 1966

[1260] Hutchison, Alan. China's African Revolution (Westview Press, 1976) pages 197-198.

[1261] Ibid, pages 197-198.

[1262] Teltsch, Kathleen. "Apartheid's Foes Ignore Trade Ban" The New York Times March 26, 1963 page 4.

[1263] "S African imports from communist countries" BBC Summary of World Broadcasts May 12, 1981

[1264] "Romania denies barter deal with South Africa" Financial Times February 18, 1982 page 5.

[1265] "East Germans in Apartheid South Africa?" July 10, 2001 Accessed From: http://www.galimoto.co.za/index.php/history/5-motoring-history/130-trabant

and were tempted to increase profitable prospects in trade with the Soviet Union. In a July 1989 interview with the Johannesburg correspondent of the Soviet publication New Times, Foreign Minister Pik Botha noted that South Africa was interested in *"fair trade relations with all countries including the Soviet Union."*[1266] The top Soviet African expert, Anatoly Adamishin, praised a meeting between liberal white South Africans and Soviet officials in West Germany. He noted that *"These contacts should continue, to find out what is happening in this important industrialized country."* As of January 1989, goods from China, Czechoslovakia, and East Germany were sold in South African shops. South African entrepreneur Clive Strugnell of B&W Motors noted that *"If the United States and Japan stop supplying us, this (increased trade with the communists) is what will happen."* Strugnell noted that his meetings with Soviet officials in Botswana in the fall of 1988 made him discover that *"our conceptions of what Russians were like were completely wrong."* Strugnell's firm imported Soviet products such as Niva jeeps and cameras into the South African market. The head of a Johannesburg-based life insurance company Frank Kruger noted that *"Only once did somebody ask me how I can be so unpatriotic as to buy a Russian car...My answer was that to me the Niva represents value for money...I didn't buy a Russian car because I like the Russians, but I think South Africa should learn not to be scared of the Russians, should develop a relationship."* Kruger noted that *"South Africa's biggest enemy is America...America has kicked us so many times it's not funny. Who first imposed sanctions? Who collapsed our currency?...Russia is like a big South Africa, and we're both changing."*[1267]

The South Africans also maintained open economic relations with the communist dictatorship of Mozambique. Before the Portuguese withdrew from Mozambique in 1975, South African goods and tourists flooded that colony. South Africa's rulers and businessmen desired to continue these profitable commercial relations even with FRELIMO communist-ruled Mozambique under its dictator President Samora Machel. The Mozambicans also grudgingly realized the benefits of a continued economic relationship with South Africa. Not unsurprisingly, this advice was provided by Mozambique's strategic ally, the USSR. Soviet President Nikolai Podgorny reportedly advised Machel to retain Mozambique's economic links with South Africa as a means of acquiring high quality goods and especially hard currencies.[1268] A Portuguese trader based in Mozambique who conducted business with South Africa commented on the hypocrisy of FRELIMO in respect to its relations with South Africa: *"We are Marxists in theory, capitalists in practice. And worse, we are capitalist partners of South Africa."*[1269]

The South Africans also contributed resources to bolster the financial and military assets of FRELIMO-ruled Mozambique. As of 1985, the *Loja Franca* hard currency shop in FRELIMO communist-ruled Mozambique stocked goods from Western countries, including South Africa. Mozambicans who were employed in South Africa were among the customers who patronized the *Loja Franca*. The *Loja Franca* earned $7,000 per day and $2.5 million per year in hard

---

[1266] "S Africa Soviet publication carries interview with Pik Botha" SAPA July 24, 1989

[1267] Masland, Tom. "Soviet 'Jeeps' On The Road In South Africa" The Chicago Tribune January 9, 1989 Accessed From: http://articles.chicagotribune.com/1989-01-09/business/8902230877_1_post-apartheid-society-anatoly-adamishin-soviet-trade-officials

[1268] Wilkinson, Raymond. "Mozambique Dependent On South Africa" Lubbock Avalanche Journal April 21, 1977 page C3.

[1269] Zucchino, David. "A Marxist Nation at the Mercy of South Africa's Capitalists" Philadelphia Inquirer August 17, 1987

currency for the FRELIMO regime.[1270] In fact, the signs over the cash registers at the *Loja Franca* stated *"Rand or Dollar. Metical Need Not Apply."*[1271] The *Loja Francas* (officially the *Interfranca* enterprise) had three checkout lines for payment in South African rands, American dollars, and American Express credit cards.[1272]

The South Africans and Mozambicans also established missions and bank accounts in their respective nations as a means of promoting trade relations. As of August 1987, the South African Trade Mission expanded its building to accommodate the increase commerce between South Africa and Mozambique.[1273] As of 1977, the FRELIMO communists maintained a bank account with the Bank of Lisbon branch in Johannesburg. This account is used to pay South African exporters in rand.[1274]

Sometimes, South African funds and goods were consumed by communist FRELIMO troops. As of 1976, it was reported that the ration cans for FRELIMO troops were marked *"Canned in South Africa."* Bulk food supplies for the FRELIMO soldiers were marked *"Made in South Africa for Use of the Portuguese Army."*[1275] In 1977, it was reported that Mozambican workers in South Africa donated 10,000 rand to the *"liberation struggle."* The money was handed over to top FRELIMO officials at an expensive dinner at a hotel in Maputo.[1276] In 1977, it was reported that the Herstige National Party (HNP) in South Africa opposed trade that was conducted by both the Nationalist government and the business community with communist Mozambique. It claimed that the Mozambican regime generated 120 to 140 million rand per year in gold from migrant workers in South African mines. HNP MPs also pointed out that South Africa exported grain and other agricultural products to Mozambique. HNP General Secretary Louis Stofberg complained that *"treason was aiding the enemy"* and felt that the government was complicit in these actions.[1277] In the early months of FRELIMO rule, the South Africans even participated in assisting Machel's forces in arresting rightwing Portuguese Mozambicans. The South African Bureau of State Security (BOSS) even suppressed an invasion of Mozambique by the right wing settler group MML.[1278]

While the South Africans naively assumed that the Incomati (or Nkomati) Accord signed with Mozambique would force FRELIMO to withdraw support for the communist ANC terrorists. South Africa, in turn, withdrew support for the anti-communist forces of RENAMO. However, Machel and his comrades viewed the Incomati Accord as their Treaty of Brest Litovsk. The Mozambicans saw the Accord as a breathing period where FRELIMO forces could regroup and crush RENAMO. After the defeat of RENAMO, then Mozambique would gain military strength to increase its support for the ANC or even to assist in an invasion of South Africa. In

---

[1270] Valpy, Michael. "Withdrawing Portuguese sabotaged city Mozambique capital's beauty fades" The Globe and Mail (Canada) May 24, 1985

[1271] Ibid.

[1272] Zucchino, David. "A Marxist Nation at the Mercy of South Africa's Capitalists" Philadelphia Inquirer August 17, 1987

[1273] Ibid.

[1274] "Mozambique" Financial Mail May 8, 1977

[1275] Wright, Robin. "Machel Keeps His Vital SA Ties" Argus April 13 1976

[1276] Dalglish, Geoff. "SA Cash Pays for Mozambique Terror" Rand Daily Mail July 1, 1977

[1277] "SA Gold Helps Mozambique" Cape Times March 6, 1977

[1278] Cabrita, Joao. Mozambique: The Tortuous Road to Democracy (Palgrave, 2000) pages 80-81.

1984, President Machel stated *"With this accord, the Mozambique people, from the Rovuma river to the Maputo river, celebrated a victory of our socialist policy of peace. Incomati closes yet another chapter of the war of aggression against our independence and our revolution. Incomati marked the failure and non-viability of the imperialist-sponsored regional strategy, which was aimed at the destruction of the independent and progressive states of southern Africa...By negotiating with the Mozambique Government, South Africa recognised the lack of any political opposition in our country. By signing the Incomati accord, the main objective-the destruction of our state-failed. By signing the Incomati accord, we confirmed the reason for our fight-peace. It is only with peace that we can carry out our objective of defending the fatherland, over-coming backwardness and building socialism. While it is true that Incomati has crowned our socialist policy of peace, it is also true that we came out of this fight with deep wounds...The accord defends revolution. It defends the cause of socialism. It defends the most profound and legitimate aspirations of peoples. It is an act of solidarity with all other initiatives which are taking place throughout the world with the same objective of peace."*[1279]

In 1984, President Machel stated *"Listen to this properly. This is the meaning of the pact (with South Africa). It is to defend our independence; it is to defend our state and our sovereignty, it is to defend our territorial integrity. With it, we are finally defending every Mozambique national. There is something else. The pact defends the revolution, it defends our social transformation, it defends our economic transformation, it defends scientific and technical transformation. We did not sign an accord with the South African party. We did not sign an accord of political and ideological coexistence. Do you understand?...Greater vigilance is required because we have signed the accord. It is not an ideological accord...South Africa has its political and economic system, which is different from ours. They are antagonistic systems. Do you understand? We are for socialism, we are against capitalism. Do you understand? Therefore, it is not a question of coexistence of systems in the ideological sense."*[1280]

Despite the trade relations and the Incomati Accord signed between communist Mozambique and apartheid South Africa, FRELIMO continued to support efforts to overthrow the Nationalists in Pretoria. Hence, arms, training, and sanctuary were provided to the ANC. At a FRELIMO Party Congress (1977) Machel stated that Mozambique would become a *"revolutionary base"* from which anti-communist white ruled governments would be overthrown.[1281] The ANC used Mozambique as a transit point to infiltrate its troops into South Africa. The Mozambican Border Guard Troops (TGF), trained by Soviet *Spetsnaz*, were used in this effort and had an operational radius of 50 km beyond the border with South Africa. ANC agents were disguised as migrant workers and infiltrated into South Africa using false passports issued by FRELIMO. South African Communist Party official Joe Slovo was used to coordinate arms shipments from the USSR to Maputo.[1282]

Despite the Nkomati Accord, aid to the ANC continued to be provided by FRELIMO. In 1986, South African Army reported that *"the banned South African Communist Party and second in command of the military wing of the ANC, Joe Slovo, had been seen on a number of occasions in Maputo since the beginning of the year after his arrival in that country from*

[1279] "Mozambique President on Accord with S Africa" Maputo home service April 10, 1984
[1280] "Machel's 17th March Maputo Rally Speech" Maputo home service March 20, 1984
[1281] Ottaway, David. "Mozambique to Be 'Revolutionary Base'" Washington Post February 8, 1977 page A14.
[1282] Cabrita, Joao. Mozambique: The Tortuous Road to Democracy (Palgrave, 2000) page 181.

Angola. It is suspected that Slovo serves as the link between ANC training camps in Angola and transit camps in Mozambique. During his visits to Mozambique Slovo is accompanied by Mozambican government officials, and he travels on a British passport...a number of terrorists who had been arrested in the past in connection with terrorist attacks in the eastern Transvaal had infiltrated the country through Mozambique. Two were caught trying to cross the border into Mozambique. Since the beginning of the year about 23 terrorist attacks have been perpetrated in South Africa from Mozambique."[1283] South African General Magnus Malan noted in 1987 that ANC *"terrorists who were based in Mozambique admitted the Nkomati Accord provided them with freedom of movement, because of restrictions placed on South Africa by the accord. They felt themselves free to carry out acts of terrorism without any fear. With the support provided by the Frelimo government, the ANC has expanded its activities in Mozambique."*[1284] In July 1989, 200 ANC terrorists arrived in Mozambique. These ANC soldiers were flown into Beira Mozambique in Soviet-made Antelope transport aircraft. These ANC terrorists were met by members of SNASP.[1285]

Despite South African support for anti-communist UNITA forces, Pretoria continued to conduct underground trade with the ruling Angolan communist party known as the MPLA. In April 1989, the anti-MPLA rebel group UNITA commented *"It is widely known that South African technicians work in Lunda province diamond mines. The international press has reported this. Luanda's tyrannical regime sought for a long time to maintain economic relations with South Africa. MPLA chiefs have always expressed appreciation for South African products in their meetings with South African officials, including comments about the products' quality that would surprise the Angolan people if ever they were broadcast on the radio. Countries on other continents maintain profitable, intimate relations with the RSA despite repeated calls for economic sanctions, which only aim to distract those who are guileless and naive and are content with words and forget international reality."*[1286] In 1988, Angola imported items such as food, mining equipment, and other products from South Africa through neutral middlemen.[1287]

The South Africans also conducted trade with other Third World Communist and anti-Western despotisms as a means of capturing or retaining existing commercial markets. In 1981, about 22% of Zimbabwe's exports were shipped to South Africa, while 20% went to West Germany, the United States, Britain, and Italy. Zimbabwe imported 25% of its goods from South Africa in 1981. As of 1982, South African firms such as the Anglo-American Corporation, Delta Corporation, and South African Breweries were present in Mugabe's Zimbabwe.[1288] In the early

---

[1283] "South African Allegations of ANC-Mozambique Links" Johannesburg home service October 10, 1986

[1284] "S Africa's Malan Warns Mozambique About Accommodation of 'Terrorists'" Johannesburg television October 16, 1987

[1285] "Mozambique accused of violating Nkomati accords by accommodating ANC 'terrorists'" Radio Truth July 3, 1989

[1286] "UNITA Radio Comments on Luanda's 'Propaganda Campaign' Angolan-South African Relations, Cuban Involvement, US Policy" Voice of the Resistance of the Black Cockerel April 18, 1989

[1287] Claiborne, William. "Rancor Aside, Trade Ties Grow Between S. Africa, Black States" Washington Post April 1, 1988 page A15.

[1288] "Zimbabwe: A Country Study" 1982 Accessed From: http://www.dtic.mil/dtic/tr/fulltext/u2/a135022.pdf

1980s, Iraq purchased G-5 155mm artillery pieces from South Africa.[1289] Starting in 1984, South Africa bought weapons and Western technology in exchange for oil from Iran via a Greek front company. Reportedly, the South Africans provided US-made Bell helicopters and spare parts to Iran in exchange for the oil.[1290]

As odious and reprehensible as the policies of the Nationalist Party government were Pretoria's concerns about the menace of international and domestic communism were clearly not unfounded. Southern Africa was also a battleground for various *"liberation movements"* and satellite nations to subjugate non-communist states to Red rule. Such *"liberation"* movements included the African National Congress (ANC) and the Southwest African People's Organization (SWAPO). Soviet plans for the intimidation and even possible invasion of South African territory were seriously drawn up from the 1960s until the late 1980s, even despite the efforts to settle the conflict in Angola. Former senior Soviet official and Politburo aide Igor Glagolev noted *"The decision to begin an offensive for the conquest of Southern Africa was taken by the Politburo near the end of the 1960s...Through the chairman of the South African Communist Party, the Soviet leadership controls not only that party but also the African National Congress..."*[1291]

While the ruling Nationalist Party regime in South Africa was clearly repressive and highly authoritarian, they were also the target of the aggressive plans of the USSR and its allies. In 1965, the Carnegie Endowment for International Peace prepared a report entitled Apartheid and United Nations Collective Measures which envisaged air and naval operations which could culminate in the invasion of South Africa which would involve 100,000 UN soldiers. Sadly, the total casualties from such an invasion were estimated to range from 19,000-38,000. Radicalized blacks would also rise up, overtax the South African Defense Force (SADF) and cause the collapse of the apartheid government. A D-Day landing of foreign invaders of South Africa would require 3 armored divisions, three mechanized divisions, and two airborne divisions with decisive air superiority and technical and logistical support. The UN may also call upon the USSR and its allies to blockade South Africa until it changes it political system and the US might be called to collaborate, resurrecting the *"popular front on a global basis."*[1292] These UN forces could conceivably be composed of soldiers and officers from radical Third World and communist bloc nations. If the Soviets and Chinese were to gain hegemony over the world in the 1960s, 1970s, and 1980s, such a UN invasion operation would not be so far-fetched. Certainly, ANC and South African Communist forces would serve as saboteurs in the event of an invasion of South Africa by the Soviets, Cubans, or an international coalition.

[1289] Fullerton, John. "S. Africa's 155-Millimeter Weapon Scores Top Marks From Experts" Los Angeles Times October 9, 1988 Accessed From: http://articles.latimes.com/1988-10-09/news/mn-5426_1_south-africa

[1290] Stokes, Lee. "South Africa, Iran secretly trading arms for oil, documents show" United Press International November 25, 1987

[1291] Morris, Robert. Our Globe Under Siege III (J & W Enterprises, 1988) page 132.

[1292] Gann, Lewis Henry and Duignan, Peter. South Africa: War, Revolution, Or Peace? (Hoover Press, 1978) pages 39-41.

According to Rhodesian and Portuguese intelligence gleaned from defectors from the communist MPLA and the Patriotic Front[1293], a three stage plan of attack directed against South Africa was drawn up by 1968. The core of the invasion force was to comprise the 38,000 to 42,000 guerrillas in camps in Zambia and Tanzania and an additional 28,000 guerrillas in camps in Algeria, Ethiopia, Soviet Union, China, and Cuba. The first phase of the plan was to create a *"citizen army"* of 100,000 men with high quality non-commissioned and higher level officers. The second phase was to introduce Chinese and Soviet troops to assist the anti-colonial communists in southern Africa. The third phase of the plan would be the invasion of southern African countries, the overthrow of their governments, and their replacement by leftist or outright communist dictatorships.[1294]

Reports of potential Soviet plans for the invasion of South Africa cropped up in the Western press in the pre-Gorbachev period. Such plans were to involve the ANC, SWAPO, and the South African Communist Party as native forces of cooperation. Based on French Army General Staff information, the West German newspaper Die Welt reported that Soviet bloc forces planned an invasion of Southwest Africa (Namibia) in 1978. Five Soviet Generals were supposedly involved with the planning process and would involve the utilization of East German soldiers. The purpose of the invasion was to allegedly derail the elections held in Southwest Africa (Namibia). The military attack was to center on the capital Windhoek and the port-industrial city of Walvis Bay. The Soviet officers who were supposed to lead this invasion included General Chakhanovich, Karpov, Shurupov, Sredin, and Gubin. Massive amounts of war material specifically dedicated this attack was allegedly airlifted to Angola. The airlifted equipment included T-62 and T-54 tanks, APCs, artillery, and small arms. This equipment in Angola was positioned at the former modern Portuguese military base of Vila Henrique de Carvalho. This base contained two runways, modern electronic underground command centers, barracks, and maneuvering areas. Soviet General Chakhanovich had a paratrooper training center built at this base. Polish and Soviet airborne divisions trained three companies of MPLA troops and two battalions of Cuban forces in paratroop tactics. Southwest Africa People's Organization (SWAPO) terrorists were to play a subordinate role in invading Namibia alongside Soviet and other communist forces. East German National People's Army (NVA) communications and pioneer companies were also tasked to participate in the attack on Walvis Bay and Windhoek. The battle plan was supposed to occur in three phases:

1) Terror attacks by SWAPO forces.
2) During a period of confusion, airborne troops from Cuba and Angola would be dropped into Southwest Africa (Namibia) under the guise of what was dubbed *"patriotic liberation."*
3) Tank units were to break through the Etosha Pan and communist planes would simultaneously bomb Walvis Bay.
4) East German airborne forces of the Fifth Paratroop Regiment would be flown from Rugen Island located in East Germany to attack Windhoek.

[1293] The Patriotic Front was the coalition of the Zimbabwe African People's Union (ZAPU) and the Zimbabwe African National Union (ZANU) which fought the Rhodesian government of Prime Minister Ian Smith.

[1294] Weyl, Nathaniel. Traitors' End (Arlington House, 1970) pages 232-233.

5) Once victory is attained, foreign experts from East Germany and other communist countries would take over the administration of several important towns in Namibia.[1295]

The USSR also commenced training of a future South African Army based on ANC cadres that were present in Red Army academies. These ANC trainees received instruction in the fields of helicopter piloting, jet fighter training, naval officers, communications officers, and political officers. The Soviets also provided the ANC with radio communications equipment.[1296] In 1986, Spear of the Nation soldiers arrived for a full course of motorized infantry officers in Simferopol, located in the USSR. In 1987, full training was organized for the ANC in helicopter and later jet piloting, aircraft engineering, naval, armor, and communications officers. The Soviets provided this training in order to develop an officer core for the future armed forces of a *"democratic South Africa."*[1297]

As *"glasnost"* and *"perestroika"* swept into southern Africa, Moscow continued to promote revolution and compile invasion plans directed at Namibia and South Africa. In December 1988, it was reported that Soviet *Spetsnaz* or East German soldiers, along with SWAPO and Cuban troops, reinforced with tanks, were based in southern Angola, for a possible invasion of Namibia. In June 1988, Cuban and SWAPO troops occupied southern Angola with tanks, armored personnel carriers, artillery, missile systems, and radar equipment. Such forces could be well positioned to invade Namibia to install a SWAPO regime.[1298]

The Soviets and their allies also had a hand in *"observing"* the elections in Namibia in 1989 and 1990. The UN transition team (UNTAG) for *"monitoring"* the 1989 elections in Namibia was partially comprised of undemocratic and/or communist states such as Cuba, Libya, Romania, East Germany, and the Soviet Union.[1299] For example, East Germany sent 30 Volkspolizei officers to Namibia as part of the UNTAG team.[1300] It was very possible that the USSR, East Germany, and the other anti-Western participants also peppered their UNTAG delegations with intelligence officers who passed information to their ideological allies SWAPO and Eastern Bloc capitals. Historical precedent backs up this claim. The Polish and Hungarian ICC delegations in Vietnam passed information to the North Vietnamese all the while posing as a disinterested monitoring organization seeking to enforce the Geneva Accords of 1954.[1301]

In early 1989, Soviet officials visited South Africa covertly and overtly at least four times in an observer capacity. The Soviets even attempted to get a KGB officer appointed as an observer. The Soviets also started to transfer its intelligence apparatus from Angola to Namibia/Windhoek. The Soviets also reportedly installed FROG ballistic missiles in southern

[1295] "Soviet Generals Based in Angola Plan Attack" Die Welt June 29, 1978

[1296] Jeffery, Anthea. People's War (Jonathan Ball Publishers, 2009) pages 143-144.

[1297]Shubin, Vladimir. ANC: A View From Moscow (Jacana Media 2009) pages 242-243.

[1298] "South African Defence Force Statement on Cuban Advance in Southern Angola" SAPA June 6, 1988

[1299] Johns, Michael. "Namibian Voters Deny Total Power to SWAPO" The Wall Street Journal December 11, 1989 Accessed From: http://thomas.loc.gov/cgi-bin/query/z?r101:E11DE9-213:

[1300] Lange, Daniel. "The GDR's UNTAG involvement 1989/90" The Journal of Namibian Studies Volume 12 (2012) Accessed From: http://namibian-studies.com/index.php/JNS/article/view/25

[1301] Nash, George H. "Dissolution of the Paris Peace Accords" National Review October 24, 1975

Angola targeted towards South African targets in Namibia.[1302] In June 1991, the USSR established an Embassy in Pretoria, in the Republic of South Africa. It was reported that *"South Africa was limiting (the number of Soviet diplomats) to 15 on the advice of Western intelligence services who feared a greater KGB presence."*[1303] After the *"collapse"* of the Soviet Union, it appeared that Red China took over the task of supporting the South African Communist Party. Since the South African Communist Party played a larger role in governance after 1994, they also acquired funds from various state investment projects.[1304]

The Soviets and their allies continued the effort to subvert South Africa through political warfare designed to divide the white population against the increasingly reformist De Klerk government. Certainly one avenue for splitting the white population against the Nationalist government was through the avenue of trade and greed. The previously discussed trade relations between the communist world and South Africa clearly illustrated such a possibility. An ANC document that dated from 1969 expounded: *"Nor must we ever be slow to take advantage of differences and divisions which our successes will inevitably spark off to isolate the most vociferous, the most uncompromising, and most reactionary elements among the whites."*[1305] A joint meeting of the entire ANC NEC (National Executive Committee) and RC (Revolutionary Council) was held in Luanda Angola in late December 1978 and early January 1979 to discuss the visit to Vietnam in October 1978 by an ANC NEC delegation. The results of the visit to Vietnam were laid out in <u>The Green Book: Report of the Politico-Military Strategy Commission to the ANC National Executive Committee</u>. It noted in part that "***It is our duty to take full advantage of such secondary contradictions within the enemy camp in order to win over sections of the white community to our cause***."[1306]

Furthermore, delegates from foreign communist countries and parties started to attend conferences in South Africa and Namibia by the end of the late 1980s. In December 1989, the anti-apartheid Conference for a Democratic Future was held in Johannesburg and hosted delegates from the leftist Mass Democratic Movement, Black Consciousness Movement, the Azanian People's Organization, the ANC, and a Soviet academic from Moscow State University, Irina Filatova. One resolution adopted by the Conference *"called on whites to break decisively with apartheid and to take to the streets, while another said that campaigns would be initiated to 'educate' conscripts and black security force members about the role of the SADF."*[1307] In July 1991, the ANC National Congress hosted delegations from the Anti-Apartheid Movement in Britain, Kairos, from the Netherlands, leftist anti-apartheid groups from the US, Europe, and

---

[1302] Vanneman, Peter. <u>Soviet Strategy in Southern Africa: Gorbachev's Pragmatic Approach</u> (Hoover Press 1990) pages 44 and 40.

[1303] "Soviets Take First Step to Establish Diplomatic Mission in South Africa" <u>Agence France Presse</u> June 10, 1991

[1304] Ware, Allan and Burnell, Peter J. <u>Funding Democratization</u> (Transaction Publishers, 2006) page 215.

[1305] Roberts, David. "Letter" <u>Commentary Magazine</u> December 1, 1988 Accessed From: http://www.commentarymagazine.com/article/the-anc/

[1306] The Green Book: Report of the Politico-Military Strategy Commission to the ANC National Executive Committee, August 1979 Accessed From: http://www.marxists.org/subject/africa/anc/1979/green-book.htm

[1307] "Anti-Apartheid Conference in Johannesburg" <u>BBC Summary of World Broadcasts</u> December 11, 1989

Scandinavia, along with communist and socialist parties from Europe, Africa, and Middle East, including delegates from Qaddafi's Libya, the Arab Baath Socialist Party of Iraq, and the PLO.[1308] In December 1991, the Communist Parties of Cuba, Portugal, China, and France attended the South African Communist Party Congress. South African Communist Party National Organizer Charles Nqakula even remarked that *"Cuba is a democratic country."*[1309] In December 1991, a delegation of FRELIMO attended the South African Communist Party Congress.[1310] After the *"collapse"* of the Soviet Union, it appeared that Red China took over the task of supporting the South African Communist Party. Since the SACP played a larger role in governance after 1994, they also acquired funds from various investment projects.[1311]

After the collapse of apartheid and the ushering in of the ANC-South African Communist Party dominated government, South Africa descended back into a dictatorial government that was also aligned against the interests of the United States. The South African government implemented the features of crony-capitalist and socialist economics that were major features of its ideological allies and military backers. However, the ANC realized that nationalizing all industries and banks and imposing a violent purge would not be in its long-range interests. The 51st National Conference of the ANC was called Preface to the Strategy and Tactics of the ANC: People's Power in Action and was drawn up in late December 2002. It stipulated that *"In this ideological struggle, the ANC needs clearly to define itself in relation to modern expressions of class and sectoral interests. The principal ideological currents, in this era of globalization, in terms of which we need to contrast our own positions are neo-liberalism and modern ultra-leftism. On the one extreme is the ideology of rampant capitalism, a system in which, as the Strategy and Tactics explains, formal democracy should be underpinned; by market forces to which all should kneel in the prayer: 'everyone for himself and the Devil takes the hindmost!' This is at the core of the ideology of neo-liberalism and other such worldviews, which dare the democratic state to emasculate itself. On the other extreme are ultra-left practices, assumptions and ideologies. A common feature of ultra-leftist tendencies is subjectivism; a confusion of what is 'desirable' with what is actually and immediately possible. This results in all manner of voluntaristic adventures, including the advocacy of impossible and dangerous great leaps forward, which reflects a systematic inability to understand the dynamic complexity of objective factors. In our South African conditions, ultra-leftism has historically been impatient with the national grievance of the oppressed and dismissive of the national democratic struggle and of the ANC-led Alliance. It fails to understand the national question as being a profoundly objective reality, shaped by centuries of colonial domination. As such, it advocates a working class struggle that should be waged purely and only in 'direct' pursuit of a system without exploitation. This would be achieved in a simplistic and dramatic abolition of the capitalist market with the state seizing the means of production."*[1312]

[1308]"ANC Spokesman on Delegates; Messages of Support" Radio RSA July 5, 1991

[1309] Chaise, Christain. "South Africa's Communist Diehards Soldier On" Agence France Presse December 4, 1991

[1310]"Mozambican Ruling Party Sends Delegation to SACP Congress" Radio Mozambique December 7, 1991

[1311] Ware, Allan and Burnell, Peter J. Funding Democratization (Transaction Publishers, 2006) page 215.

[1312] 51st National Conference: Preface to the Strategy and Tactics of the ANC People's Power in Action December 20, 2002 Accessed From: http://www.anc.org.za/show.php?id=2496

This did not mean that South Africa moved from the strict state controls of apartheid to a relatively free market economy. Jim Peron noted that *"The government of Mandela's African National Congress (ANC) was imposing policy on the country. The de facto deregulation of the last years of NP rule gave way to the re-regulation of the ANC. Censorship laws that had been declared unconstitutional were rewritten, and the Board of Publications was once again in operation. In some ways its powers were expanded. The new board can also place legal restrictions on films, videos, and computer games for material that is deemed to be stereotypical or prejudiced regarding race, sex, ethnicity, or religion."* Peron also observed that *"The mom-and-pop casinos were replaced with a few licensed operations favoring ANC supporters."* The ANC partners in the South African government were the Congress of South African Trade Unions (COSATU) and the South African Communist Party (SACP). At a COSATU rally, ANC Secretary General Kgalema Motlanthe urged workers *"to intensely hate capitalism and engage in a struggle against it."* Motlanthe noted that the ANC is *"not a bourgeois organization. The country's leading socialist minds are in the ANC. Anyone who argues for socialism will find allies in the ANC."* The Employment Equity Act of 1998 (EEA), banned *"unfair discrimination"* in private businesses on 19 grounds including race and sex. Companies were required to draw up and submit to the ANC government its plans for the setting of numerical goals for equitable representation of specified races. Peron noted that *"More than one commentator noticed that the new legislation was quite similar to the old apartheid laws, with the favored categories changing places with the previously unfavored groups."* The ANC regime announced its support for the Communist Cuban health care system. Cuba sent medical personnel to South Africa under the ANC regime. ANC/South African President Zuma ordered South African youth to perform one year of service to the state. This was dubbed *"service training.* " The large element of avowed Marxists within the ANC regime opposed any privatization of state companies. The state-owned telephone company ESCOM was turned into a private corporation owned by the state. The ANC government was the majority stockholder. Twenty percent of the government-owned South African Airways was sold to Swissair. The remaining 80% was government-owned. The *"black empowerment"* companies were owned by ANC and trade union officials. ANC negatively branded free market economics as *"mutant liberalism"* or *"libertarianism."*[1313]

Meanwhile, the ANC demanded labor discipline from South African workers. This was not an uncommon feature of communist regimes who sought foreign investment to bolster their economic position. Mandela also warned the workers that they needed to *"tighten your belts"* and *"accept low wages so that investment would flow."* Mandela also had an *"attachment to the glamour of the very rich…Money was dazzling. Hence, once freed, he holidayed at the Irish businessman Sir Tony O'Reilly's Caribbean island and gave the go-ahead for his takeover of South Africa's biggest newspaper group, in anticipation of his 'magic money' providing black empowerment in the media. He allowed the casino king, Sol Kerzner, to host the wedding of his daughter Zinzi. He borrowed rich men's houses and flew around South Africa in their aircraft."*[1314]

[1313]Peron, James. "South Africa's Polarized Politics" <u>The Freeman</u> January 1, 2001 Accessed From:http://www.fee.org/the_freeman/detail/south-africas-polarized-politics#axzz2mo61RVH6

[1314]O'Connor, Patrick. "Former South African President Nelson Mandela Dies" World Socialist Website December 6, 2013 Accessed From: http://www.wsws.org/en/articles/2013/12/06/mand-d06.html

Even the hard-line SACP/ANC official and Minister of National Defense Ronnie Kasrils was concerned about the repression of dissent in ANC-ruled South Africa. He wrote that "*I had become concerned long before the Macia incident of reports of beatings and torture in police cells. There had also been almost 800 reported deaths in police custody in 2010-2011, constant attacks on protest demonstrations, 'shoot to kill' exhortations of police ministers, numerous reports involving police corruption, the use of conspiracy theories to deal with opponents of government and the move to strengthen the powers of the government security cluster by dubious means. Add to this the bizarre occasion where six young would-be recruits perished in a Pietermaritzburg recruitment drive recently and one has a picture of a force bordering on chaos.*"[1315] After the transition to ANC rule in 1994, elements of the white South African police and SADF were integrated into the Spear of the Nation forces and hence the new SADF. ANC commanders such as Chris Hani and Joe Modise encouraged this. Captain Dirk Coetze, a police assassin, was also welcomed into the new police forces.[1316] The "*New South Africa*" soon became similar, in some respects, to the old Nationalist Party, with all of the cronyism, quasi-socialist economics, and repression of dissent. Plus, the "*New South Africa*" became a reliable ally of Russia, China, and other anti-Western powers.

Malawi Under President Hastings Banda (1965-1991)

In 1965, Great Britain granted Malawi independence with Dr. Hastings Banda as the new president of that country. Banda ostensibly represented a fraction of the anti-colonial forces that were still pro-Western and anti-communist. President Banda ruled as an iron fisted authoritarian who maintained trade, military, and intelligence relations with the United States, Great Britain, West Germany, and even apartheid South Africa. Banda's movement, the Malawi Congress Party (MCP) became the only governing party in Malawi. It established various official organizations, such as the Young Pioneers, that mobilized various segments of civil society. President Banda portrayed himself as a stalwart opponent of socialism and communism and a believer in capitalism. However, one must ask: was Banda's public image truthful?

In reality, while the economy of Malawi under Banda was not technically communist or socialist, it was subjected to state control and vast amounts of governmental cronyism. State interventionism in Malawi arose as a result of economic nationalism, political authoritarianism, and the desire for top government officials to line their pockets. The Banda government even created the legal machinery for unjustified confiscation of private property. Private businesses were acquired by the government through the Forfeiture Act of 1966. Party officials, Young Pioneers, and party workers acquired the property from Asians and dissidents that were expelled from Malawi after independence. It was estimated that 300 properties were confiscated by the Forfeiture Act between 1966 and 1984. Many of these confiscated properties were absorbed by Banda's personal, quasi-state enterprise called Press Holdings. By 1977, Press Holdings gross turnover was 1/3 of the GDP in Malawi. The state sector was also quite large in allegedly capitalist Malawi. State-owned companies in Malawi included ADMARC, ESCOM, MDC, Air

---

[1315] Kasrils, Ronnie. "Mr President, Arrest This Descent Into Police State Depravity" <u>Mail and Guardian</u> March 6, 2013 Accessed From: <u>http://mg.co.za/article/2013-03-06-mr-president-arrest-this-descent-into-police-state-depravity</u>

[1316] Trewhela, Paul. "Inside Quadro" <u>Searchlight South Africa</u> July 1990 Number 5 Accessed From: <u>http://www.marxists.org/history/etol/revhist/supplem/hirson/quadro.html</u>

Malawi, Malawi Housing, the Malawi Book Service, the Malawi Broadcasting Corporation, the Export Promotions Council, and the various tobacco, sugar, and coffee small holder's authorities. The Malawi state-owned banks provided funding to a favored group of wealthy Malawians under President Banda. Lawanda accurately noted that *"The MCP and indeed Dr. Banda's government was in many respects like the Russian Politburo was under the strong leaders like Stalin and Khrushchev. What capitalism the Party permitted was only for those allowed to participate…"* He also wrote that *"Within what was perceived as an efficient and capitalistic Malawi economy there was a streak of Stalinism. In fact the present commentator likens the Malawi economy under Banda to an East European economy except for the name. The Malawi parastatals for example ADMARC and even Press Holdings itself were run like the monopolized industries would be run in East Europe or sixties Britain."*[1317] Managers at David Whitehead and Sons (DWS) and the Eastern and Central African Railway Ltd claimed that *"the MCP government viewed companies as state property as the party relied on companies to fund conventions; public functions and party cards drive campaigns."*[1318]

The labor unions and workers in general were severely controlled by the MCP and President Banda's government. Private and state-owned corporation boards appreciated the fact that labor was strictly controlled in Malawi, thus assuring maximum production. MCP functionaries on the shop floor ensured the ideological loyalty of the workers to the concepts of unity, loyalty, obedience and discipline. At the 1965 Malawi Congress Party (MCP) convention, the Trade Union Congress (TUCM) was recognized as the only labor organization that was approved by the state. In October 1986, the official <u>Daily Times</u> noted that *"Everyone holding a responsible position in the party, Government or any organisation associated with the party would be in that position as long as he/she worked within the framework of the party."* The Chairman of the Employers Consultative Association remarked at its April 1979 annual general meeting in Blantyre that they were thankful for the *"continued industrial peace under the wise and dynamic leadership of His Excellency Ngwazi Dr Kamuzu Banda."*

In May 1966, TUCM general secretary Kelly Zidana warned that *"our demands must be economically possible, supported by solid economic facts and morally justified…they must not be selfish demands which make progress at the expense of equally needy people."* At a closing ceremony of the Trade Unions' Seminar at Chancellor College in August 1970, TUCM Chairman Justin Liabunya remarked that the *"primary aim (of the unions) was to find out how they could help the President Ngwazi Dr Kamuzu Banda, to develop the country."* In February 1986, the Plantation and Agriculture Workers Union Acting General Secretary warned members to follow the order of employers so that they *"could help the Ngwazi develop the country economically."* In July 1972, the Minister of Labour ordered a group of migrant workers destined for South Africa: *"Don't copy the bad behaviour of your friends from neighbouring countries, instead obey your employers' orders and work hard."* In August 1991, the Minister of Labor urged trade union leaders to not emulate foreign ideologies that were not in line *"with the tradition and aspiration of our leaders and Governments."*[1319]

[1317] Lwanda, John. <u>Kamazu Banda of Malawi</u> (Glasgow: Dudu Nsomba Publishers, 1993) pages 91-94.

[1318] Dzimbiri, Lewis B. "The State and Labour Control in Malawi: Continuities and Discontinuities Between One-party and Multiparty Systems" <u>Africa Development</u> Volume XXX Number 4 2005 Accessed From: http://community.eldis.org/.59dbaaff

[1319] Ibid.

Even the ideological statements of Banda and MCP officials explicitly did not endorse free market capitalism. President Banda noted that "*In Malawi, we can not have capitalism of the American type where railways, airways, electricity and water facilities, the telephone and telegraph system are all in private hands, to say nothing of shops and industry…On the other hand we could not have the communism of the Russians and Chinese, where the state owns everything and people are not allowed to own anything at all, not even their own children…So we have to have something mid-way. The government has to do certain things. Let the government through statutory bodies own the railway, airways, water, electricity. But the people must own their own land on which to have their own houses; people must be allowed to have shops, to have farms and estates."* A high-level MCP official Dunduzu Chisize remarked that "*We pursue happiness by rejecting…individualism…and by emphasis on a communal way of life.*"[1320]

Despite the harsh repression of the Left and alignment with the noncommunist world, President Banda also maintained some relations with various communist powers. Some like Mozambique was a neighbor of Malawi, while other communist powers were known for creating highly regimented and disciplined societies that were models for President Banda and the MCP. Initially, the Banda dictatorship desired to maintain proper relations with its newly independent neighbor in FRELIMO-ruled Mozambique. Sometimes this translated into assisting FRELIMO in deporting and arresting anti-communist Mozambicans. The Banda regime in enticed Mozambican exile activist Simango to Malawi from Kenya and handed him over to FRELIMO troops at the Milange border post. Banda also handed over PCN officials and members to FRELIMO soldiers at the Milange border post, where the Frelimo security chief Joao Honwana awaited them.[1321]

While Malawi later assisted anti-FRELIMO guerrillas by the 1980s, MCP and FRELIMO delegation continued to meet at annual party congresses. Both sides expressed a degree of political solidarity with each other. Other African communist and radical leftist parties and guerrilla movements were also in attendance at MCP congresses. In October 1979, a Mozambican FRELIMO delegation attended a Malawi Congress Party convention.[1322] In September 1983, a FRELIMO Party delegation led by Mozambican Ambassador Daniel Mbanze attended a Malawi Congress Party conference. Other ruling parties that attended the conference included delegations from the Revolutionary Party of Tanzania, the United National Independence Party of Zambia, the African National Union Party of Zimbabwe, the Democratic Party of Botswana, and the Popular Revolutionary Movement of Zaire.[1323] In September 1984, delegations from Mozambique, Tanzania, Zambia, and Zimbabwe attended the convention of the Malawi Congress Party.[1324]

In October 1986, FRELIMO Major-General Bonifacio Masamba noted at the Malawi Party Congress convention that the "*Mozambicans will work closely with Malawians to improve the standard of living of the people in the two countries.*" A report indicated that President

---

[1320] Pryor, Frederic L. <u>Malawi and Madagascar</u> (Oxford University Press, 1990) page 38.

[1321] Cabrita, Joao. <u>Mozambique: The Tortuous Road to Democracy</u> (Palgrave, 2000) pages 80-81.

[1322] "Frelimo delegation's visit to Malawi" <u>BBC Summary of World Broadcasts</u> October 9, 1979

[1323] "Frelimo delegation at Malawi Congress Party conference" <u>BBC Summary of World Broadcasts</u> September 7, 1983

[1324] "Malawi Congress Party convention" <u>Blantyre radio</u> September 5, 1984

Machel instructed Major-General Bonifacio Masamba *"to tell the delegates that the people of the two countries are brothers and sisters. He said the boundaries separating the two countries were created by colonialists."* Masamba noted that *"Now that the two countries are independent, President Machel would like the women, the youth and the soldiers to be united and work together for the benefit of the two countries."* General Masamba urged *"the people of the two countries to be vigilant against those elements which tried to cause confusion among the people of the two states."* He also *"wanted the people of Mozambique and Malawi to observe unity, loyalty, obedience and discipline."*[1325]

In September 1989, President Banda met with the Mozambican delegation to the Malawi Congress Party convention led by Frelimo Central Committee member Feliciano Gundana.[1326] In September 1989, delegations from Tanzania, Zaire, Zambia, and Zimbabwe also attended the congress of the Malawi Congress Party. President Banda noted that *"people from other countries were most welcome in Malawi."* Banda *"expressed happiness that ruling parties in the neighbouring countries represented at the convention were able to send delegations...This afternoon, delegations from sister parties in Tanzania, Zambia, and Zaire addressed the convention, delivering fraternal greetings from their parties. In their speeches, the leaders of the delegations praised the friendly relations between Malawi and the respective countries. They praised the country's leadership, noting that under the Malawi Congress Party Malawi remained the shining example...in terms of economic and political stability. The three delegations hoped that this regional co-operation would continue for the benefit of the people and governments of these countries."*[1327] In September 1991, a delegation from the ANC attended the convention of the Malawi Congress Party.[1328]

It also appeared that Malawi under President Banda maintained close relations with the allegedly *"independent"* communist regime of President Ceausescu in Romania. Perhaps Banda fell into the trap that Romania represented a *"maverick"* and *"anti-Soviet"* member of the Warsaw Pact, and thus worthy of political relations. In October 1985, a delegation from the Romanian Communist Party Central Committee led by Maxim Berghianu attended the congress of the Malawi Congress Party. Blantyre radio reported that Berghianu *"praised the life president's policies which he said enabled the country to develop in various fields within a short period of time. He also expressed the hope that bilateral relations between Romania and Malawi would grow from strength to strength."*[1329] In September 1986, a delegation from the Romanian Communist Party Central Committee led by Alexandru Szabo attended the Malawi Congress Party convention.[1330]

While FRELIMO espoused solidarity and a general desire for positive relations with President Banda and MCP dictatorship, Mozambique also chose to subvert and even draw up

---

[1325] "Mozambican Delegate Addresses Malawi Party Convention" <u>Mana/PANA</u> October 2, 1986
[1326] "Malawi Banda Closes Party Convention Defends Women's Movement Against Criticism" <u>Malawi Broadcasting Corporation</u> October 3, 1989
[1327] "Malawi Banda receives foreign delegates to party congress" <u>Malawi Broadcasting Corporation</u> September 27, 1989
[1328] "Malawi Banda Opens Party Convention; ANC Delegation Attends" <u>Malawi Broadcasting Corporation</u> September 24, 1991
[1329] "Romanian delegation to Malawi Party convention departs" <u>Blantyre home service</u> October 12, 1985
[1330] "Romanian party delegation arrives in Malawi" <u>Blantyre home service</u> September 30, 1986

invasion plans with Malawi as the target. Attempts were made to manipulate the Malawian youth and armed forces through cultural and cooperation exchanges. Mozambique opened their borders to leftist anti-Banda guerrillas coming from Tanzania.[1331]

A Soviet trained FRELIMO commander Daniel Caetano defected and revealed that Machel was turning Mozambique into a springboard for the communist conquest of Africa. He stated that *"Machel has turned the country into a training base for blacks from African moderate states, labeled by him as puppets of the capitalist and imperialist forces."* Caetano revealed that leftists from Zimbabwe, Malawi, Swaziland, and Kenya trained at these camps. He stated: *"There they receive military training and communist indoctrination and are later sent back to their countries to foment uprisings against their governments."* Caetano also claimed that the planes, tanks, and missiles were to be used by FRELIMO and allied communists for the conquest of Africa: *"Machel's ambition is to turn the African continent into a continent of communist states against the will of the peoples of those countries."*[1332]

According to captured documents, former Mozambican communist president Samora Machel recommended that: *"Mozambique and Zimbabwe must bring into being a new force in Malawi. Banda is worn out. We must not allow South Africa to set the course in Malawi. We must not allow the English, Americans and the Federal Republic of Germany to choose the Malawi leaders. The Army knows how these things must be done…We can also organize a Malawi Liberation Front, equip ourselves and infiltrate into Malawi in order to destroy the bandits (the Renamo guerrillas) who are there. We may also define the targets for such a front for the liberation of Malawi."* Machel laid out this aggressive plan against Malawi to a secret conference with the Zimbabwean Minister of State Security Emmerson Munangagwa, the Zimbabwean Ambassador to Mozambique H.E. Mvundura, Minister of Defense E.R. Kadungure, Zimbabwean Army Commander General Rex Nhongo, Air Marshal J. Tungamirai, Maj-Gen Maseko, and Lt-Col Shumba, of the Zimbabwe National Army. Soviet and Cuban officials were also present at this planning meeting. Machel noted that *"'military men' had to place 'all available means in Zambezia,' the province bordering Malawi…'We have some special forces for special operations, we have about 41 MiG-21 (jet fighters)…the victory is being planned…it demands cold-bloodedness.' The transport of troops and equipment of Zambezia and Tete provinces was discussed, with the vital role Zimbabwe's transport facilities would play here, and the organization of medical services and food."* Machel also stated that *"The military action had to be backed by political action and Malawi had to be persuaded to allow Zimbabwean troops to cross its territory into Zambezia. The people of Malawi had to be convinced the Mozambique and Zimbabwe forces were in 'solidarity' with them and not their government. Mr. Munangagwa told President Machel, 'there is a force ready to go,' but that there were preparations that had to be jointly made with Zimbabwe. Problems with the transport of military hardware from Mozambique harbours were also raised…"*[1333]

Rhodesia Under Ian Smith and the Rhodesia Front

[1331] Cabrita, Joao. Mozambique: The Tortuous Road to Democracy (Palgrave, 2000) pages 80-84.

[1332] "Resistance Leader Hits Out" To The Point January 19, 1979

[1333] South African Press Association "South Africa Says Zimbabwe and Mozambique Planned to Attack Malawi" BBC Summary of World Broadcasts November 6, 1986

In 1965, the white minority population in British Rhodesia launched its Unilateral Declaration of Independence (UDI). This exercise in declaring Rhodesia an independent nation was carried through by the nationalist Rhodesia Front (RF) under the leadership of Ian Smith. Much of the international community isolated Rhodesia from political and economic relations. Furthermore, Soviet and Chinese-supplied and trained communist rebels fought against Rhodesian government troops. These rebels of ZANU/ZAPU (later united as the Patriotic Front) won much sympathy within international liberal and progressive circles. Soon the United States and Great Britain slowly encouraged the Smith government to hold elections and grant increased power to the native African population. Meanwhile, American anti-communists were largely sympathetic to the plight of Rhodesia and its battle against ZAPU/ZANU forces. Smith's government was the subject of admiration and the Rhodesian economy was viewed as an example of free enterprise in action.

In reality, the Smith government and the Rhodesian economy were both rigidly controlled systems. This reality was the product of two factors: international sanctions and the siege mentality that developed henceforth and an ideological bias towards highly statist formulas for economic nationalism. It appeared that pre-1965 British Rhodesia was following the paths set by the socialist Labor Party in the mother country. By 1945, the Rhodesian state created various industries such as electric power plants, Cold Storage Commission, the Rhodesia Iron and Steel Corporation, and the Sugar Industry Board and its Triangle Estate. The government also subsidized the production maize and other types of products through price supports. These measures had the effect of undercutting the African producers in Rhodesia. In the early 1950s, the Rhodesians enacted comprehensive price controls. The government guaranteed the prices of farm products and purchased the crops from the producers. Industrial plants were protected by high tariffs and had access to cheap laborers. One historian referred to this state of affairs as *"Socialism for the Whites."* In 1971, the Rhodesian Permanent Secretary for Internal Affairs W.H.H Nicole stated *"the strength of our position soon revealed itself because we became masters in our own house through the good fortunes of sanctions which had so effectively removed the villains who had previously manipulated our development and had dictated our progress through the fraudulent device of international capital."* One Rhodesian government official during UDI justified these *"dictatorial powers"* to protect the *"financial and political security"* of Rhodesia. Meanwhile, the Rhodesian Front (RF) controlled the political process during the UDI period.[1334]

The Rhodesians also mimicked their South African allies and communist adversaries in utilizing propaganda operations to sway global public opinion in favor of the Smith government. In 1966, Rhodesian Front member Brigadier Skeen noted Rhodesia's *"best weapon in the Cold War"* against her was propaganda and approved a Rhodesian budget for the Ministry of Information, Immigration, and Tourism and an additional budget for *"publicity."*[1335]

In February 1966 the Rhodesians opened an Information Office in Washington DC with Henry J.C. Hooper as its head. It disseminated propaganda such as Rhodesian Commentary which attacked British *"fiddling"* in Africa. The publications were printed by the Rhodesian

---

[1334] Herbst, Jeffrey. State Politics in Zimbabwe (University of California Press, 1990) pages 19-27.

[1335] Laurence, John. The Seeds of Disaster (Gollancz, 1968)

Ministry of Information, Immigration, and Tourism.[1336] Rhodesian Information Office head Hooper noted that 12 US groups were established as of March 1966 to oppose the British-US embargo on Rhodesia.[1337] There were two or three Rhodesian Information Offices in the world in the 1960s. They were located in the United States, France, and Australia. The Rhodesians also maintained formal diplomatic relations with only South Africa and Portugal.

Despite the international embargo, the United States also maintained trade relations with Rhodesia under the Smith government. The Byrd Amendment of 1971 allowed the United States to import *"strategic and critical materials"* from Rhodesia into the United States. According to May 1973 testimony by former British Foreign Minister official Barbara Rogers, American firms such as RCA, ITT, and Reuters Ltd supplied Rhodesia with communications facilities and equipment. Air Rhodesia and the Rhodesian National Tourist Board operated offices in New York City. Hertz and Avis Rent-a-Car companies also maintained operations in Rhodesia. South African Airways, Air Rhodesia, and Air Malawi operated directly in Salisbury. In 1972, the Journal of Commerce noted in an advertisement that *"The Rhodesian Promotion Council ... which aims to promote knowledge of Rhodesia's economic development and potential ... please write to the Director who will be glad to supply you with the appropriate information and, if desired, to assist in travel arrangements and appropriate appointments. Industrial Development Corporation of Southern Rhodesia, Ltd...Interested industrialists are invited to contact us. Whatever your product, the most profitable way to enter the Rhodesian market is via The Standard Bank...Rhodesia Exports, too...Rhodesia's Information Office in Washington...knows a lot about the country-economics, trade, finance, raw materials and the people who count Bulawayo...a fine City for any industrialist to establish himself. The Associated Chambers of Commerce of Rhodesia ...Rhodesian businessmen believe in the country's future and the growth potential is such that foreign businessmen can make profitable investment in confidence."* These advertisements were paid for by Rhodesian companies through the Rhodesian Promotion Council.[1338]

Amazingly, while Moscow and Beijing were pouring resources into the ZANU/ZAPU arsenals and war chests, trade relations were also occurring between communist regimes and the Smith regime. Trade sources in Zambia informed Alan Hutchison that China imported Rhodesian tobacco through West Germany. Officials in the mining trade in Sudan also informed Alan Hutchison that China imported Rhodesian chrome as of 1972.[1339]

As of 1979, the UN Sanctions Committee reported that the USSR bought chrome from Rhodesia through Swiss front companies. This chrome was resold by the Soviets to the US at a high profit. The trade began in 1970. A captain of a Soviet ship docking in Mozambique noted *"Russia is interested only in doing business."* In the early years of UN sanctions, Rhodesian exports to the USSR were channeled through Portuguese Mozambique and as of 1979, South African ports were used. Rhodesian exports were also sold to Bulgaria, Romania, and Czechoslovakia. Even after Frelimo closed the border with Rhodesia, the white minority regime shipped tobacco and maize through the port of Maputo in Mozambique. For example, in March

---

[1336] "Rhodesia Opens An Office in US: Information Center Causes Distress in Washington" New York Times February 5, 1966 page 3.

[1337] Welles, Benjamin. "U.S. May Deport Smith Aide" New York Times March 2, 1966 page 19.

[1338] Park, Stephen and Lake, Anthony. "Business as Usual: Transactions Violating Rhodesian Sanctions" Issue: A Journal of Opinion, Volume 3, Number 2 Summer, 1973 pages 7-17.

[1339] Hutchison, Alan. China's African Revolution (Westview Press, 1976) pages 197-198.

1976, the Soviet ship Mikhail Kedrov was loaded in a Maputo port with Rhodesian tobacco. Officials of a Swiss front company visited Moscow and Sofia to arrange sales of Rhodesian tobacco to Bulgartabac and Razndexport.[1340] The USSR sold Rhodesian chrome to the United States at double the price in violation of the UN sanctions as of May 1979. Rhodesian chrome was sold to the USSR as far back as 1970 and then resold to the United States at a profit. The Soviets bought the Rhodesian ore at $32 per ton and the USSR sold it to the US at $58 per ton.[1341]

The United States under President Carter and Britain under Prime Minister Thatcher greased the diplomatic skids for the transition in Rhodesia to Marxist-Leninist rule. Mugabe himself praised President Carter for his "*solo effort*" of 1978-79 in blocking American recognition of the coalition government of Prime Minister Abel Muzorewa government. Mugabe also added that "*we need the friendship and solidarity of the United States just as we needed it during the struggle.*"[1342] Other American officials downplayed the Marxist ideology of ZANU and ZAPU. Assistant Secretary of State for African Affairs Richard M. Moose testified before a subcommittee of the United States Congress on March 27, 1980 about the nature of the nascent Mugabe dictatorship. Moose noted "*In the past Prime Minister Mugabe was labeled a dedicated Marxist in many circles…However, I believe we should judge him in an African context and deal with him both on his presently stated intentions and his future actions…he has adopted a moderate and conciliatory approach in recent months, and his initial steps in the post-election period have been encouraging.*" Even as evidence of ZANU communist repression mounted in the newly independent Zimbabwe, the American government chose not to speak out on behalf of the oppressed. Author Geoff Hill criticized President Carter for keeping "*quiet as Mugabe nationalized the press, committed genocide against minority tribes and subverted (Zimbabwe's) constitution to make himself the sole source of authority.*"[1343]

The Zimbabwe African National Union (ZANU) and the Zimbabwe African People's Union (ZAPU) were both communist guerrilla movements that fought to overthrow any noncommunist government-black or white-run-and replace it with a Marxist-Leninist dictatorship. The literature of ZAPU and ZANU were very explicit in their promotion of communism. The official political programme of ZANU supported, as of 1975, the creation of "*A truly socialist, self-supporting economy would be established and organized on broad principles enunciated by Marxism-Leninism.*" The publication, Basic Information about ZANU, noted that "*ZANU is guided by the principles of Marxism-Leninism. It aims at achieving a socialist revolution.*" Edward Ndhlovu, the ZAPU Deputy National Secretary, stated in December 1974 that "*As for ZAPU, it is no secret that we base our work on the principles of Marxism-Leninism and that our ideological position is rooted in the masses. The struggle to create a new society such as we are striving for must be based on the principles of scientific socialism. We are committed to a programme of establishing a socialist state and society in*

[1340] McDonald, Larry P. "Russia Defies Rhodesia Trade Boycott" Congressional Record June 5, 1979 pages 13580-13581.

[1341] "Russia Reported Selling U.S. Rhodesian Chrome" New York Times May 28, 1979 page A11.

[1342] Zimbabwe: A Country Study (Foreign Area Studies, American University August 1982) Accessed From: http://www.dtic.mil/dtic/tr/fulltext/u2/a135022.pdf

[1343] "United States-Zimbabwe Relations" Accessed From: http://en.wikipedia.org/wiki/United_States%E2%80%93Zimbabwe_relations

Zimbabwe, and this we will do."[1344] In December 1985, ZANU and ZAPU unified and dissolved their differences. In a speech on this alliance, Mugabe noted that "*We all agreed that it would be socialism based on Marxism-Leninism. But we still differ on the fundamental issue of what form this will be that will constitute the unity forum for ZANU (PF) and ZAPU.*"[1345] Even into the 1990s and beyond, Mugabe and ZANU clung to Marxism-Leninism and anti-capitalism as its guiding ideologies. For example, Mugabe noted in September 1990 "*The (ZANU) party leadership must, however, not lose their political and ideological bearings and embark on selfish adventures or ventures as they seek for themselves green pastures in the land of capitalism where the masses would forever remain hewers of wood and drawers of water, for even the claim they have to their god-given land would vanish as our socialist approach is dropped in favour of capitalism.*"[1346]

Mugabe and his government also had a penchant to openly encouraged brutality and mass human rights violations directed at anti-communist opponents and class enemies. Didymus Mutasa, a ZANU party official remarked in January 2003 that "*We would be better off with only 6 million people, with our own people who support the liberation struggle. We don't want all these extra people.*" In July 2004, when the communist land confiscations were in full steam, Mugabe commented that "*Absolute power is when a man is starving and you are the only one able to give him food.*"[1347]

The Soviets, Chinese, North Koreans, various African leftwing dictatorships, and the Eastern European Communist countries all provided weapons and training to the ZANU and ZAPU terrorists.[1348] In addition, plans were laid for a conventional communist invasion of Rhodesia as a means of overthrowing the Smith government. In 1979, Rhodesian intelligence sources reported that the Soviets held a high-level meeting in Lusaka, Zambia. The topic covered at the meeting was a conventional invasion of Rhodesia. The Soviets planned the invasion with tanks, APCs, and MIG fighter jets. The pilots and troops were to be from ZIPRA, Cuba, East Germany, and the USSR. The USSR event sent MIG-25s into Rhodesian airspace to test their reactions to a clear Soviet provocation.[1349]

After Mugabe took power after the betrayal of Zimbabwe-Rhodesia and its coalition government of Prime Minister Abel Muzorewa in 1980, relations were deepened with Red China and North Korea. Despite initial mistrust of the Soviet Union, Mugabe sought to cooperate with that communist power as well. In December 1985 Mugabe signed a party to party agreement

---

[1344] Information Section Ministry of Foreign Affairs Rhodesia SLB/CGR 28 November 1975 "Communist Support and Assistance to Nationalist Political Groups in Rhodesia" Accessed From: http://www.rhodesia.nl/commsupp.htm

[1345] "Reported agreement between ZANU and ZAPU over ideology" SAPA January 1, 1986

[1346] "Zimbabwe Mugabe warns party meeting on dangers of capitalism" SAPA September 26, 1990

[1347] Bogdanor, Paul. "The Communists As They Really Are" Accessed From: http://www.paulbogdanor.com/left/communists.html

[1348] Information Section Ministry of Foreign Affairs Rhodesia SLB/CGR 28 November 1975 "Communist Support and Assistance to Nationalist Political Groups in Rhodesia" Accessed From: http://www.rhodesia.nl/commsupp.htm

[1349] War in Rhodesia Books on Ebay Accessed From: http://www.militaryphotos.net/forums/showthread.php?49154-War-in-Rhodesia-Books-on-Ebay/page2

with Gorbachev and he also met with Konstantin Katushev who handled Soviet arms exports to the Third World. The USSR sent Zimbabwe 20 T-54 tanks. Out of 62 Soviet Embassy staffers in Harare, 22 were KGB and GRU agents. Zimbabwe also negotiated with the USSR to buy MIG-29 jet fighters.[1350] The Zimbabwean Central Intelligence Organization (CIO) was trained by the East German Stasi.[1351] The Zimbabwean Army's Fifth Brigade was financed by Red China and trained by North Korean soldiers and officers.[1352]

In October 1980 Mugabe signed an agreement with the North Korean leadership that stipulated that 106 North Korean military advisors would train and equip 3,500 soldiers loyal to Mugabe's political party, the Zimbabwe African National Union (ZANU). Mugabe was supposedly having trouble with internal *"malcontents."* In August 1981, the advisors arrived in Harare, Zimbabwe's capital, and though the North Koreans were reputed for their toughness, they became infamous for their lavish lifestyles and lack of personal discipline. Subsequently, the first group of North Koreans was phased out in 1982. The second group, under the command of Major General Sin Hyon Dok, trained the notorious Fifth Brigade that would carry out the brutal Gukurahundi campaign. The Fifth Brigade answered to only Mugabe and consequently saw themselves as above the law.[1353]

As stated previously, Mugabe was a strategic pragmatist and maintained trade relations with apartheid South Africa, the United States, and other Western countries. Mugabe did not wish to threaten his power base by moving to full communism, thus potentially setting off an economic collapse. Zimbabwean anti-communists did not look kindly upon Western aid and trade with the ZANU communist dictatorship of Mugabe. Zimbabwe's opposition Radio Truth noted in 1985 that *"The ZANU-PF regime must be congratulated for they have been pulling the wool over the eyes of the Americans in a very cunning manner and guaranteed themselves a measure of support by so doing. They have discovered the secret of continuing aid by the West and the secret is communist rhetoric. The more you stamp and threaten, the more you run down the West and capitalism, the more money you can expect."*[1354]

Such cooperation with the Western and domestic capitalists was supported in the theoretical statements of the ZANU party leadership. In 1981, the Zimbabwean news agencies reported that: *"The Prime Minister, Comrade Mugabe, says Zimbabwe does not intend to nationalize any industry despite being a socialist state. He told leaders of commerce and industry in Bindura that Zimbabwe had inherited an economy which was privately controlled and that it was not the intention of the Government to control the industries. The Prime Minister said we found this economic system and we would like to carry on with the same system. Comrade Mugabe however said the Government intends to improve on this system along*

[1350] Vanneman, Peter. Soviet Strategy in Southern Africa (Hoover Institution Press Stanford University 1990) page 76.

[1351] Schlink, Leo. "Murders in Mugabe torture camps, paper reports" Hobart Mercury (Australia) March 4, 2002 page 12.

[1352] Bloom, John. "Yes, he has no bananas: Mugabe runs out of time...and everything else" The National Interest Number 75 2004 page 103.

[1353] Young, Benjamin R. "Zimbabwe and North Korea: Uranium, elephants, and a massacre" Zimbabwe Situation October 30, 2013 Accessed From:http://www.zimbabwesituation.com/news/zimsit_zimbabwe-and-north-korea-uranium-elephants-and-a-massacre/

[1354] "Radio Truth Criticizes US UK Support for Regime" Radio Truth February 28, 1985

socialist lines and industrialists would be expected to play an important role. He said commerce and industry should not fear anything from the Government as long as it abides by what the state requires them to do. "[1355]

In a New Year's Day Message Mugabe noted in 1983 *"Because the next three years constitute too short a time scale for the implementation of our socialist programme, we have planned that during this period there shall be a role for private enterprises. However, it will be one of our functions as a state to ensure greater control and regulation of this sector so that it is geared to achieving the goals and objectives of the overall plan."* [1356]

In December 1989, the South African Press Association reported that *"Mugabe said 'It has been necessary in our experience to capitalise on the positive gains from the old order where necessary. While we must be clear as to the ideological direction we take and the principles we espouse, namely Marxist-Leninist socialist principles, we must also take full cognisance of the environment and the concrete realities in the context of which we seek to achieve social transformation.'"* [1357]

In the pre-1980 period, ZANU and ZAPU issued statements that expressed tremendous hostility towards Western multinational corporations. For example, one ZANU party statement noted that *"In ideology ZANU is guided by the Marxist-Leninist Principle. ZANU aims to achieve a socialist revolution...All the means of production and exchange will be publicly owned by the people of Zimbabwe...Economic cooperation will be established and strengthened with the socialist world so as to bring capitalist USA, Britain, West Germany, etc., to ultimate doom."* [1358]

However, from the start, Western corporations and governments funneled millions of dollars of aid and trade to the communist regime of Mugabe. In 1981, about 22% of Zimbabwe's exports were shipped to South Africa, while 20% went to West Germany, the United States, Britain, and Italy. Zimbabwe imported 25% of its goods from South Africa in 1981.[1359] As of 1982, South African firms such as the Anglo-American Corporation, Delta Corporation, and South African Breweries were present in Mugabe's Zimbabwe. As of 1982, American investment in Zimbabwe comprised 20% of the total foreign capital in that country. Union Carbide had a large stake in the Zimbabwean chrome mining and refining industry in that country.[1360]

The West also exported armaments to Mugabe's communist armed forces during the 1980s and 1990s. In the period 1980 to 1992, communist Zimbabwe received 13 Hawk-60 jet trainers, 2 Canberra bombers, and 9 Hawker Hunter jet fighters from the British.[1361] As of 1980,

---

[1355] "Mugabe on Government policy on industry" BBC Summary of World Broadcasts November 3, 1981

[1356] "Mugabe's New Year Message" Harare home service January 3, 1983

[1357] "Zimbabwe Mugabe's Address to Inaugural Congress of United Party" SAPA December 21, 1989

[1358] Zimbabwe: A Country Study (Foreign Area Studies, American University August 1982) Accessed From: http://www.dtic.mil/dtic/tr/fulltext/u2/a135022.pdf

[1359] Zimbabwe: A Country Study (Foreign Area Studies, American University August 1982) Accessed From: http://www.dtic.mil/dtic/tr/fulltext/u2/a135022.pdf

[1360] Zimbabwe: A Country Study (Foreign Area Studies, American University August 1982) Accessed From: http://www.dtic.mil/dtic/tr/fulltext/u2/a135022.pdf

[1361] Jeuck, Lukas. "Arms Transfers to Zimbabwe" SIPRI Background Paper March 2011 Accessed From: http://www.nonproliferation.eu/documents/other/lukasjeuck4e9eb3953e58d.pdf

the Zimbabwean Air Force inherited from the old Rhodesian Air Force 17 Hawker Hunter jet fighters, C-47 transport planes, BN-2A transport planes, Italian-made SF-260 training planes, 10 Canberra bombers, 40 Alouette helicopters, and 11 Bell AB-205 helicopters.[1362] In 1988, the British sold Zimbabwe BAe-146 transport aircraft to Mugabe's air force.[1363] During a meeting with Robert Mugabe in 1987, Prime Minister Thatcher agreed to supply Hawk and Harrier jet fighter aircraft to the Zimbabwean Air Force.[1364] A number of these British-made aircraft were inherited by Mugabe after the American and Western pressured the Smith and Muzorewa governments to surrender power to the communists of ZANU.

As the human rights situation deteriorated further and ZANU launched a campaign to confiscate and nationalize farmlands in the 2000s, the West and the United States started to impose partial sanctions in Zimbabwe. The United States first imposed sanctions on communist Zimbabwe in 2003 in response to the so-called "*land reform*" program that nationalized private farms. President George W. Bush signed an order that banned 77 Zimbabwean individuals from conducting business with American corporations. The sanctions did not prohibit general trade and humanitarian assistance funding. In 2012, the United States was Zimbabwe's 11th largest trade partner and total two way commerce totaled $110 million. Despite sanctions, Zimbabwe's trade with the European Union (EU) continued. In 2012, EU-Zimbabwe trade totaled $875 million. The United States and the EU also disbursed hundreds of millions of dollars in aid money.[1365]

Youde commented that "*...for all the talk of Western neocolonialism, Zimbabwe still engages in significant trade with the United Kingdom, the United States and other countries that it has labeled predatory.*" Despite sanctions, trade between the United States and Zimbabwe doubled between 2003 and 2008. Britain imported $1.62 billion in goods from Zimbabwe in 2011.[1366]

Sometimes, Zimbabwean trade with the West was carried out in a surreptitious manner that violated the sanctions. The Och Ziff Company reportedly was the "*silent*" financier of a $100 million loan that was disbursed to the Mugabe regime. The Och Ziff Company paid out the loan as a part of a "*share purchase*" in a mining corporation (CAMEC) that had connections with the ruling party, ZANU-PF. The loan itself was paid to the state-owned Zimbabwe Mining and Development Corporation (ZMDC).[1367]

[1362] "Air Force of Zimbabwe" Aeroflight Accessed From: http://web.archive.org/web/20070704065721/http://www.aeroflight.co.uk/waf/aa-africa/zim/zim-af-home.htm

[1363] "Government Said Buying Arms from PRC, UK, USSR" Radio Truth March 9, 1988

[1364] "UK Reportedly Offers Harrier, Hawk Aircraft" Johannesburg Star July 7, 1987

[1365] "Do Western Sanctions Really Hurt Zimbabwe's Economy? African Leaders Call For A Rethink" International Business Times August 19, 2013 Accessed From: http://www.ibtimes.com/do-western-sanctions-really-hurt-zimbabwes-economy-african-leaders-call-rethink-1390131

[1366] Youde, Jeremy. "The Active Pariah: Zimbabwe's 'Look East' Policy" World Politics Review April 2, 2013 Accessed From: http://www.worldpoliticsreview.com/articles/12825/the-active-pariah-zimbabwes-look-east-policy

[1367] Bell, Alex. "US and UK urged to probe 'sanctions busting' ZANU PF loan" SW Radio Africa May 6, 2014 Accessed From: http://www.swradioafrica.com/2014/05/06/us-and-uk-urged-to-probe-sanctions-busting-zanu-pf-loan/

Zaire under General Mobutu Sese Seko

In 1960, the Congo received its independence from Belgium. The reins of government were turned over to the leftwing, pro-communist leader Patrice Lumumba of the MNC. It was a known fact that the Belgian Communist Party maintained links with Patrice Lumumba and the MNC. After 1960, the Belgian Communists served as intermediaries between the MNC and the Soviet Embassy. Lumumba and his associates/ministers established direct links with the USSR.[1368] Pieter Lessing also personally viewed and reported that crates of Czech arms were destined in early 1960 for Lumumba's MNC and Gizenga's *Parti Solidaire Africaine*.[1369]

Lumumba's governance was both brief and very brutal. One of Lumumba's former Cabinet Ministers Joseph Yav admitted that behind the nationalist veneer, Lumumba was a diehard communist: "*Yes Lumumba is a communist! I know it. I have proof...On his visit to Russia and East Germany he was given money, girls, and lavish hospitality. He never looked behind the glitter to see the real foundation of these slave states.*" Lumumba himself wrote: "*I am convinced that with the unreserved support of the Soviets I shall win the day in spite of everything.*" The Soviets provided Lumumba's MNC with 300,000 rand per month subsidy for the MNC. Even before independence, the MNC possessed 38 cars and 1.3 million rand in Swiss bank accounts. The Soviets also provided the new Congolese Army with 7 officers. A document captured by UN troops that was dated from March 20, 1961 highlighted Lumumba's repressive and bloody plans for the Congo. This document quoted confidential instructions from "*P. Lumumba, Prime Minister*" to the heads of the Congo's provinces. It called for "*terrorism, essential to subdue the population*" and the establishment of an "*absolute dictatorship.*" All oppositionists were to be arrested by the Army, with Lumumba being personally responsible for the arrest of anti-communist separatist leaders Tshombe and Kalonji. Captured rebels were to be flogged 10 times morning and evening for seven days. Repeat offenders were to be imprisoned in underground prison cells and exiled to countries where Lumumba had arranged agreements with to handle these recalcitrant oppositionists.[1370]

He was eventually overthrown and a civil war ensued in the Congo between pro-communist and pro-Western forces. By the mid-1960s, the communists were defeated. In 1965, the pro-Western Congolese President was overthrown by General Mobutu Sese Seko, who proceeded to establish a fascist-collectivist dictatorship. While it presented itself as anti-communist, Mobutu's government did not close relations with the Red nations. The characteristics of the economy were clearly socialistic with a heavy dose of cronyism thrown in the mix during Mobutu's dictatorship.

Mobutu sought to create a revolutionary movement based on a pseudo-leftist, yet anti-communist ideology. In April 1967, Mobutu created the Popular Revolutionary Movement (*Mouvement Populaire de la Revolution* or MPR). In May 1967, the Manifesto of N'Sele was issued by Mobutu, which declared nationalism, revolution, and authenticity as the pillars of the MPR. Revolution was described as a "*truly national revolution, essentially pragmatic*" that

---

[1368] Greig, Ian. The Assault on the West (Foreign Affairs Publishing Company, 1968) page 141.

[1369] Greig, Ian. The Communist Challenge to Africa (Foreign Affairs Publishing Company 1977) page 151.

[1370] Metrowich, F.R. Africa and Communism (Voortrekkerpers, 1967) Accessed From: http://www.rhodesia.nl/Africa%20and%20Communism.pdf

meant *"the repudiation of both capitalism and communism."* One of the main slogans of the Mobutu regime were *"Neither right nor left"* and *"authenticity."* Mobutu noted that *"in our African tradition there are never two chiefs…That is why we Congolese, in the desire to conform to the traditions of our continent, have resolved to group all the energies of the citizens of our country under the banner of a single national party."* Mobutu's MPR also supported the legacy of the communist dictator Patrice Lumumba.[1371] The First Congress of the MPR (1972) opposed capitalism and communism and instead advocated a state-controlled private economy.[1372] The newspaper <u>Salongo</u> confirmed in 1977 that Zaire was in the throes of an *"authentic revolution"* and *"10 years of struggle against capitalism and communism, against imperialism."*[1373]

Even as President Mobutu and his government accepted the IMF-recommended reforms as a condition for the disbursement of loans, the Zairian state still dominated the economy. Increasing the role of the private sector in Zaire did not translate into blind de-regulation and anarchy. In May 1984, the Zaire Press Agency reported that *"On the economic front, the MPR Founding Chairman reaffirmed the choice of liberal economy underway in Zaire, but he specified that this new trend was not tantamount to the death of the state, which would continue its supervisory role aimed at avoiding anarchy."*[1374] In November 1986, Mobutu noted that *"…on the contrary, will continue to see to it that unbridled liberalism does not take root in the country. For this is contrary to the interests of the masses…"*[1375]

The Central Committee noted in 1986 that the MPR economic policy was *"based on economic nationalism"* whose purpose was *"economic independence and the economy in the service of man"* in contrast to the policy of *"economic liberalism"* which existed under the previous periods in Zaire. The Central Committee noted that *"economic liberalism ignored the realities of the country…led to monetary reform whose effect has been to destabilize the Zairian currency…did not take into account the international environment…tried to take over the state's authority as regulator of the economy in the service of man…led people in Zaire to believe, wrongly, that economic liberalism is opposed to the safeguarding of national industry and even the national labor force, for no country, whatever its level of development, can open its national market without any restrictions…has contributed to impoverish, if not to strangle our economy, even more so given that concrete measures taken have been principally dictated by the IMF…"*[1376]

Mobutu denounced the corrupt, individualistic business practices of the Zairian business community in March 1987: *"…despite the liberal system of trade, it is becoming more and more difficult to rely on the economic operators both national and foreigners whose only objective is making profits, speculating and systematically sapping the country's economic base. In this way,*

[1371] "Zaire: A Country Study" Accessed From: http://memory.loc.gov/cgi-bin/query/D?cstdy:2:./temp/~frd_erKJ::
[1372] "Zaire: A Country Study" Accessed From: http://memory.loc.gov/frd/cs/zrtoc.html
[1373] "Salongo Attacks Soviet Policy, African Lackeys" <u>Kinshasa Domestic Service</u> March 23, 1977
[1374] "Interview with Mobutu Sese Seko" <u>Zaire Press Agency</u> May 24, 1984
[1375] "Zaire; Mobutu Speaks on Economic Measures" <u>AZAP</u> November 11, 1986
[1376] Lalevee, Mary. "Zaire Condemns IMF, Economic Liberalism" <u>Executive Intelligence Review</u> November 21, 1986 Accessed From: http://www.larouchepub.com/eiw/public/1986/eirv13n46-19861121/eirv13n46-19861121_013-zaire_condemns_imf_economic_libe.pdf

the economic operators reduce the people to misery and push them to revolt against authority..."[1377] In March 1988, Mobutu noted that *"...as practised in his country, economic liberalism could very easily cause confusion and anarchy which could lead the country into a disastrous socio-economic situation...Both nationals and foreigners, in the name of false liberalism, increase the prices of their goods in a disorderly way, thus substantially decreasing the purchasing power of the working masses. The Zairian President asked the officials of the economic and financial sectors of his government to take all the necessary steps to prevent this evil.*"[1378]

Private businessmen were told to serve the needs of the state and its people. For example, in August 1985, Mobutu noted that *"If a Zairian entrepreneur thinks about the welfare of Zaire before everything else, there will never be any constraints."*[1379]

By the early 1970s, the Zairian experiment in its unique form of socialism was well underway. In November 1973, the Mobutu regime announced the expropriation program called Zaireanization. Zaireanization enriched the MPR and military elites under Mobutu. Under this program, foreign-owned businesses were nationalized by the government. Nationalized properties included commercial buildings, light industry, and agricultural holdings. Many of these properties were acquired by Mobutu and held in partnership with Belgian business interests.[1380]

Before 1983, the government controlled economic policies through the ownership of major enterprises such as Gecamines and the Zairian Commerce Company (Sozacom). In 1972, the Zairian government formed state marketing companies to purchase farm products such as coffee and cotton for export. By the early 1990s, the only state-owned marketing company that existed in Zaire was the Zairian Coffee Board. Zaire: A Country Study noted that *"Although by the early 1990s the government still owned or held a majority interest in many enterprises, including the national railroad and airlines, major mining and petroleum companies, and utilities, in theory the private sector was expected to lead economic growth."*[1381]

The labor unions were also regimented by Mobutu's dictatorship and ultimately became an arm of the ruling MPR. In 1967, the Mobutu regime forced all of the independent trade unions into the National Union of Zairian Workers (Union Nationale des Travailleurs Zairois or UNTZA). The UNTZA was a support arm for Mobutu and was controlled by the MPR leadership.[1382] The UNTZA was also a stalwart opponent of any privatization and liberalization of the Zairian economy. In November 1990, Zairian UNTZA criticized the stagnating wages and prices increases as a result of *"a certain economic liberalism. The result thereof is the catastrophic loss of purchasing power for the working masses."*[1383]

[1377] "Zaire: Mobutu on Profiteers, His Foreign Tours" Kinshasa home service March 25, 1987

[1378] "Mobutu discusses economy at meeting of new cabinet" AZAP/PANA March 22, 1988

[1379] "Zaire; Mobutu Notes Continuing Structural Difficulties" Zaire Press Agency August 6, 1985

[1380] "Zaire: A Country Study" Accessed From: http://memory.loc.gov/cgi-bin/query/r?frd/cstdy:@field(DOCID+zr0108)

[1381] "Zaire: A Country Study" Accessed From: http://memory.loc.gov/cgi-bin/query/r?frd/cstdy:@field(DOCID+zr0113)

[1382] "Zaire: A Country Study" Accessed From: http://memory.loc.gov/cgi-bin/query/r?frd/cstdy:@field(DOCID+zr0163)

[1383] "UNTZA Chief Calls for Anti-Inflation Plan" Kinshasa ELIMA November 27, 1990

Since the Mobutu regime and the MPR did have an anti-Western streak and sought to maintain its nonaligned image, relations were re-opened with the communist world. Mobutu and his followers also admired the regimentation of communist bloc countries like Romania, Red China, and North Korea. It was reported that "*Mobutu appeared to have been so impressed by what he saw in China and in North Korea that his rhetoric became noticeably more radical. He instituted the takeover of schools by the party and began advocating the establishment of agricultural cooperatives.*"

The Soviets established closer ties with Mobutu in the late 1960s and early 1970s. The USSR supported Zaire's nationalization of the operations of foreign mining companies and the anti-Western tilt of the Mobutu regime. In 1967, Mobutu established diplomatic relations with the Soviet Union. By 1974, Mobutu visited North Korea and Red China. In November 1972, Mobutu established full diplomatic relations with East Germany, Red China, and North Korea. In 1974, Mao Tse-tung and Mobutu discussed joint assistance to the socialists of the Angolan FNLA.[1384]

Even during the 1980s, Mobutu maintained relations with the USSR, China, and Romania. A delegation of Soviet trade unionists visited Zaire in 1985 on a "*friendship visit.*"[1385] Romania under Ceausescu had close relations with Mobutu and the MPR and Romanian Communist Party had party-to-party ties.[1386] In March 1986, a Zairian National Union of Workers (UNTZA) delegation was visited by a delegation of the All-China Federation of Trade Unions led by Wang Xun.[1387] In the mid-1970s, the North Koreans stationed a 400 member military mission in Zaire. It was withdrawn and then returned in 1985 to train the Kamanyola Division.[1388]

In the 1980s, Red China provided weapons and spare parts to the Zairian Armed Forces. In February 1990, a Chinese military delegation arrived to oversee the training of the 41st Commando Brigade of the Zairian Armed Forces.[1389] In 1983, China cancelled Zaire's $100 million debt with Beijing. In the late 1980s, Red China provided Zaire with arms and military training.[1390]

Clearly, the Zairians and Red Chinese engaged in some level of strategic military cooperation, given a certain level of ideological compatibility of the two nations. In August 1984, PLA General Zhang noted that "*expressed complete satisfaction with the co-operation between both countries in the common struggle to safeguard world peace.*"[1391] In September 1986, Red Chinese PLA Colonel Zhou praised the "*frank and sincere friendship between the Zairian and Chinese armies continuing on the same basis.*"[1392]

Mobutu's Zaire had few supporters within the political landscape of American public opinion. One political extremist group that provided propaganda support for Mobutu and the MPR were the LaRouchians. In 1986, the LaRouche publication Executive Intelligence Review

---

[1384] "Zaire: A Country Study" Accessed From: http://memory.loc.gov/frd/cs/zrtoc.html

[1385] "USSR Trade Union Arrives on Visit" Kinshasa AZAP November 30, 1985

[1386] "Zaire: A Country Study" Accessed From: http://memory.loc.gov/frd/cs/zrtoc.html

[1387] "PRC Trade Union Delegation Continues Visit" AZAP March 16, 1986

[1388] "Zaire: A Country Study" Accessed From: http://memory.loc.gov/frd/cs/zrtoc.html

[1389] Ibid.

[1390] Ibid.

[1391] "Zaire's Military Co-operation with China" Zaire Press Agency August 3, 1984

[1392] "Chinese military adviser ends term in Zaire" AZAP/PANA September 25, 1986

(EIR) reproduced the text of Mobutu's speech to the Central Committee of the Popular Revolutionary Movement (MPR). The LaRouche movement praised Mobutu's fascist regime. The Central Committee noted that the MPR economic policy was *"based on economic nationalism"* whose purpose was *"economic independence and the economy in the service of man"* in contrast to the policy of *"economic liberalism"* which existed under the previous periods in Zaire. The Central Committee noted that *"economic liberalism ignored the realities of the country...led to monetary reform whose effect has been to destabilize the Zairian currency...did not take into account the international environment...tried to take over the state's authority as regulator of the economy in the service of man...led people in Zaire to believe, wrongly, that economic liberalism is opposed to the safeguarding of national industry and even the national labor force, for no country, whatever its level of development, can open its national market without any restrictions...has contributed to impoverish, if not to strangle our economy, even more so given that concrete measures taken have been principally dictated by the IMF..."*[1393]

While the Soviets and some of their allies sought to improve relations with Mobutu's Zaire, efforts were undertaken to sabotage his regime through guerrilla attacks. Perhaps the most well-known force that attempted to undermine the Mobutu regime were the pro-Marxist separatists in the Shaba Province in Zaire (the FLNC). It was reported that these leftist rebels in the Shaba Province received support from the communist world. For example, Arnaud de Borchgrave reported that Cubans and Portuguese Communists trained these leftist rebels from the Shaba Province in Zaire.[1394] Former Cuban political prisoner Armando Valladares also recalled that *"During my detention, I recall having heard that the United States had accused Castro of having sent troops to Zaire-an accusation hotly denied by the Cuban regime. Yet one of my prison wardens, Mariano Corrales, a sergeant and a Communist Party member, was sent to Angola with a special Interior Ministry unit. Corrales told me in detail how his battalion was ordered to invade Zaire and how, during a clash with Belgian and French troops, he lost 70 of his companions."*[1395] The East Germans also played a role in training and arming the FLNC in their invasions of the Shaba Province in 1977 and 1978. The USSR tasked East Germany with the subversion of the Mobutu regime in 1976. The East Germans were to provide the FLNC with weapons, including surface to air missiles (SAMs) to destroy the Zairian Air Force. The East Germans also advised the FLNC to create 45 bases inside the Shaba Province to launch attacks Mobutu's forces. Czechoslovakia also provided the FLNC with APCs to transport soldiers into the Shaba Province. One hundred East German military personnel under the command of Lt-

[1393] Lalevee, Mary. "Zaire Condemns IMF, Economic Liberalism" Executive Intelligence Review November 21, 1986 Accessed From: http://www.larouchepub.com/eiw/public/1986/eirv13n46-19861121/eirv13n46-19861121_013-zaire_condemns_imf_economic_libe.pdf

[1394] "The Front Line States: The Realities in Southern Africa" Heritage Foundation March 26, 1979 Accessed From: http://www.policyarchive.org/handle/10207/bitstreams/9523.pdf

[1395] Valladares, Armando. "Cuba's new elite cracks the whip 'Swamped by deep economic crisis, Castroism unleashed the political police against the people'" The Globe and Mail (Canada) September 13, 1983

General Helmut Poppe arrived in Angola to train FLNC cadres, with specific instructions not to penetrate into Zaire (Shaba Province).[1396]

Conclusion

Based on the evidence presented in this book and the political spectrum that I subscribe to, one can reasonably conclude that the anti-communist dictatorships mentioned above have more in common with the Left than what is known as the *"Right."* This was particularly true in the fields of economy, aspects of the official, ideological discourse, and the centralization of government authority. One can properly refer to these governments as *"anti-communist, nationalist collectivists"* who reject small government and balance, free market economics in favor of the heavy hand of statism. The purpose of this book is to lay out the evidence for the reader to judge the validity of my thesis and to provide a defense to the *"Right"*[1397] who are unfairly lumped into the same category as the Trujillos, Chiang Kai-sheks, and Francos of the world. If a General Francisco Franco or a Shah Mohammed Reza Pahlavi imposed their policies on the United States, many citizens (including conservatives and libertarians) would be on the streets shouting *"big government tyranny,"* *"socialism,"* and *"fascism."* Solid conservative anti-communists should offer a more balanced explanation of their historiography and commentary on various regimes such as General Franco, Dr. Salazar, the Shah, and many other like-minded dictators. They should not be whitewashed as constitutionalists or advocates of free enterprise. Instead, the dictatorships outlined above should be classified as anti-communist collectivists who maintained a certain level of an intersection of interests with the United States.

While many of these anti-communist collectivists undertook quiet dealings with Moscow and Beijing, they were still ideologically aligned against China, Russia, and its allies all over the world. In the case of Iran, Cuba under President Batista, and Nicaragua under President Somoza, there was simply no excuse for the United States to betray these governments to the ever worse Islamists and communist forces. Unfortunately, with the Sandinistas back in power in Nicaragua and the mullahs ruling Iran since 1979, we are living with the consequences of failed American policies to this day.

In conclusion, it would be helpful for the reader to summarize the key features of the anti-communist, collectivist dictatorships:

Greece Under Colonel Papadopoulos
1) State control over the private economy.
2) Subsidies for farmers.
3) Promotion of a collectivist nationalism that was simultaneously anti-communist and anti-individualist.
4) While anti-communist, the Greek colonels sought to expand trade with many Eastern Bloc nations. It appeared that the prime motivation for this trade was economic (i.e. new markets for Greek goods).

[1396] Butler, Shannon R. <u>Brotherhood in Arms: East German Foreign Policy in Africa</u> (Naval Postgraduate School 1978) Accessed From: https://archive.org/stream/brotherhoodinarm00butl/brotherhoodinarm00butl_djvu.txt

[1397] The *"Right"* as defined in this sentence is supportive of balanced government of checks and balances, free market economics, and large amounts of personal freedoms (speech, assembly, movement, etc.)

Spain Under General Francisco Franco
1) Creation of a corporative, fascist-style economic superstructure.
2) Inauguration of nationalized industrial sector (INI).
3) Government controls over the private economy.
4) Forced collection of crops from farmers and landowners in the early years of the Franco regime.
5) Quiet trade with communist countries, which became more prevalent by the 1960s. The prime motivations for such commerce with the Soviet bloc and Cuba were profits for Spanish state-owned and private industries generated by exports and a desire to assert Spain's independence from a sole adherence to the NATO alliance. Some Spanish Falangist theorists desired the creation of a Fourth World alliance, which rejected liberal capitalism and communism.
6) While proclaiming neutrality, Spain allied itself with the Axis Powers during World War II.
7) Creation of a superstructure for a mass movement in the form of the FET, which was the result of a merger between the Carlist royalists and the fascist Falangists and National Syndicalists (JONS).

Portugal Under Dr. Antonio Salazar
1) Creation of a corporative, fascist-style economic superstructure.
2) Government controls over the private economy.
3) Quiet trade with communist countries, which became more prevalent by the 1960s. The main motivation for this trade was commercial and an effort to aggravate the United States and NATO. The Salazar regime was perturbed at America's criticism of Portugal's colonialism in Africa.
4) Partial alignment with Red China over its conflicts with India and Nationalist China.
5) While proclaiming neutrality, Portugal aligned itself with both the Allies and Axis Powers during World War II.
6) Creation of a superstructure for a mass movement in the form of the National Union (UN).

Chile Under General Augusto Pinochet
1) While ostensibly privatizing aspects of the Allende era socialist economy, a number of Chile's industries and financial institutions remained under government control or ownership.
2) There was a split between the statist-nationalists/fascists and free market reformers within the Pinochet regime regarding the administration of public economic policy.
3) Chilean state-owned and private companies engaged in trade relations with the communist world. The chief motivation for such trade was commercial (i.e. profits). Some of the trade even involved arms transfers from Chile to the communist world (e.g Vietnam and Sandinista Nicaragua).

Argentina Under the Military Junta
1) While ostensibly privatizing aspects of the Peron-era economy, a number of Argentina's industries and financial institutions remained under government control or ownership. In fact, there was a general increase in government spending and expansion of the state sector in Argentina under the military junta.

2) There was a split between the statist-nationalists/fascists and free market reformers within the Argentina military junta regarding the administration of public economic policy.

3) The Argentine military junta also expanded trade with the communist world, especially with Cuba, the Soviet Union, and Sandinista Nicaragua. Such trade stemmed from commercial motivations (i.e. profits for Argentine firms) and a shift away from the alliance with the United States in response to President Reagan's alignment with the British during the Falklands war in 1982. Powerful elements of the Argentine military also clung to anti-American sentiments, which in turn, paved the way for a partial rapprochement with the communist world.

Bolivia Under Generals Barrientos, Banzer, Garcia-Meza

1) All three regimes expanded the state sector in various aspects. Banzer and Garcia Meza rejected liberal capitalism, while Barrientos openly indentified himself with the *"Christian Left"* and allegedly supported a purge of unions, businessmen, and politicians. Banzer was on record for increasing the size and scope of the public bureaucracy of the Bolivian state and expanded the number of government agencies administering the economy.

2) Garcia-Meza also slowly opened relations with the Soviet Union in response to souring relations with the United States over Bolivia's complicity in drug trafficking and massive human rights violations.

3) Garcia-Meza also adhered to a leftist-sounding *"anti-imperialist"* nationalism which spoke of his 1980 takeover of Bolivia as a *"revolution."*

4) Barrientos, Banzer, and Garcia-Meza strictly controlled the labor unions.

The Dominican Republic Under General Rafael Trujillo

1) Trujillo utilized the government apparatus of the Dominican Republic to directly profit from the production of average workers and peasants.

2) Trujillo expanded the size and scope of the state economic agencies and expanded the number of government-owned enterprises and crony capitalist firms.

3) The Dominican labor unions were placed under strict control and became propaganda mouthpieces for the Trujillo regime.

4) In response to American criticisms of corruption and human rights abuses, Trujillo officiated a shift to the Left. Subsequently, the Trujillo dictatorship reached out to Cuba and the Soviet Union in 1960 and 1961.

5) Trujillo implicitly and sometimes explicitly blasted capitalism and called for the development of a planned economy.

Haiti Under Presidents Francois and Jean-Claude Duvalier

1) Duvalier smashed the independent unions and extorted/controlled private businesses.

2) Duvalier expanded the number of state agencies and enterprises, which became the personal piggy-banks of the regime and its cronies.

3) The Duvalier regime also employed social-revolutionary rhetoric to solidify its support amongst the black masses. Some of this rhetoric even assumed a Marxist tinge.

4) Duvalier also briefly toyed with the idea of moving to the Soviet bloc camp in response to American opposition to his government's atrocious human rights record. French and Haitian Communists penetrated the Duvalier regime and even attempted to move Haiti in the direction of a socialist republic.

Paraguay Under General Alfredo Stroessner
1) Stroessner opposed free market capitalism in theory and practice.
2) The Stroessner dictatorship also expanded the size and scope of the state bureaucracy and the number of state-owned enterprises.
3) Stroessner used the statist-collectivist nationalist Colorado Party to consolidate mass-based support for his dictatorship.
4) When Presidents Carter and Reagan opposed Paraguay for its government's horrendous human rights records, the propaganda apparatus of the Stroessner dictatorship launched anti-American campaigns. Some of the regime's propaganda assumed a leftist form, which complained about the poverty and imperialism of the United States.

Venezuela Under General Marcos Perez-Jimenez
1) Perez-Jimenez expanded the size of the state sector in Venezuela.
2) Perez-Jimenez included communists in top administrative and state security posts in Venezuela.
3) He also adhered to a collectivist nationalism which was authoritarian in nature and known as the New National Ideal.

Nationalist China Under General Chiang Kai-shek
1) The KMT under Chiang Kai-shek espoused a collectivist nationalism which adhered to socialist (People's Livelihood) and fascist (Blue Shirt Society and the New Life Movement) principles.
2) Massive expansion of state-owned enterprises throughout the reign of Chiang Kai-shek.
3) Ideological identity and kinship with the Nazis during the 1930s.
4) Ideological identity with the methods of the Soviet Union (especially by Chiang Ching-kuo). The KMT under Chiang also employed social revolutionary rhetoric during the 1930s and 1940s. Often, such rhetoric exhibited a Marxist tone.
5) Massive subsidies for farmers and social welfare programs.
6) Very limited trade relations between Chiang's Taiwan and Mao's China.

South Korea Under Syngman Rhee, Generals Park Chung-hee, and Chun Doo-hwan
1) Crony capitalism flourished under the Rhee government.
2) Rhee employed socialistic rhetoric during his campaigns in the postwar period in South Korea.
3) The role of the state in the economy increased in the Rhee years. Such *dirigisme* ensured the nurturing of a crony capitalist sector in South Korea.
4) Under Generals Park Chung-hee and Chun Doo-hwan, social revolutionary and even pseudo-Maoist/Marxist rhetoric was employed against real and allegedly corrupt businessmen and high level government officials.
5) Both Park and Chun also imposed and sustained the corporative superstructure called Saemaul Undong as a tool to regiment the working classes, foster social harmony, and to increase production.
6) Both Park and Chun expanded trade with the communist world for commercial reasons.
7) Park increased the number of state-owned enterprises and the number of public bureaucracies, which oversaw the South Korean economy.

8) The Chun dictatorship also established Maoist-style *"re-education camps"* to brainwash and repress the enemies of his revolution.

Indonesia Under General Suharto

1) The dictatorship of General Suharto repudiated liberal capitalism (referred to as *"free fight capitalism"*) and supported the creation of an economy based on the nationalist collectivism of Pancasila.

2) A mass based movement led by the military was inaugurated by General Suharto. It was known as Golkar and it espoused the principles of Pancasila.

3) The labor unions were controlled by the state and became tools of Suharto.

4) A corporative labor-management setup called Pancasila Industrial Relations was inaugurated by the Suharto regime.

5) Trade relations were continued by Suharto with much of the communist world. These commercial relations were motivated by profit, an urge to maintain the image of *"nonalignment"* in the Third World, and continuity of the previously close trade and military relations between Moscow/Beijing and the old Sukarno dictatorship.

Pakistan Under General Mohammed Zia ul-Haq

1) The Zia regime imposed a radical Islamic dictatorship that was ideologically opposed to Western culture and political ideologies.

2) While advancing some level of privatization, the Zia dictatorship controlled the private economy, labor unions, and maintained many of the nationalized industries leftover from the Bhutto government.

3) Zia and his colleagues were opposed to liberal capitalism and sought to create an Islamic economy.

4) At times, Zia also aligned Pakistan with anti-Western, anti-American interests. This stemmed from anti-Zionism/anti-Israel fervor, a desire to project an image of anti-colonial *"nonalignment,"* and a suspicion of American involvement in the Middle East (i.e. opposition to the Iran hostage rescue mission in 1980 and government sanctioned riots against American diplomatic missions). North Korea and Red China also maintained close military and intelligence relations with Pakistan during the Zia years.

Saudi Arabia Under the Wahhabis

1) The Saudi regime imposed a radical Islamic dictatorship that was ideologically opposed to Western culture and political ideologies.

2) The Saudis also developed a state capitalist economy, which was heavily subsidized and controlled by the government. A number of state-owned enterprises such as Aramco and SABIC were created by the Saudi royals.

3) Business associations were controlled by the government, while labor unions were banned.

4) The Saudis also supported anti-Western, even anti-American interests out of a lingering hostility to imperialism, Israel/Zionism, and to gain support amongst various Middle East governments (Iraq, Syria, and Sadat's Egypt). Saudi Arabia also funded the purchase of Soviet weapons for Syria, Iraq, and Sadat's Egypt in an effort to smash Israel. Riyadh also expanded trade relations with the communist world, while Moscow sought to develop a united front with the Saudis based on a common hostility to Zionism and Israel.

Iran Under Shah Mohammed Reza Pahlavi

1) The Shah repudiated capitalism and supported a hybrid of the world's major economic systems. On several occasions, the Shah claimed that his dictatorship was based partially on socialism.

2) The Shah also developed an ostensibly mass based movement called the Rastakhiz Party which attempted to consolidate support for his dictatorship. A number of Iranian communists led the Rastakhiz Party, since they believed that the Shah would lead Iran into a socialist paradise.

3) Under the Shah, the Iranian government also developed a number of state-owned enterprises, while private shopkeepers were controlled and even harassed by the Rastakhiz Party.

4) The state controlled the Iranian labor unions, which repudiated Marxism and supported corporative arrangements between workers and employers.

5) The Shah increased trade relations with their powerful Soviet neighbor to the north. The motivations behind such trade included commercialism (i.e. profit) and a desire to be somewhat independent of the United States.

South Africa Under the Afrikaner Nationalist Party

1) The Afrikaner Nationalists opened a number of state-owned enterprises from the late 1920s to the 1950s.

2) The Nationalists subsidized South African agriculture.

3) Black entrepreneurship and labor organizing were severely controlled and restricted by the apartheid state.

4) Marxism was stamped out of white labor unions. The philosophy of the white union leaders was based on a fascist-racialist based corporative ideology.

5) Despite the restrictions on business and initial hostility toward capitalism, the Afrikaners intensely lobbied for American and Western investment and trade.

6) The Nationalists also forged commercial ties with the communist world and various anti-American Third World regimes. This was based on a hunger for profits/new markets and a desire to spite the United States for its opposition to apartheid.

15929986R00149